On Location in Cuba

ENVISIONING CUBA

Louis A. Perez Jr., editor

On Location in Cuba

Street Filmaking during Times of Transition

ANN MARIE STOCK

THE

UNIVERSITY

OF

NORTH

CAROLINA

PRESS

Chapel Hill

© 2009
THE UNIVERSITY OF
NORTH CAROLINA PRESS

Designed by Courtney Leigh Baker and set in The Serif,
The Sans, and Press Gothic by Tseng Information Systems, Inc.
Manufactured in the United States of America

The paper in this book meets the guidelines for permanence
and durability of the Committee on Production Guidelines
for Book Longevity of the Council on Library Resources.

The University of North Carolina Press has been a
member of the Green Press Initiative since 2003.

Library of Congress Cataloging-in-Publication Data
Stock, Ann Marie.
On location in Cuba : street filmmaking during
times of transition / by Ann Marie Stock.
    p. cm. — (Envisioning Cuba)
Includes bibliographical references and index.
ISBN 978-0-8078-3269-1 (cloth : alk. paper) —
ISBN 978-0-8078-5940-7 (pbk. : alk. paper)
  1. Motion pictures—Cuba—History—20th century.
  2. Motion pictures—Cuba—History—21st century.
  3. Motion pictures—Study and teaching
     (Graduate)—Cuba. I. Title.
     PN1993.5.C8.S86 2009
     791.43097291′090511—dc22
     2008045196

CLOTH   13 12 11 10 09   5 4 3 2 1
PAPER   13 12 11 10 09   5 4 3 2 1

FOR MY FAMILY

AND *ESPECIALLY*

FOR DAVID

In my judgment,

our culture—today

as much or more than ever—

is something that's alive.

—AMBROSIO FORNET

Cinema—and culture in general—

are immensely important

in bringing us togcther ...

Culture can unite us.

—FERNANDO PÉREZ

CONTENTS

Credits xv

Preface xix

Abbreviations and Acronyms xxiii

Introduction: Screening an Island Nation in Transition 1

DOLLY BACK //

1 Documenting Tumultuous Times: New Culture Organizations
   Proffer Alternatives 35

2 Establishing Community Media in the Mountains: Televisión
   Serrana Strengthens Highland Identity 77

3   Balancing Tradition and Innovation: The National Animation
Studio Negotiates the Global Marketplace   106

CLOSE-UP //

4   Opening New Roads: Juan Carlos Cremata Malberti
Redefines Revolutionary Filmmaking   149

5   Promoting Popular Genres: Pavel Giroud Revises
Conceptions of Cuban Cinema   175

6   Filming in the Margins: Esteban Insausti Explores Life
and Art amidst Chaos   206

JUMP CUT //

7   Making Space for New Interventions: A Montage
from the National Exhibit of New Filmmakers   237

Epilogue: Reflections on Cuba, Filmmaking,
and the Times Ahead   279

Notes   289

Works Cited   317

Index   329

ILLUSTRATIONS

Larita (Laura de la Uz) looks out to sea in *Madagascar* 3

Fernando Pérez provides direction to a young actress on the set of

   La vida es silbar 5

Tomás Gutiérrez Alea converses with filmmaker Juan Carlos Tabío 8

Humberto Solás in a recent documentary by Carlos Barba 10

Alejandro Pérez filming in the streets of Havana 25

Carlos Barba prepares to film in Santiago de Cuba 25

Jorge Luis Sánchez in the ICAIC 51

Gloria Rolando at home in Centro Habana 63

Inti Herrera, Alejandro Brugués, and Diego Javier Figueroa 69

Jorge Perugorría in Manhattan 73

Daniel Diez Castrillo in Havana 82

Poster promoting one of Cuba's mobile cinema initiatives 85

Coffee-grinding instrument featured in *In Step with the Mortar* 89

Carlos Rodríguez prepares to film in the Sierra Maestra 90

Men and boys catch fish in *Freddy, o el sueño de Noel* 93

EICTV students gain practical training at the TVS installation as
     Daniel Diez Castrillo mentors 95

Elpidio Valdés y el fusil poster by Eduardo Muñoz Bachs 115

Filminutos poster by Eduardo Muñoz Bachs 119

Image from "We Are All Champions" by Karel Ducases Manzano 138

"Family Violence" publicity spot by Yurina Luis Naranjo 140

Ernesto Piña Rodríguez flanked by two of his creations 141

El Propietario by Ernesto Piña Rodríguez and Wilber Noguel 141

Filming the Varadero Beach scene for *Viva Cuba* 161

The day-for-night sequence in *Viva Cuba* 163

Juan Carlos Cremata Malberti, Orlando Rojas, and Daisy Granados
     in New York City 168

Tres veces dos poster by Aquino 188

Pavel Giroud at the International Festival of New Latin
     American Cinema 192

Samuel (Iván Alberto Carreira Lamothe) and his grandmother
     (Mercedes Sampietro) in *La edad de la peseta* 195

Ana Victoria "Bebé" Pérez contemplates the future in
     La vida es silbar 201

Existen poster by Samuel Riera 209

Image from *Luz roja* 217

Alejandro Pérez and Esteban Insausti consult
     while filming *Luz roja* 219

Esteban Insausti and Alejandro Pérez filming a

    street scene for *Luz roja* 219

Angélica Salvador and Esteban Insausti in Havana 225

Esteban Insausti and Angélica Salvador at home 230

Publicity poster from the Muestra Nacional de Nuevos Realizadores 241

An image from *Despertando a Quan Tri* 249

Gustavo Pérez self-portrait 251

Carlos Barba during the filming of *Ciudad en rojo* with Rebeca Chávez,

    Yoraisi Gómez, and María Teresa García 254

The protagonists in *Personal Belongings* ponder their

    competing desires 257

Enrique Colina shares his opinion with a gathering

    of film specialists 267

CREDITS

Instituto Cubano del Arte e Industria Cinematográficos
(ICAIC), Havana
Fundación Ludwig de Cuba, Havana
College of William and Mary, Williamsburg, Virginia
Collegeville Institute for Ecumenical and Cultural Research,
Collegeville, Minnesota
St. John's University, Collegeville, Minnesota
Fulbright Scholar Program
Program for Cultural Cooperation between Spain's Ministry
of Culture and U.S. Universities
Robert and Polly Dunn Foundation
Rockefeller Foundation
MacArthur Foundation

American Friends of the Ludwig Foundation of Cuba
Harold Leonard Memorial Film Fund at the University of Minnesota

For opening doors in Cuba

Helmo Hernández   Susana Molina
Wilfredo Benítez   Rosa María Rovira
Omar González   Marisol Rodríguez

For proffering access to images, films, photographs,
books, and other documents

Kathy Cassanova   Lola Calviño
Alejandro Pérez   Raulito Mendoza
Luis González Nieto   Marta Díaz
María Caridad Cumaná   Cláudia Nunes
Abel Pino   Pablo Pacheco López
Alberto Ramos   Daniel Diez Castrillo
Luciano Castillo   Carole Rosenberg
Mario Naito López   Nancy Berthier

For contributing valuable experience in interviews and conversations

Ambrosio Fornet   Gloria Rolando
Fernando Pérez   Aram Vidal
Esteban Insausti   Gustavo Pérez
Angélica Salvador   Humberto Solás
Alejandro Pérez   Daniel Díaz Torres
Jorge Luis Sánchez   Julio García Espinosa
Juan Carlos Cremata Malberti   Gerardo Chijona
Enrique Colina   Daniel Diez Castrillo
Paco Prats   Samuel Riera
Aramis Acosta   Karel Ducases Manzano
Armando Alba   Carlos Barba
Ernesto Piña Rodríguez   Alejandro Rodríguez Fornés
Orlando Rojas   Johanhnn Ramírez
Pavel Giroud   José Eduardo García
Juan Antonio García Borrero   Lester Noguel
Inti Herrera   Wilber Noguel
Alejandro Brugués   Marcelo Martín

Lázara Herrera

Mario Rivas

Joel del Río Fuentes

Rosana Cuba

Hilda Elena Vega

Jaime David

José Antonio Jiménez

Alfredo Guevara

José Luis Lobato

Tané Martínez

Amado "Asori" Soto Ricardo

Zulema Clares

Dania Iliesástegui

Laura de la Uz

Giovanni Federico

John Della Penna

Martica Araujo

Senel Paz

For support crucial to the completion of this study

P. Geoffrey Feiss

Karen Wilbanks

Shirley Aceto

Marvin D'Lugo

Gillian Cell

Heidi Mayor

Guru Ghosh

Fernando Sáez Carvajal

Karen Dolan

Darsy Fernández

Mitchell Reiss

Camilo Vives

David Dessler

Lia Rodríguez

Joel Schwartz

Tania Delgado

M. Troy Davis

Ernesto Rodríguez

Marlene Brummer

Carlos Rafael Solís

Cecilia Newton

Diego Javier Figueroa

Stephen Rivers

For assistance with everything from filming and transcribing interviews to arranging logistics and tracking down elusive information, and for helping me weather a hurricane

Luis Enrique Prieto Armas

For insights shared during the "Contemporary Cuba" program

Sarah Belpree

Bill Casterline

Fran Borgenicht

Harriet Fulbright

Jack Borgenicht

Bernard Rapoport

Michael Carver

and all participants

For hospitality in Havana, San José, Collegeville, and Campeche

Silvia Gil

Mario Mora Quirós

Pablo Fornet

María Eugenia Fornés

Zaida Capote

Jorge Fornet

Santi Armas

Enrique Prieto

Yairys Salcedo Cañizares

Laura González

Oscar Suárez García

Héctor Alberto

Antonio Montero Campos

Marilynn Yaekel de Dent

Kari Meyers de Riggioni

Wilfred Theisen

Kilian McDonnell

Elisa Schneider

Carla Durand-Demaris

Carlos Sánchez Gamboa

For critiquing a chapter in preliminary form as part of the Collegeville Institute seminars

Carole George

Brian Hartley

Kathleen Hughes

Margaret O'Gara

Donald Ottenhoff

Carmel Pilcher

Mary Schertz

Susan Sink

Susan Smith

Michael Vertin

For reading early versions of the manuscript and sharing thoughtful comments

Pablo Fornet

Edna M. Rodríguez-Mangual

Several anonymous readers

For editorial guidance and assistance

Elaine Maisner

Lou Pérez

and the rest of the Press staff

Stephanie Wenzel

Courtney Baker

For solidarity and sound advice

Kirsten Kellogg

Francie Cate-Arries

Teresa Longo

Neal Devins

For being a part of this project from the very beginning

Ambrosio Fornet

Fernando Pérez

David Campagna

Caminante no hay camino,
se hace camino al andar.
—Antonio Machado

I did not set out to write this book. That is to say, when I first traveled to Havana for the International Festival of New Latin American Cinema in 1989, I had no way of knowing where that trip would take me. I never suspected I would return to the island nearly fifty times over the next twenty years, witnessing firsthand the dramatic changes occurring there. Initially, it was the festival and the films that drew me back. But then, finding myself connected through professional relationships and personal friendships, I returned to Cuba for all sorts of reasons—to participate in cultural events and to present my scholarship at conferences, to design and then direct a dozen installments of a study program, to mentor the research of my students and support that of my colleagues, to develop an initiative distributing Cuban documentaries in the United States, to serve as a consultant for foundations and nongovernmental organizations, to select films and curate programs for U.S. festivals, and so on. Only after a decade and a half of takeoffs and landings, of moving back and forth between Miami—or Nassau or Cancún or Mexico City or San José—and Havana, only after repeated experiences on the island and sustained contact with its inhabitants, did I undertake this project. Or perhaps more accurately, it was then that the project took hold of me.

A great deal has changed during the course of this study. The contents of my luggage over the years attest to a series of shifts—in Cuba's economic situation, in changing film industry standards, and in my own professional engagement. Only first-time visitors to Cuba travel light. On my initial trip to the island, my single suitcase attracted attention. Frequent fliers to Cuba lug huge duffels; it is not uncommon for overweight surcharges to exceed the cost of the airline ticket. While the contents of these shrink-wrapped bags vary, they always include medicines, the labels of aspirins and antacids, diaper rash ointment and children's cold remedies, vitamins, and antibiotic cream showing through. Remaining space is taken up by assorted sundries and supplies, depending on the purpose of the visit and the needs of friends and colleagues. Through the years, my bags have contained spark plugs and a fan belt for a friend's car; printer cartridges and a scanner for a cultural agency; numerous books and videos for a library; hundreds of pens donated by my students; some canvases and paints for a hospital art project; baseball uniforms and equipment provided through a people-to-people initiative; a digital camera for an archive; a toilet flush mechanism and a shower curtain for one apartment where I sometimes stayed, and towels and bed linens for another; and a bolt of fabric to make into tablecloths and napkins for a friend's *paladar* when family-run restaurants were first introduced. During the depths of the economic crisis, when virtually everything was in short supply, I stuffed in multipacks of soap, light bulbs, writing paper, and pencils and dozens of bottles of vitamins.

When traveling to Havana, I always pack films—new releases, especially by independent U.S. filmmakers, and international classics. On the way back home, this space is taken up by books, journals, posters, and films for my research and teaching. Over time, the VHS format gave way to DVD; now I simply carry an external drive onto which I can transfer entire directories of filmed material, photographs, and articles. The process through which I conduct the interviews has evolved as well; my notebook and pencil were replaced first by a small tape recorder and then by the digital video camera on which I now rely.

As I reflect on two decades of goings and comings, my dominant impression of Cuba is one of constant movement. Nothing, it seems, has stayed in place. This perpetual motion is particularly evident in the audiovisual sphere. Film projects move forward. What begins as an idea gives way to casting actors and scouting locations, which in turn leads to filming, editing, sound-mixing—and then the premiere of a new film. Facilities deteriorate. And sometimes, as in the case of the film institute elevators and the Cine Chaplin, they get repaired. Directors come and go. A few leave permanently—but most return to their home base on the island. Traveling to festivals, leading workshops, and advancing their next projects in various sites around the world have translated into numerous stamps in the passports of these cineastes. Cuba's media world has not held still for an instant. Like a restless patient, it has fidgeted and shifted constantly ever since I began examining it in the late 1980s. The splicing together of the clips herein is designed to illuminate the ever-changing panorama of Cuba's audiovisual landscape. And detain it for an instant.

While developing this project, I have been privy to tales and testimonies. Filmmakers have reflected on their creative process, vented their frustrations, aired their concerns, celebrated their accomplishments, and shared their dreams. These stories—and especially the friendships with their tellers—have left me enlightened, inspired, and deeply moved. They have touched me in profound ways. So much so, that long after I have walked out of the José Martí Airport and across the tarmac to the waiting plane, and long after I have cleared U.S. customs and returned home, they persist. Like a sultry summer evening on the Malecón, they envelop me.

ABBREVIATIONS AND ACRONYMS

AHS   Asociación Hermanos Saíz (Saíz Brothers Association)

CNC   Consejo Nacional de Cultura (National Council of Culture)

EICTV   Escuela Internacional de Cine y Televisión
(International School of Film and Television)

FLC   Fundación Ludwig de Cuba (Ludwig Foundation of Cuba)

FNCL   Fundación del Nuevo Cine Latinoamericano
(Foundation of New Latin American Cinema)

ICAIC   Instituto Cubano del Arte e Industria Cinematográficos
(Cuban Institute of Cinematographic Art and Industry,
or Cuban Film Institute)

ICRT   Instituto Cubano de Radio y Televisión
(Cuban Institute of Radio and Television)

ISA   Instituto Superior del Arte

NGO(s)   nongovernmental organization(s)

SGAE   Sociedad General de Autores y Editores
(General Society of Authors and Editors of Spain)

TVS   Televisión Serrana

UNEAC   Unión de Escritores y Artistas de Cuba
(National Union of Writers and Artists of Cuba)

ON LOCATION IN CUBA

The meaning of revolution is
embodied in culture, that is where the
transformation process is evident.
—Tomás Gutiérrez Alea

Screening an Island Nation in Transition

The camera frames a faded newspaper clipping that depicts a tremendous gathering. The place is Havana, and the time is the 1960s. Tens of thousands of people crowd together in Revolution Square. Zoom out to a woman moving a magnifying glass over the photo. She seeks to focus on familiar faces, but the attempt is futile; the lens reveals only a gray mass. As an extreme close-up obliterates the image altogether, the female voice cries out, "Where am I, *Dios mío*, where am I?" The woman in this 1994 Cuban film cannot place herself in that photograph, nor in that moment. Her dislocation in Cuba's Revolutionary past resonated for Cubans floundering in a sea of change.

The 1990s were a time of dramatic transformation for Cuba. With the collapse of the Soviet Union, the island nation plummeted into a full-scale crisis. Severe shortages penetrated virtually every facet of life for Cubans:

Frequent blackouts left families without electricity for hours at a time; food scarcity resulted in widespread hunger and undernourishment; basic products once plentiful—soap, light bulbs, paper—disappeared altogether; and the lack of fuel paralyzed private autos and dramatically reduced the public transportation upon which most islanders relied. As a result, scores of frustrated Cubans constructed makeshift rafts and drifted away from the island—some to wash up on the shores of south Florida, and others to be engulfed by the sea.

This Período Especial, or Special Period, yielded extreme measures most Cubans never imagined possible: the legalization of U.S. currency, the marketing of the island as a tourist destination, the encouragement of entrepreneurial activities and small businesses, and even the pope's celebration of Catholic mass in Revolution Square. During this moment of accelerated change, Cubans struggled—both to make ends meet and to reckon with an uncertain future. Given the sudden and dramatic insertion into the global marketplace, what would become of the nation's Revolutionary ideology and the island's socialist structures? How would Cuba's economic system, political mechanisms, and cultural apparatus fare? Answers to these questions were as elusive as basic supplies were scarce. Cubans watched their world turn upside down; it was all they could do to hang on—and hope.

Fernando Pérez documented this time on film. With honesty and courage, he relied on his personal experiences to illustrate the impact of Cuba's abrupt entrance into the global arena and the ongoing evolution of what it means to be Cuban. *Madagascar* was made against all odds, during the summer of 1993, the lowest point during the Special Period. Cuba's state-sponsored film institute was experiencing shortages of film stock, fuel to transport crews and equipment, food to provide a meal to those working long days, and the hard currency necessary to edit, produce, and distribute films. Pérez, a filmmaker in Cuba's national institute for more than forty years, recalls thinking this might be the last work he'd ever make—that at any time the country could become paralyzed and the film project stalled out. Yet, he forged ahead and completed *Madagascar*, a film deemed by the Cuban critic Ambrosio Fornet to be "an X-ray exposure of the prevailing state of our soul."[1] For his poignant reflection of Cubans' reality during that difficult time, Pérez was named the Cuban

Larita (Laura de la Uz) looks out to sea in Fernando Pérez's Special Period film, *Madagascar*. Courtesy of the director.

filmmaker of the 1990s. And for capturing the existential uncertainty of that moment, *Madagascar* is considered *the* film of the Special Period.

The young protagonist, Larita, seeks to embrace the unknown, to simultaneously be "here" and "elsewhere." In one scene, she stands with arms outstretched looking out to sea. Behind her lies the city, a once familiar space that is now alien. Before her the open water spans to an empty horizon. In another sequence, she stands atop a multistory building in Havana, arms outstretched once again. With her body forming a cross, she chants, "Madagascar, Madagascar, Madagascar." The editing reveals similar figures across the city, human cruciforms interrupting the urban skyline. In an essay I wrote on the film shortly after its premiere, I likened these human forms to television antennae, awaiting distant signals, each one a medium for receiving and transmitting.[2] Each stands alone, but they are connected by their joint invocation of the unknown, "Madagascar, Madagascar." Through this mantra, Larita and the other young people seek to connect themselves with one another, to locate themselves vis-à-vis a nation undergoing rapid transition, and to reimagine their place in the world.

The film's double ending reaffirms the uncertainty of this "special" moment and contributes to a guardedly hopeful vision. The sequence opens with Larita and her mother, who earlier struggled to place herself in the past. The women lead their bicycles into the tunnel that crosses under the Havana Bay, as did thousands of Havana residents at that time. Darkness engulfs them. The image fades to black, and we read the filmmaker's dedication of this very personal work to his three children. While expecting the credits to roll, we're surprised by another sequence: A train moves slowly across the screen, past dilapidated buildings in a stark industrial zone. This long take is accompanied by the popular song "Quiéreme mucho" ("Yours"), in a rendition by the legendary Cuban singer Omara Portuondo. Paraphrased loosely, the lyrics go like this: "When love is real, like ours, it's impossible to live apart. . . . I'll be yours . . . here or on far distant shores!" This Cuban love song underscores the resilience of love—love of family, love of community, love of *patria*, or homeland. And, in this context, it reimagines the community; in this rendition, the nation is unbounded.[3]

Cuban audiences were buoyed up by the film's hopeful message during hard times. At the premiere of *Madagascar* in Havana, viewers left the cinema not in silence but in song. Hundreds of voices lifted together in singing the tender love song. As a member of that audience, filing out amidst the clasped hands and embraces and tears, I shared the filmmaker's hopeful vision. In the midst of scarcity and uncertainty, what prevailed was a spirit of solidarity. And hope for better times ahead. And love. "Quiéreme mucho." In commenting on the film at that time, Pérez said to me, "I believe that in present-day Cuba there is a great deal to love, and also a lot that can still be improved—slowly, but steadily."

As global tides washed over the island in the early 1990s, Cubans did their best to remain anchored. How did they manage to survive this moment of transition? How did they adapt to their nation's abrupt entrance into the current world system? And how have they faced one of the greatest challenges posed by this era of globalization—preserving their sense of home and community while engaging with an increasingly connected world? *On Location in Cuba: Street Filmmaking during Times of Transition* probes these and other questions. This study employs cinema—defined broadly to include film, video, and audiovisual art—to analyze this piv-

Fernando Pérez provides direction to a young actress on the set of *La vida es silbar*. Courtesy of the director.

otal moment in the island's history, this "special period" of accelerated change and great uncertainty. It will be through the lens of cinema that we observe the ending of the Cold War and, with it, Cuba's abrupt loss of both political model and financial patron; the ensuing economic crisis exacerbated by the tightening of the U.S. embargo; islanders' concomitant reliance on multinational finances, global communications networks, and transnational cultural practices; and the reconfiguration of the state's role amidst an expanding civil society.

In *On Location*, I interrogate Cuba's collision with the world system. I am interested in what happens when autochthonous culture is confronted by global forces. More specifically, I track the transformation of a concertedly national cinema into a decidedly transnational audiovisual praxis—one emanating from new technologies, taking shape on multiple geopolitical and aesthetic terrains, financed by multinational capital, and directed at consumers around the world. Whereas the globalization of cinema renders opaque the geographic boundaries of nation-states, we will see herein that it need not obfuscate or occlude cultural identity. In fact, as the context of Cuba reveals, transnationalism can actually contribute to a reassertion of "a sense of cultural self-hood."[4] I use the Cuban case, then, to demonstrate how culture workers in a precise context have activated global processes and mobilized transnational linkages in order to sustain, strengthen, and reshape national identity.

And this leads to a second issue driving this study: the scrutiny of the *process* through which the Cuban community has been reimagined. *On Location in Cuba* tracks the emergence of multiple and varied notions of *cubanía* that emanated from the realignment of state authority and the expansion of civil society. The Cuban state responded to the crisis by implementing policies that "created the spaces within which people could mobilize in less restricted ways." As a result, there emerged new social sectors with fewer connections to the state. The growth of these sectors begged the question, as articulated by Geraldine Lievesley, of "how the state would respond to these voices for change" and produced tensions as culture workers "vied to convert their own labor into financial capital by entering directly and individually into contractual agreements with transnational stakeholders."[5] As this study reveals, the expansion of civil society yielded a shift in the state's authority; the hegemony previously espoused gave way to greater heterogeneity. Cuban identity, once crafted by the revolutionary collective, became more of a "coproduction," growing out of the efforts of actors working both within and outside the state apparatus. No longer would Cubanness emanate primarily from island institutions; from this time onward it would emerge from the mediation between state actors and individuals working on their own, oftentimes aligned with international and nongovernmental organizations based outside Cuba. And that would mark a significant change. This resultant *cubanía* would retain Cuba's socialist values of justice and solidarity while integrating the emerging values of individualism and tolerance of difference. Before zooming in on the audiovisual sphere to examine islanders' shifting relationships to one another, to the nation, and to the world during this Special Period, we will flash back to a foundational moment in order to establish the centrality of filmmaking in the forging of a revolutionary consciousness in Cuba.

Culture workers have, for the past half-century, documented and participated in the construction of *cubanía*.[6] The acclaimed Cuban cineaste Humberto Solás articulates the key role of culture in constructing a revolutionary community. "Artistic culture is an essential element in the configuration of the idea of nationhood," he contends. "I used to think it was political ideas and the economic system that determined and defined the nation. Certainly they are critical contributing elements, but the concept of the nation is configured in film, literature and poetry, and is not definitively articulated until signified through the images and sounds of the country."[7]

Within the realm of culture, cinema would lead the charge to promote the new ideology and shape cultural practices. Film has been a key arbiter of Cuban revolutionary identity. It is through the medium of cinema that notions of citizenship have been defined and promoted, that relationships to the state have been negotiated, and that alliances—both island-based and international—have been forged. "I remember that during those years I went to the cinema not to see films but to become Cuban," recalls renowned screenwriter Senel Paz. "I saw the movies of the Cuban Film Institute (ICAIC) with the same emotion that I felt when I went out to greet the *barbudos* led by Che, who had freed my town."[8] Over the past half-century, film has to a great extent defined what it means to be Cuban. After all, as Tomás Gutiérrez Alea reminds us, "Cuban cinema was really born with the revolution and thanks to it."[9] Historical circumstances positioned cinema as the quintessential mode for imagining the Cuban nation.

From the dawning of Revolutionary Cuba in 1959, cinema was deemed central to implementing the new ideology. The second decree of the new government authorized the establishment of a national film institute to be called the Instituto Cubano del Arte e Industria Cinematográficos (Cuban Institute of Cinematographic Art and Industry, or ICAIC). Dated 20 March 1959 and put into effect on 24 April 1960, this blueprint would guide the creation of Cuba's national film institute. The first two assertions in the Ley No. 169 would be critical in charting the institute's course over more than a half-century. First, "cinema is art," and second, cinema

Tomás Gutiérrez Alea (left), one of the founders of Cuba's revolutionary cinema, converses with accomplished industry filmmaker Juan Carlos Tabío. The two collaborated on *Fresa y chocolate* (*Strawberry and Chocolate*) and *Guantanamera*. Courtesy of the ICAIC.

constitutes "an instrument of opinion and formation of individual and collective consciousness" and can therefore contribute to deepening the revolutionary spirit and sustaining its creative impulse.[10] Building the Cuban Film Institute, a state entity widely known by its acronym, ICAIC, constituted the first step toward establishing a new revolutionary cinema, one that would link aesthetic concerns with ideological aims.

A 1960 newsreel heralds the founding of the ICAIC, marking the moment when Cubans embarked on an ambitious project of representing themselves—their island, their people, their experiences. They began to reject depictions from the outside, instead constructing images of their own reality. *Noticiero 49* (*Newsreel 49*) blends in a dizzying montage the icons of major U.S. studios—MGM, 20th Century Fox, and United Artists. While the soundtrack blasts "Rock around the Clock," a voice-over commentary notes that "for many years North American films poisoned Cuban screens, advocating imperialism and preaching violence and crime." This sequence outlining the problem gives way to the next one celebrating its resolution. We see the first president of the ICAIC, Alfredo

Guevara, framed in close-up and hear of the success in driving out the Yankee distribution companies: "Now we can see the revolutionary films from around the world that were previously hidden and destroyed by these companies." Images of smiling, hammer-wielding Cubans accompany this declaration. From their position atop the buildings previously occupied by U.S. film distributors, they demolish the Hollywood logos and cheer the demise of the U.S. film conglomerates. Hammers in hand, the Cuban multitudes have cleared space for the revolutionary culture to come.

The ICAIC charged this first generation of revolutionary filmmakers with developing a cinematic language capable of helping to bring about sociopolitical transformation. It was clear that cinema would constitute a form of liberation—freedom from the artifices of Hollywood and from the saturation of cinema screens with faraway places and unfamiliar faces. No longer would singing-and-dancing, ruffle-clad actors speaking broken English be the predominant purveyors of "Cubanness" on the silver screen.[11] And it was clear that this powerful form—a weapon of liberation—had the potential to help release Cuba from the hold of U.S. imperialism. What remained far less apparent, though, was just *how* this would be achieved. As cultural critic Ambrosio Fornet recalls of that time, "This would have to be discovered along the way."[12] Cuban filmmakers set out boldly on this journey of discovery. Their trek—sometimes exhausting, sometimes exhilarating—would continue into the next century.

From the very beginning in revolutionary Cuba, cultural production was aligned with larger social, political, and economic agendas. As Humberto Solás has commented, "The revolution may appear as a monolithic event, unique and uniform," but in fact, "it has always been as much cultural as it is economic, reflecting multiple and opposing polemics."[13] In Cuba, then as now, all these spheres are inextricably linked. The prominence of culture and its centrality to political and economic forces can surprise those unfamiliar with it. I recall one consulting trip early in this century, when our delegation was invited to the Presidential Palace for dinner with Fidel Castro and several members of his cabinet. As we milled about informally, the discussion ranged from golf games to the Gulf War and included Cuban films and Disney cartoons. One U.S. visitor, impressed by Castro's knowledge on a wide array of subjects, asked the then-commander-in-chief how much time he devoted to politics and

A pioneer of revolutionary filmmaking in Cuba and director of the Cine Pobre festival, Humberto Solás, in a recent documentary by Carlos Barba. Courtesy of Carlos Barba.

how much to culture. The response was immediate and unequivocal: "In Cuba, these two cannot be separated. Culture and politics are one in the same." To track the experiences of several filmmakers and developments in the audiovisual sphere is, then, to traverse cultural, political, and economic territory. In *On Location in Cuba*, I acknowledge and interrogate this convergence so as to make sense of this recent time of accelerated transformation on the island.

The cultural project that began a half-century ago—wielding a camera to help construct a new nation—has continued into the present. In recent years, however, it has changed markedly. For one thing, circumstances on the island have necessitated a revision in how things are done. What this meant for Cuba's film realm was a new mode of production. No longer would state funds underwrite the costs of making features, documentaries, and animated films. Financing through coproductions, involving at least one partner from another country, would help stretch the institute's limited resources. And no longer would the principal goal be to serve domestic audiences. From now on, the tastes and expectations of international viewers would have to be factored in. Cuban directors and producers would continue advancing their film projects, but they would proceed in ways vastly different from their earlier mode of operating.

The same period also witnessed a technological revolution. Digital cameras and PC-based editing proliferated around the world. So, too, did VCRs, DVDs, PCs, CDs, and the Internet. The introduction of new technologies in Cuba provided an attractive alternative to the unwieldy industry equipment and infrastructure. It brought new ways of making, circulating, and accessing films. Satellites now beam films to Cuba from all over the world; island entrepreneurs have tucked their receptors into rooftop water tanks or camouflaged them with vegetation. (Several cine-files shared with me the fact that they frequently see first-run Hollywood films on the island even before their public premiere in Los Angeles.) A network of official and unauthorized video and DVD rental shops cropped up across the island. Films now pass easily from one hand to another, one home to the next. With a few keystrokes, a feature or documentary can be reproduced directly on the hard drive of any computer or the flash drive of any user. The Internet also constitutes an important avenue: Audiovisual artists in Cuba upload their work; film fans around the world download it. Dissemination through Portalatino, YouTube, and a host of other websites connects Cubans with local and global audiences. Since 1990, then, waves of new options for producing and disseminating audiovisual material have washed up onto Cuba's shores.

These factors coincided with ICAIC's own transformation in terms of personnel and practices. A "changing of the guard" occurred in 2000 when Alfredo Guevara retired from his role as leader of the institute he helped found and directed for more than thirty years, and Omar González moved over from the Instituto del Libro to assume the presidency.[14] Almost immediately, new modes of producing and disseminating films were introduced. Whereas the ICAIC had previously underwritten the vast majority of films made by Cuban directors, now it sought coproduction opportunities with other countries. The Animation Studio, granted greater autonomy and allocated additional resources, grew significantly. The circulation of Cuban films increased—through new festivals organized on the island, the transfer of films onto video and DVD, and new partnerships with overseas allies. The creation of an ICAIC website and a weekly electronic bulletin communicated these and other developments. Coinciding with and contributing to this momentum were shifting demographics. Industry filmmakers had aged; with increasing frequency, headlines lamented the loss of a pioneer of Cuban cinema.[15] The 1990s, then, marked the dramatic transformation of the ICAIC.

Culminating from all of these changes was a shift in the state's role in film production and circulation. Whereas the national film institute constituted the principal venue for Cuba's filmmakers from the 1960s through the 1980s, this ceased to be the case by the mid-1990s. A series of innovative audiovisual endeavors began to take place outside the industry's purview and beyond the capital. This transformation away from a state-centered film industry has yielded benefits at the same time it has posed challenges. Filmmakers working within the ICAIC collaborate more closely with their counterparts in other organizations—some governmental and other nongovernmental, some located on the island and others based overseas—and with those working on their own. Resources have been maximized, and space has been created for new voices. Greater access to the medium has yielded multiple and sometimes contradictory visions of Cubans' imagined community. Predictably, some of the works created within these "alternative" spaces have clashed with industry representations and practices. Overall, however, the dynamic between those working within and outside the national film institute has been one of synergy and coexistence. The state has, in fact, actually contributed to helping bring about many of these changes. As this study reveals, state actors in the national film institute and other government agencies appear less intent on imposing a preexisting agenda than on generating new initiatives and empowering artists. Evidence suggests that we should view the Cuban state not as a "repressive centralized apparatus that enforces its dictates on citizens from the top down" but, rather, in the words of Sujatha Fernandes, as a "permeable entity that both shapes and is constituted by the activities of various social actors."[16] In querying contemporary audiovisual praxis, *On Location* will reveal how Cuba's state industry has actually contributed to its own decentering.

This is not to suggest that the shift away from a centralized culture apparatus has proved effortless. In fact, in Cuba's film sphere we see the contrary to be the case. At times, ICAIC officials experienced discomfort and felt threatened. They responded with measures deemed extraordinary by some. (Proposals during the past few years include the levying of a thousand-dollar fee for anyone filming in Cuba, whether a student working on a graduation thesis or a media conglomerate filming a high-budget feature; such a move would have made it impossible for most Cubans—who earn the average annual wage equivalent to less than three hundred dollars—to film in their own country.) The ICAIC film-makers themselves were concerned. Some feared their artistic autonomy was slipping away. Others wondered if the stalwart structure steeped in more than three decades of tradition by that time could adapt to rapid technological innovation, the influx of global capital, and transnational communications networks. Regardless of their stance on the role of the national film institute, all recognized that change was imminent. And indeed it was, for a generation of audiovisual artists was about to script the next chapter in Cuba's film history.

On Location in Cuba examines the ways in which global processes affecting film creation and circulation relate to the broader questions of cultural identity. Cuba provides an interesting case. As we have seen, revolutionary cinema and the nation-building project moved forward in tandem from 1960 onward. Some thirty years later, the vicissitudes of the Special Period resulted in their decoupling. State funds would no longer support island filmmakers and finance their projects to the extent they once did. Filmmakers would no longer create primarily for local audiences. And films would no longer have as a key objective the disseminating of revolutionary ideology. Despite these sweeping changes, autochthonous culture would continue to be valued; the difference is that now *cubanía* would be constructed by audiovisual auteurs intent on meeting the demands of the world market. Through their filmmaking endeavors, these artists would construct a new discursive place in the world. Located between past histories of the nation and emerging narratives of a global community, they would draw upon Cuba's "foundational fictions" to problematize and critique national identity. In doing so, they would craft a conception of *cubanía* characterized by transnational linkages and responsive to global processes—an identity retaining some of the socialist values promulgated throughout the revolution while resisting dogmatism and the reach of state authority. The utopian vision of the New Man would be jettisoned so as to acknowledge, as does *Life Is to Whistle*, that "nobody's perfect."

Writing from Havana in 1998, Fernando Martínez Heredia envisioned a notion of national identity engaged with the past and committed to the future. In his words, "A national identity that does not renounce the heritage of the past decades but that is capable of revising itself from within, without lies or cover-ups, would be an extraordinary force, be-

cause of the profound anchorage that identity has in the people and because of its capacity to lift us above narrow interests to prefigure utopias
and to summon us to give a more transcendent sense of life and to the
search for well-being and happiness."[17] As will become apparent in subsequent chapters, Cuban culture workers—filmmakers and audiovisual
artists principal among them—will manage to contribute to just such a
"revising" of traditions and in doing so project a broader notion of what
it means to be Cuban.

Street Filmmaking: A New Generation Heads Out to Film

Cuba's Special Period would engender a new mode of filmmaking. It
was during this turbulent time that a generation of audiovisual artists
emerged. Born in the 1970s and 1980s, these aspiring filmmakers came of
age at a unique time when "the revolutionary process achieved substantial gains in the conditions of material and cultural life."[18] This golden
age gave way, seemingly in an instant, to an acute crisis proffering extensive suffering and extreme hardship. The circumstances produced by
this rupture marked the young men and women of this generation—and
prepared them to alter the course of Cuba's cinema.

Upon completing their formal studies at the university and/or in art
and film schools, these graduates stepped out of the classrooms into the
street. And that is where they stayed. There were no jobs to be had during this Special Period. Everything was empty—refrigerators, markets,
gas pumps, shop windows, water tanks, pharmacy shelves, and even
the state coffers. Many government agencies, unable to meet payroll, reduced the workweek, cut salaries, and slashed benefits. Hearty employee
lunches, once an institution in Revolutionary Cuba, shrunk to only a few
sips of broth or a few mouthfuls of rice. And many of the *guaguas* that
had shuttled Cubans to work remained immobile, leaving workers to
make their way on infrequent and overcrowded buses, while standing
in the bed of a truck, on a bicycle, or on foot. It was not uncommon during this time to hear that someone whose breakfast consisted of a cup
of sugar water had awakened at four o'clock in the morning to wait in
long lines for a bus, to stand on the roadside with arm outstretched to
hitch a ride, to ride a bicycle for nearly two hours, or to walk six or eight
miles in order to report to work on time. If Cubans *with* jobs experienced

these harsh conditions, it is not at all surprising that recent graduates had little possibility of procuring employment. Unemployment rates soared; whereas only 3.4 percent of the population was deemed "economically inactive" in 1981, the percentage increased to 5.4 in 1990 and 8.1 in both 1993 and 1995.[19] Talent, tenacity, and the successful completion of an advanced degree did not translate into a job during this time, for the island's largest employer, the state, was broke. New opportunities were virtually nonexistent for these artists. So lacking a professional home—that is, sponsorship by a state institution—they had no choice but to remain in the street. To break into filmmaking, they would have to pound the pavement.

And pound the pavement they did. Intent on making movies, but lacking opportunities within the industry, these aspiring filmmakers set out to seek funding, establish contacts, and procure equipment. Out of necessity, working with limited budgets and without industry infrastructure, this generation became adept at *resolviendo* and *inventando*—figuring out creative ways to make do. One strategy was to forge partnerships with institutions and individuals at home and abroad; through collaboration and connectedness, they could stretch scarce resources and capitalize on synergistic momentum. Another consisted of experimenting with new technologies, thereby increasing the audiovisual options open to them for producing and disseminating their work. They ventured down paths never before trod in Cuban cinema. And their efforts revolutionized the ways in which films would be made in Cuba and marketed the world over.

I have devised the term "Street Filmmaking" to denote this new mode of audiovisual expression that emerged in Cuba around 1990, when lightweight portable equipment began to replace the unwieldy industrial models and young media artists began producing films with only a few friends and a handful of *fulas*. Works created in the Street Filmmaking style share common features: All have relied on new technologies for their creation, often in conjunction with traditional approaches; all have been financed with low or no budgets; all have benefited from partnerships with allies on the island and in other countries; and all reveal a commitment to experimentation and innovation. These films have all been made by audiovisual artists adept at *resolviendo*, or making do. They combined footage filmed with a variety of cameras, filmed night scenes during the day, colored on and scraped away the celluloid, and actually invented new techniques every step of the way. It bears mentioning that these low-budget films do not generally reveal their humble origins. On the contrary, as one photographer will attest in a subsequent chapter, Street Filmmakers seek to produce the impression of high-budget films even when working with only a few pesos. Impatient and passionate, propelled by their perseverance and entrepreneurial spirit, these artists pursued new avenues in creating and disseminating their work. With urgency and audacity these young people would represent their world, forge new relationships, and anchor themselves in a present-becoming future.

Street Filmmakers do not tend to see themselves as part of the collective Revolutionary project in the way that their elders did. Born after 1959, they are inheritors of the Cuban Revolution rather than its architects. Not surprisingly, their sense of citizenship and national identity differs dramatically from that of their parents' and grandparents' generations. This is not to say they have distanced themselves from explorations of what it means to be Cuban—in fact, many of their films tackle this very topic. But we will see that the nature and scope of their inquiry differs significantly. Having jettisoned politically charged constructions of nation, utopia, revolution, and the "New Man," they reflect on identity in a variety of ways. They are interested in what it means to be gay, straight, sane, crazy, in love, alone, disenfranchised, an artist, and so on. They turn their cameras toward the margins to recover the disenfranchised, those who have been left behind by Cuba's hegemonic socialist project. And they are rethinking conceptions of "home" and the "world" and reflecting on their connection to both spheres.[20] Being "Cuban" for these audiovisual artists is to pertain to an increasingly connected world. Recall that the Berlin Wall came down before they ever reached adulthood. And during their lifetime, the problems plaguing our world grew ever graver: Poverty worsened, epidemics intensified, violence escalated, and wars were waged. The proliferation of communications technologies brought them into contact with previously unknown peoples, remote places, and distant issues. As a result, Street Filmmakers jettison dichotomies delineating "us" from "them" and "here" from "there." The island's upheaval and its collision with the global marketplace positioned this generation to negotiate the coming together of local and global forces. They also understand the constructed nature of identity and self-consciously enact *cubanía* for their own purposes. Products of a new era, they embrace identity as an ongoing process—one more individual than collective, more dynamic than static, more personal than political.

The body of material they produced, taken as a whole, reasserts a sense of Cuban identity not defined and promulgated by the Revolutionary state apparatus but emanating instead from the visions and experiences of individual artists. What do films produced in the Street Filmmaking mode look like? It would be convenient to report that all of these films are cut from the same cloth. But they are not. They vary greatly—in style and subject matter and approach. Among them are included features, experimental works, animation, documentaries, and video clips. Some of these new artists underscore the resilience of islanders as they struggle to get by during difficult times. In *Habanaceres* (*Havana Dawns*, 2001), Luis Leonel León interviews four of Cuba's leading culture workers: novelist Leonardo Padura Fuentes, playwright Alberto Pedro, filmmaker Fernando Pérez, and musician Carlos Varela. Their collective impressions and experiences illuminate the changing role of Cuban artists during this time of transition. In *Jugando al Timeball* (*Playing Timeball*, 2004), Susana Patricia Reyes captures the frustration of Cubans who feel forced to waste time every day—waiting for the bus, waiting for their turn to buy a movie ticket, or waiting to buy the newspaper. In this short, interview footage and takes of long lines combine to underscore the pervasive problem.[21] These works, like industry productions *Suite Habana* (Fernando Pérez, 2003) and *Rey y Reina* (*King and Queen*, Julio García Espinosa, 1994), highlight the dignity of the protagonists in their struggle to *resolver*, or get by in present-day Cuba.

Other filmmakers experiment with the medium to engage with issues affecting people the world over. In *Video de familia* (*Family Video*, 2001), Humberto Padrón employs the home video as his structure for exploring family dynamics and dysfunction. What begins as a simple taped message to an expatriate son unveils the complexity and challenges of a contemporary Cuban family. Although dedicated to "Cuban families wherever they may be," this film touches on experiences all families encounter—conflict, intolerance, disappointment, forgiveness, and love.[22] In *Existen* (*They Exist*, 2005), a film that will be discussed at length in a subsequent chapter, Esteban Insausti recovers the stories of Havana residents deemed crazy by some. The clever weaving together of their experiences and impressions provokes a solemn reflection on the part of viewers. *Existen* implores us to ask the question, To what extent can any of us remain sane, given the poverty, violence, contamination, and increasing dehumanization plaguing our world? These works, like the avant-garde documentaries of Nicolasito Guillén Landrián and Sara Gómez, test the limits of cinematic representation while probing universal conditions and concerns.

Still other films employ humor and satire. In *Utopía* (2004), Arturo Infante relies on a double discourse to critique his nation's cultural literacy agenda. The beer-drinking, domino-playing men and gum-chewing, nail-painting women debate the finer points of Italian opera and baroque aesthetics. In *Monte Rouge* (2004), Eduardo del Llano tackles the subject of state security. This piece simultaneously pokes fun at Cuba's secret police and those islanders whose paranoia runs rampant. Both call to mind the deft use of humor by such established industry directors as Gerardo Chijona, Enrique Colina, Daniel Díaz Torres, and Juan Carlos Tabío.

Despite their diversity, these films do share common elements. Oftentimes, the focus is individuals and their idiosyncrasies. Personal stories, frequently drawn from the filmmakers' own experience, prevail over historical epics.[23] Subjects once considered taboo in Cuba—inconsistencies between official policies and actual practices, sexuality, domestic violence, drugs, prostitution, housing shortages, censorship, discrimination, and so on—now figure prominently. The films employ a broad range of protagonists, including children, disenchanted urban youth, the mentally ill, campesinos, transvestites, graffiti artists, and other disenfranchised sectors. And transnational topics abound. These works frequently feature migration and movement; border-crossing protagonists oftentimes appear in their narratives. Some films even take shape out of images filmed in multiple locales. In *Fuera de Liga* (*Out of Their League*, 2008), for example, Ian Padrón spliced footage filmed in Havana together with interviews of the legendary baseball pitcher Orlando "El Duque" Hernández filmed in the United States.[24] Works by these Street Filmmakers cease to celebrate the Revolution's triumphs and idealize its subjects, as did many ICAIC classics of the 1960s and 1970s. Instead, they explore the tensions provoked by the island's accelerated transformation—the pervasive absences and exodus, the topsy-turvy values and ethics, and the omnipresent *doble moral*. Taken together, they proffer a reflection on what it means to be Cuban in times of transition.

And yet, it is not the films, per se, that characterize Street Filmmaking. Rather, it is the mode of production and dissemination forged by a particular generation. The young cineaste Tupac Pinilla sums this up effectively. "We are defined," he asserts, by "the effort it takes to make films in the street."[25] He and his counterparts differ in their aspirations and aesthetic approaches, but they share the common experience of mediating the governmental structures and the growing public sphere. Street Filmmakers craft these projects from an in-between position; they are not wholly connected to the state-sponsored apparatus but not completely disconnected from it either. For this reason, *On Location in Cuba* goes beyond mere analysis of the film texts to interrogate the conditions of production and circulation in a precise locale. Examining the material conditions of cultural creation and dissemination is, I believe, crucial for making sense of how social actors operating increasingly outside the state's purview have helped transform a concertedly national cinema into one driven by transnational linkages and global forces, and how they have contributed to the imagining of a more heterogeneous Cuban nation.

Attention to the artistic process marks a key contribution of this book. Many studies of national cinema take a body of films as their objects of inquiry; a reading of these texts determines, in great part, the nature of the nation being narrated. Such an approach is valuable, particularly in articulating the centrality of representation to identity formation. After all, to reiterate Stuart Hall's influential remark, "Identity is constructed inside not outside representation."[26] My interest lies not only in the films, however, but in the larger context of their conception, creation, and circulation. I am committed to querying the *process* through which these texts come into being and scrutinizing the routes along which they move. I am intent on tracking Cuban culture workers in the tumultuous 1990s and early into the twenty-first century so as to interrogate the forces that collided in that particular place and time. Cubans of this generation were cast into the role of mediators. Moving back and forth between state structures and the public sphere, they would negotiate the limits of government authority and global market forces. As they chronicled this time of transition and sought to make sense of their ever-changing circumstances, they would introduce emerging values into the existing social-ist structure and thereby participate in imagining a national community characterized by greater diversity.

A number of terms have been employed to denote the creative output of this generation—"*cine de aficionados*" ("amateur"), "*cine submergido*" ("underground" or "alternative"), and "independent" filmmaking.[27] Each contributes to understanding the phenomenon analyzed herein. Yet all fall short in my estimation. "*Cine de aficionados*" rightly captures the youthful spirit of many aspiring filmmakers. And it certainly attests to their passion for cinema—watching films from all over the world, staying abreast of media news and technological innovations, and always work-ing toward their next project. But while it succeeds in capturing the ideal-ism and energy of this generation, it obliterates altogether the serious-ness of purpose characterizing these artists. Filmmaking is not a hobby for them, some activity to fill evenings and weekends. Rather, it is a voca-tion. These audiovisual artists see themselves as bona fide cineastes and approach their work with a great degree of professionalism. To dub these filmmakers "amateurs" is, I believe, to give short shrift to their passion and commitment.

"Underground" and "alternative" are sometimes used to denote the efforts behind these homemade films. Indeed, both terms account for the ever-increasing practice of making films outside the ICAIC and of employing a mode different from that used by the national industry. And both correctly suggest that this generation of filmmakers poses challenges to the status quo. They constantly push the limits, whether developing themes or refining techniques or negotiating distribution deals. Their formal audiovisual training has translated into confidence and contacts permitting them to resist extant norms. "Underground" and "alternative" may be preferable to the more paternalistic and dis-missive "*cine de aficionados*," but I still find them inadequate. One rea-son is that these terms set this generation of filmmakers in opposition to their predecessors. Whereas these Street Filmmaking projects do demon-strate a commitment to innovation and experimentation, in fact, many resemble those made within the state-sponsored institute—they depict faces and places familiar to Cuban film fans, scrutinize island situations and circumstances, and draw inspiration from the nation's revolutionary film tradition. The filmmakers of this generation are, almost without exception, quick to credit Cuba's rich film tradition as a significant source of inspiration. They readily express admiration for their ICAIC counterparts, many of whom are mentors and friends. So, in fact, these artists and their work continue rather than contradict the island's industry tradition. While members of this generation tackle some topics heretofore not treated in Cuban films and explore new production channels and dissemination avenues, their stance vis-à-vis the industry is decidedly not an oppositional one. Another reason is more straightforward still: For readers in the United States, whose access to information about Cuba is both limited and biased, the terms conjure up dissident production. "Underground" and "alternative" suggest "counterrevolutionary." Such a reduction occludes the complex ways in which members of this new generation are employing expressive culture to reflect on and reconfigure their identities—as artists, revolutionaries, Cubans, and citizens of the world.

"Independent" has also been used to characterize this new audiovisual mode, but I find myself wary to do so. Part of my rationale echoes that of one filmmaker comprising this generation. Juan Carlos Cremata Malberti contends that very few directors—in Cuba or anywhere for that matter—can be considered truly independent. He notes that only Robert Redford, Francis Ford Coppola, and a handful of others have sufficient wealth to finance their own films. Deep pockets certainly do facilitate independently made films. But capital alone does not account for my reluctance to label this new mode of filmmaking "independent."

It is the reach of Cuba's extensive cultural infrastructure that poses, for me, the greatest impediment to notions of independent production. Individuals working in state-sponsored entities invariably contribute expertise, provide equipment, and facilitate contacts. The rubric of "independent" filmmaking obliterates this critical support from government organizations. Oftentimes, it is a close friend or family member who lends a hand—a member of a theater troupe offering the use of a hard-to-re-create period costume or item, the chauffeur of a state agency taking a circuitous route to assist a filmmaker in scouting a distant location, a policeman agreeing to reroute traffic in order to facilitate filming, and so on. Family connections between the state culture industry and the Street Filmmakers abound and contribute further to this collaboration: Juan Carlos Cremata Malberti is the son of Cuban Institute of Radio and Television director Iraida Malberti Cabrera; Danielito Díaz is the son of ICAIC director Daniel Díaz Torres; Pavel Giroud is the nephew of Iván Giroud, director of the International Festival of New Latin American Cinema; Inti Herrera is the son of ICAIC actress Eslinda Núñez and director Manuel Herrera; Ian Padrón is the son of renowned ICAIC animation director Juan Padrón; and so on. These connections in no way diminish the talent and tenacity of these young filmmakers; what they do, however, is suggest the potential of "independent" to mislead. In Cuba, the state and public spheres are interconnected. As this study reveals, civil society is indeed expanding in Cuba, but it does not exist separate from the state. In this transitional moment, the growing public sphere is buoyed up by and taking shape in collusion with governmental policies and practices.

With the Cuban state's investment in education, its significant role in training and supporting artists, and its overt agenda of fomenting au-tochthonous culture, virtually all filmmakers have derived benefits from it. Perhaps their work has not received direct funding from the ICAIC (al-though in many cases it has), but that is not to deny the audiovisual art-ists' training in state-subsidized facilities, participation in government-organized trips around the island and sometimes even overseas, and lifetime of exposure to government-funded cultural events. And as with the earlier terms, "independent" constructs false dichotomies; it suggests Cuban filmmakers work *either* inside the ICAIC *or* outside it, that they align themselves *either* with the industry *or* against it. In fact, the bor-ders between industry-produced and other films have become more fluid as filmmakers increasingly occupy the interconnected worlds. The "in-dependent" moniker remains inadequate, then, for making sense of this recent audiovisual activity.

I have coined "Street Filmmaking" in order to analyze the island's re-cent audiovisual transformation without reproducing the dichotomous thinking that is all too prevalent in critical studies of Cuba's culture. Be-fore proceeding, however, I must acknowledge that the "street" adjec-tive is also imperfect. For one thing, it may conjure up the 1980s graffiti movement in Cuba. And indeed Street Art (Arte de la Calle) shares some elements with Street Filmmaking: The works emerge from spontaneity, and the artists communicate their creative visions without institutional infrastructure or backing some of the time. And there is an element of rebellion, a resistance to tried-and-true approaches and aesthetics. But whereas Street Artists worked outdoors, employed public spaces, and directed their message to a local audience, Street Filmmakers do not limit their work to outdoor public spaces, generally do collaborate with institutions on and beyond the island, and seek to communicate with a local and international viewing public. The two cultural phenomena are distinct, then, emerging during different times, responding to diverse sets of issues, and proffering widely divergent expressions. Another drawback of the term is that "street" can connote the disenfranchisement of the noun it modifies, such as a "street person." That is clearly not the intention here. All of these filmmakers consider themselves to be actively contributing to their nation's cultural scene; many manage to earn a living from their artistic endeavors, some with incomes far greater than those of their industry counterparts. Despite these limitations, I have opted to employ the term "Street Filmmaking." One reason is simply the prominence of the streets in Cuba. It is on the streets where news is shared, business transacted, and affection shown. The island's climate has always drawn people outdoors, but during the Special Period, when blackouts silenced televisions and radios and darkened houses for hours on end, most Cubans preferred the streets. And many still do. It is not by accident that Fernando Pérez set his recent film, *Suite Habana*, in the capital's streets. For him, it is in the streets where one best gets a feel for life in Cuba. The most compelling reason, though, has to do with the filmmakers themselves. In conversations, they often articulate their creative efforts in terms of the streets. Whether pounding the pavement or going door-to-door, they tend to talk about working "on the street." As Pavel Giroud remarked to me, "I work with the industry, but I continue considering myself a filmmaker *on the street*"; or as Esteban Insausti interjected during our conversation, "If there's something that differentiates my generation from previous ones, it's that we're making films '*in the streets*.'" Industry professionals, too, occasionally employ the "street" designator in referring to the practices of this new generation. Longtime producer Camilo Vives expressed hope that the ICAIC would move forward quickly enough to catch up with these emerging filmmakers; "I believe that more is being produced *in the streets* than in the industry," he remarked, emphasizing the importance of capitalizing on the "*street experience*" of these artists in order to streamline the industry production process (emphasis mine).[28]

To sum up, then, Street Filmmakers of this generation are individuals with formal training in filmmaking or a related field who came of age in the late 1980s and early 1990s. Products of the Special Period and emboldened by their impatience and passion for making films, they developed an entrepreneurial spirit in order to *resolver*. Seeing themselves as active agents in charting their future, this generation asks questions, takes risks, and poses challenges. They are comfortable using celluloid, video, and digital media and sometimes combine all of them in a single project. Many are involved in some way with the national film institute, but virtually all operate as "free agents," carrying out nonindustry projects as well. Whether working within or outside the industry, they succeed at mobilizing contacts and capital from the island and far beyond. Adept at negotiation, they serve as mediators between Cuba's autochthonous traditions and international culture producers and consumers. This generation is plugged in to the global communications networks—and connected. Street Filmmakers are industrious, ingenious, and innovative. Juan Carlos Cremata Malberti, Esteban Insausti, Pavel Giroud, Léster Hamlet, Arturo Infante, Luis Leonel León, Humberto Padrón, Ian Padrón, Gustavo Pérez, and Waldo Ramírez are among the Street Filmmakers who have helped change the course of Cuba's revolutionary cinema. And their efforts are already influencing up-and-coming audiovisual artists like Carlos Barba, Susana Barriga, Alejandro Brugués, Karel Ducases Manzano, Sandra Gómez Jiménez, Inti Herrera, Ernesto Piña Rodríguez, Jeffrey Puente García, Alejandro Ramírez, Alina Rodríguez Abreu, Asori (Amado Soto Ricardo), Hilda Elena Vega, Daniel Vera, Aram Vidal, and dozens of others.

Tracking Images, Telling Stories: A Postcolonial Approach

How to tell the Street Filmmaking story? I have opted to create a work of cultural history in the vein of Eduardo Galeano, the Uruguayan historian who characterizes his efforts in this way: "Each fragment of this huge mosaic is based on a solid documentary foundation."[29] Like Galeano's narrative, mine is crafted from bits and pieces gathered here and there. Instead of a mosaic, though, a montage results herein. In this project, I have juxtaposed films and facts with memories and experiences—those of numerous filmmakers as well as a few of my own. *On Location in Cuba* reels off like a film—with dolly backs, close ups, and jump cuts exhibit-

Alejandro Pérez with his digital camera filming in the streets of Havana.
Courtesy of Pérez.

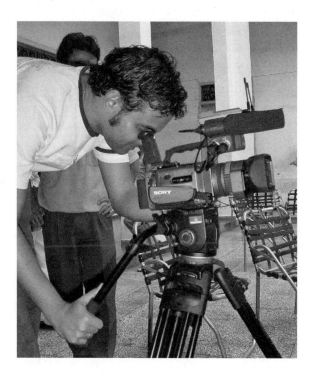

Carlos Barba prepares
to film in Santiago
de Cuba. Courtesy
of Barba.

ing the *process* of making and circulating films as well as the *products* or film texts. The transformation of Cuba's state cinema into a multifaceted audiovisual praxis did not occur in a neat chronology. Nor was the process smooth, seamless, and devoid of conflict. The cinematic structure of this study, therefore, is designed to depict its complexity; *On Location* retains contradictions and collisions so as to reveal some of the nuances—of both recent audiovisual activity and the island's larger transformation over the past two decades.

My project differs significantly—in structure, method, and scope—from other critical assessments of Cuba's cinema. The first three decades of the island's revolutionary cinema are fairly well documented. The *Cine Cubano* journal traces the development of the island's film tradition through in-depth essays, interviews, film reviews, and images. Recently published volumes of correspondence and essays make available documents crucial to understanding Cuba's film policies, practices, and theories from the 1960s and 1970s.[30] Several editions focus on the founding fathers of Cuba's revolutionary cinema, such as Santiago Álvarez, Julio García Espinosa, Tomás Gutiérrez Alea, and Humberto Solás.[31] A catalog of ICAIC productions spanning forty-five years and a study of Cuban cinema from 1897 to 1990 round out the principal resources in Spanish.[32] In English, Michael Chanan's *The Cuban Image*, first published in 1985 and then updated and rereleased in 2004 as *Cuban Cinema*, remains the primary source on island filmmaking between 1960 and 1990. With industry production predominating in Cuba until only recently, it is understandable that Chanan focuses his discussion around ICAIC films and state-supported filmmakers.

Very little attention has been paid to Cuba's film production in recent years, and even less to the audiovisual activity by a new generation of artists mediating national strictures and transnational forces. A few single-author studies address components of the island's recent activity,[33] and some thoughtful compilations on Cuban culture integrate reflections of one or more filmmakers.[34] In addition, Sujatha Fernandes devotes one-third of *Cuba Represent* to island cinema; her emphasis on film reception expands cultural criticism in a meaningful way, but the compelling study does not treat films made outside the national film institute. All of these contributions are valuable, but none proffers a sustained examination of Cuba's audiovisual output from 1990 to the present. And none moves beyond industry initiatives to analyze audiovisual activity outside the state-sponsored ICAIC. Given the plethora of changes that have occurred in Cuba over the past two decades—including the erosion of state hegemony, the rapid expansion of the public sphere, the stepped-up engagement with global markets and cultures, and the reconfiguration of *cubanía*—there is a pressing need to examine the dramatic transformation of island filmmaking within *and* outside the state institute. *On Location in Cuba*, then, represents the first book-length study in any language to interrogate the island's changing audiovisual landscape in recent years so as to make sense of these larger shifts. In showcasing the efforts of Street Filmmakers, this study reveals the increasing importance of social actors working outside of—but not out of synch with—the state apparatus. In considering efforts with the ICAIC as well as "on the streets," *On Location* heeds the call of Cuban film critic Juan Antonio García Borrero to move beyond "ICAIC-centric" approaches.[35] In proffering glimpses of groups and individual artists working outside the capital, the volume takes into account Daniel Díaz Torres's insistence that Cuba's filmmaking—and by extension the criticism of that work—should not be limited to Havana. And in highlighting border-crossing artists, this project repositions this national cinema on decidedly transnational terrain.

On Location in Cuba: Street Filmmaking during Times of Transition provides a window through which to view an island in flux and a series of audiovisual artists navigating the waters between a state-controlled system and a market mechanism. The first section of *On Location* begins with a "dolly back" to the late 1980s and early 1990s. Chapter 1 brings into its frame several culture organizations established at that time that helped pave the way for new modes of producing and distributing films. The Escuela Internacional de Cine y Televisión (International School of Film and Television), the Asociación Hermanos Saiz (Saíz Brothers Association), the Movimiento Nacional de Video (National Video Movement), and the Fundación Ludwig de Cuba (Ludwig Foundation of Cuba) all helped prepare conditions for the emergence of Street Filmmaking. The impact of each of these organizations is examined, as is their influence on individual filmmakers. We will observe the precedents they set—in embracing video as a viable mode of documenting a nation in transition, in establishing partnerships with island and international organizations, and in working outside but in tandem with state-sponsored film and television—and their importance for the island's audiovisual future. Chapter 2 is devoted to Televisión Serrana, a media collective located in the remote Sierra Maestra region. Televisión Serrana is considered a community media success story for its achievements in empowering local residents and employing video to strengthen highland identity. Emanating from alliances among community-based, national and international entities, this organization attests to the effectiveness of local-global collaboration and to the ways in which individuals working on grassroots initiatives can effect change. Chapter 3 shifts from the countryside to the capital, and from a nongovernmental organization to a state agency. The trajectory of the ICAIC Animation Studio permits us to see the potential for new technologies to coexist with traditional ones. In order to survive, this operation migrated from hand-drawn to computer-generated images without sacrificing its principal mission—that of serving the Cuban public. Just as innovation need not obliterate tradition, so, too, can engagement with the global marketplace actually sustain and strengthen "local" culture. Despite the key contributions of all these cultural organizations, not only in Cuba but also in the broader media sphere, information about them is scarce. It is fitting, then, to profile these entities herein and to underscore their influence on the audiovisual artists to be featured in subsequent chapters.

The next section zooms in on three notable Street Filmmakers. Juan Carlos Cremata Malberti, Pavel Giroud, and Esteban Insausti are featured in Chapters 4, 5, and 6, respectively. In their creative output, they explore a series of questions relevant for making sense of the island's transformation and changing notions of *cubanía*: What does it mean to make "revolutionary" or "Cuban" films today? How are Cuban artists and culture workers to negotiate an increasingly connected—and chaotic—world? What are the forces that drive individuals and cultural products beyond the borders of the nation and cast them into new roles? To what extent has the crafting of auteur identities helped satisfy producers and viewers at home and in other countries? In each of these cases, textual analyses and contextual frameworks are augmented by the filmmaker's testimony. Their experiences of getting by during Cuba's tumultuous Special Period—their struggles as they collide and collude with myriad local and global forces—yield a collective portrait of Street Filmmaking, one revealing how this new generation of audiovisual artists has altered the direction of Cuban cinema, pushed the limits of the state's authority, and broadened conceptions of *cubanía*.

A final section presents a montage of audiovisual artists and issues. Chapter 7 focuses on the National Exhibit of New Filmmakers (Muestra Nacional de Nuevos Realizadores), a showcase of work by emerging media-makers that takes place each year in Havana. Within this precise context, we see once again the diversity of perspectives and approaches characterizing present-day audiovisual activity on the island. We witness the ways in which these artists draw upon and deviate from Cuba's revolutionary dogma so as to communicate their values of social justice and individualism. And we observe the interventions of these cineastes in Cuba's cultural politics and their collusion with government actors who tolerate and even heed their criticism. Finally, in an epilogue, I highlight some of the ongoing challenges and speculate on the island's audiovisual future.

As Cuban revolutionary cinema turns fifty, it is fitting to focus on the Street Filmmakers who, like previous generations of Cuban cineastes, are wielding cameras to construct their nation. Unlike their predecessors, however, many work without ongoing support from the state-sponsored industry. Employing new technologies and connected to global networks, they focus on persistent problems in their midst and question long-held truths. From their position in the street—that is, straddling state structures, public spheres, and the global marketplace—these filmmakers are intervening in the island's cultural politics.

This study—taking shape over two decades and growing out of sustained contact with film colleagues and friends in Cuba—required a unique approach. In *On Location*, I develop and employ "tracking." The technique of tracking, in cinematic practice, keeps the camera in motion as the action unfolds. It differs from a snapshot, in which a click of the camera shutter produces a static shot of life. It also differs from panning, in which the camera is rotated, on its axis, across a scene. Tracking frames a scene as it unfolds over time, and it links the camera and operator with the subject. Tracking entails movement as well as connectedness to one's subject. As a postcolonial critical approach, tracking permits us to move *with* our objects of inquiry—not out front as guides or behind as followers but, rather, alongside cultural texts and in dialogue with their producers and consumers.

My mapping of Cuba's shifting audiovisual landscape relies heavily on the perspectives of numerous filmmakers and other audiovisual professionals. Like Dean MacCannell, I believe that "any discovery of a new critical subject necessarily begins and ends ethnographically, with observations of real people, events and relations," that "it cannot be contained in advance in philosophy, theory, or hypothesis, unless it is condemned to produce, or to fail to produce, only that which the investigator already knows."[36] At the center of this study, then, are the experiences of those who lived through these staggering changes. The reflections and recollections of dozens of audiovisual artists, gleaned from our conversations and correspondence as well as through the interviews I conducted and filmed, capture the complexity of making and marketing films in a precise locale. *On Location in Cuba* reveals how a "special" generation of Cuban filmmakers has adapted to drastically shifting circumstances at home and around the world.

Several factors motivated my decision to track the emergence of both a new notion of *cubanía* and a new audiovisual era through the eyes of island filmmakers. One decisive objective was to humanize these artists. A prevalent tendency, particularly pronounced in the United States, is to depersonalize Cubans. This became exceedingly evident to me during the tug-of-war over Elián González. For many in the United States, the appearance of Elián on network news constituted their first glimpse of a "real" Cuban. Prior to this, it had not really occurred to many—perhaps most—that Cuba was comprised of children and men and women. U.S. citizens had been conditioned by the media to collapse Cuba with Castro, a reduction that effectively obliterated from view 11 million inhabitants. The image of the six-year-old boy, together with footage of his concerned father expressing his desire to be reunited with his young son, left no doubt that the island was populated by individuals who experienced joy and sadness, whose lives were filled with love, loss, and longing.

Another related goal of integrating these perspectives is to highlight the diversity of Cuban artists and other social actors. During two decades of traveling back and forth between the United States and Cuba—and also disseminating information about Cuban culture in the United States by teaching university courses, delivering lectures at professional conferences, addressing audiences at film festivals and cultural events, and so on—I have become painfully aware of how little we know about Cubans, despite our geographical proximity and common histories.³⁷ Policies and practices in Washington, D.C., and Havana limit our contact with one another and widen the gulf. As a consequence, people in the United States have a simplistic notion of what it means to be Cuban. *On Location in Cuba* introduces a range of filmmakers who enact their identities very differently. Some see themselves as artists above all. Others are more intent on the business of cinema. Some characterize themselves as revolutionaries. Others steer clear of labels altogether. Most are based on the island, but some "commute" to distant locales while still considering Cuba to be home. The experiences of Street Filmmakers featured herein reveal their diversity and dynamism. The juxtaposition of their divergent attitudes, approaches, accomplishments, and dreams is designed to present the multifaceted nature of the island and its inhabitants.

It is, ultimately, to accord agency to these individuals that I rely on their testimony. Generally, only a handful of Cuban voices are heard, those of émigrés and dissidents. Rafael Hernández has commented on the tendency to disregard the perspectives of Cubans on the island. In "Looking at Cuba," he identifies a paradox: In order "to be credible, the author of a work on Cuba must be outside the country or be a 'dissident' within it." He goes on to note the pervasive view that "Cuban intellectuals lack their own perspectives for reflective thought. Either they are faint-hearted or they are mere bureaucrats repeating official discourse. Dissidents . . . are deemed to be far more credible."³⁸ The stories and memories and experiences contained herein cast Cuban audiovisual artists as active agents committed to the island's culture and its future. Whether working inside or outside governmental channels, this generation has helped chart Cuba's course. And, as we will see in the pages that follow, they intend to continue doing so.

As ideas and individuals increasingly move across geopolitical territories and traverse disciplinary spaces, the articulation of multiple and varied perspectives has become indispensable. In proffering the stories of numerous tellers, the tracking method complicates issues instead of simplifying them. It embraces rather than erases dissonance. I have tracked the experiences of dozens of audiovisual artists around Havana and across the island as well as in sites as diverse as Montreal and Madrid, Mexico City and New York, San José and Williamsburg. Whether "on location" in Cuba for a week or a month or more, whether based in Havana or in outlying areas, I have experienced firsthand this rapidly changing world. And I share some of those moments herein. My self-conscious use of the first person from time to time is intended to acknowledge the ways in which my own perceptions and experiences shape this study. By reflecting on my process of inquiry, I reveal—at least to the extent possible—my position of enunciation. What routes did I follow in seeking information? What questions did I ask? How might those have evoked particular answers? I am convinced that there is no neutral zone reserved for critics. To track a culture in transition is to take a stand. It is to assist and advocate. It is a political act. The insertion of my own perspectives into this narrative acknowledges that fact. I close this introductory chapter and open the next with an admission echoing the words of Eduardo Galeano: "What is told here has happened, although I tell it in my style and manner. . . . I take sides: I confess it and am not sorry."[39]

DOLLY BACK

The task of a revolutionary cineaste
is to revolutionize cinema.
—Julio García Espinosa

Documenting Tumultuous Times

NEW CULTURE ORGANIZATIONS

PROFFER ALTERNATIVES

Filmmaking activity in Cuba's national film institute declined dramatically in the 1990s. In the midst of the economic crisis and concomitant scarcity, it became exceedingly difficult to sustain the resource-intensive production. The Noticiero ICAIC Latinoamericano (ICAIC Latin American Newsreel) ceased to exist, after thirty years of uninterrupted production under the direction of Santiago Álvarez. The Animation Studio managed to keep its doors open, but only by contracting with foreign firms, and while the selling of services constituted a lifeline, it did nothing to guarantee the studio's survival. Production of feature films and documentaries slowed dramatically—and then stalled out. When, in 1996, not a single feature film was completed, the absence marked a first in the ICAIC's history.[1] This significant decline in film production during Cuba's Special Period rendered the future of the island's national film institute tenuous. Coproduction agreements helped, but they alone could not move the precarious industry back onto solid ground. At stake, then, was nothing less than the nation's ability to represent itself.

Despite the bleak panorama, some hope for Cuba's cinema glimmered from outside the ICAIC. The late 1980s and early 1990s witnessed the founding of several organizations devoted to fomenting the island's cultural expression. As the ICAIC's film production was slowing down, these organizations were gearing up. They trained audiovisual artists and provided the equipment, resources, and infrastructure that helped keep Cuban cinema afloat. This chapter examines four organizations whose efforts contributed to diversifying the island's cinema: the Escuela Internacional de Cine y Televisión (International School of Film and Television, or EICTV), the Asociación Hermanos Saíz (Saíz Brothers Association, or AHS), the Movimiento Nacional de Video (National Video Movement of Cuba), and the Fundación Ludwig de Cuba (Ludwig Foundation of Cuba, or FLC). Each made important inroads into transforming Cuba's cinema into a more complex audiovisual culture; collectively, they paved the way for a new era in media-making that would engender Street Filmmaking.

The entities examined herein represent both governmental and nongovernmental organizations (NGOs). While they took shape out of varied individual and institutional efforts and responded to diverse sets of circumstances, all shared key characteristics that would nurture mediamaking on the island. First, all had at the center of their mission the strengthening of Cuba's culture; all sought to train and empower culture workers—audiovisual artists among them—and all promoted concertedly local creation. These organisms occupied ground familiar to existing Cuban organizations. That is not to say that all proffered a single vision or employed identical strategies. Rather, they emphasized a common cultural mission, one compatible with the aims of the Revolution. So while the creation of NGOs and the reconfiguration of some governmental organizations could have proved threatening, that possibility was mitigated by their shared goal of strengthening Cuba's cultural sector and promoting the production and circulation of autochthonous representation.

A second characteristic of all these new entities was their willingness to embrace alternative methods and test new technologies. Participating artists experimented with video, for example, a mode far less expensive and far less cumbersome than industry-style filmmaking. Although works created during this time reveal varying degrees of success, the artists made the most of the emerging mode. Mastering the new medium required a marked investment of time, a great deal of patience, and a willingness to make mistakes. But it was worthwhile; the accessibility and spontaneity afforded by video proved appealing. In a period of accelerated change, video was the ideal medium for capturing the rapid transformation. Images filmed in the morning could be projected later that same day in a roughly edited form. These artists' forays into video technology added another option for communicating through moving images. From this time onward, industry film production would cease to be the sole mode of filmmaking, audiences would begin to adapt to a different kind of viewing experience, and aspiring filmmakers would not hesitate to pick up a camera and set out to film.

A third feature characterizing these four organizations—and several others like them[2]—was their emphasis on building coalitions. Aware of the synergy derived from joining forces, they identified domestic and international allies and oftentimes secured capital from beyond the island. During a time when virtually everything was in short supply, these organisms constituted lifelines—for audiovisual artists *and* for the national film industry. They helped the ICAIC overcome mundane as well as momentous challenges—from procuring paper to printing publicity fliers to underwriting the cost of entire events. While the financial support was critical, even more important was the sense of connectedness these partnerships proffered. Despite widespread uncertainty, the audiovisual artists working in these spaces felt connected to their counterparts in Cuba and beyond the island. Linked to local *and* global networks, these emerging Cuban filmmakers remained grounded; they did not have to choose between being "here" or "there" in tough times. Alliances like these, forged during a crisis period, would continue to nurture media activity on the island for years to come.

By furthering one of the Revolution's key aims, embracing the then-new video technology, and creating partnerships, these organizations succeeded in documenting this period of accelerated transformation. Significantly, it would be filmmakers in spaces like these—outside the film industry—who would produce a substantial portion of the nation's visual archive of the Special Period.[3] Given the dire economic straits at the time, the ICAIC could not invest scarce resources in documentary productions unlikely to yield any return. Instead, they relied increasingly on coproductions; feature-length films made in partnerships with other nations provided both resources for production and expanded markets for dissemination. So the bulk of the documentary material filmed during this time emanated from individuals working in a series of organizations. No longer was the state-sponsored industry the sole purveyor of images. The EICTV, the AHS, the National Video Movement of Cuba, and the FLC, taken together, would set a precedent for making films and videos outside of—but not necessarily out of synch with—the national institute. It was with lots of spontaneity and very little infrastructure that groups of emerging artists documented their context. This would inspire subsequent filmmakers to pick up their cameras and pound the pavement in search of ideas, capital, and collaborators. Indeed, the efforts and accomplishments of these organizations helped pave the way for Street Filmmaking in Cuba.

Training Filmmakers to Depict Regional Realities: The EICTV

It was while attending the International Festival of New Latin American Cinema in Havana in 1991 that I heard the story of Manuel Marcel, a young Cuban bent on learning to make films. A new training facility was about to open in Cuba, but Marcel's odds for admission were anything but favorable. The EICTV sought to attract a diverse student body, so despite its location on the island, only a handful of spaces in the inaugural class were reserved for Cuban students. In order to compete for one of the highly desired slots, applicants had to submit a sample of their work. And Manuel Marcel had nothing to show. Nor did he have access to equipment for making a film in the traditional industry fashion. What he did have, however, was ingenuity and a friend receptive to his predicament. Fernando Pérez helped the aspiring artist procure discarded footage, strips that had broken during projection or takes that ended up on the editing room floor. Then Marcel, seated at his kitchen table, alternately colored on this used celluloid and scratched away at it with a razor blade. He spliced the bits to create a highly innovative and eminently successful homage to the Canadian animation artist, titled *A Norman McLaren (To Norman McLaren*, 1990).

I begin my discussion of the EICTV with this anecdote because it reveals several important features about the school. First, an entrepreneurial spirit prevails among EICTV students and alumni. They bring a passion for filmmaking that propels them forward. The great majority of graduates from the EICTV launch impressive careers in the field, thereby affirming the efficacy of experimenting and venturing beyond established boundaries. Second, the school has effectively built a coalition with partners on and beyond the island. Cuba's industry filmmakers have, for example, been engaged in supporting the school from the outset. The EICTV and the ICAIC have enjoyed a mutually beneficial relationship from the time of the school's founding. And the EICTV has teamed with Televisión Serrana (TVS); students have the opportunity to work in the Sierra Maestra, training with this community media initiative. This collaborative spirit has helped attract allies from many regions of the world—individual film professionals, festivals, state agencies, and NGOs. Third, conditions on the island and across Latin America have affirmed the importance of creating a film language that responds to and is engendered by the region's precise circumstances. Autochthonous elements and familiar traditions make their way into these new forms, demonstrating the school's faithfulness to one of its founding premises—that of training aspiring filmmakers to develop projects appropriate for their local contexts.

Even before the EICTV was founded, Cuba had promoted autochthonous cinema across Latin America. The principal motivation for developing a regional cinema was to counter Hollywood; filmmakers from Latin America would participate in representing their realities from within, rather than permitting themselves to be depicted—and their identities constructed—from without. Cuba's Revolutionary agenda to create a concertedly autochthonous culture contributed to and gained momentum from the region's politically charged film movement, New Latin American Cinema. The relocation of the International Festival of New Latin American Cinema from Chile to Cuba in 1979 helped consolidate Havana as a hub for the region's cinema, a movement Zuzana Pick has aptly called "a continental project." Each December since that time, Cuban filmmakers have joined their counterparts from Latin America and beyond to showcase their recent work, experience the cinema traditions of various nations, and collaborate on producing and marketing their future films. It was out of this context that the proposal for a film school emerged, a Cuba-based institution that would promote the production of local images and further consolidate a regional cinema.

The vision for a regional film school took shape during a meeting of the Comité de Cineastas de América Latina (Latin American Filmmakers Committee). Together, members of this group masterminded the creation of the EICTV, a training center designed to address a very specific need: that of equipping Latin Americans to depict their own realities on-screen. The school would provide an alternative to Hollywood-style production. It would prove that "another cinema is possible" by building on the strong grassroots media initiatives in the region. The need for Latin Americans to generate homegrown culture was articulated by the renowned Cuban filmmaker and theorist Julio García Espinosa, who served as both director of the ICAIC and the EICTV during his career. His words greet virtual visitors to the school on its website: "It is indispensable and possible for us to exercise our right to promote and develop national films on our Continent. A country without images is a country that doesn't exist. Everything we do, everything we want to do, is to have the right to be the protagonists of our own image. Another cinema is possible . . . because the visibility of our countries is necessary." The institution would be led by the accomplished Argentine filmmaker Fernando Birri, as director, and the acclaimed Colombian writer Gabriel García Márquez, as rector.

Just a year after this founding meeting, in December 1986, the school opened its doors. The process of the school's construction and inauguration is recorded in the documentary *Nace una escuela* (*A School Is Born*, Melchor Casals, 1987). Viewers see the dormitories go up, the classrooms and production studios being equipped, the swimming pool take shape, and the gardens being landscaped. Calendar pages establish the sequence of events and create anticipation as the opening draws near. The energy and excitement revealed in this documentary hark back to ICAIC productions from the 1960s and 1970s in which euphoric Cubans go about the labor of constructing housing projects, parks, and government buildings. In addition to serving as a record of the school's physical emergence, *Nace una escuela* depicts some of the key members involved in turning the dream of an international film school into a reality—Ambrosio Fornet, Julio García Espinosa, Gabriel García Márquez, and Dolores "Lola" Calviño among them.

Initially named the Escuela de Tres Mundos (School of Three Worlds), the institution was envisioned to serve Latin America, Africa, and Asia, "three regions of the world gravely affected by underdevelopment and transculturation." Along the way, students and filmmakers from Spain and other countries in Europe and America became involved, so the name was changed to the Escuela Internacional de Cine y Televisión. The variation in name in no way altered the mission, which continued to be "the formation of artists" whose "high aesthetic and technical level" is accompanied by "a concept of ethics, a critical vision of the world, and the ability to dream."[4]

The EICTV campus, located an hour south of Havana in San Antonio de los Baños, provides work space as well as living accommodations. Open-air corridors connect classrooms and production studios with dormitory rooms, a cafeteria, and administrative offices. The attractive grounds, featuring a swimming pool amidst artful landscaping, evoke a verdant oasis. Distractions are minimal, since the airport is located thirty minutes away and the city center lies another thirty minutes beyond that.

In order to provide hands-on training to aspiring filmmakers, students are mentored by practitioners rather than pedagogues. Active directors, editors, producers, sound technicians, and other experts from around the world have been brought to the island to share their expertise with the apprentices. Among the numerous notable directors affiliated with the school during its twenty-year history are Francis Ford Coppola (U.S.), Daniel Díaz Torres (Cuba), Milos Forman (Czechoslovakia–U.S.), Constantino Costa Gavras (Greece), Danny Glover (U.S.), Peter Greenaway (U.K.), George Lucas (U.S.), Fernando Pérez (Cuba), Robert Redford (U.S.), Walter Salles (Brazil), Martin Scorsese (U.S.), Ettore Scolla (Italy), Mrinal Sen (India), Fernando "Pino" Solanas (Argentina), Stephen Spielberg (U.S.), Hsván Szabó (Hungary), and a host of others. It is from highly accomplished international filmmakers that new generations of Latin Americans are being trained.

The reflections of Alejandro Brugués, an EICTV graduate specializing in scriptwriting, attest to the importance of this instructional model. When I interviewed him, he remarked on the multiple points of view among the instructors. "Sometimes we had professors who worked in Hollywood, and other times we had Cuban or Argentine professors, who worked more independently." He went on to share an anecdote from his thesis experience: "One week I had a tutor who told me there were certain things in the script that were fine, and others that didn't work. And the next week I had another adviser from another place who told me exactly the opposite. 'You can delete all this. This part here is what works.' They said diametrically opposed things," he exclaimed, adding, "and that's where you realize that you have to learn to choose your own path. Everyone is going to make suggestions and express opinions but, in the end, you're the one who decides what to keep and what to eliminate." Through their exposure to a variety of perspectives from filmmakers with vastly different experiences and philosophies, EICTV students learn to chart their own course and develop their own style in documenting their realities.[5]

One factor that helps ensure the school's success is the productive relationship it enjoys with Cuba's film industry. Numerous ICAIC directors have served on the faculty; Daniel Díaz Torres, Belkis Vega, Enrique Colina, Orlando Rojas, Miriam Talavera, Julio García Espinosa, Jorge Luis Sánchez, Fernando Pérez, and a host of others have invested their time and talent to advise and train the emerging filmmakers. ICAIC film professionals also collaborate on the students' films. In the bulk of the works produced by the EICTV, the ICAIC figures prominently in the credits. At times, these credits acknowledge the direct participation of industry personnel, such as Mirta Ibarra playing a lead role, Raúl Pérez Ureta serving as photographer, Julia Yip editing footage, or Paco Prats in the role of coproducer. At times, they are an expression of gratitude for other kinds of support, such as lending equipment, providing advice, helping secure permissions, and arranging interviews and press conferences. Industry venues like the Cine Chaplin and the Fresa y Chocolate screening room, both located only steps from the ICAIC, routinely exhibit material produced at the school. The effective partnership of the two filmmaking entities is also evident by their sharing of opportunities: When a renowned international filmmaker visits the ICAIC, the EICTV community receives an invitation, and when the EICTV is hosting an accomplished audiovisual artist, ICAIC personnel are included in the event. From the time of the school's inception, then, Cuba's national film institute has been steadfast in its support of this international training facility.

Studying filmmaking at the EICTV was then—and remains today—a remarkable opportunity. Aspiring audiovisual artists vie to enroll in the highly competitive program. And their work attests to the formidable training. Films created there reveal a tendency toward stylistic innovation and technical acumen, as one work from the first generation of students illustrates. The thesis project of Juan Carlos Cremata Malberti, whose career trajectory will be traced in Chapter 4, heralded the success of the first class of EICTV graduates. *Oscuros rinocerontes enjaulados (muy a la moda)* (*Dark Jailed Rhinoceroses [Very Much in Style]*, 1990) earned accolades on the island and beyond. Evident in this sixteen-minute debut are signs of what would define the subsequent work of this filmmaker and many other EICTV graduates: a fascination with film genres and mastery of techniques from various traditions, irreverence for established modes of thinking and acting, and a penchant for experimentation. *Dark Jailed Rhinoceroses* flaunts its fascination with film, television, and youth culture—a feature common to the films and videos produced by EICTV students. Youthful perspectives and a zeal for innovation characterize much of the school's output.

This work nods to a range of international films and a variety of cultural forms, most of which correspond to the 1960s. References to Hollywood genre films, French New Wave, and Cuba's revolutionary cinema coexist with allusions to superhero comics, television ads, and news broadcasts from the time. Cremata Malberti's parody of bureaucracy harks back to an early film by Tomás Gutiérrez Alea, *La muerte de un burócrata* (*Death of a Bureaucrat*, 1966). The subject matter constitutes a parallel as does the setting; the suite of offices where Alea filmed his humorous critique is the same location selected by Cremata Malberti for his film. Interspersed are images of Marilyn Monroe, Bugs Bunny, and scores of other legendary screen figures; a sound bite from a Humphrey Bogart film; a rendition of "You Ain't Nothin' but a Hound Dog"; and action expressions—"*plin*," "*plan*," "*cataplun*," and "*aúúúúúú*"—nodding to superhero comics. Making their way into this pastiche are advertisements promoting mostly invented health products: for sweaty feet, Acetolia; for asthma, Maico; for pain relief, Defensol; to calm the nerves, Nerveza; for an upset stomach, Uriceden; for a cold, Vicks Vaporub; and for low energy, Neurosofato Skay. This humorous convention mimics radio and television from bygone days. Further evoking the era are the characters filling the screen—miniskirted women sporting Twiggy hairdos and Jackie-O sunglasses, and suited-up men with slicked-back hair. Many of these period people were actually EICTV students, delighting in their debut as actors and extras.

The film is replete with self-conscious references to the past that merge with the present. An introductory sequence informs us that this is "a film from the archive of the Cuban Cinemateca." The black-and-white notice, appearing out of focus on the screen, gives way to a disclaimer: "The film that you are about to watch has been reconstructed from various used copies. We thank you in advance for excusing any deficiency in their projection." The "deficiency" alluded to becomes apparent; it results from the deterioration of the found footage, but also from the filmmaker's own manipulation of the celluloid. So while this film is indeed comprised of some recycled footage—film clips from several decades earlier—it also contains many sequences filmed expressly for this project. Old and new merge in *Dark Caged Rhinoceroses*, blending the 1960s with the 1990s. The final credits sequence once again conjoins past and present. The year "1960" is crossed out with a red hand-painted "X" and replaced with "1990."

In *Dark Jailed Rhinoceroses*, Cremata Malberti colored and scratched directly on the celluloid. The black-and-white design is occasionally interrupted with bright red, as when a woman applies the color from a tube of lipstick or when a dot appears on the screen. The intermittent splash of red breaks up the predominant color scheme and adds to the film's whimsical tone.[6] It also reminds viewers that the product being displayed before them has been carefully manufactured. A particularly effective montage depicts a woman seated in different positions—arms crossed, hands folded in lap, shoulders hunched, head bowed, body turned sideways. The images, artfully filmed and effectively edited, are accompanied by a hymn. This poignant sequence has the potential to absorb viewers. Before it does, however, a red dot appears in the lower right corner of the screen. The somber mood is interrupted as the dot blinks and an off-screen voice blurts out, "Get that fucking red dot off the screen." This application of paint to a succession of individual frames and the extra-diegetic sound reinforcing its intrusion remind viewers that film manipulates and the medium is a constructed one. The same effect achieved by adding a layer to the celluloid is obtained by removing some of its surface. Shapes created by scratching directly on the film serve to "age" the image, rendering ambiguous the era to which this film corresponds. The contrast of the old and the new underscores the process through which films are made — the selection, framing, juxtaposition, and manipulation of sounds and images. Just before the film ends, the assertion "Hecho en Cuba" ("Made in Cuba") offers a final testament to the fabricated nature of this film.

Cremata Malberti rejects staid conventions in *Rhinoceroses*, preferring instead to amuse and shock the viewer. Production credit goes to CAG-ARTE, a play on the word *"cagarte,"* meaning "to shit yourself." The body and its functions are flaunted throughout; a cartoon-style penis fills the screen early on, and boogers, boobs, and blow jobs follow. As the hidden is revealed, what was once improper is now rendered screenworthy. The cleaning woman sneaks her peeks where she can — through one keyhole she sees an underwear-clad woman dancing, and through another she observes a finger stuck up a nostril. She spies with her binoculars, too, and uses her flashlight to search through drawers and on desktops. This voyeurism at the narrative level is created by and reinforced through Cremata Malberti's handheld camera penetrating people's privacy.

The irreverence in *Dark Jailed Rhinoceroses* extends beyond the body to politics. In one sequence, the distinctive voice of Fidel Castro proclaims, "What the imperialists can't forgive is that we're here … with our dignity, our values, our ideological convictions, our spirit of sacrifice, our revolutionary spirit." The accompanying images are of office employees, decked out in party hats and sunglasses, dancing in a conga line through their workplace. Again, costumed EICTV students fill the frame. The disjunction between image and sound, and between frivolity and authority, produces a parody of official discourse emphasizing productivity. Yet, the critique is decidedly lighthearted. This sequence is interspersed among numerous others poking fun at everything from advertising and bodily functions to sex and fashion. It even makes the viewers the butt of a joke. In a final sequence, the cleaning woman is aroused by an obscene phone call; her moans of pleasure give way to credits beginning with the on-screen question, "Do you know what an orgasm is?" The answer follows, "Lean your head sideways," and then the credits roll — sideways from right to left across the screen rather than vertically. The point is not to criticize in any serious way but, rather, to amuse and entertain. The film managed to do so, pleasing viewers at the EICTV and elsewhere in Cuba as well as on the international festival circuit. With *Dark Jailed Rhinoceroses*, Juan Carlos Cremata Malberti and the EICTV succeeded in impressing diverse audiences.

Recent works demonstrate that the school has maintained its high quality of production. *Radio Belén* (2005), by the Peruvian Gian Carlos Juanchini, develops out of a compelling structure of juxtaposition. Commentary from a local radio program emphasizes the importance of good nutrition and hygiene while the screen reveals people wading knee-deep through murky water, men hauling blocks of ice on their backs and women weighed down by bunches of plantains on their head. They lunch at outdoor food stalls, brushing flies away from tortillas and starchy rice before taking a bite. The counterpoint between soundtrack and images, between what's being broadcast over the radio and what appears on-screen, produces the irony driving the work. The result is an unmistakable social critique. Another impressive EICTV film from recent years is titled *José Manuel, la mula, y el televisor* (*José Manuel, the Mule, and the TV*, 2003). The short is dedicated to "José Manuel," a campesino who has participated in several documentaries made by the TVs, a community media organization that will be examined in the next chapter. Filmmaker Elsa Cornevín employs the trope of a TV to create an interesting narrative and point of view. The majority of the sequences are filmed through the wood box that once contained a television screen. Her innovative framing and masterful narrative yield a dignified portrait touched with humor.[7]

The collective accomplishments of EICTV students and alumni are noteworthy. Some graduates of the school have gone on to nurture nascent film industries in their home countries: In filming *El dirigible* (1994), for example, the Uruguayan Pablo Dotta created the first feature film in his nation's history; Rogelio Chacón returned home to Costa Rica after graduation and, upon taking over direction of the national film center in San José, led efforts to preserve his country's earliest films from the 1930s. Other graduates have garnered scholarships for their successful works. Miguel Coyula, who completed his EICTV training in 2001, earned several prizes for his highly original shorts and a humorous musical comedy titled *El tenedor plástico* (*The Plastic Fork*, 2001). These accolades at the Muestra Nacional de Nuevos Realizadores (National Exhibit of New Filmmakers) in Havana propelled him into new terrain. Coyula was awarded a scholarship to study at the Actors Studio in New York, where he filmed *Cucarachas rojas* (*Red Cockroaches*, 2003).

Still other EICTV graduates have enjoyed considerable success on the festival circuit; EICTV films have earned more than 100 awards at international events. Some of the more celebrated works include *Habana Blues* (Benito Zambrano, Spain, 2005); *Cuestión de fe* (*Question of Faith*, Marcos Loayza, Bolivia, 1995); *Amor vertical* (*Vertical Love*, Arturo Sotto, Cuba, 1997); *Las horas del día* (*The Hours of the Day*, Jaime Rosales, Spain, 2003); and *Los debutantes* (*The Debutantes*, Andrés Waissbluth, Chile, 2003). Many of these emerge from the collaboration of EICTV alumni long after they have graduated and returned to their respective countries. Indeed, the students-turned-filmmakers constitute a web covering the world. From their locations across Latin America and beyond, they share opportunities, exchange ideas, and lend support to one another's projects — and to the projects of subsequent generations. The EICTV has fulfilled its mission of fomenting filmmaking among Latin Americans and others and of generating an alternative vision of the region — one filmed from inside.

The EICTV also performs an important function as an information clearinghouse, compiling and disseminating news about audiovisual activity in Cuba and in Latin America. The school has hosted numerous conferences and workshops and has sponsored the publication of a series of journals and books.[8] In addition, with the launching of *Miradas* audiovisual bulletin in 2001, the institution has furthered its reach in promoting Latin American cinema.

The EICTV is eminently international. Partnerships with individuals and institutions from around the world lend diversity to this unique learning facility. Allies help recruit promising students from their respective countries, facilitate the exchange of ideas and experts, and donate films and books to the ever growing library. Participating universities and film schools include Ferris and the Schools of Art and Media in Cologne (Germany), the Film School of Barcelona (Spain), and the School of Media and Acting at the University of Salford (England), among others. The EICTV has also managed to establish formal collaboration agreements with an array of international media institutions. Foremost among them are the ICAIC, the General Society of Authors and Editors of Spain (Sociedad General de Autores y Editores, or SGAE), Canal Plus (Spain), ARCI-UCA (Italy), Sundance Institute (U.S.), the British Consulate, and the Ministry of Foreign Affairs of France. By plugging into a far-reaching network, the EICTV has greatly enhanced its scope and impact.

In 2006, the EICTV turned twenty years old. An ambitious schedule of activities marked the momentous occasion in various sites around the world. Hundreds of film professionals came together, expressing their gratitude for the ways in which this institution had shaped them— whether as students or faculty or visitors. At film festivals held in Mar del Plata, Guadalajara, Cartagena, New York, Havana, and elsewhere throughout the year, the school was paid tribute in special screenings and events. A video was created underscoring the impact of the EICTV on filmmakers as well as on viewing audiences in numerous countries.[9] The activities culminated in an anniversary celebration in Cuba in December 2006; Gabriel García Márquez and Fidel Castro participated, as did other luminaries instrumental in founding and sustaining the school. The director at that time, Julio García Espinosa, remarked with his characteristic good humor that getting to the twenty-year mark was something, particularly when one works every day not only as director but also as mayor of a town.[10] And indeed, for those who spent a significant period in San Antonio over the years, the EICTV is more than a site for learning. It constitutes a unique international village to which they remain connected.

The EICTV, envisioned as a training ground for filmmakers across Latin America and beyond, has remained true to its mission. What could not have been predicted in the late 1980s, as the school was opening its doors, was just how influential it would be for subsequent generations of Cuban audiovisual artists. Many of the school's principal practices and strategies parallel those employed by Street Filmmakers. At the EICTV, youthful rebellion was accepted and even embraced. The student body challenged the status quo—whether by rejecting entrenched methods, experimenting with new techniques, or finding fault with the establishment. Wary of conventional wisdom and tired truths, these individuals questioned and critiqued. They adopted an activist stance, valuing critical thinking as essential to their artistic output. Not surprisingly, they tackled new technologies with gusto, all the while continuing to experiment with traditional ones. While many delighted in filming on 35 millimeter, they eagerly picked up video cameras and quickly learned to employ them to creative ends. And they were entrepreneurial. Working together with students and faculty film professionals from around the world, they developed partnerships and alliances key for advancing their projects and enhancing their skills. Finally, the school's congenial relationship with the ICAIC proved the efficacy of collaboration between state and nongovernmental organizations. All of these ingredients will figure in the Street Filmmaking formula.

Promoting Filmmaking among Cuba's Youth: The AHS

The AHS was founded in Cuba in 1986 with the purpose of serving young writers and artists. The AHS emerged from the fusion of several groups working to foment the creativity and cultural awareness of the island's youth: the Brigada Raúl Gómez García, comprised of teachers and technicians; the Brigada Hermanos Saíz, made up of young writers and artists, many affiliated with the Unión de Escritores y Artistas de Cuba (National Union of Writers and Artists of Cuba, or UNEAC); and the Movimiento de la Nueva Trova (Movement of New Troubadours). Together they supported the ongoing development of musicians, writers, artists, and audiovisual creators under the age of thirty-five.

The name of the organization attests to its political nature and close alignment with Cuba's revolutionary culture agenda. The AHS honors two brothers, Luis and Sergio Saíz Montes de Oca, who were gunned down in 1957 for their support of the Revolution. The mission of the AHS, displayed on the *Juventud Rebelde* website, is to foment and disseminate revolutionary culture among Cuba's youth; the organization strives to engender among young writers and artists the concept of "an authentically revolutionary culture."[11]

At present, some 3,500 Cuban youth across the country belong to the AHS. Headquartered in the Pabellón Cuba, an outdoor pavilion centrally located on La Rampa thoroughfare in the Vedado district, the organization has access to numerous cultural centers. Next door is the Instituto Cubano de Radio y Televisión (Cuban Institute of Radio and Television, or ICRT), and it is an easy walk to the UNEAC, the Casa de las Américas, and the ICAIC. In addition, an extensive network of regional centers, called Casas del Joven Creador, or Young Creators' Houses, serves the island's youth. Among the initiatives undertaken by AHS members are organizing exhibitions and concerts, sponsoring grant competitions, and promoting participation in cultural offerings across the island.

Making and disseminating films constitutes one area of AHS activity. And it was here that emerging filmmaker Jorge Luis Sánchez would have a unique opportunity in the late 1980s. Sánchez credits the experience of making an "independent" film with this organization as key to his formation as a filmmaker and his subsequent trajectory in Cuba's industry. Born in 1960, Sánchez grew up with the Revolution. In the 1980s, he and his contemporaries were eager to "try out their wings." During my interview with him in Havana in January 2006, Sánchez described to me the prevalent attitude of his generation at the time: "When you get to be twenty years old, you start looking for spaces. . . . We said the Revolution gave us wings—meaning instruction, education, culture—and we wanted to fly. I had a wonderful childhood. I don't know what it means to be poor. My family wasn't rich, but I had a uniform to wear to school and a snack every day and opportunities to participate in lots of artistic and cultural activities—all for free. So they gave me wings. . . . They gave me tools, they gave me a compass." Sánchez entered the ICAIC in 1981, working first as an assistant cinematographer and then moving up to assistant and eventually director.

During those early years in the industry, he was uninspired by the majority of the films being produced. He found many documentaries "boring," characterized as they were by the same vision and the same aesthetic point of view. "They were like sausages," he recalls, turned out one after another. Fiction films weren't any better; Sánchez considered them "foolish" for the most part. He yearned to try his hand at making different kinds of films. The newly founded AHS would provide him with just such an opportunity. As a member of that organization, Sánchez lobbied for the creation of an audiovisual workshop—and succeeded. He managed to secure the participation of the ICAIC, which loaned them an obsolete camera that had been replaced by a newer model, gave them some virgin film that was past its expiration date, and allowed them to use a Moviola for editing. Sánchez's initiative resulted in the creation of the Taller de Cine y Video (Film and Video Workshop) in the AHS.

Within this space, Sánchez and other young aspiring filmmakers tackled their projects. Deeming ICAIC films to be increasingly uniform,

Jorge Luis Sánchez in the ICAIC (2006). Photo by the author.

they sought to make different kinds of works, to introduce new issues and styles into Cuba's film repertoire. Sánchez and his contemporaries resisted the dominant representation of the time. Part of their eagerness to distance themselves from extant industry production emanated from their youthfulness. They represented a new generation. In marked contrast to their parents, they did not come of age under the Batista regime. Nor did they help in initially forging a new Revolutionary context. Sánchez and his contemporaries had few—if any—memories of the euphoria of the early 1960s and no direct involvement in effecting radical change on the island. They were too young to have participated in initiatives like the literacy campaign and other activities that helped fuel Cuba's transformation. Inheritors rather than creators of the Cuban Revolution, their values, perspectives, and desires differed from those of their parents' generation. It was with some skepticism, then, that they approached the island's culture at that moment.

Sánchez and his cohorts resisted ICAIC norms. They generated ideas for subjects and styles vastly different from those in the industry. And they did so with the "confidence and complicity" of the ICAIC, then under the direction of Julio García Espinosa. "We began to develop by opposing the status quo," explains Sánchez, who characterizes his vision as "diametrically opposed to the more official gaze," as going beyond that which was printed in the party newspaper, *Granma*. "I read *Granma*, but wasn't interested in taking that and filming it. I wanted to look for my own truth, to make mistakes." Sánchez and his contemporaries insisted on the right to experiment, even if it meant making mistakes. "We said this in conversations with everybody—even with Fidel. We needed to be able to make mistakes." His participation in the Film and Video Workshop compelled Sánchez to make several highly effective documentaries, works that would influence industry production and Street Filmmaking in subsequent years.

It would be an experience far from home that would inspire this young filmmaker's first documentary. In 1988, Sánchez had the opportunity to travel to the Soviet Union. He tells of being in Leningrad, now St. Petersburg, and having his eyes opened to those who lived on the margins of society. While hosted by a Communist youth organization, Sánchez and other Cubans were ushered up some stairs and into a room where the event would take place. Just outside the building, he noticed a group of young people "like punks, with their hair standing up and all kinds of body piercing." Playing the fool, he asked why they did not come inside. One of the hosts explained that the activity was not for them. Sánchez kept thinking about the "outsiders" and, despite his limited English and nonexistent Russian, went down to converse with them. Upon learning that they liked the music of Elvis Presley and others from the 1950s, he was struck by their outdated cultural references and limited access to information. "We had always idealized the Soviet Union, considered it a perfect country," he reflected. "So to suddenly come upon these kids, many of whom were on the fringes—rockers and punkers and half-crazies—and to learn that the Communist organization that should have made a space for them excluded them, well, that got under my skin."

Shortly after his return home to Havana, Sánchez was in the Parque Central where preparations were under way for a concert. A group of young people called *friquis* (freaks)—with long hair, tight jeans, and body piercings—passed by. Sánchez observed that one turned around and came back to look at the band's sheet music. He was struck by this gesture. With this image in mind, he picked up a camera and set out to find the *friquis*.

Thus began a documentary project. Sánchez recalls that filming was no easy task. The young people were elusive, moving from one place to another and sometimes sleeping in the parks. Eventually, though, he managed to compile the footage necessary for the documentary *Un pedazo de mí* (*A Piece of Me*). The filmmaker admits to doing little preparation for this project. He was most interested in filming. It was from his encounter with this sector of the population that the documentary emerged. Sánchez's friends at that time told him he was making a very visceral work. The observation initially bothered him, but when he mulled it over, it seemed to make sense. "If I don't make something visceral that claws at my insides, something born deep within," he wondered, "what am I going to make?" *Un pedazo de mí* was, for this up-and-coming filmmaker, a work that simply "had to come out."

The documentary was well received. It earned prizes, including one at the International Festival of New Latin American Cinema in Havana, and was programmed in island cinemas and broadcast over Cuban television. Sánchez credits its widespread dissemination on local TV with helping to change the perception of the *friquis*. After his film, these disenfranchised young people joined some of Cuba's youth organizations, including the AHS. In fact, Sánchez would later meet several of these same young people in the countryside and film them working there. He went on to incorporate these images into his documentary homage to *Memorias del subdesarrollo* titled *El cine y la memoria* (*Cinema and Memory*, 1992). By that time the *friquis* were no longer mentioned. While these young people were on the fringes, Sánchez explains, they stood out; but when society made room for them, they blended in. "In the end, they were just kids with family problems who liked rock music. When rock went out, they had less to differentiate themselves from others. I think they took refuge in these things as a way to protest, as a way to be rebels because they had a cause. Without a cause, they ceased to be rebels." In drawing attention to the plight of the *friquis* and portraying them in a humanizing way, *Un pedazo de mí* helped integrate these young people into Cuban society.

The conditions in the country at that time were such that Sánchez and his AHS collaborators could produce their own films. A pizza cost about a peso and a bus ride was only a few centavos, so the energetic young filmmakers could make their way around the city compiling their desired footage. Sánchez considers *Un pedazo de mí*, made in 1989, an independent film. For this project, the ICAIC lent Sánchez a camera and provided him with some outdated film. (The latter explains the film's unique texture, one highly appropriate for the subject matter.) In exchange for this support, the institute expected nothing. They allowed the filmmaker complete autonomy, never once asking to see the script. "A benefit enjoyed by my generation is that we worked with lots of liberty," notes Sánchez. "We said, 'We've got nothing to lose' in terms of status, and naturally that bothered a lot of people. We were rebellious—I haven't stopped rebelling, although over the years I've become more mature. But we were rebels and we managed to move forward."

The self-proclaimed rebel would undertake his next projects from inside the ICAIC. Initially, he had some trepidation about how his films would be received, emphasizing as they did "the negatives" that those in charge did not want to acknowledge. "One of our great unknowns was whether those of us making documentaries through unofficial channels but who aspired to work in the ICAIC could sustain our efforts once we were recognized as inside directors," he recalls. "I've been able to sustain it," he affirms. "In other words, I haven't changed my discourse because I'm now in the ICAIC." Sánchez insists that he continues to develop projects that interest him, ones coherent with his earlier work made outside the institute. Indeed, his next two undertakings would again address people in the margins: *El fanguito* (1990) deals with the residents of one of Havana's slums, and *Donde está Casal* (*Where Casal Is*, 1990) portrays the poet Julián del Casal, whose life and work have been relegated to the margins of Cuban literature and history.[12]

These films made by Sánchez and other young members of the AHS had a lasting impact. Not only did they inspire young would-be filmmakers; they also influenced accomplished industry directors. Sánchez recalls inviting Fernando Pérez to see *Un pedazo de mí*. Pérez was so moved by the piece that he arranged for his ICAIC colleagues to watch it. Daniel Díaz Torres and Rolando Díaz were equally impressed. "Perhaps a window had opened," Sánchez explained to me, one revealing another view of society. Sánchez eschews characterizing his work as a "rupture"— "that's for others to say," he notes with a smile—but he does acknowledge that his documentaries laid bare the circumstances of this tumultuous time, coinciding as they did with the late 1980s and early 1990s in Cuba when Revolutionary values were being challenged, resisted, and revised.[13] Sánchez describes his efforts and those of his AHS cohorts at the time: "To some extent we helped dust off the gaze. God or nature or Darwin or Whomever invented the succession of generations so that each one would add something. And I believe in the harmony—and the discord—of the generations."

Jorge Luis Sánchez would continue the trajectory he began with the AHS—that of creating space for young people to develop their ideas on film and thereby "opening new windows" on Cuban society. He would do this by helping to establish the Muestra Nacional de Nuevos Realizadores in 2000. This annual exhibition, to be discussed more fully in Chapter 7, features the projects of Cuba's audiovisual artists under age thirty-five. For many aspiring cineastes, the Muestra constitutes the first public display of their work and the first opportunity to discuss it with a diverse audience. Virtually every Street Filmmaker in Cuba has had his or her work exhibited in this venue. Sánchez's leadership in helping create the Muestra and his ongoing support of emerging directors have earned him respect as a maestro and mentor. Street Filmmakers welcome Sánchez's input on their works in progress and seek out his company at cultural and social events. Several of them credit him as a major influence in their development. While organized under the ICAIC's auspices, the Muestra serves young people that do not work in the industry for the most part. The vision and leadership of Sánchez in founding this event— one bringing together ICAIC filmmakers and those working on their own to exchange ideas and materials and work out strategies for making and marketing their films—has been instrumental in helping promote media activity on the island.[14]

Jorge Luis Sánchez has been a rebel with a cause. In deeming the space for new filmmakers to be insufficient on the island, he developed a film and video workshop for the AHS, one still in existence some two decades later. Then he contributed to creating the first Muestra. When I interviewed Sánchez, he was putting the finishing touches on his first feature film about the legendary Cuban musician Benny Moré. We met in one of the postproduction studios in the ICAIC, where technicians were adding sound effects. More than fifteen years had elapsed since he had made his first documentary with the AHS, and it was a quarter-century since he had entered the ICAIC. He alternated between not wanting to answer questions about the film before it was finished, claiming he was superstitious, and talking about the project with unfettered enthusiasm. Less than a year later, *El Benny* premiered in Havana to favorable reviews. As the film began its sojourn on the international festival circuit, it was clear that this rebel was enjoying considerable success with his long-awaited first feature. At the International Festival of New Latin American Cinema, when the reporter Salvador Salazar Navarro asked Sánchez about awards the film might garner, he responded, "The best prize was given to me several months ago—it was being able to make the film."[15]

Making Space for a New Medium:
Movimiento Nacional de Video de Cuba

The projection of celluloid images on the big screen has, for more than a century, captivated audiences the world over. When video began to make inroads in Cuba in the 1980s,[16] film aficionados were wary. The medium's accessibility appealed—videocassettes could be inserted into VCRs and watched in school classrooms, as part of public events, and in private homes. But video did not hold the same magic as its predecessor. Videotape was considered inferior to celluloid for making films, and television sets were diminutive for viewing when compared to expansive movie house screens. So while video technology was deemed better than nothing, the medium still left a great deal to be desired. Rather than being considered a unique form of cultural expression, with discreet characteristics and still-to-be-discovered potential, video was more often dismissed as a second-rate substitute for film. It seemed to make sense for didactic purposes but fell short in the artistic realm. Industry filmmakers the world over tended to steer clear of video.

Despite this initial bias against the medium, its appeal began to grow across Latin America. The 1980s were a decade of turmoil and transformation in which civil wars were waged (in El Salvador, Guatemala, and Nicaragua), terrorism reigned (in Peru), and military dictatorships ruled (in Argentina, Chile, and Uruguay). Widespread poverty, the marginalization of indigenous peoples, and repeated U.S. intervention fueled turmoil and violence. Struggles for liberation grew up across the continent and, with them, an awareness of culture's importance to sociopolitical transformation. One needed to look no further than Cuba, a country that had successfully employed expressive culture to forge a sense of identity and consolidate a national consciousness. The promotion of a concertedly local culture constituted an important strategy for bringing about change. As the Cubans had effectively modeled, sociopolitical liberation went hand in hand with cultural autonomy. Engaging local populations in documenting their own realities was a tried-and-true way to integrate them into the transformation agenda. As a result, familiar faces, sometimes with indigenous features, made their way onto the screens. While they never completely replaced the Anglo actors proffered by Hollywood, they certainly provided alternatives. Spectators in Latin America could see themselves reflected on the screen; that vision translated into an increased valorization of their experiences, their surroundings, and their traditions.

Video cameras, with their mobility and ease of operation, were utilized widely to document happenings "at home" across the continent. Given the pervasive sociopolitical upheaval, they captured instances of brutality, violence, and injustice—acts that would otherwise go unseen, for state-controlled television stations often presented views diametrically opposed to those glimpsed by residents of the zone. As a result, video became highly politicized. From its inception, it was a medium of resistance—resistance to state-controlled television that often colluded with military governments in sanitizing the stories told, and resistance to the cultural imperialism purveyed by Hollywood. In this way, video in the region came to be seen as a weapon to battle oppression; the camera, in Frantz Fanon's influential formulation, was an arm in the struggle for liberation.[17] Video's ease of access and potential for contestation would have extraordinary repercussions in Latin America, ones that would endure into the present.

Filmmakers across Latin America teamed up on a series of media initiatives designed to promote autochthonous representation and employ culture as a tool for change. The cross-fertilization of ideas and experiences resulted in the creation of several regional entities. One of these, as noted earlier in this chapter, was the International Festival of New Latin American Cinema. Another, also mentioned previously, was the establishment of the EICTV, where aspiring directors would be trained to document their local environs. Still another important regional film initiative was the creation of the Mercado de Cine de América Latina, a market designed to promote and disseminate Latin American films within the region as well as the world over. Representatives from the key national film institutes on the continent signed on; the market also sought to attract independent producers who would use it as a platform to promote their films and establish coproduction agreements and sales. Cuba, with a strong cinema tradition and a commitment to revolutionary transformation, served as a leader in the regional movement to foment the production and dissemination of Latin American films and videos.

During the late 1980s and early 1990s in Cuba, increasing economic pressures and the concomitant industry crisis rendered filming on celluloid next to impossible. Industry filmmakers found their options exceedingly limited: They could either film on video or cease filming altogether. By turning to video, some ICAIC filmmakers, like Belkis Vega[18] and Gloria Rolando, were able to continue wielding the camera to tell their stories. Employing the then-new video technology constituted an effective strategy for capturing audiovisual ideas and communicating them to viewing audiences. Video became an increasingly viable option.

Precedents for filming on video existed in the country prior to this time. During the late 1970s and early 1980s, Cuba's state organizations — many of which had already supported an active film production agenda — began to experiment with video technology.[19] By the mid-1980s, when video cameras, cassettes, and players became widely available in Cuba, these agencies would migrate to the new technology, creating numerous video production arms: Mundo Latino (Cuban Communist Party), RTV Comercial (Cuban Institute of Radio and Television), Televisión Latina (Information Agency of Prensa Latina), Hurón Azul (Cuban Writers and Artists Union), and Producciones Trimagen S.A. (from the armed forces' film and television studios). Videographers in virtually all the groups faced the same challenges: first, the lack of detailed information about equipment operation and troubleshooting; second, the lack of a cohort of colleagues who were knowledgeable about audiovisual production; and third, the lack of a venue for disseminating the work beyond the state agencies in which they worked. Many of these problems would be addressed by an organization that was about to emerge.

The Movimiento Nacional de Video de Cuba (National Video Movement of Cuba) was founded in 1988. José Antonio Jiménez spearheaded the nongovernmental organization in order to create a space for audiovisual artists interested in video. The Movimiento served to train media-

makers, foster autonomous production, and forge alternative dissemination channels, he noted during my interview with him in Havana in
January 2006. It was envisioned to be a hub where audiovisual artists
in various sectors could share insights and infrastructure, circulate their
work, and promote the medium. The Movimiento, like the other organizations outlined in this chapter, sought to strengthen Cuban culture—in
this case through the production and circulation of video.

The Movimiento Nacional de Video engaged inexperienced and accomplished media-makers in a variety of activities. Principal among these
was the organization's signature event, the annual Encuentro Nacional de
Video (National Video Encounter). Also important was the *En video* (*On
Video*) program, a television series broadcasting videos made by Cubans
and Latin Americans. And the video debates introduced aficionados to
a variety of material and fostered lively discussions. The Movimiento's
positive relationship with both national television and the national film
industries bolstered these and a host of other activities.

Ideas were exchanged and resources shared. With only two or three
people and one lightweight portable camera, a respectable documentary
or short work of fiction on video could be created. What resulted was a
cohesive community of media-makers, one comprised of individuals
experienced at making films and videos in various state agencies and
others with no such background or affiliation. As the crisis mounted during the Special Period, this camaraderie would be critical. Jiménez characterized the Movimiento as a product of the Special Period. "People began
by helping one another. . . . They developed solidarity among themselves,"
he explained to me. During meetings, one member would agree to lend
a camera, and another would chime in with an offer to help manage the
editing. This solidarity, for Jiménez, helped the Movimiento gain its momentum. Together, these audiovisual artists and aficionados generated
interest in video; they organized festivals and events, encouraged production, and developed partnerships across the island and beyond.

The organization made tangible and long-lasting contributions to
Cuba's audiovisual landscape. Media artists aligned with this group
recognized video's potential; their confidence grew as their abilities developed. The Movimiento members identified themselves as bona fide
audiovisual artists and the then-new medium as legitimate. Their foray
into video-making under the rubric of the Movimiento enhanced their

technical ability and consolidated their identity as audiovisual creators. Without a doubt, the Movimiento picked up some of the slack left by the industry's decline.

The impact of the Movimiento Nacional de Video can be best illustrated through the trajectory of one of its members. Gloria Rolando is an ICAIC filmmaker whose career was shaped by the Movimiento.[20] Born in Havana in 1953, she studied music at the acclaimed Amadeo Roldán conservatory and then completed an art history degree at the University of Havana. Rolando came of age during the politically charged 1960s, a time when battles were being waged the world over to resist oppression and redress injustice. Cubans were rethinking their relationships to one another, to structures of authority, and to nations beyond their borders. Rolando joined in the struggle.

Gloria Rolando began working in the ICAIC in 1976. Her foray into filmmaking was influenced by her academic and artistic training and by a heightened sensitivity to her African heritage. Immediately she began to develop a passion for Afro-Cuban traditions and a commitment to African diaspora cultures in the Caribbean. During her first decade at the ICAIC, in the capacity of scriptwriter, researcher, and assistant director, Rolando treated themes of Afro-Caribbean identity. While writing the script for *Tumba francesa* (Santiago Villafuerte, 1979), she investigated the origins of French *tumba* drum societies in eastern Cuba, particularly the slave festivals and dances brought to Cuba by the French as a consequence of the eighteenth-century Haitian revolution. *Haití en la memoria* (Santiago Villafuerte, 1986) provided her with another opportunity to examine Haitian traditions in Cuba. *Algo más que el mar de los piratas* (*Something More than the Pirates' Sea*, Bernabé Hernández, 1976) afforded her the opportunity to participate in shaping a film about cultural identity in the Caribbean. She teamed up with Rigoberto López on several occasions to assist in creating various documentaries depicting the Afro-Cuban experience; among these are *Semilla de hombres*, *El viaje más largo* (*The Longest Journey*, 1987), *Esta es mi alma* (*This Is My Soul*, 1988), and *Mensajero de los dioses* (*Messenger of the Gods*, 1989). Predictably, when preparing a synopsis for her first project, Rolando would structure it around a topic of Afro-Cuban import.

In 1989, the ICAIC announced a competition to fund low-budget short films. Despite the fact that the institute sought projects of ten to fifteen minutes in duration and comprised exclusively of interior shots, Rolando decided to participate. She submitted the script for a fifty-minute documentary on Yoruba gods. The length of Rolando's project coupled with the need for extensive exterior takes prepared her for the subsequent rejection, for the film she envisioned simply did not fit the criteria outlined in the call for proposals. Determined to proceed, the director sought other avenues for advancing her project. During this time she learned of Video América, a Havana-based initiative seeking material on Cuba's culture. Through this entity, she secured funding for her first film, *Oggún: The Eternal Present* (1991). *Oggún* recounts the *patakin*, or myths of the Yoruba gods. The fifty-two-minute documentary sets out to answer the question "Who is Oggún?" and goes on to introduce significant gods in the Afro-Cuban Santeria tradition. The legend of Oggún and other deities is told by Cuba's renowned Yoruba singer Lázaro Ross. Seated at the foot of the sacred *ceiba* tree, this son of Oggún describes his initiation into the world of the Santeria religion. These sequences are interspersed with scenes from a *toque* Yoruba ceremony in Havana. The video evokes the beauty and passion of the dance and worship, whether performed by professional dancers or members of the community. African threads are woven throughout. Rolando's participation in the Movimiento Nacional de Video de Cuba provided her with all she needed to make this film; she had willing partners, know-how, and access to equipment. During the subsequent fifteen-year period, she would make a total of six documentaries—all but one produced outside the ICAIC.[21]

In her documentaries, Rolando pays homage to her Africa-descended ancestors. She believes that to reveal the essence of this culture is to contribute to its ongoing relevance. As she expressed in her "Artist's 1998 Statement of Purpose and Biography," "It is my belief that the men and women of Lázaro's generation and others much older are the last bridge tying us to the Africa that gave birth to its roots in America since the time of slavery. . . . It is necessary not only to film the dances and songs, but also to reveal the essence of this culture. We must recognize that it contains legends and universal values that explain the world. My personal experience with Oggún demonstrates to me that this is possible." These same objectives inform Rolando's entire oeuvre.

In *My Footsteps in Baraguá* (1996), the filmmaker examines the African diaspora in the Caribbean. The work treats the assimilation of British cultural patterns in Cuba due to the presence of immigrants from Barbados, Jamaica, and Trinidad and Tobago. As further evidence of her vision of a pan-Caribbean African identity, the filmmaker created two versions of this film, one in Spanish and another in English. *Eyes of the Rainbow* (1998) probes the African diaspora in another context, focusing on the Black Panther and Black Liberation Army leader Assata Shakur, who took refuge in Cuba after years of struggles in the United States. The video testimonial demonstrates the protagonist's connections to her African American roots *and* her Afro-Cuban context after living for nearly twenty years in Cuba. It is a pan-African version of identity that Rolando's next work espouses. *El alacrán* (*The Scorpion*, 1999) deals with one *comparsa*, or Afro-Cuban carnival, founded in Havana in 1908. Although the event had evolved over the preceding century, it remains a living tribute to Yemaya, the god to which it is dedicated. Black-and-white archival photos interspersed with colorful sequences of present-day festivities effectively conjoin past and present. In the same way, the short feature *Raíces de mi corazon* (*Roots of My Heart*, 2000) revisits the past in order to reinterpret the present. This documentary depicts the massacre of members of the party Independents of Color in 1912. In doing so, it has added a chapter of Cuba's history that has been overlooked for the most part. With *Los Marqueses de Atarés* (2003), Rolando returns to the *comparsa*, rescuing and preserving another Afro-Cuban event. More recently, *Nosotros y el jazz* (*The Jazz in Us*, 2004), outlines the cross-fertilization of Cuban and U.S. jazz. Whereas most music documentaries feature the performers, this one shines the spotlight on the fans of Cuba's rich jazz tradition. A group of friends reflect on their devotion to the musical form from the 1940s and 1950s up to the present day.

Rolando's films reveal an unwavering commitment to African beliefs and traditions.[22] Her work frames Afro-Cuban identity as part of the larger African tradition, one not limited by geopolitical boundaries. The structure of these works consistently connects the past to the present, history to current-day perspectives and practices. Rolando's videos insert Afro-Cuban traditions into Cuba's Revolutionary culture. Each one of her documentaries demonstrates her passion for Afro-Cuban identity and her commitment to making room for traditions and histories that have been ignored or pushed aside. Significantly, the filmmaker inserts African themes and traditions into Cuba's national film culture but refuses

Gloria Rolando at home
in Centro Habana (2005).
Photo by the author.

to set them against their European counterparts. In her formulation of
identities, the island where she makes her home is comprised of a blend
of cultures. Transculturation and syncretism—not separation and division—characterize Cuban identity for this artist.

Rolando's professional projects emanate from her personal beliefs
and experiences. Life and art, for her, are inextricably linked. When I contacted her in Havana to arrange an interview, she suggested I attend a
commemoration of the anniversary of her initiation into Santeria. By
visiting Rolando at home—meeting her mother and friends and neighbors and helping mark the momentous occasion, she believed I would
develop a greater understanding of her work. And she was right. On the
evening of the celebration, I made my way to her address and was welcomed into a small ground-floor apartment. Gloria was upstairs, meeting
with guests one by one. Her uncle handed me a glass of rum and orange
soda and directed me to one of the benches along the wall. After convers-
ing with a few of the guests, I took my turn visiting Gloria in a small room
up some narrow stairs. Dressed all in white, she welcomed me warmly
and thanked me for coming. She then invited me to pay homage before
the altar where tropical fruits shared space with stones and shells and
pesos and numerous other offerings. Without a doubt, experiencing this
special moment in Rolando's life—a reaffirmation of her adherence to the
beliefs and practices of Santeria—provided me with greater insight into

her work, and into the Africa-descended traditions that are integral to *cubanía* in the present day.

The Movimiento Nacional de Video served as the umbrella under which Gloria Rolando continued to document the history of African cultural traditions in Cuba and the Caribbean. Under this rubric, in 1995 she created an independent video group called Imágenes del Caribe (Images of the Caribbean). Imágenes is comprised of Cuban television professionals, industry filmmakers and specialists, and artists. With this group, Rolando develops her projects independently and secures the financing necessary to produce them. No one tells her what she can or cannot do. Yet, she remains affiliated with the industry. She entered the ICAIC in the late 1970s and has earned a salary ever since. So even though Rolando has not worked on an industry-sponsored project for more than a decade, she still picks up a weekly paycheck at ICAIC headquarters. Her stance, with one foot inside the ICAIC and the other outside, will be replicated—albeit somewhat differently—by the subsequent generation of Street Filmmakers.

The location of Rolando's home, in the dilapidated Centro Habana neighborhood abutting Chinatown, on the margins of the fashionable Vedado neighborhood, parallels the filmmaker's peripheral place in Cuba's film industry. Despite having worked in the ICAIC since 1976, Rolando characterizes herself as an outsider there. She is hard pressed to explain why, but she does have some theories. Perhaps it is because the Afro-Cuban themes she treats hold little appeal to members of the ICAIC selection committee. Perhaps it can be attributed to gender, for female filmmakers in the institute have always been a minority and have had to struggle harder than their male counterparts. Or perhaps it emanates from the industrywide crisis; tight budgets and obsolete equipment have left most filmmakers—even the most established—wondering when they will be able to tackle their next project.

Although Rolando does not mention this, it may also have to do with her creative vision, with how she tells her stories. The works of this filmmaker differ in style from many ICAIC productions. Cultural traditions—that is, the content—rather than formal considerations drive the documentaries. This filmmaker alludes to her preference for an anthropological over an artistic approach. She confesses that colleagues often find her documentaries to be overly long. On several occasions, while she was working on a project, ICAIC mentors and peers urged her to edit out some sequences in order to streamline the documentary. Rolando resisted, and she explained to me her reasons: "I'm a musician, and for me the music is a protagonist. When I include a song or dance number, I want it to be complete. I don't want to hack it up with a machete (*machetearlo*). When I hear a song cut off, I say, 'Man, but why?' Huh-uh, I like to finish a musical phrase, because I know what a musical phrase is."

Rolando has opted to film subjects that interest her in the ways she deems most appropriate. Her unwillingness to make concessions—or even to consider suggestions, in some cases—has come at a cost. Her video output documents important cultural phenomena and pays homage to significant traditions and figures. Rolando's documentaries are replete with hard-to-access information. Yet, they leave some viewers wanting more—more carefully crafted scripts, more consistent sound quality, and above all, more judicious editing. This filmmaker has produced a body of work more significant for the information imparted than for its formal acumen. And yet, given Rolando's commitment to showcasing her nation's African heritage, a subject that has received far less attention than European culture, it is understandable that she insists on privileging the story. Dualities that separate form and content, past and present, and truth and lie have no place in the oral sharing of traditions. Storytelling, as Trinh T. Minh-ha reminds us, relies on the integration of structure and narrative rather than their separation.[23] Given her particular vision, Rolando realized early in her career that in order to make films according to her preferences, probing topics of personal interest and employing film conventions in ways she deemed most appropriate for telling her stories, she would have to work on her own. And that compelled her to develop her own production entity.

Having her own team has permitted Rolando to produce and disseminate her work. She has collaborated with a number of partners: the West Indian Welfare Center, an NGO based in Guantánamo; the Artex society, devoted to marketing Cuban literature, music, art, and crafts; Mundo Latino and Televisión Latina; and numerous others. Perhaps most notable—given the complicated political and economic circumstances— is the support she has garnered in the United States. African diaspora networks based in the United States have come to the aid of this filmmaker. The AfroCubaWeb promotes Rolando and markets her work over the Internet.[24] Through this venue and others, she has been able to procure invitations, travel widely, and disseminate her work in the United States. Alliances like these have permitted Rolando to continue transforming her ideas into video documentaries.

The increasing difficulty Cubans have in getting visas to enter the United States has left this filmmaker concerned about her future. She misses the valuable encounters with university students and faculty— whether in New York, California, Florida, or elsewhere—and hearing firsthand their impressions of her work and discussing issues of mutual import. She can no longer acquire items critical for future projects, such as cloth for sewing period costumes, makeup, and props that are either unavailable in Cuba or priced out of her range. And Rolando has lost her major source of financing. It was with U.S. dollars—honoraria and cash donations generated on the lecture circuit—that she funded her previous films.

Gloria Rolando promotes and preserves Afro-Cuban identity by examining her own life. In her words, "With each film, I try to look at myself a little in the interior mirror. This is my response to globalization." Rolando is less involved in the Movimiento these days. Her *compañero* and collaborator emigrated, causing a slight shift in her circle of friends. Her mother is aging, compelling Rolando to devote more time to caregiving. And, frankly, she seems to need the Movimiento less today than she once did. Gloria Rolando is, as Cubans would say, *encaminada*; she is on her way.

The Movimiento has evolved over time as members have come and gone. Yet, the group remains active. For the past several years, it has partnered with the National Museum of Natural History and the Sociedad Cubana Pro Naturaleza (Cuban Pro-Nature Society) to sponsor the Images of Nature Video Festival. It teamed up with the Latin American Video Archive, based in New York, to circulate the work of Cuban video artists in the United States.[25] And it celebrated its twentieth anniversary in June 2007 with an exhibition of nearly 100 works. The ICAIC *Boletín Digital* of 19 June 2007 reported membership at 455. Two decades after its founding, the Movimiento remains effective in promoting media-making and in bringing together audiovisual artists and aficionados.

It was a vision of German art collectors that engendered the FLC, an organization devoted to supporting Cuban arts and promoting Cuban artists by connecting them with their international counterparts. Peter and Irene Ludwig became interested in the creative output of young Cubans upon seeing the Cuba OK exhibition in 1990. Cosponsored by Cuba's Center for the Development of Visual Arts and the Kunsthalle in Düsseldorf, this collective exhibition brought together some of the most significant artworks made by Cubans in the 1980s. The show's content as well as its timing proved exceedingly powerful. Fernando Sáez Carvajal and Wilfredo Benítez Muñoz explain the impact of Cuba OK as follows: "At a moment when the fall of the Berlin Wall was still very recent, these works, which were officially sanctioned, but, paradoxically shared characteristics of some dissident art from former Socialist countries, explored themes with a critical point of view about Cuban society."[26] The Ludwigs were impressed by the vision and talent of the young Cuban artists, and by the candor with which they treated their subject matter.

Compelled by their fascination with contemporary Cuban art, Peter and Irene Ludwig began a series of trips to the island. While seeking to develop a greater understanding of island art, they purchased numerous works for their collection. They then disseminated these pieces across Europe through exhibitions. As their interest in Cuban art grew, so, too, did their commitment to the island's artists. So when the dire conditions of the Special Period threatened Cuba's vibrant arts scene—when numerous cultural centers lacked the resources necessary to operate and dozens of artists contemplated emigrating—the Ludwigs stepped in to help. In 1994, they established the Fundación Ludwig de Cuba.

The creation of the FLC—a nongovernmental organization in Revolutionary Cuba—required great care.[27] For the FLC to make a meaningful contribution to the island's cultural sphere, it would have to differ significantly from its state-sponsored counterparts and enjoy a great deal of autonomy. At the same time, it would require the full support of the host country to ensure effective collaboration with governmental organizations and guarantee smooth operation. In short, the FLC had to get the Cuban government to "buy in" enough to permit the organization's creation and sustainability, and yet be hands off enough to allow its new directors and international partners to chart its course. Reflections on the FLC's genesis by its president, Helmo Hernández, reveal this delicate balance:

> This Cuban institution was born of the friendship and feelings of goodwill between the Ludwigs and the Cubans. Cuba's cultural policy already vigorously sustains the visual arts and has a tradition of supporting institutions for education and exhibition. The Ludwig Foundation seeks to augment the strengths of Cuba's artistic establishments. We aim to bring together diverse sectors that, within the limits of a substantial community of interests both in Cuba and abroad, are willing to work for the promotion of an art characterized by earnest experimentation and a ripe and reflective adoption of the responsibilities of creation.[28]

Situated in the capital's Vedado district, the FLC began by curating and mounting group exhibitions to showcase the talent of young artists. The first of these, One of Each, involved more than forty artists and consisted of a set of installations in various sites across the capital. The principal purpose of this display was to prove that art in Cuba was alive and well, for the exodus of several leading artists in the 1980s—José Bedia, Arturo Cuenca, and Elso Padilla among them—had cast a shadow on Cuba's art world. In affirming the continuity of Cuban art, One of Each demonstrated the likelihood of a vibrant future for island art. Exhibitions of photography, design, and printmaking followed shortly thereafter.

Since its inception, the FLC has contributed in concrete ways to shaping new generations of Cuban artists and educators. One key strategy for building capacity among young creators has been through scholarships. Backed by this NGO, numerous Cuban artists have traveled abroad; they have lived, learned, and worked in Germany, Switzerland, Denmark, Hungary, Canada, the United States, and elsewhere for periods ranging from one to six months. This exposure to artists and students in other cultural contexts has energized and enhanced the island's art scene. It has also permitted these young creators to develop relationships overseas, contacts critical for their ongoing professional development and the marketing of their work. Equally important to Cuban artists are the modest grants and awards designed to help cover living expenses and/or materials costs while working in Cuba.

The FLC provides the setting for the author's 2006 interview with Inti Herrera (center) and Alejandro Brugués (right); Diego Javier Figueroa (left) records sound. Courtesy of the author.

The FLC takes seriously its mission of performing outreach to artists, educators, scholars, and others. Groups of art teachers meet there regularly to be apprised of currents in island and international art. Artists stop by to receive English instruction from a language professor. And here many international visitors learn about Cuba's art scene. Whether a day or semester in duration, the instruction on art and culture provided by foundation specialists invariably consists of presentations, site visits, and conversations with artists. Various U.S. universities have selected the FLC as their host in Cuba for educational programs. On several occasions, while directing study programs in Havana, I arranged for my students to gather at the FLC. Each session differed, but virtually all included a discussion of Cuba's art history and a tour of whichever exhibition happened to be mounted at the time in the foundation's attractive gallery. Particularly memorable was one display of old cameras set alongside a projector of stereoscopic images, the present-day invention of Paul Chaviano. Another impressive show compiled artifacts from Cuba's sugar industry, including a tower of ink-stamped burlap sugar sacks. Yet another consisted of objects from the travels of the artists and specialists working at the FLC, a collage emphasizing movement and migration. Regardless of the subjects addressed and exhibits experienced, all learning sessions culminated in a dinner on the balcony; with an aerial view of the city and sea beyond, we would converse with poets, painters, actors, playwrights, critics, educators, and foundation specialists.

Among the FLC's notable contributions—and the one of greatest relevance for this study—is its foray into media art. The expansion of the organization's mission to serve media artists responded to difficulties facing filmmakers. If the economic crisis had left painters, sculptors, dancers, and performers lacking necessary resources, it had virtually paralyzed audiovisual artists whose work required far more costly equipment and materials. In 1997 and 1998, the FLC sponsored a series of workshops led by Canadian video artists; this Cuba–Canada initiative served up-and-coming artists in significant ways. Pavel Giroud and René Peña, for example, were afforded their first opportunity to wield a camera for artistic purposes. Other *talleres* and training sessions followed.

To serve these media-makers in a variety of ways, the FLC acquired basic equipment—several televisions, VCRs, and DVD players—for viewing films on video and works of video art. They installed an audiovisual lab with digital video cameras and an AVID editing system. And they inaugurated a series featuring premieres of local audiovisual projects. With this infrastructure in place, emerging filmmakers could visit the FLC to screen films from Cuba and around the world, gain insights from the experienced artists who offered workshops, and, in a few cases, even do some filming and editing on the equipment there. Ernesto Rodríguez made his five-minute documentary on the carnivals in Remedios, titled *Parranda* (2004), with FLC equipment; Arturo Infante used the FLC as the backdrop for his short titled *El intruso* (*The Intruder*, 2005); and Esteban Insausti and Angélica Salvador edited *Luz roja* in the FLC lab.

Some up-and-coming media artists have received grants to continue their work: Waldo Ramírez (director of several award-winning shorts and longtime participant in the TVS community media initiative); Arturo Sotto (graduate of the EICTV and writer-director of *Amor vertical* [*Vertical Love*, 1997]); Arturo Infante (director of *Utopía* [2004], *El Intruso* [2005], and *Flash Forward* [2005]); and various young Cubans whose work has been featured in the Muestra Nacional de Nuevos Realizadores (Yemelí Cruz Rivero, Marcel Echevarría, Tamara Castellanos, and Roberto Renán, among others). The FLC has acknowledged the new opportunities proffered by digital media and low-budget production. By supporting emerging artists interested in exploring this alternative mode of media-making, this NGO has fomented audiovisual activity in Havana and helped expand options available beyond the industry.

To some extent, the FLC's move to integrate media art was a natural outgrowth of its alliances. Early on, the FLC and the ICAIC teamed up on a series of workshops and other initiatives. The two entities — one state supported and the other an NGO — developed a productive partnership that has endured into the present. Together they curate displays of graphic arts and photographs that are mounted in the Cine Chaplin gallery adjacent to the ICAIC. The FLC regularly contributes modest financial support to industry film events such as the Festival Documental Santiago Álvarez in Memoriam and the Muestra Nacional de Nuevos Realizadores. And it offers prizes in the form of scholarships to participants in these and other domestic festivals. The fact that FLC activities are frequented by industry filmmakers and specialists — including the ICAIC president and vice presidents — further attests to this effective alliance.

The FLC also collaborates closely with the Instituto Superior del Arte (ISA), Cuba's premiere advanced art school. When the ISA added a program in audiovisual media arts, complementing its offerings in visual arts, music, theater, and dance, the FLC began partnering on initiatives in this area. This alliance naturally drew attention to linkages between the plastic and the audiovisual arts, with the result being a series of installations and videos fusing techniques from the two art arenas.

One young audiovisual artist who has benefited from FLC support is Amado Soto Ricardo, who goes by "Asori." Even before making his acquaintance, I had the opportunity to view a few of his shorts. FLC personnel invited me to screen *Zona afectada* (*The Affected Zone*, 2005); *Mosquitos, el documental* (*Mosquitos, the Documentary*, 2005); and *Good Bye, Lolek* (2005). All three evoke their Cuban context. The first depicts a young man repeatedly hauling buckets of water up several flights of stairs, underscoring the perpetual water shortages in Havana. The second tackles the topic of fumigation, obligatory in Havana dwellings; the practice is considered intrusive and inconvenient even while its importance for public health in the tropics is acknowledged. And the third short nods to the Polish cartoons that Cuban baby boomers grew up with. Each of

Asori's projects is structured effectively to build suspense, elicit humor, and drive home a message. When I visited this twenty-something artist in his Havana apartment early in 2007, he was putting the finishing touches on a feature-length documentary. *Del Tosco* (*About El Tosco*) is devoted to one of Cuba's contemporary musicians, José Luis Cortés, better known as El Tosco. Asori showed me the trailer, and as we conversed, I learned that he had benefited from FLC support for this project. His tenure as a grantee had ended, but he had filmed several sequences with an FLC camera.

Audiovisual artists require support not only to create but also to disseminate their work. Aware of this need, the FLC has instituted a series showcasing the digital and analog videos of Cuba's emerging filmmakers. It was there that Esteban Insausti's film *Existen* (*They Exist*) premiered in December 2005. That evening, the FLC's reception room and open-air terrace were packed with aficionados eager to see this new work. Esteban Insausti attended, as did the film's editor, Angélica Salvador, and other members of the production team. Joining them were friends—several filmmakers among them—family members, specialists from the ICAIC, and poets, artists, and musicians from Havana's cultural scene. So many people showed up, in fact, that a second screening had to be offered to accommodate all the guests. *Existen* was received with great enthusiasm. Audience members commended the innovative filming and editing techniques, the respect accorded to the film's subjects, and the homage it paid to some of Cuba's avant-garde filmmakers. As a member of that audience, I applauded the film and lauded the FLC's vision in hosting its premiere. The gathering had brought together artists from a range of disciplines, affording them membership in this cultural community. Without a doubt, the FLC makes a meaningful contribution to Cuba's cultural sphere by convening creators and critics and educators—those sponsored by various state and nongovernmental organizations and their self-reliant counterparts.

Strong partnerships have been the hallmark of the FLC's success. Collaboration with Cuba-based organizations like the ICAIC, the ISA, the TVS, and Cine Educativo (Educational Cinema, or CINED) are complemented by others beyond Cuba's borders. Through transnational alliances, emerging artists and filmmakers connect with the international art sphere. The FLC maintains close ties with its counterpart in Germany, which provides some programming funds as well as support for special needs. There is

Jorge Perugorría, the acclaimed actor who starred in *Fresa y chocolate* and *Guantanamera*, among other films, being interviewed in Manhattan during the 2007 installment of the Havana Film Festival of New York. Courtesy of the festival.

also a sister organization in the United States. The American Friends of the Ludwig Foundation of Cuba, a nonprofit directed by Carole Rosenberg, strives to build cultural bridges between the United States and Cuba through exchange programs in the arts. While the U.S. embargo has limited the nature and scope of the collaboration between the two organizations, the New York–based entity has helped host Cuban artists undertaking short-term studies in the United States and has put artists from both sides of the Straits of Florida in touch with one another. American Friends has also teamed up with a partner of the FLC; with the ICAIC they sponsor the Havana Film Festival of New York. Held each April, the event showcases many of the prizewinning films from the Havana-based International Festival of New Latin American Cinema and provides space for screenings of classic and contemporary works from Cuba and elsewhere in the Americas.

Central to the FLC's mission is the dissemination of Cuban culture. It willingly offers in-kind support for initiatives compatible with its goals. The FLC provided logistical support for this study as well as my other Cuban culture projects.[29] One evening during the International Festival of New

Latin American Cinema in 2005, a dozen people gathered at the FLC for a special event. Minister of Culture Abel Prieto Jiménez hosted the group. Attendees included the president and vice president of the FLC, the president and vice president of the ICAIC, Chilean filmmaker Silvio Caiozzi, U.S. activist-philanthropist Julie Belafonte, and me. Over dinner on the terrace, the minister (who arrived late because he had come from a screening of a newly released Cuban film) led us in debating a series of issues related to the coordinates of culture, politics, identity, and education. We aired our individual and collective concerns about cultural homogenization, the digital divide, the depoliticization of art in some contexts, and the crisis in education. While perspectives varied and viewpoints differed, we were aware of our shared commitment: employing culture to foster tolerance and understanding. Conversation was animated and continued long into the evening. Just before dawn we dispersed, not through any desire to end the lively discussion but reluctantly, because the once balmy breeze had become a biting wind. It seemed appropriate that the FLC served as our base for this event; the gathering of leaders from Cuba's governmental and nongovernmental cultural sectors and partners beyond the island clearly corresponded to the organization's mission of connecting Cuban arts to broader issues in a range of geopolitical contexts. Apparent was the camaraderie and shared vision among those promoting Cuban culture through governmental and nongovernmental organizations in Cuba and those working elsewhere, as was the centrality of the FLC and other newly created organizations to Cuba's cultural agenda.

Paving the Way: A New Audiovisual Era

The organizations examined in this chapter contributed to creating the conditions that would foster Street Filmmaking. A series of borders had been crossed; the boundaries blurred between governmental and nongovernmental organizations, local and global entities, artists working in the ICAIC and those making films in other spaces, and film and video. The way was paved for a new audiovisual era on the island.

These groups began to engender a new mind-set, one that empowered individuals to pursue their audiovisual projects, embraced partnerships and collaboration, demonstrated the effective coexistence of various technologies, and, above all, eroded dichotomous thinking. Making films in these spaces was perceived not as oppositional but as merely a sensible way to pursue projects through one of the increasing number of channels available. Audiovisual artists proved that nongovernmental or independent endeavors need not assume adversarial positions. While it was (and to some extent still is) assumed that "alternative" initiatives might resist the establishment, this need not be the case. On the contrary, collaboration by governmental and nongovernmental organizations in the cultural sphere, as we see here, has helped build human capacity, affirm identities, and strengthen autochthonous culture. As various state-sponsored and nongovernmental organizations worked together, they advanced their shared vision. Building alliances and leveraging resources has generated momentum. The synergy among these local-local and local-global partners has propelled them further than if each entity had been working on its own.

Previously, filmmaking had taken place almost exclusively within state agencies. Foremost among them was, of course, the ICAIC, known for its "artistic" filmmaking where cineastes have had the opportunity to experiment with the medium, creating works for local and international dissemination. The ICRT also produced filmed material, principally for Cuban television. ICRT filmmakers have had to adhere closely to a series of norms. Some limitations are inherent to the medium of television—the requisite duration for a particular program slot, the reliance on serials, the need for quick turnaround, and the importance of reaching a wide viewing audience. Others emanated from the ICRT's status as an organ of the Revolution and the concomitant expectation of proffering the party perspective. Other state agencies such as CINED and the Ministerio de Fuerzas Armadas (Armed Forces Ministry, or MINFAR) also produced films that have tended to value didactic over aesthetic concerns. The efforts of entities like these would be augmented by those of the newly created organizations.

These new organizations demonstrated that audiovisual materials could be produced in alternative spaces. Although these entities existed separately from state agencies in general and the ICAIC in particular, they never competed. On the contrary, they actually complemented industry efforts. In the chapters that follow, we will observe many instances of crossover: the industry acquisition of distribution rights for an "extra-industry" production, the allocation of ICAIC funds for a feature film made by self-reliant filmmakers, the state sponsorship of an event designed to serve young artists working on their own, and so on. The cross-fertilization of talent and resources—back and forth between the ICAIC and these other entities—served in concrete ways to energize the ICAIC. Filmmaking efforts from these spaces reaffirmed some of the key functions of Cuba's Revolutionary cinema. The audiovisual medium documented local realities, entertained and educated, and also fostered innovation and experimentation.

Significantly, an archive of the Special Period was created because these artists ventured into new terrain. Audiovisual activity from outside the ICAIC, emanating from these organizations, served to revise and renew the telling of stories on film and video. And, before long, the resultant practices—these new ways of seeing—would make their way into the industry. This new style of filmmaking would reinvigorate Cuba's state-supported cinema. In the pages that follow, we will see that the relationships between film professionals working within and beyond the industry need not be competitive or adversarial. ICAIC productions can and increasingly do coexist with other media-making initiatives. After all, in a country the size of Cuba, to "take sides" would be to jeopardize the future of the nation's culture. It would also be to overlook the ways in which Cuba's national film industry, in collaboration with other governmental and nongovernmental organizations, has contributed in very concrete ways to ushering in a new audiovisual era on the island. Ignoring the state's role in the creation of this new media moment, or setting recent audiovisual activity in opposition to the state, would jettison a critical development in Cuba's Revolutionary culture. It would be to overlook the state's own efforts in decentralizing the island's cultural sphere.

In the snapshots thus far we have glimpsed organizations founded in the late 1980s and early 1990s whose inroads would prepare the way for Street Filmmaking. We will now examine the evolution of two entities: the media collective TVS and the Animation Studio of the ICAIC. The respective trajectories of these collectives—one a nongovernmental organization located in a remote region of the island, the other a state agency based in the capital—will permit us to track recent changes in Cuba's film and video world and assess their impact. In this way, we will continue to map the contours taking shape on the island's audiovisual landscape.

It's good that they see this in Havana.

—Nicolasito Guillén Landrián

Establishing Community Media in the Mountains

TELEVISIÓN SERRANA STRENGTHENS HIGHLAND IDENTITY

As Cuba's economic crisis worsened in the early 1990s and the ICAIC's film production continued to plummet, a new community-based media organization came into being. In 1993, Televisión Serrana put down roots in the Granma province of the Sierra Maestra. Its mission: to "rescue the culture of peasant communities" in the region and "facilitate alternative communication for communities to . . . participate in the search for solutions to the problems that affect them." TVS emerged to give voice to the local highlanders and affirm their identities, and it did so precisely when Cuba was stepping up its engagement with world markets and international communications networks.[1]

During its first decade, TVS made some 350 videos totaling more than 600 hours of running time. Since opening its doors in San Pablo de Yao, a small community in the Buey Arriba municipality, TVS has had a widespread impact on individuals and communities. More than 32,000 people reside in the area of influence of TVS. Others have gained access to the material through presentations at community video clubs and screenings at local, regional, and international film festivals.[2] Still others have tuned in when the programming is aired on national television. The documentaries made by this community media group have been lauded across the island and beyond. Audiences from Buenos Aires to New York and elsewhere in the Americas have responded favorably to the material, as have viewers in Europe.

The success of media organizations is anything but guaranteed; in fact, virtually all community-based media initiatives fear for their very survival at some point, and many eventually dissolve. Their precarious situation parallels that of "circus performers who walk on the tightrope in delicate balance," according to audiovisual specialist Alfonso Gumucio-Dagrón. Community media projects, like these acrobats, "sometimes fall into the net only to ascend to start all over again." More often, however, "there is no net to cushion the fall. Many projects face too many challenges too soon after they begin, and so never have the opportunity to stabilize in the community," asserts the author of the comprehensive study titled *Sustainability of Community Media*.[3] Given the tenuous position of community video and television initiatives, and the precarious situation in Cuba when this entity was founded, it is remarkable that TVS has managed to produce award-winning documentaries, reach a large and diverse audience, and influence the local communities it is committed to serving.

This chapter will examine the trajectory of TVS. How did the community media initiative manage to emerge in a time of economic uncertainty and sociopolitical upheaval on the island? How has it continued to thrive, given the decline in community-based media initiatives around the world? And how has it succeeded in building human capacity, preserving and promoting a unique sense of identity and community, and establishing alliances across the island and beyond? We will see that the project's success emanates, in great part, from the balance achieved among international, national, and local partners. Rather than emphasize difference and divisiveness—pitting local residents against national institutions, for example, or driving a wedge between national entities and potential allies from the international arena—founding director Daniel Diez Castrillo sought to identify common ground. He aligned this initiative's mission with the agendas of international funding organizations, Cuban governmental and nongovernmental agencies, and local organizations and communities. By creating this coalition, he built a strong foundation for the media project, one that has transformed TVS into what it is today—a formidable structure on Cuba's audiovisual landscape. In the discussion that follows, we will see illustrated George Yúdice's contention that "the most innovative actors in setting agendas for political and social policies" may very well be "grassroots movements and the national and international NGOS that support them."[4]

Laying the Foundation: A Clear Vision and Common Goals

Three goals drove the development of this community media initiative: first, accomplish a technology transfer by training the residents to use cameras and editing equipment; second, enhance the residents' self-esteem by depicting their realities on-screen; and finally, disseminate this reality via television to others across the island. The objectives of TVS dovetailed with those of national and international entities. At home in Cuba, the rural population was deemed essential to the Revolutionary agenda. In fact, one of the platforms upon which the Revolution was implemented was the strengthening of rural sectors and their integration into the national project. No longer would agricultural workers be marginalized, lacking access to education, health care, expressive culture, and basic necessities. Instead, schools, clinics, and cultural institutions would be constructed for them, making accessible resources previously enjoyed only by the urban population. Revolutionary rhetoric was soon transformed into reality as the newly created state organizations began to make sweeping changes. One of the most notable initiatives was the massive literacy campaign. In the fall of 1960, Fidel Castro announced a program designed to eradicate illiteracy. At that time, more than 20 percent of Cuba's population could not read or write. The challenge was particularly pronounced in remote areas. Nearly 270,000 teachers and students were dispatched to remedy the situation, and within a year they returned home triumphant. More than 700,000 people had learned to read and write in what is considered one of—if not the—most successful literacy campaigns in the world. The island's literacy rate soared to 96 percent, putting Cuba's population on par with highly developed nations. The impact of this intensive project on teachers and learners alike, and the euphoria following the campaign's success, is captured in an early ICAIC documentary. In *Historia de una batalla* (*History of a Battle*, 1962), Manuel Octavio Gómez takes us far from Havana to observe reading lessons; the teachers, often not yet twenty years old, train their pupils—children, their parents, and even their grandparents. These close-ups of the effort of pairs and small groups give way to long shots of celebratory parades in Havana. Another work devoted to the literacy campaign is José Massip's *El maestro del Cilantro* (*Teacher of Cilantro*, 1962). In it, the established industry filmmaker Enrique Pineda Barnet is captured in the act of teaching. Both of these documentaries attest to the ambitious scope of this countrywide undertaking—for the individuals who participated and for the emerging Revolutionary nation. This successful initiative helped narrow the gap between the island's urban and rural populations.

Empowering rural communities was also the aim of international development organizations, specifically UNICEF and UNESCO. They were making funds available for initiatives that would foster development—the building of schools and clinics, the training of teachers and health care workers, the installation of public works (water, sanitation, and electricity), and so on. Community media initiatives were deemed to be an effective tool for fostering development and enhancing lives.

The proposal for the community media project, aligned as it was with both national and international development agendas, resonated for all concerned. The green light was given, and support was promised that would be crucial for creating and sustaining TVS. The provincial government set aside land and contributed the building. The ICRT took responsibility for training the staff. The nongovernmental National Association of Small Farmers (Asociación Nacional de Agricultores Pequeños), having already succeeded in building rural community networks, agreed to serve as the hosting agency. And UNESCO's International Programme for the Development of Communication granted $78,000 for the purchase of video cameras, editing equipment, and supplies. It was through the collaboration of governmental and nongovernmental entities in Cuba and abroad, then, that TVS came into being. At a time when state-sponsored filmmaking was dwindling, this new alliance stimulated the creation and circulation of community documentaries.

With partnerships forged and resources secured, the vision for TVS could become a reality. The Sierra Maestra, a region of great symbolic weight for Cubans as the cradle of the Revolution, was selected as the location for this project. It was in these mountains that Fidel Castro, Ernesto "Che" Guevara, Camilo Cienfuegos, and other rebels converged to plan their ousting of the Batista regime and implementing of a new revolutionary agenda. Moreover, development momentum in the region was strong. Prior to the Revolution, the area lacked basic infrastructure and social services; there were no roads, no electricity, no running water, and no access whatsoever to mass media. Daniel Diez Castrillo describes the region at that time as characterized by silence; its residents were isolated from one another and from the rest of the island. To illustrate, he notes that the closest doctors worked in Bayamo, the small provincial capital some eighty kilometers away on a dirt trail that was often impassable. Not surprisingly, the region experienced one of the highest incidences of infant mortality on the island.[5] Education was as elusive as health care; schools were too far away and too costly for rural children. Today, in marked contrast to pre-Revolutionary times, there is one doctor for every 800 inhabitants in the region. Schools are free and serve all children; they have been established in even the most remote areas of the Sierra. Residents can access two national and one regional television channel.[6] The Sierra Maestra has come a long way over the past half-century.

The site appealed for other reasons. Daniel Diez Castrillo first visited the Sierra Maestra while on assignment with the ICAIC. As a filmmaker working alongside the legendary Santiago Álvarez, he had the opportunity to travel through remote areas and align himself with rural people. Connections to Cuba's campesinos were also consolidated through his participation in the literacy campaign; Diez Castrillo taught reading and writing to his illiterate compatriots in the mountains of Caney in the island's eastern region. Through his experiences in these remote mountainous areas, he developed an affinity with highland peoples. Some fifteen years after founding TVS, Daniel Diez Castrillo shared with me the motivation behind his desire to form a space for artistic creation that was tied to these highland communities. He considers these mountain

Daniel Diez Castrillo
in Havana during the
seventh National Exhibit
of New Filmmakers (2008).
Courtesy of Cláudia Nunes.

communities to be "bases" for what later became the culture of a country. From the outset, he envisioned disseminating the results of this creativity over national television, in the cinemas, through local broadcasts, and especially at events organized where the filming had been done.

Filming in the Countryside: The ICAIC's Depictions of Rural Cuba

The notion of filming in the countryside was not new for Cuba. In fact, the ICAIC had been representing Cuba's rural communities for more than three decades by the time TVS was launched. An early and ongoing aim of the ICAIC was to project Cuban places and people on-screen. This emphasis on autochthonous culture in remote areas is evident in several early works. Some depict campesinos as model revolutionaries, others illustrate the vastly different experiences of Cuba's rural dwellers versus *habaneros*, and still others suggest the disenfranchisement of the island's less advantaged population living in remote areas.

Oscar Valdés pays tribute to the Cuban cowboy in *Vaqueros del Cauto* (*Cowboys of the Cauto River Region*, 1965). Long panoramic takes of cattle and cowboys serve as establishing shots. Through the framing, editing, and voice-over narration, this documentary underscores the danger faced by the vaqueros in working with cattle and highlights their strength and passion. Significantly, the protagonist is a collective one comprised of men from adolescence to retirement; a predominance of long and medium shots features the group of cattlemen on horseback among the herd. The thirty-minute black-and-white documentary concludes with a statement on destiny: The cowboy will always be a cowboy, even if life tries to take him in other directions. Valdés's admiration for Hollywood westerns comes through, as does his celebration of the "New Man," the model of revolutionary masculinity.

Another documentary, *Pedro cero por ciento* (*Hundred-Percent Pedro*, Luis Felipe Bernaza, 1980), features a legendary animal advocate. Pedro Acosta runs a dairy farm that produces 400,000 liters of milk per year. This exemplary manager has purportedly not permitted even a single cow to die for seven years running. His passion and commitment have earned him the national record for milk production and a reputation as an exemplary farmer and revolutionary. In the documentary, Pedro's talking head is interspersed with images of him at work—feeding the cows, pulling them out of molasses, artificially inseminating them, and assisting as they give birth. The thesis is clear: Hard work and unwavering dedication yield dividends for the individual and the nation. *Pedro cero por ciento* introduces rural viewers to Pedro and urban viewers to farming practices. This devoted citizen labors to meet the production quotas established by his metropolitan compatriots. His efforts translate into personal satisfaction and contribute to the collective good. Through his efforts and the work of others like him, residents of the provincial capitals and Havana can count on a steady stream of milk and other agricultural products.

A classic of Cuba's revolutionary cinema, *Por primera vez* (*For the First Time*, Octavio Cortázar, 1967) also focuses on islanders living far from Havana. The ten-minute black-and-white documentary attests to the ICAIC's mission to bridge the city and the countryside through culture; it traces the experiences of campesinos in the remote community of Los Mulos as they prepare to watch moving pictures for the first time. A mobile cinema unit has arrived from the capital bringing with it the opportunity to project films. Local men, women, and children appear in the foreground, often arranged in groups in front of the camera in family-picture style. Their humble homes against the rural landscape provide the backdrop. In the culminating sequence, the generator brings the projector to life; clips from Charles Chaplin's *Modern Times* are juxtaposed with expressions on the faces of viewers as they witness the wondrous spectacle. Michael Chanan, in *Cuban Cinema*, comments on how this work "has produced for the audience a vision of its own self-discovery *as an audience.*"[7] He argues convincingly that this film gives Cuban viewers "a new awareness" of their status as audience. While his analysis is compelling and the documentary is delightful in many ways, the depiction of rural subjects in *Por primera vez* remains problematic. They are relegated to the position of passive consumers of images produced by their more informed counterparts in the metropolis. Even though the campesinos appear in front of the camera, their interventions only reaffirm their alleged "lacks." Industry filmmakers from Havana drive the dialogue, with a male interrogator posing questions to the rural residents: Have they ever been to a cinema? Have they ever seen a movie? What do they imagine it to be like? Their answers reveal the rift between the urban and rural experiences and perspectives. No, they have not been to the cinema. "Is cinema a movie?" wonders one little boy. No, they have not seen a movie. The response of one woman highlights the disparate worldviews; she remarks, "They [the films] must be something important, since you're so interested in them; they must be something very beautiful." *Por primera vez* casts campesinos in a subordinate position relative to their *habanero* counterparts.[8]

In stark contrast to these works is *Ociel del Toa*, a stunning documentary depicting life in Cuba's remote Toa River region.[9] Nicolasito Guillén Landrián focuses on a solitary campesino named Ociel. In extreme close-ups as well as languid pans we observe the man portrayed not as a beneficiary of or contributor to the Revolution but, rather, as an individual struggling to combat adversity—the powerful current of the Toa River as he poles his homemade boat across it, the stifling heat of the midday sun as he trudges over gravel roads during a political rally, and the relentless monotony of everyday life. By relying on intertitles rather than Ociel's recorded voice, this highly innovative documentary underscores the protagonist's lack of agency. In the same way that the current of the Toa River propels his craft, so does the Revolutionary momentum sweep him along.

The ICAIC did pay attention to the countryside, then, both by filming in remote regions and by dispatching mobile cinema units to the prov-

Poster promoting one of Cuba's mobile cinema initiatives. By Eduardo Muñoz Bachs. Courtesy of the ICAIC.

inces.[10] Yet, a review of the institute's output over the past fifty years attests to the relative scarcity of films on rural topics. Images of Cuba's outlying areas were few and far between, and representations created by the campesinos themselves were nonexistent. Industry filmmaker Daniel Díaz Torres affirms this fact. He acknowledges that although the Revolution has penetrated the mountain communities and has managed to change and transform society even in very remote areas, this has not translated into a greater screen presence. The interior of the island continues to be a territory rarely explored cinematically, despite its potential to express the depth of *cubanía*. According to this ICAIC filmmaker, recent national film production has done little to help alleviate "the fragmentary and insufficient metropolitan vision of our Island and the lives of its inhabitants." Díaz Torres reminds us that "Cuba isn't Havana," despite our tendency to believe—consciously or unconsciously—otherwise. For those who think it is, he cautions, it is worth considering at the very least that the "urban asphalt" would be "monotonous, asphyxiating and brutal" without the balancing contrast of the countryside. From his position within Cuba's film institute, he recognizes the need for more and different depictions of the countryside. Not surprisingly, he lauds TVS filmmakers for presenting "this other image of ourselves" with "validity and with artistic authenticity."[11]

TVS sought to provide an alternative view of rural communities, one that filled gaps in extant programming in Cuba. "In my country," TVS founder Diez Castrillo explains, "television shows rural folks only as producers of [food] staples; nothing is said about their dreams, their conflicts, their culture." With all television programming in Cuba once coming only from the city of Havana, Diez Castrillo observed that the rural world was being reflected simplistically. "The campesinos are part of Cuban culture," Diez Castrillo recalls thinking, "and their culture is part of us, too." He believed that television screens needed to reflect "their happiness, their hardships, their conception of life, their music—how they sing it, how they play it, how they dance."[12] Daniel Diez Castrillo envisioned a new way of depicting rural residents on film and engaging communities in that endeavor. To that end, TVS began to augment Cuba's revolutionary film tradition. Diez Castrillo resisted the facile approach sometimes used to introduce new initiatives, whether in media or politics or academe or some other sphere, that of creating a rupture with one's predecessors. Rather than emphasizing what the ICAIC had not managed to achieve, he focused on its strengths. By building on rather than dismantling earlier efforts, Diez Castrillo positioned TVS to succeed. The media initiative's adherence to revolutionary filmmaking practices contributed to its effectiveness and ensured its survival: It kept in mind the importance of developing a film language appropriate for the circumstances; it accorded prominence to local faces and places on-screen; and it respected the medium's power to teach and inform as well as to entertain. It also did a whole lot more. An examination of TVS programming and production strategies will allow us to glimpse the foundation upon which the Street mode of filmmaking would be constructed.

Screening Highland Experiences: Local Landscapes, Familiar Faces

TVS filmmakers have, for more than a decade, strived to develop local content and create programming relevant to communities in this mountain region. In working toward this end, they have integrated rural residents into nearly every stage of the process. Before examining how this was carried out, we will consider the material TVS has produced. Video documentaries address topics of local import in the realms of culture, identity, public health, the environment, and children's rights. The documentaries express the highland context in which they are produced—whether by featuring members of the local communities who narrate their stories with expressions and pronunciation unique to the zone, or by treating and thereby valorizing existing ways of doing things.

"There were those who said that Televisión Serrana wasn't going to last more than two or three months," recalls Diez Castrillo, "because in these parts there wasn't much to film. But the highland people are human beings with . . . all the contradictions, all the happiness, all the virtues, everything." He elaborates on the complexity of this local culture and its resonance for all Cubans, regardless of their location on the island: "The mountain man is a human being and his entire life is there: And this gave us the possibility . . . of demonstrating to the rest of the country that these human beings existed and they were also working to construct a society." Diez Castrillo believes this is important, given that many urban dwellers were born in the countryside and grew up there. Some forget, he notes, and others perhaps choose not to remember. TVS also provides an opportunity to "reflect the cultural world" of these zones, adds Diez Castrillo, citing musical traditions as an example. TVS has been consistent in creating programming that captures the richness of this context and responds to community demands and interests.

One format commonly employed to feature individuals from the region is the portrait documentary. *Las cuatro hermanas* (*Four Sisters*, Rigoberto Jiménez, 1998), for example, takes us to the home of four sisters who have lived together for most of their lives. Now in their seventies and eighties, the elderly sisters share responsibilities for maintaining the simple cabin, caring for the animals, tending the garden, and making occasional trips to town. Their memories of the past—"We were always working . . . always"—are interwoven with images from their daily experience. They cook with wood and eat by candlelight, as their home has no electricity. They haul water from the outdoor pump and carry their clothes to the river for washing, as they have no running water. Very infrequently, one of the women is depicted at rest—smoking a cigarette on the porch, sipping a cup of coffee in the kitchen, or surveying the mist as it settles on the mountains. This fifteen-minute piece offers the women's stories as a testament to their strength, solidarity, and self-reliance.

The documentary personalizes the represented subjects. In the opening sequence, each sister appears in a still image above her first name: Dolores, Gelacia, Cira, and Josefa. The selection and editing of their stories permit their unique traits to emerge. While their personalities vary—industrious, mischievous, pensive, and melancholy—they share common experiences. All shun charity, believing in hard work and independence. All recall respecting and even fearing their father. All left the farm at one point to pursue a relationship with a particular man. And all returned, ultimately deeming their humble life in the mountains preferable to the hassles of their ill-fated partnerships.

The concluding sequence, like the opening one, features the still image of each woman. Here, though, the four portraits dissolve into one another, with each woman contributing to the composite. In the end, then, *Four Sisters* is not so much about these particular women (whose surname is never given) but, rather, about the intersection of their lives and experiences with one another—and presumably with the highland viewers. It is significant that self-sufficient campesinas are featured here, in con-

Coffee-grinding
instrument featured
in the documentary
*In Step with the
Mortar*. Courtesy of
Daniel Diez Castrillo.

trast to most depictions of rural people that cast the farmer as male. The
documentary never draws attention to this alternative representation; it
merely inserts the female dimension, thereby revising the portrayal of
the rural community. This reframing so as to integrate women's experiences is further underscored by the soundtrack; the Camerata Romeau, an
all-female chamber group based in Havana, performs the musical score.

Complementing these portraits of Sierra residents are documentaries
structured around a unique object and its relevance in everyday life. *La
cuchufleta* (*The Whatyoumacallit*, Luis Ángel Guevara Polanco, 2006) centers on a microelectric generator. Through testimony of neighbors and
the inventor, we learn that this homemade device can power the radios
and television sets of several households. *Al compás del pilón* (*In Step with
the Mortar*, Carlos Rodríguez, 2002) focuses on the instrument used in the
Sierra Maestra for removing the husk from coffee beans. Sequences showing this process are deftly interspersed with humorous vignettes relating
tall tales and bits of hearsay. In a succinct nine-minute project, a familiar
utilitarian object serves as the portal to coffee traditions and local lore. *La
chivichana* (*The Go-Kart*, Waldo Ramírez, 2000) is a testimonial of campesino creativity. This fourteen-minute documentary highlights the cre-

Carlos Rodríguez prepares to film in the Sierra Maestra (2008). Courtesy of Daniel Diez Castrillo.

ation and use of go-karts by the residents in the mountainous Brazón area of the Sierra Maestra. During the Special Period, Cubans developed ingenious solutions to everyday problems; they became experts at *resolviendo* (getting by, making do). The innovative form of transportation depicted in this documentary constitutes one colorful example.

Opening and closing sequences compare the mule and the *chivichana*. An elderly campesino astride a mule admits his preference for the traditional flesh-and-bones beast. Between these sequences framing the documentary, footage features *chivichanas* in motion and their makers in action. In a light tone, the talking heads and voice-overs enumerate the benefits of this mode of transportation: The versatile carts can be used to haul heavy loads (illustrated by bunches of plantains on one, a bundle of firewood on another); they can serve as taxis (some speed downhill carrying three, four, or even six people); and they have even been employed as ambulances (the image of a white-smocked doctor attests to the public health function of this contraption). Constructed of basic materials (wood scraps, nails, and rope) and capable of careening downhill at speeds of up to sixty miles per hour, the *chivichana* has indeed helped alleviate transportation problems in the region. It also attests to the ingenuity of the mountain residents, for when the gasoline shortage removed motorized vehicles from the roads, these people developed a solution to their dilemma. Rather than lamenting the loss of their locomotion, they created a new mode of transportation.

The documentary takes full advantage of the local landscapes; outdoor settings filmed with natural light predominate. Panoramic views depict the mountains enveloped in dense forest. The expanses of trees are interrupted only by the roads along which mules, pedestrians, and *chivichanas* move; gasoline-powered vehicles are notably absent. Enhancing the charm of this work is the rendition of the song "La chivichana" played by local musicians comprising the Grupo Musical Aficionado Sonido Providencia.

The natural surroundings serve as the leitmotif unifying virtually all of the works produced by TVS. The filmmakers and community members emphasize their ecological concerns in numerous projects. *La tierra conmovida* (*The Saddened Earth*, 1999) is one of the most innovative in this genre. Daniel Diez Castrillo shared with me his ongoing interest in making a film about drought. Every time he tried, though, it rained. So the years passed, until one day he was scouting locations for a different project. Suddenly, he found himself "amidst sand and dust" in a "desolate landscape," one that had previously been replete with trees, animals, insects, and "marvelous" vegetation. Upon seeing so much devastated land, Diez Castrillo experienced a profound sadness. He was struck by the fact that we always think about how "our senseless acts of destruction" affect ourselves, never considering the suffering imposed on the flora and fauna. So Diez Castrillo set out to capture "nature's cry of desperation and alert."

The six-minute documentary opens with a sequence of languid pans across a series of landscapes—mist rising off the water, mountains towering and birds soaring against a cloudless sky, grasses blowing, and palm trees standing in fog. Biblical verses from Isaiah 24 overlay the images, foreshadowing the destruction to follow:

All the earth is saddened
infected by the inhabitants therein
because they have transgressed the laws
they have changed the ordinance
they have broken the everlasting covenant.

The results of this havoc are evoked succinctly through a metonymic sequence: Men fell trees with large saws, and the noise of their falling bleeds into an image of frightened horses running away. The biblical verses continue, giving way to images of barrenness. A dead tree stands alone on a solitary hellish landscape. Insects bore into its branches. Two horses butt heads. A crab lies motionless in the sand. A reptile displaced to dry land slowly lifts its head skyward. One last verse of Isaiah calls out: "Oh inhabitants of the earth!"

This final lament creates space for spectators to reflect on the condition of our environment. Through an evocative rather than didactic approach, we are engaged in a meditation on the sorry state of the planet. The director jettisons dialogue and voice-over narration, and with it the "preaching" and finger-pointing characteristic of many ecology films. The images of our natural world, the biblical text, and the soundtrack with strands of Jan Garabek's "Officium" resonate for viewers in the Sierra Maestra and elsewhere in the world. We are invited to reflect together on the magnitude of this destruction. Although the degradation is localized—the credits connect the images to the Río Cauto municipality of Granma province—*The Saddened Earth* situates the challenge facing a specific community within a broader context. This work succeeds, then, in connecting viewers across landscapes and national territories and in positing a local problem within a larger global framework.

Another work conjoining the local and the global is *Freddy o el sueño de Noel* (*Freddy or Noel's Dream*, Waldo Ramírez). This "fictionalized documentary," set to the sounds of Queen's "Bohemian Rhapsody," blurs dreams and reality. The piece opens with the image of a young boy on the dry side of a dam. The empty reservoir parallels the absence of life and lack of activity. He seems to recall the lifting of the gates and the ensuing rush of water. As the dam opens and water rushes out of the reservoir, tremendous schools of fish flail over the structure. Men stand waist-deep in the swirling water below, swinging clubs and flinging nets. The once dry hole has become filled with raging water; it has been transformed into a fishing paradise. As the rhythm of "Rhapsody" begins its decrescendo, the dream sequence evaporates and reality returns. Once again, the young boy stands alone, dwarfed by the concrete structure. This eight-minute piece employs with artistic precision the format of the video clip. The fantasy of a local boy is made accessible to an international audi-

Men and boys catch fish as water rushes over the dam in *Freddy, o el sueño de Noel*.
Courtesy of Daniel Diez Castrillo.

ence, moved by the simultaneously violent and exhilarating rendering. Ramírez's reliance on the recognizable video clip form and the popular song appeals to viewers across cultures. In order to see it, however, they must travel to Cuba. Dissemination of *Freddy* is limited because permission to use the Queen song has not been obtained. Copyright compliance is a challenge facing many filmmakers in Cuba. They are aware of artistic property rights but lack the resources to pay for costly permissions. As a result, works like this one are destined to a limited circulation.

TVS programming stresses the ingenuity of the mountain peoples, the importance of the land in their lives, and the richness of their culture and traditions. The programming consistently emphasizes their connected-ness—to the land, to others in the surrounding areas, and to individuals extending far beyond their community.

Connecting with Local Communities: Both Sides of the Camera

In order to permit the highland communities "to see themselves reflected," TVS had to avoid a pitfall common to many media initiatives—

that of failing to connect with the social actors they purport to represent. From the very beginning, the support of the community was sought; highlanders were integrated fully in the production and dissemination of videos. Diez Castrillo recalls that early on some of the local authorities did not understand the value of a cultural video project. TVS had to work to establish a rapport with its principal constituency in the Sierra Maestra and earn community support. Their alliance with the local farmers' organization helped integrate some members of the community at this initial stage, and other partnerships lent them legitimacy and expanded their contacts: The television of Holguín helped train the first generation, for example, and the Festival de Cine de la Montaña provided an avenue for the work's dissemination.

One key strategy for connecting with local residents was the recruitment and training of area youth. Although the initial TVS crew hailed from Havana, they were soon joined in their training workshops by aspiring media-makers from the Granma province and the city of Bayamo. Now, the team consists almost exclusively of highland residents. In 2002, the staff numbered 15—3 camera operators, 3 directors, 2 editors, 2 producers, 2 sound assistants, and 3 drivers who doubled as lighting specialists when shoots required illumination. Numbers fluctuate, depending upon the audiovisual activities on site. A partnership with the EICTV brings students from San Antonio de los Baños to the TVS enclave. There they team up to create video portraits of individuals in the region. More recently, young filmmakers have done their obligatory social service with the collective. Hilda Elena Vega, the maker of the award-winning *La Bestia* (*The Beast*, 2007), was preparing to leave for the Sierra Maestra when I interviewed her during the seventh Muestra Nacional de Nuevos Realizadores in Havana. The media-makers at TVS work closely with one another; their collaboration ensures ongoing mentoring and the cross-fertilization of ideas and approaches.

TVS filmmakers value their work with the community media project. In an installment of TV Yumurí's *Quédate conmigo* program, several media-makers reflected on the importance of TVS for their professional development and personal well-being. One young woman credits TVS for training her and giving her a profession. Another concurs, saying, "I'm developing as a professional and so are many others." Her neighbors "who have never seen what a camera is, who have never seen what cinema

EICTV students gain practical training at the TVS installation as Daniel Diez Castrillo (left) mentors (2008). Courtesy of Daniel Diez Castrillo.

is, what making video is" have benefited from having access to this experience. She sums up her remarks by noting, "Televisión Serrana has opened the road for me and many young people." A male colleague expresses his gratitude to the organization for introducing him to the world of television, saying, "For me, a hick from here, working in television is . . . the most enriching experience I've had." Another echoes this sentiment, stating that encountering TVS was "finding meaning in life." By fostering the development of young professionals, TVS has fulfilled its objective of building human capacity and transferring technological skills to area residents. At the same time, the reliance on local youth has permitted TVS to represent highland experiences in ways that resonate in the mountains and far beyond.

The involvement of local residents extends beyond the filming process. They actively participate at video screenings as well. In order for TVS programs to reach their intended audience, videos are often packed onto mules along with a generator, monitor, and VCR and hauled to remote mountain communities. There the documentaries are shared in a public event generally consisting of two parts. During the screening, viewers see documentaries reflecting their own circumstances: Faces and places are familiar to them; the linguistic patterns resemble their own. And when songs accompany the voices on the soundtrack, they are often renditions by local musicians. During the postscreening discussion, residents share their impressions and expand on the issues raised in the documentary.

Diez Castrillo compares this kind of filming and viewing experience with that of industry efforts. In both cases, "You work with cameras, [and] you work with sound." The key difference has to do with the role of the spectator: "It's not the same for a man to go to the cinema to watch a movie or [to be] at home watching TV," he contends, "as it is for a man in the community watching this material to see his community, his reality, and have the opportunity to say things, the things on his mind." In fact, it is this very "feedback" that helps to generate new topics; these community conversations yield ideas that later make their way into documentaries.

It was during one of the postscreening discussions, for example, that the TVS crew met an elderly man who had been writing poems on the Sierra Maestra for twenty years; eighty-five-year-old Abel Rodríguez, with a corpus of more than 1,400 poems, became the subject of a video directed by Diez Castrillo. In *Como una gota de agua* (*Like a Drop of Water*, 1998), we hear the poet reading from his work—"between the cradle and the grave we enjoy life"—as we experience images of the lush landscape with forests, waterfalls, and ponds. The images of nature are interspersed with close-ups of handwritten pages of poetry and of the elderly man seated on the porch of his humble dwelling. The montage places poetry in the countryside. When the poet reflects on his creative process, poetry and the local landscape are conjoined. At times the poet sits down and is able to write, and at other times, as he explains, inspiration is absent: "I was writing and in the struggle to find the rhyme in meaning and word I felt something like a drop of water fall into my brain and there was the word." With *Como una gota de agua*, Diez Castrillo sought to show that the artist who has something to say will say it, regardless of where he is. The creative spirit of this wizened mountain poet inspires all who create—including community members generating ideas for new programs or trying their hand at documentary production.

One format particularly effective in engaging residents and affirming local ways of life is the *video carta*, or video letter. These testimonials feature people of the Sierra Maestra telling about their daily lives, the nature surrounding them, their families, and their work or school. The production of *video cartas* has fomented a sense of local identity, according to Diez Castrillo. "Just the fact of being filmed is meaningful for the people of Sierra Maestra," he notes. "When a video crew comes to their community and stays with them, their self-esteem increases." In public screenings of video letters, the audience may respond with a video letter of their own. This common response, according to Diez Castrillo, attests to the "enormous need" of the rural people to say, "We are here." Through TVS, they embrace their experiences as camera-worthy.

Rural children are often involved in sending their impressions on video to other young people in Cuba and beyond the island. The young protagonists ask questions of the children who will "receive" or view the *video carta*. In many cases the *video cartas* are addressed to a group of children in a particular country. A key feature of the *video carta* is its emphasis on fostering communication. Through these documentaries, images of everyday rural life are disseminated on the island and beyond. The circulation of their voices and culture to other communities in Cuba and the world accords these people recognition and respect. The local residents are integrated into the communication process; their input permits the creation of these informative and often entertaining documentaries that are, above all, exceedingly relevant. They also participate in developing linkages with viewing communities in other sites on the island as well as elsewhere across the Americas.

TVS relies on low-cost and easy-to-use equipment; technological resources are appropriate for the community's needs. Small cameras—nonprofessional VHS, Super VHS, and Beta—and basic editing equipment can be used effectively with relatively little experience. They are manageable for individuals of all ages, including children. This straightforward technology facilitates participation. The small size and relative ease of operation also makes the equipment relatively unobtrusive and therefore more compatible with the TVS mode of filmmaking. "Real" experiences of "live" people can be captured with spontaneity. This accessible technology enables highland residents to communicate in a new way. By demystifying the technology and strengthening the audience's critical capacity, TVS fosters ownership of the communication process. Local residents participate in shaping the communication agenda.

TVS emphasizes the coordinates of education and communication in promoting development. The TVS mission corresponds to the aims of the community; the people behind the cameras and those in front of the screen share a common agenda. The organization does not speak for the people. Instead, it provides them with the space and means to tell their stories and narrate their experiences. Through this audiovisual initiative, highland communities are empowered; they are encouraged to employ media to shape their future—not to rely on outsiders for help but, rather, to tackle problems collectively and work out solutions at the local level.

Effecting Transformation: Identity Affirmed, Ownership Conferred

The community media initiative has focused on a sector of Cuba's population whose experiences have rarely been depicted. At the same time, it has engaged the residents of one of the country's most remote areas in representing their surroundings. Not surprisingly, TVS has earned high marks from its partners on and beyond the island. Cuban television and film festival audiences seek out and applaud TVS programming. During its first decade, members of the TVS team earned more than 200 awards.[13] When a recent installment of the *Pantalla Documental* program aired on Cuban television, the moderator, acclaimed documentary filmmaker Octavio Cortázar, described TVS as nothing less than an "extraordinary artistic and cultural experiment."

International organizations consider TVS a model of effective community media. In the 1996 projects report of the Intergovernmental Council of the International Programme for the Development of Communication (IPDC Council), UNESCO evaluated the collective as fully achieving its objectives "regarding the development of remote areas and information transfer as well as the active participation of rural communities in the creation of community television." The report deemed TVS to be "an efficient vehicle for progress among rural populations."[14] In a 2002 evaluation summary, TVS once again impressed the reviewers. The IPDC Council reiterated that "project objectives were fully achieved"—that highlanders had participated in creating community television, thereby improving the flow of information and the development of the zone. The report stated, "The utilization of allocated funds has been optimal," noting that the quality of TVS productions is appreciated throughout the country, and that few initiatives with such a limited budget turn out to be as successful as this one. On the tenth anniversary of its founding, TVS was heralded as "one of the most original and innovative social communication projects in Latin America" with great successes in effecting positive transformation and educational development.[15]

UNESCO funding was critical in establishing this organization. Yet, TVS does not depend on outside contributions. Instead, the initiative seeks to generate revenue to sustain some of its activities. TVS provides services, including training workshops available through the Centro de Estudios para la Comunicación Comunitaria, created in 1996. In addition, TVS specialists consult with communities seeking to foster participatory development and democratic communication through video. Other services include transferring and copying videocassettes. While this media organization still requires subvention, it has assumed responsibility for covering some of its operating expenses.

For an independent media organization to be truly effective, it must support the development objectives of the community. "It is not enough that a community medium is recognized," asserts Alfonso Gumucio-Dagrón; "it also has to have impact and concrete actions in support of the objectives of community organization and development."[16] Indeed, TVS has contributed in concrete ways to mitigating local problems and fostering social, economic, and cultural development. The sensitivity of TVS to the problems of its residents has permitted it to have a positive impact. During one of the postscreening discussions, for example, individuals expressed concern over the contamination of the River Yao by a coffee processing plant. Their plight became the subject of a subsequent documentary, and this filmed criticism provoked action. Community members are changed through this process, becoming active agents in shaping their futures.

At times the individuals featured in a TVS documentary derive concrete benefits from the experience. *Tocar la alegría* (*Playing Joy*, Marcos Bedoya, 1996) attests to the commitment of children from the Pilón municipality who came together to make music. The short depicts them loading their crude instruments—some fashioned from tin cans and kettles and scraps of wood—into two dilapidated wheelbarrows and transporting them to various nearby locales, where audiences applaud their performances. The camera closes in on the homemade cymbals, advertising the group's name, *Super Salsa*. Banana fronds and drying laundry flutter around the children as they answer the narrator's questions: "What would you like to be?" "A drummer," comes the answer from one. "If you were famous, who would you like to be like?" "Like Selena," says one girl. "Like the *Originals*," offers one boy. "What do you want to tell Cuban musicians and music teachers?" Here multiple voices chime in, all expressing their desire to continue making progress toward becoming musicians. One child implores the spectator, "Please help us move forward." The documentary captures their aspirations. And the experience of participating in the project actually propels them toward that goal. After appearing in *Tocar la alegría*, the budding musicians had the opportunity to go to Santiago de Cuba and play with the internationally acclaimed composer-performer Adalberto Alvarez.[17] So this TVS project launched them onto the stage, providing them with a formative experience in the music world.

Arguably the most significant contribution to the community has been enhancing its highland identity. Sierra Maestra residents often credit TVS for their increased knowledge of local traditions and their strengthened connection to the land and the community. In a television special devoted to the community media project, one local resident emphasizes all that she and her neighbors have been able to observe, thanks to Televisión Serrana. "I've seen many things that we never thought we'd see, we've discovered—or they've discovered—things, too, that are very much a part of the mountains," she noted on the TV Yumurí *Quédate conmigo* program.[18] Another community member cites as a plus the increased "momentum of cultural work and the discovery of all that exists in these mountains."

Producers of TVS documentaries recognize the value of their work for the communities and for themselves. One young man reflects with poignancy on the appeal of the programming to area residents: "People get used to seeing the work of Televisión Serrana here and . . . they like what we do. Why? Because they recognize themselves. In these documentaries, in these stories, they recognize themselves and see themselves reflected. The people say, 'Well, I feel happy because all of us—even the chickens— get to appear on screen' and I think this is the way to influence others." Several members of the team affirm their renewed connection to the countryside and their community though their work. One young woman sums up by saying, "Well, the most important thing I've learned . . . is how to love and respect others, especially the people who live in the Sierra Maestra. That's one of our objectives." Another credits TVS for increasing her appreciation for rural life. The media collective taught her "to admire the people of the countryside, because I'm from the country. But, well, one always . . . tries to move away . . . to look for other things. . . . However, I didn't have to leave here. I stayed right here and learned to see things in all their beauty." One highlander recalls seeing TVS material and being struck by how different it was from other programming. Now, working with TVS, he has found a way to "connect with nature" and feel useful. "I like [José] Martí's work a lot," he comments. "For me Martí is the paradigm . . . the paradigm of Cubans and his 'With the poor of the earth I would cast my lot' always seemed like one of the goals of my life." Another team member reflects on the central role of his TVS work in strengthening his sense of Cubanness and further consolidating his national identity: "I'm reaffirmed as a Cuban in the Sierra Maestra. I believe that in some way the Sierra Maestra . . . wasn't only the cradle of the Revolution but . . . [also] the cradle of Cuban nationality. I've been reaffirmed as a Cuban because I'm recovering traditions. I've been learning from the people a way of living, especially in matters dealing with family . . . with objects, with music, with everything. . . . In the lives of the campesinos, everything has meaning." The residents of the Sierra Maestra have affirmed their highland identity through their interaction with TVS. Community members do not merely consume images passively; rather, they actively participate in their creation. By blurring the boundary between producers and consumers, TVS engages Sierra Maestra communities in representing their reality; it accords them ownership of the communication process.

Televisión Serrana has had a transformative impact on highlanders. The project has fostered community participation in one of the island's most remote areas. It has helped create a new generation of Cuban videomakers who value alternative media and community ownership of communication tools. And it has affirmed local identities. No longer are Sierra residents marginalized through the communication process—either ignored altogether or represented from without. Instead, they actively participate in showing their lives, land, and labor. These depictions are neither idealized nor simplified; rather, they present highlanders as creative agents capable of representing their own surroundings, identifying and addressing their problems, and developing ingenious solutions. The impact of TVS extends beyond the Sierra Maestra to Havana and other urban areas. In "Más allá de La Habana," Daniel Díaz Torres notes the broad sphere of TVS influence: "That the gaze of the city spectator is surprised and recreated through contemplating the mountain landscapes like those offered by the Televisión Serrana filmmakers . . . is positive and refreshing. It's the first step towards helping us to recognize the richest and most complex spaces in our make-up as an island and as a nation, and they should also be integrated into our conception of 'Cuban-ness.'"[19] In creating programming for their neighbors as well as for others in Cuba and afar, highland residents are reconfiguring the relationship between consumers and producers of images and between the capital and the countryside. Rural residents are generally considered producers of only the most basic of all commodities—food. The creation of cultural content most often takes place in the urban centers, with this programming then transmitted out to remote areas. In this case, however, the flow is interrupted. The production of cultural content takes place in the countryside. Images generated by rural media-makers are disseminated locally though community discussions and events, regionally through festivals, nationally on television, and internationally through various networks. No longer is Havana perceived to be the sole producer of island images and, therefore, the sole arbiter of Cuban identity. Through the efforts of TVS, rural experiences figure more prominently in the concept of Cubanness. The national imaginary has been altered.

Extracting the Formula for Success: Lessons from Televisión Serrana

TVS teaches a series of valuable lessons about the sustainability of community media, the importance of local-local and local-global partnerships for Cuba's future, and strategies for countering the homogenizing force of global communications. Regarding community media, we see illustrated Gumucio-Dagrón's recipe for success: While there is no "magic formula," he insists on the importance of balancing three elements—economic, social, and institutional—if community media initiatives are to take root and thrive. The use of inappropriate technology is the single most common cause of failure. For success, "the political commitment of social agents" is necessary. And indeed, the impressive trajectory of TVS is inextricably linked with the passion and ongoing efforts of founding director Daniel Diez Castrillo. Initiatives like TVS do not merely "emerge"; they come into being through collaboration, hard work, and a certain degree of selflessness on the part of one or more individuals. Daniel Diez Castrillo exhibited these traits over more than a decade guiding TVS. While conceptualizing the project, he kept in mind the agendas of all potential players and identified the common ground on which he would build the media initiative. In formulating the objectives, he resisted the temptation to undermine the Revolutionary agenda and built upon it to strengthen his project. During the implementation phase, he adhered to the objectives he and his partners had identified, and he embraced the arduous task of building consensus and earning the respect of local communities. And throughout the decade of production, he consistently sought to empower others. Content to remain in the background, Diez Castrillo strived to create the space into which others could insert themselves and achieve their collective goals. We see here the importance of the individual to the success of the initiative.

We see also that "alternative" or "independent" initiatives need not take an adversarial position to be effective. It is sometimes assumed that nongovernmental and state-sponsored entities are necessarily at odds. Indeed, community media projects in some locales often take shape without support from and/or in conflict with governments. That is not the case in Cuba, however, where the TVS project and the state share common development goals of building human capacity, affirming local identity, and strengthening rural communities. Recall that the Cuban government backed this project in concrete ways. So while state support for an independent media initiative may seem paradoxical, and indeed funding for community media generally emanates from not from governments but from national and international NGOs (or in Latin America, from the progressive Catholic Church),[20] in the case of TVS the Cuban government participated as a significant ally. This came about in great part through the commitment of TVS to build on the state agenda. Independent initiatives are uniquely positioned to forge alliances and leverage resources; the synergy of local-local and local-global partnerships yields greater results than if each entity worked independently. Had the Cuban state apparatus insisted upon maintaining exclusive rights over media, TVS would never have come into being. The residents of the Sierra Maestra would never have benefited from this capacity-building initiative, Cubans across the island would not have enjoyed and gained from the alternative highland programming, international viewers would not have glimpsed this facet of life and culture in Cuba, and UNESCO would not have been able to showcase Cuba's TVS as an example of effective community media. Important Revolutionary aims and international development objectives would have gone unmet.

TVS has increased community participation. It has given voice to more highlanders. And it has provided an alternative to extant programming. In short, it has democratized access to the media and expanded depictions of the national imaginary. TVS has engaged more individuals in charting their future. This decentralized grassroots initiative has provided highland residents with the space in which to represent. And in that space, they have developed an agenda not incompatible with that proffered by the state. Some skeptics of Cuba's political structure might argue that state involvement impedes local residents from creating truly autonomous programming. Others might speculate that with limited access to the media in general, these people have no models other than those of the state from which to work. Both of these suppositions are limited, it seems to me, in that they deny agency to these social actors.

Another and perhaps the most significant lesson that TVS teaches is that community media programming can participate in affirming and creating local identity and culture while resisting the cultural homogenization produced through the globalization process. TVS came into being during a unique moment when Cuba's first NGOS were being piloted and the nation's unstable economy necessitated external capital. That TVS was created and thrived during Cuba's Special Period suggests that the island's economy and Cubans' identity has been and can continue to be strengthened through transnational partnerships. Through this initiative, we glimpse a Cuba connected to larger media networks and global capital without being consumed by them. We see here that Cuba has engaged with these partners without letting go of its own agenda. It has met them on its own terms. International solidarity is increasingly important for economic, political, and cultural stability. Cooperation increases synergy, steps up momentum, and leverages resources. In an era of increasing connectedness, the question is not one of whether to engage but rather how to preserve a sense of identity, remaining anchored to concepts of home and community, while navigating globalized waters.

TVS has managed to do just this. This community media initiative proves that an alternative communication outlet can indeed access global flows without jeopardizing local concerns, traditions, and expressions. While the globalization of media tends to decouple the national imaginary from fixed geographical territories, it need not erase and homogenize cultural identity. In fact, as we see in this case, transnationalism actually supports cultural diversity and strengthens identities.

The trajectory of TVS, particularly its adaptation to and relevance for the changing context in which it thrives, has earned it a reputation as one of the most accomplished community media initiatives in the world. The skills and commitment of the organization's founding director have been widely recognized. Not surprisingly, Daniel Diez Castrillo was tapped to contribute his expertise more widely. After a decade in the Sierra Maestra, he returned to Havana to help train filmmakers there. He began teaching documentary filmmaking at the ISA, mentoring and advising students at the EICTV, and working with the ICAIC to develop new production modes and better integrate young audiovisual artists. Many of the practices and strategies employed by TVS will be adopted by Cuba's new generation of filmmakers. Before turning to the Street Filmmaking phenomenon, however, let us consider the evolution of one other organization. The government-funded ICAIC Animation Studio, which underwent extensive transformation during the tumultuous 1990s, will provide a useful counterpoint to TVS as we continue mapping recent changes in island filmmaking.

I don't work for a market. I don't work to
sell a product. The purpose of the work I
do is to give pleasure to Cuban children.
—Armando Alba

3

Balancing Tradition and Innovation

THE NATIONAL ANIMATION STUDIO

NEGOTIATES THE GLOBAL MARKETPLACE

Memories of my first visit to the ICAIC's Animation
Studio are alternately bright and dim. It was in 1994,
during the depths of the Special Period, when I first
entered this modest facility. As I walked through it,
the lights flickered on and off. Each time the darkness engulfed us, we
stopped and waited. And each time the rooms brightened, the artists
picked up their ink pens and paintbrushes and we resumed the tour. I
recall being impressed by the beauty of the works in progress, the passion
and perseverance of the animators despite difficult conditions, and the
attentiveness of my hosts, producers Paco Prats and Aramis Acosta. And I
remember being particularly intrigued at seeing an old animation camera and listening to its story. Early one morning in 1959, an elaborate camera was loaded into the cargo hold of a U.S. plane bound for Havana. By

noon, the camera was unloaded, uncrated, and installed. Only a few hours later that same day, the Revolution was declared a victory. This anecdote made clear that film animation in Cuba grew up with the Revolution. It emerged from and contributed to the transformation of a nation.

That afternoon in the ICAIC's Animation Studio more than a decade ago provided me with a glimpse of the traditional animation process as practiced by world-renowned specialists. Even then, I knew I was witnessing a dying art. What I didn't appreciate was just how imminent its demise would be. Cuba's film animation would decline markedly during the 1990s when the vicissitudes of the Special Period would all but paralyze the studio. Production statistics tell the somber story. In 1991, ten animated films totaling fifty-seven minutes were completed. The following year, nine films totaling fifty-one minutes were completed. Then, in 1993, production levels plunged. That year, only three works were produced, with a total running time of eighteen minutes. So in the course of a single year during this devastating time, animation production had declined by two-thirds. Elsewhere in the world, the mode of making animated films was changing. Newly developed cameras, computer hardware, and software programs were transforming the animation industry. Shortly after my visit to the studio, the island began migrating from hand-drawn to computer-rendered images, as ICAIC artists embraced what had become the dominant production mode in the international sphere. The economic crisis and ensuing shortages forced the Cubans to adapt in order to survive.

This chapter traces the dramatic change in the production and dissemination of Cuban animation. Over the past decade alone, computer-generated images have replaced much of the hand drawing and painting, the ICAIC's Animation Studio has expanded from a suite of rooms in a house to a seven-story building, and the staff has grown to include a host of young artists working alongside their experienced counterparts. Perhaps most significantly, the entity has stepped up its efforts to engage with the international arena—participating in and hosting festivals more frequently, entering new markets, and providing services to clients around the world. Without a doubt, Cuba's animation operation has undergone sweeping changes. Yet, this transformation has not meant a complete rupture with the institution's past. The studio's original mission—contributing to the creation of a uniquely Cuban culture created from within by island artists—remains intact. And its commitment to the Revolution has not wavered. Animators continue to perceive their primary role as serving their compatriots, especially the children of their nation, and resisting U.S. domination by proffering alternatives to Disney cartoons. So while digital technology and international market forces have had a major impact on Cuban animation in recent years, the island's local tradition has not been usurped by the global industry. On the contrary, Cuba's animation operation is thriving.

Of particular interest to this discussion is how this art form has been employed—in different ways at multiple junctures—to further the goals of the Revolution. It will become apparent that the success of animation on the island has to do, in great part, with its ability to adapt to an ever-changing context. And crucial for this adaptation has been the careful balancing of political aims with aesthetic concerns, local needs with global market forces, and tradition with innovation. The talent and tenacity of studio personnel have been put to the test as new challenges have emerged repeatedly over the past half-century. Time and time again, animation artists, directors, and producers have revised their modes, redirected their efforts, and retooled their skills in order to remain effective. The studio has demonstrated a knack for reinventing itself—but never at the cost of abandoning its mission or denying its history.

To set the stage for examining recent developments, I begin with a review of the island's Revolutionary animation tradition. And to capture the nuances of the studio's history, I rely extensively on the impressions and recollections of animation professionals. While some of these individuals have worked in the field for more than forty years, others are just starting their careers; while most reflect on Cuban animation from Havana, one does so from Miami; and while the majority share experiences about working in the ICAIC's studio, a few reflect on making films from their homes. When I spoke with animation artists in Havana on several occasions, they expressed surprise and pleasure at the fact that their work would be featured in this book. "We usually get left out," remarked longtime director Mario Rivas.[1] The inclusion of these voices underscores a basic tenet of this book: Filmmaking in Cuba engages culture workers in a variety of ways. Films do not emerge from monolithic institutions but, rather, from the talent and commitment of people working together—inside and outside state structures—to achieve their goals. By acknowledging the complex and contradictory nature of these individual experiences, we can begin to understand the dawning of a new audiovisual era. Before tracking recent developments, however, we will flash back to the studio's founding moment.

Laying the Foundation: The First Decade of an Animation Industry

The early history of animation in Cuba consists of a series of false starts—efforts by a handful of individuals in different island locales at various times during the 1930s, 1940s, and 1950s.[2] Animation made a comeback on the island in the 1950s with the advent of television and the proliferation of advertising agencies. Short works of twenty to sixty seconds appeared as television commercials. Among the most important agencies producing these animated shorts was Publicitaria Siboney. Two artists from this organization—Jesús de Armas and Eduardo Muñoz Bachs—would form the nucleus of the national film institute's animation department.

The Animation Studio was established in Cuba in 1959, immediately after the triumph of the Revolution.[3] Joining de Armas and Muñoz Bachs were Nicanor González, Manuel Lamar (Lillo), Hernán Henríquez, Tulio Raggi, and José Reyes. These animation artists, like culture workers in many sectors at this time, placed themselves at the service of the Revolution. Taking as their task the shaping of a new society through their work, they organized into three groups with de Armas, Raggi, and González each directing one of them. Together they sought to develop a uniquely Cuban form of animation. With limited professional training and virtually no precedents to guide them, they began to experiment and drew extensively on the dramatic changes taking place in their midst. Their first two films tackled topics relevant to the nation-in-transition: *El maná* (*Manna*, 1960) addresses the need for land reform in the countryside, and *La prensa seria* (*The Serious Press*, 1960) denounces the corruption in the country's private press.

During these early years, film animation artists learned on the job. Both Jesús de Armas and Eduardo Muñoz Bachs hailed from the arena of visual arts. Although talented at drawing, they had to develop their animation skills through trial and error. Lamar worked in advertising, and Reyes helped run his family's printing business. Henríquez was self-taught, having sent away for a kit, "How to Learn Animation," from a magazine advertisement. Although the mail-order method taught him little or nothing, he credits it with inspiring his career choice. Animation artists in Cuba did not have the luxury of drawing from a strong animation tradition or of benefiting from the guidance of more seasoned practitioners. Instead, they had to learn their craft and refine their skills along the way. They managed to do so through lots of trial and error—and an occasional bit of serendipity. Henríquez recalls a "lucky mistake" from which he learned a valuable lesson. During the filming of *La prensa seria*, the camera operator was panning a sequence of a character walking. Instead of moving the background in the direction opposite to that in which the character was walking, so as to simulate forward movement, he had them both going in the same direction. As a result, the sensation produced was of the character walking backward, "like when Michael Jackson moonwalks." Henríquez remembers his dismay upon seeing this: "The day the print arrived from Mexico, we were in ICAIC's theater along with Alfredo Guevara [then president of the institute]. When I saw the scene that was incorrectly shot, I was shocked. Imagine that in our first test there was an error. Nervously, I looked at Alfredo and with great surprise he turned to us and said: 'How clever! This man is going against the flow.'" From that time onward, Henríquez vowed to "convert all mistakes into effects."[4] These early animated shorts served as a training ground for the emerging animation filmmakers. They also helped pave the way for the development of this form of cultural expression.

Select works from the early 1960s demonstrate themes relevant for adults that address political, historical, cultural, and social issues: *Remember Girón* (de Armas, 1961) combines filmed footage and animated sequences in a satirical reconstruction of the Bay of Pigs invasion; *Los indocubanos* (Modesto García, 1962) traces the indigenous groups that lived in Cuba before the arrival of the Spanish conquistadors; *El cowboy* (de Armas, 1962) employs humor to deconstruct the heroic image of the cowboy in Hollywood westerns; and *Niños* (Henríquez, 1964) reflects on the relations between parents and children. These shorts and others like them were created principally for the edification and enjoyment of adults. A decade would go by before animation artists would revise their mission to meet the needs of Cuba's youth.

Working conditions during this time were exceedingly favorable. The animation department was located in the upscale Cubanacán suburb, a district formerly home to diplomats and wealthy Cuban families as well as the island's most exclusive country club. There the artists worked in an opulent mansion amidst lush gardens. The studio counted on an Oxbury camera, the best available at the time. As soon as the camera was installed, the Cuban government hired a Czech technician to train the animation filmmakers. Hernán Henríquez, who left Cuba for the United States in 1980, recalls his enthusiasm at working in the studio. "We were privileged at Dibujos Animados," he asserts. "We have to recognize that. If you say to a young lad, 'You will have a job for the rest of your life. You will have the best equipment in the world, and the most beautiful building designed exclusively for you,' isn't this the perfect paradise?" The Cubanacán facility became a showcase for international dignitaries and tourists. Visitors expressed their surprise and enthusiasm after touring the studio. Many of them would exclaim, "How is it possible that in a country like Cuba, where a Revolution is happening . . . people are doing animation? Animation is a specialty of developed nations, like Canada!" In the early years of the Revolution, the Animation Studio served as proof that a small island nation in the Caribbean could foster a vibrant culture. Producer Paco Prats refers to these years as "the golden age" of animation in Cuba; in a conversation with film critic Joel del Río Fuentes, he deems this a time of "fantastic designs," critical thinking, satire, and extensive innovation. But as the decade drew to a close, the "gold" had ceased to glitter so brightly.[5]

For one thing, the studio's isolation began to take its toll. The remote location, several miles from the city center, impeded interaction between the animation artists and other ICAIC filmmakers housed in the Vedado headquarters. It also limited recruiting and hiring, since many professionals preferred jobs in the heart of the bustling capital. "The moment came when being in that luxurious fish tank was annoying," recalls Henríquez. So after eight years in Cubanacán, animation personnel appealed to the ICAIC's board of directors for a new location. Their request was granted, and the studio was relocated to the Vedado district, a couple of blocks from ICAIC headquarters. The converted home on Twenty-third Street would house the Animation Studio for the next thirty years. With the move, Henríquez and his colleagues returned to "civilization"; in the heart of Havana, they could "see people, go to the coffee shops," and take full advantage of the lively social and cultural scene.

At the same time, the perspectives of the animation artists had evolved, but not necessarily along the same lines. Prats recalls vigorous debates on the role of the artist and the purpose of culture in a society undergoing transformation. These heated discussions often ended in vehement disagreements. Director Jesús de Armas found himself at odds with the artistic visions of his colleagues and the direction in which the studio was heading. So after having directed some fifteen animated films, de Armas resigned and returned to painting.[6]

The change in locale and leadership coincided with a shifting focus in Cuban animation. By the late 1960s, animated films had become more didactic. More projects grew out of commissions by various state agencies, and more artists relied on documentary filmmaking techniques in their animation. During this time, the first series featuring a local hero debuted. Harry Reade and Harry Tanner created *Pepe cafetómano* (*Pepe the Coffee Maniac*, 1968) on the campaigns to harvest coffee; *Pepe trinchera* (*Pepe in the Trenches*, 1969), a work made for Civil Defense; and *Pepe voluntario* (*Pepe the Volunteer*, 1969), on the virtues of volunteer work. With an emphasis on the message, however, the medium began to suffer. Cuban animation lacked its earlier dynamism. Animation historian Giannalberto Bendazzi attributes this "decline" to two major factors: First, the influence of foreign animation "dampened the original spontaneity of Cuba's animated works," and, second, the "didactic objective" came to be valued over "political, artistic and other aims."[7] At the same time animation was losing its luster, the national spotlight was shining on education and culture. This would have a profound impact on the future of island animation.

Altering the Blueprint: Animation for Children in the 1970s

Significant changes in the Animation Studio were just around the corner. The Primer Congreso de Educación y Cultura (First Congress on Education and Culture) was held in April 1971. During this nationwide event, it was decreed that aesthetics and culture be important aspects of all education. A proclamation devoted to mass media singled out animation as deserving prominence: "The production of animated films within world cinema is scarce and limited even further in terms of [work consistent with] our ideology. This form of expression is ideal for the young spectator, and consequently the production of animated films should be stimulated."[8] Very little film material for children existed at the time in Cuba, and animation was prescribed to remedy the situation. (A similar call would be made nearly three decades later when, during the Battle of Ideas, the Animation Studio would reaffirm its commitment to the Revolution and respond once again to the nation's changing needs.)

ICAIC authorities embraced this charge and, in 1972, altered the course of the institute's animation operation. The industry would develop new themes and direct its production at much younger viewers. In order to fulfill its commitment to this new audience, the ICAIC sought international expertise. Animation specialists came from Eastern Europe, Canada, and elsewhere to provide guidance as the Cubans retooled their operation. International culture workers, inspired by Cuba's vision and tenacity in forging a new society, eagerly shared their expertise. The Canadian animator Grant Munroe was sponsored by his nation's film board to help reorganize ICAIC's animation department. World-acclaimed animation artists visited Cuba and exchanged ideas with their counterparts on the island. Hernán Henríquez recalls meeting another well-known Canadian animation artist, Norman McLaren: "One day in the afternoon, I was sitting at my desk working . . . when suddenly, a tall gentleman dressed in black, with grey hair and a very pink face stood next to me. . . . He told me that he was Norman McLaren and that he came directly from Canada just to visit us. We spent three days with him, and showed him all the films we had made. . . . McLaren sympathized with socialism and wanted to help developing countries produce their own animation." The experience of these outsiders combined with homegrown perspectives to help revive Cuba's animation industry.

Another strategy engaged the studio in establishing a dialogue with the public it was to serve. New modes of communicating with children were developed, primarily through an alliance with the Organización de Pioneros José Martí (José Martí Pioneer Organization).[9] Children in Havana and in the provinces were integrated into the creative process; conferences were held in various sites on the island to determine what young viewers would find meaningful and appealing.[10] Two distinct yet related audiences were identified: Children aged two to seven would be encouraged to develop fantasy through animation that brought plants and animals to life and employed only limited dialogue, and children aged eight to fourteen would be served by works of action and adventure with multidimensional characters and a well-defined plot. Tulio Raggi and Mario Rivas would focus on the younger group, while Juan Padrón would specialize in material for the older children.

These artists generated numerous works on a range of subjects. Tulio Raggi created entertaining educational films including *El cero* (*Zero*, 1977); *El tesoro* (*Treasure*, 1977), on geography; and a Cuban history trilogy, *El negrito cimarrón* (*The Little Black·Runaway Slave*, 1975), *El trapiche* (*The Cane Mill*, 1978), and *El palenque de los esclavos cimarrones* (*The Shelter of the Runaway Slaves*, 1978). Mario Rivas made his debut with *Parque forestal* (*Forest Park*, 1973) and went on to create *Feucha* (*Ugly Little Girl*, 1978) and *La guitarra* (*The Guitar*, 1978). And Juan Padrón brought to the screen his popular cartoon figure, Elpidio Valdés, thus initiating what would become an immensely popular series.

Elpidio had appeared on the pages of the weekly *Pionero* in comic strip form throughout the 1970s and was therefore familiar to Cuban audiences. Colonel Elpidio Valdés is a *mambí*, or soldier of the liberation army. He fights alongside the compatriots in his squadron—María Silvia, Pepe el Corneta, and Marcial—and rides his brave horse Palmiche. The machete-wielding freedom fighter is depicted in several shorts of six to eight minutes. Elpidio's knack for outsmarting his enemies and getting out of tight spots time after time can be appreciated from the titles: *Una aventura de Elpidio Valdés* (*An Adventure of Elpidio Valdés*, 1974); *Elpidio Valdés contra el tren militar* (*Elpidio Valdés against the Military Train*, 1974); *Elpidio Valdés asalta al convoy* (*Elpidio Valdés Assaults a Convoy*, 1976); *Elpidio Valdés contra la policia de Nueva York* (*Elpidio Valdés against the New York Police*, 1976); *Elpidio Valdés encuentra a Palmiche* (*Elpidio Valdés Finds Palmiche*, 1977); *Elpidio Valdés está rodeado* (*Elpidio Valdés Is Surrounded*, 1977); *Elpidio Valdés contra los rayadillos* (*Elpidio Valdés against the Spanish Stripes*, 1978); *Elpidio Valdés fuerza la trocha* (*Elpidio Valdés Forces the Battle Line*, 1978); and *Elpidio Valdés y el fusil* (*Elpidio Valdés and the Rifle*, 1979).

This series narrates the history of Cuba's struggle for independence from Spain.[11] Its creator believes in historical accuracy. "If I'm making [a film] about a past epoch, I'd like it to be true to life," Padrón confided to Xenia Reloba. So while developing the Elpidio series, he visited museums, studied photographs, and read Spanish army manuals and journals from

Elpidio Valdés y el fusil (*Elpidio Valdés and the Rifle*) poster by Eduardo Muñoz Bachs. Courtesy of the ICAIC.

the era. "Subjects for the Elpidio Valdés films would come out of those findings," he recalls. And the filmmaker's research often taught him a thing or two. With the Elpidio films, he found himself teaching children things he himself had learned during his research. Young viewers would get a better sense of their nation's history in this way. In Padrón's estimation, "They would have a good time and learn something in the process."[12]

In addition to proffering history lessons, the Elpidio series also imparts values defined within Cuban society. The films affirm courage, honor, integrity, and devotion to the *patria*. The lyrics of the refrain in the theme song allude to these:

> For Elpidio Valdés, patriot without equal
> There's no Gallego that can scare him.
> In combat, he's energetic and lively,
> Facing every bullet that comes his way.[13]

Elpidio can always be counted on. He's brave and reliable, with a great sense of humor. Fans have their favorite episode. The producer of the Elpidio films, Paco Prats, confesses that while he enjoys the entire series, he adores *Elpidio Valdés contra la policia de Nueva York*. He credits this work, in particular, with sowing the seed from which an Elpidio feature film would grow.[14] *Elpidio Valdés contra el tren militar* also appeals; the voice of troubadour Silvio Rodríguez sets a lyrical tone for the energetic Elpidio to save the day.[15]

Delighting children and adults alike, Elpidio was so successful he "starred" in Cuba's first feature-length animated film titled simply *Elpidio Valdés* (Juan Padrón, 1979). This seventy-minute version presents the now-familiar hero's life and escapades from birth to adulthood. In *Cuban Cinema*, Michael Chanan characterizes *Elpidio Valdés* as a "delightful picture" and a "highly effective demonstration that an animation factory like Disney's is not a prerequisite of producing a cartoon feature." He goes on to note that despite Padrón's reliance on a very small team consisting of three principal animators and a half-dozen assistants, this animation director created in Elpidio "a character of strong popular appeal not only to children in Cuba but wherever the film was seen in Latin America."[16] Statistics further attest to the film's popularity. In 1990, *Elpidio Valdés* was sixth on the list of Cuban films viewed by the largest audiences; 1.9 million Cuban spectators saw the film in the island's theaters.[17] Since that time, innumerable fans have watched it on television and video. Children and adults alike have embraced this popular national figure. Elpidio appears painted on the walls of school playgrounds; parks and day care centers bear his name, and fans can purchase t-shirts, puzzles, and even mouse pads with Elpidio's image. A series of limited-edition prints was commissioned.

Thanks in great part to Elpidio's adventures, film fans around the world became aware of the high-quality animation emanating from Havana. Work produced in the Animation Studio competed in the International Festival of New Latin American Cinema and traveled to festivals in Spain and Portugal, the Soviet Union, and elsewhere. The recognition satisfied Padrón and team and inspired the studio's other artists, directors, and producers. As important as the accolades and prizes, it seems to me, were the valuable lessons learned from this series.

Elpidio brought to the big screen characters coded with Cubanness. The Elpidio films narrated a key period in the island's history through the experiences of a hero communicating in a distinctively Cuban Spanish. When the mustachioed *mambí* looks viewers in the eye and winks knowingly, his comment—"*eso, habría que verlo, compay*"—is unmistakably Cuban. The success of the Elpidio installments demonstrated that a homegrown character could resonate on the island and around the world. Although award-winning animation had been created in Cuba before Elpidio, it was hard to pinpoint *cubanía*, or Cubanness in the studio's production prior to this series. With Elpidio, Padrón introduced Cuban idiosyncrasies and histories into island animation in a highly effective way.

Elpidio also proved the efficacy of a series. A great deal could be gained by varying an existing theme rather than creating completely new ones. For one thing, brief installments could pave the way for a subsequent feature-length film. The familiarity of the characters and popularity of the short films would virtually guarantee packed viewing venues. For another, it was exceedingly efficient to "recycle." The Elpidio story required both an investigation into the historical period and an assessment of children's knowledge and expectations. As this investment had already been made, why not continue to exploit it? Similarly, effort had been expended to identify voice actors, illustrators, painters, editors, and other project participants. Why not continue drawing upon their expertise, given their familiarity with the story line and characters? And, of course, the artwork—backgrounds, figures, and sequences of movements—had been created. Why not recycle some of what already existed rather than beginning from scratch? So while Elpidio delighted audiences, the series also held great appeal for ICAIC artists, directors, and producers. They recognized the potential of this mode to streamline production and elicit positive audience reception. By the time the 1970s came to a close, Cuban animation had hit its stride. The island's children welcomed Elpidio as their own and, along with their parents and other adults, eagerly awaited each new installment. The Animation Studio also considered Elpidio a hero and moved forward on the momentum he generated.

Building on Success: Filminutos, Quinoscopios, and Vampires in the 1980s

In the early 1980s, as artists explored new techniques and refined existing ones, the studio continued to produce notable animation. Juan Padrón introduced still another Elpidio installment, *Elpidio Valdés contra la cañonera* (*Elpidio Valdés against the Cannon Embrasure*, 1980), and completed *Viva Papi* (*Long Live Daddy*, 1982), a film depicting a father teaching his child the importance of work. Mario Rivas took a phrase from José Martí to outline the challenges a boy faces in trying to enlighten other children in *Al venir a la tierra* (*When Coming to the Earth*, 1982). And Tulio Raggi drew on José Martí's New York exile experience to create *El alma trémula y sola* (*The Trembling Lonely Soul*, 1983). Impressed by these animated pieces and the momentum of Cuba's industry at this time, Roberto Cobas Arrate asked whether these successful films mark merely "a moment of splendor" or whether they constitute a "sustainable advance in quality." The answer, he speculated at the time of his writing in 1984, lay in "the future work" of ICAIC's animation department. As if responding to his question, several award-winning films were released that very year, likely just after the critic's essay had gone to press: *El bohío* (*The Hut*, Mario Rivas); *Una leyenda americana* (*An American Legend*, Mario Rivas); and *Yeyín y la ciudad escondida* (*Yeyín and the Hidden City*, Ernesto Padrón).[18]

This decade would engender several new series as well as an award-winning feature-length film. The first new series, Filminutos (Film-

Filminutos poster by Eduardo Muñoz Bachs. Courtesy of the ICAIC.

Minutes), appeared in 1980. These animated shorts are numbered sequentially, with each volume containing four or five minute-long vignettes. Early installments featured vampires, elves, and hangmen. In theory, production at this time was geared toward children, but Juan Padrón designed these humorous sketches for adults. Padrón recalls showing three Filminutos to his colleagues. They were thrilled and subsequently organized a screening for ICAIC board members. The filmmaker describes the experience: "Board members . . . watched with a deadpan and then asked, 'How many of these are you planning to make per year?' We replied, 'Just one'; and they went, 'No way, you have to make twenty of them!'"[19] The concept was given the green light. With that gesture, programming for adults was reintroduced into the studio's agenda. Over the years, as new filmmakers have begun to create their own Filminutos installments, the subject matter has expanded considerably. The short length, flexibility of themes, and participation by a range of directors and artists have yielded a series as prolific as it is popular. By 2007, the Studio had released *Filminuto 67*, and several more were in the works;[20] even after more than twenty-five years, the popularity of the series among viewers *and* among animation artists shows no signs of waning.

In 1980, another series made its debut. Cecilio Avilés created Cecilín, a boy and his sidekick, the parrot Coti. In the first episode, *Cecilín y Coti contra dos pillos* (*Cecilín and Coti against Two Rascals*, 1980), Coti is kidnapped by two would-be robbers. Cecilín rescues his feathered friend and turns the troublemakers over to the police. Three years later, two more installments appeared—*Cecilín ayuda a almiquí* (*Cecilín Helps an Almiquí*, 1983) and *Cecilín y el gordo* (*Cecilín and Fatty*, 1983).

Still another series debuted this decade. In 1985, Juan Padrón introduced Quinoscopios. These animated cartoons are based on the drawings of Joaquín Lavado, the renowned Argentine humorist known as Quino. With a format similar to that of Filminutos, the Quinoscopios series consists of brief volumes that could be created relatively quickly; *Quinoscopio 2* appeared in 1986, and *Quinoscopio 3* and *Quinoscopio 4* followed a year later.

Juan Padrón did not rest on his laurels but, rather, completed a feature-length film. *Vampiros en La Habana* (*Vampires in Havana*, 1985) tells the story of Professor von Dracula, inventor of an anti-sun potion that has the potential to revolutionize vampire life. His nephew, the trumpet-playing

Pepe, is oblivious to the fact that he is a vampire, thanks to the power of the potion. The good-hearted professor prepares to give his "Vampisol" formula away to vampires the world over, thus liberating them from the wealthy elite vampires on whom they depend for a fix of artificial sunlight. But some winged schemers have other ideas. The Vampire Mafia from Chicago and the European Vampire Alliance from Düsseldorf plot to steal the recipe. Their attempts to intercept the formula drive the lively narrative. Pepe's goodwill compels him to share the formula, and he broadcasts it over the radio. A distinctly Cuban atmosphere is created through the depiction of locally coded sites like the Hotel Nacional, Plaza de Armas, and cathedral, as well as by the flavors of rum, piña coladas, and an abundance of sugar. The strains of Arturo Sandoval's trumpet accompany the bright palette of primary colors in *Vampires*.

Nearly two decades after completing the film, Padrón expressed satisfaction with the outcome. Despite initial reservations on the part of some colleagues and critics, it appears that *Vampiros en La Habana* has indeed stood the test of time. In a conversation with Joel del Río Fuentes, Padrón recalled what happened when the "experts" saw the film: "They said it wasn't at all what they had expected from me, that it was very vernacular, confusing and noisy; no press conference was scheduled to announce the film, nor was there a premiere. A review published in a magazine treated it poorly. I was depressed for several days, until it broke box office records (of the time) in a week and people were enthusiastic about it. I've felt like Spielberg when hundreds of students in Valparaiso who loved the film came out to greet me or in Puerto Rico where they knew it by heart."[21] This animation feature has become a classic among vampire buffs and animation fans alike. In Cuba, it has been shown in theaters, on television, and on video at film clubs, and it can be purchased or rented from state-owned as well as independently operated video stores. Elsewhere, *Vampires* can be ordered online from commercial, academic, and cult distributors, including Amazon, Cinema Guild, and Vanguard; it has continued to please crowds and garner prizes.

These films from the late 1970s and 1980s were exceedingly popular. When the *Cine Cubano* journal conducted a survey of the top ten Cuban films in the categories of fiction, documentary, and animation, it came as no surprise that critics chose works from this dynamic period. The poll, conducted to commemorate the ICAIC's thirtieth anniversary in 1989, listed the most outstanding works of animation as follows: the Quino-scopios and Filminutos series, *Vampiros en La Habana*, the Elpidio Valdés series, and *El paso del Yabebirí* (Tulio Raggi, 1987).[22] The future of animation in Cuba had never looked more promising. During the effervescent 1980s, it would have been hard to predict that in only a few years, production would have dwindled dramatically and the studio would be limping along.

Struggling to Get By: Scarcity and Uncertainty in the 1990s

Virtually every sector on the island experienced massive changes following the breakup of the Soviet Union. As already noted, the resource-intensive realm of film suffered dramatically. And of all the film forms, perhaps animation—already considered by many to be less serious or less important than its feature and documentary counterparts—suffered most. Production dwindled in the early 1990s, until it came to a complete halt. In 1995, not a single work was produced for Cuban audiences, not even installments of the Filminutos series. These *chistes*, or jokes, were among the least costly and easiest material to produce due to their short duration, absence of dialogue, and wide range of topics. The form was versatile in that it did not rely on a single director but had been employed successfully by several studio filmmakers. The fact that even these works had ceased to be produced, then, attests to just how dire the situation was.

During this time, the studio kept its doors open by providing animation services to foreign firms. Cuba collaborated with Spain on two films, *Mafalda* (Juan Padrón, 1994) and *Más se perdió en Cuba* (*We Lost So Much in Cuba*, Juan Padrón, 1995). The selling of services constituted a lifeline, something to grab onto. But it did nothing to guarantee the studio's survival. As Associate Producer Armando Alba Noguera recalls, "It was like buying sand to make cement blocks and selling the blocks to buy sand in order to make more cement blocks to sell so as to buy more sand."[23] In sum, providing services did indeed keep the operation afloat in turbulent waters, but this contract work did nothing to buoy up the primary mission of the studio: contributing to Cuban culture by educating and entertaining local viewers. Nor did it afford the artists opportunities for innovation. Moreover, it posed serious logistical challenges. The very nature of traditional animation requires pounds of paper and transparencies. Illustrations for a single project could fill ten cartons that would then have to be shipped overseas. With all the boxes coming and going, some of the drawings were invariably damaged by water or careless handling. Others never reached their destination. And since all the cells shipped from Cuba were originals—each an artwork in its own right—their damage and disappearance constituted a staggering loss.

Hard lessons were learned as the animation producers, like their documentary and feature film counterparts at the ICAIC, stepped into new terrain with these service-provider agreements. Alba recalls that in 1998, Spain offered to give the ICAIC a computer in exchange for animation artwork. The equipment would facilitate the transfer of materials between the countries, for the images could be duplicated and saved on a CD. The drastic reduction in the shipment's weight and the ability to retain the originals appealed for reasons of cost savings, ease, and peace of mind. It seemed that both parties would benefit. The Cubans completed the animation work and submitted it to their client, thereby holding up their end of the bargain. The Spaniards signed for the shipment but never delivered the promised computer. The investment of artist-hours and materials did not yield the desired dividends. It became all too clear to the studio that relying on a revenue stream from beyond the island was risky business. Never before in Cuba's animation history had the future of this film form appeared so precarious. The studio limped along as the millennium came to a close. It seemed unlikely that Cuban animation would see the new century.

Despite this dark panorama, some light glimmered on the horizon. For one thing, the animation team demonstrated remarkable ingenuity. Lacking basic supplies, the artists made do and often invented solutions. When the animation paint ran out and new supplies could not be procured, the artists used latex and enamel intended for houses and cement walls to fill in the line drawings. Their creativity was put to the test time and time again. The producers were demonstrating their ingenuity as well, engaging more fully with film markets beyond Cuba. Paco Prats, Aramis Acosta, and others were developing expertise that would be critical for the future of the country's filmmaking enterprise. By negotiating coproduction agreements, they were gaining familiarity with the transnational mode of making movies that was quickly becoming an industry standard. So despite the challenging conditions on the island, the studio did not give up. "Cubans don't sit around and wait for the problems to work themselves out," muses Prats. "Cubans invent. That's how we've managed to survive all these years."[24]

Another ray of light emanated from the continuity of the experienced animation team. Many sectors lost personnel during this time of accelerated emigration; Antonio Aja Díaz, a specialist in the International Migration Research Center in Havana, reports that between 1990 and 1994, some 70,000 Cubans left the island for the United States, the vast majority as a result of economic hardship. Despite this exodus, nearly all of the seasoned animation artists stayed in Cuba.[25] The talent of Ernesto Padrón, Juan Padrón, Tulio Raggi, Mario Rivas, and others would be fundamental for any recovery; their experience would be invaluable in training the next generation of artists.

Still another light beam emanated from the fact that digital animation technology was slowly making its way into the studio. A small cadre of artists was experimenting with the studio's one computer, a 486 with eight megabytes of memory. Armando Alba created a computer program to check the movement of the drawings. Until this time, it had been necessary to check the flow of the drawings by shooting them in 35 millimeter and processing the black-and-white film. Now a jump or inconsistency could be detected before the outlines were filled in and the rest of the process completed. Replacing the film checks with computer checks saved money and materials. Of equal or greater importance to stretching scarce materials was the artistic benefit. By leapfrogging the laboratory processing, animators could see the results of their work far more quickly. No longer did they have to wait days, weeks, or even months to detect an error and make corrections. The savings of time and money pleased artists and producers alike.

Subsequent steps continued to prepare the way for digital technology. Ernesto Padrón had by this time become familiar with using a computer for some stages of the animation process. He and others created the first computer-assisted animated shorts in 1998 and 1999. These *Historias con hipo* (*Hiccup Stories*), made for the national electricity service, helped inspire confidence in the new mode and demonstrate its potential. So, too, did the reliance on tradition, even when combined with innovation. During the Special Period, numerous animation projects had been designed and prepared for filming—and then shelved. The lack of film stock and irregularity of electrical power had relegated them to storage. Among these were complete sets of artwork for two Elpidio Valdés installments. Alba consulted with Paco Prats, and they agreed that it made sense to test the new technology with *Elpidio Valdés contra el fortín de hierro* (*Elpidio Valdés against the Iron Fort*, Tulio Raggi, 2000) and *Elpidio Valdés se enfrenta a Resoplez* (*Elpidio Valdés Meets General Heavy Breather*, Tulio Raggi, 2000). Alba characterizes these works as somewhat "primitive" but notes their importance in permitting him and his colleagues to hone their skills as they learned "on the fly." The completion of these animated shorts was important symbolically; they represented both continuity and change. Rather than starting from scratch, the studio wisely began with something familiar. While the new products did not look exactly like earlier Elpidio installments, and the process did not develop identically to that of past projects, the content was recognizable. With these two films, then, the studio tiptoed further into the terrain of computer-generated images. Soon, Cuba's animation artists would find firm footing on this new ground.

As the 1990s came to a close, basic computer equipment was in place, and artists were experimenting with its use. The studio began to envision a move toward computer-generated images. For the first time in several years, it appeared that Cuban animation might just survive.

Regaining Momentum: Animation Reaffirms Its Revolutionary Role in the New Century

The year 2000 marked a turning point for the Animation Studio. As the new century dawned, Cuba and the United States were at yet another political impasse. The conflict revolved around six-year-old Elián González. After washing up on the shores of south Florida, his mother and the other rafters lost at sea, the boy was being held by distant relatives in Miami. His island-based father—and the vast majority of those in Cuba and the world over—believed his rightful place was with his natural father on the island rather than with relatives he had just met in Florida. Children had featured prominently throughout the Revolution, and special initiatives had been established to ensure their nourishment, education, and development. The case of Elián served to reaffirm the nation's commitment to its youth. It also widened the rift between the United States and Cuba. This political standoff reverberated in Cuba's cultural sphere; in the midst of the struggle for Elián's return, a nationwide plan began to take shape that would move island animation to center stage.

The Batalla de Ideas (Battle of Ideas), initiated in 2000, was conceived as a strategy for defending the island from external aggression and re-affirming Revolutionary values. The plan was to revitalize those sectors perceived as crucial to sustaining the country's domestic accomplishments and stepping up Cuba's international outreach. By 2005, some 700 construction projects were completed, many of them benefiting the nation's youth. Hospitals were refurbished and neighborhood clinics were built. School buildings were repaired, and the curriculum was enhanced through the installation of new audiovisual and computer equipment. Nearly 200 computer clubs were created for the purpose of teaching basic computing skills. The Revolutionary commitment to Cuban youth was strengthened.[26]

Animation was identified as important for Cuba's young people. The spotlight was shining brightly on this cultural form, which was called upon to counter the hegemonic diffusion of Disney cartoons.[27] The journalist Pedro de la Hoz contended that "what's most important is that with animation and other graphic media ... we have an extraordinary weapon for the formation and transmission of revolutionary, patriotic and human values, and for cultivating the sensitivity, love and intelligence needed to help us conquer the future."[28] At the service of the Revolution from the outset, animation would become even more important as a tool to foster learning and reaffirm revolutionary values, and as an arm in the struggle against external aggression.

The state's renewed commitment to animation pleased film fans and energized animation artists. But some ICAIC filmmakers were displeased with the decision to channel scarce resources into the operation's expansion. Feature and documentary production were also in jeopardy, argued some, and any investment made should bolster this component of the film industry. After all, these directors had already proven themselves by winning hundreds of awards at international festivals, thereby bringing recognition to Cuba. Moreover, how could a new building, high-tech equipment, and an expanded workforce for animation be justified when the rest of the film institute was in such bad shape? The building housing ICAIC headquarters had deteriorated; only one of the two elevators functioned and then only intermittently. The cameras, editing equipment, and sound studio were outdated. Only a few vehicles remained in service, and the scarcity of gasoline and spare parts left them parked most of the time. Workers had to make do without basic office equipment and supplies; toner cartridges, paper, and even pens and pencils were hard to come by. The greatest concern of all had to do not with material conditions but with the workforce. More than a decade had passed since a new generation of filmmakers had been brought into the ICAIC. Cuba's seasoned filmmakers, many of whom joined the institute during the early years of the Revolution, were nearing the end of their careers. And the number of younger directors and technicians being hired and trained was woefully inadequate to sustain Cuba's film tradition.

Momentum was strong, however, and resources were allocated to bolster Cuban animation. The relationship between the ICAIC and the Animation Studio was altered, giving the latter greater autonomy. Luis González Nieto was appointed vice president and, among other responsibilities, tasked with setting the Animation Studio on this new course. Blueprints were drawn up for a new state-of-the-art facility. And the decision was made to experiment with digital technology in order to streamline the animation process and step up production. Armando Alba was dispatched to Barcelona, where he spent a month refining his computer animation skills and acquiring the first six animation computers loaded with the software necessary to get started.

In 2003, the Animation Studio moved to its current location on Twenty-fifth Street adjacent to the Columbus Cemetery. The facility marks a stark contrast to the former suite of rooms in an aging house as well as to the neighboring ICAIC headquarters. Abundant natural light streams in the large windows, setting off the freshly painted walls. Lighting fixtures and controls correspond to the preferences of individual artists. Spacious workstations are equipped with ergonomically designed furnishings and state-of-the-art technology. The building's seventh story, added during the renovation, opens to a terrace where artists and other employees visit outdoors after their noon meal. In the adjacent physiotherapy salon, employees receive massages. Public relations specialist Nilza González guided me through the new facility and noted that plans are in the works for a fitness center on the premises. The studio's physical transformation is readily apparent. Less obvious, however, is the impact of these changes on the producers and animation artists and their creative output.

Assessing Change: Reflections on the Migration to Digital Technology

Such far-reaching changes predictably had an impact on the studio's personnel and productions. The demographics of the workforce have changed considerably. A small staff once comprised of some of the original founders and seasoned veterans—Aramis Acosta, Mario Rivas, Tulio Raggi, Ernesto Padrón, Juan Padrón, and Paco Prats—has grown quickly to include dozens of young people in their thirties, twenties, and even teens. The average age of ICAIC animation artists is thirty-four. At present, the studio employs 180 people, 125 of whom work in the artistic sphere.[29] Whereas animation on the island was once reserved for men, more women are moving into the arena. It is a twenty-something woman, Yemelí Cruz Rivero, for example, who excels at stop-motion animation. Some artists are graduates of arts and design schools—including the ISA, San Alejandro, and the Instituto Superior del Diseño Industrial—but many learn on the job as apprentices.[30] Present-day animators, like their predecessors, work their way up the ranks; a young artist might enter as a second assistant, advance to first assistant, and then eventually direct his or her own project. Workshops are offered on-site, permitting artists to refine their skills in the various areas, including scriptwriting, sound, and direction. "With each project, I learn something new," offered Johanhnn Ramírez, a twenty-five-year-old animation artist with whom I spoke in Havana. "It's one of the things that motivates me and the others."

As in the past, the maestros train the novices in the history of animation; now, however, the young people are coming in with computer aptitude and experience, and the transfer of knowledge moves in both directions. The artists consult with one another, across generations, on virtually all phases of a given project. Whereas present-day animation artists still learn by doing, they enjoy benefits not available to their predecessors. They have mentors who train them and provide ongoing feedback, and they are inheritors of an established animation tradition. This is not to say that the studio is devoid of tension. "The young people see things differently," explained Prats, "just as we saw things differently from our parents and their generation." The producer notes that having so many young people work in animation is a great asset. Although training new artists and facilitating collaboration among colleagues ranging from age eighteen to sixty-something requires time and patience, the investment is definitely worthwhile, for Prats. Young artists agree that having personnel with varying years of experience and diverse approaches is a plus. In the words of Johanhnn Ramírez, "One of the best things this place has is the relation among the workers of all ages. We all share the same goal—animation. We all love our work."

The migration to new technology left some artists lacking necessary skills. Rather than clearing out the computer-illiterate, the studio opted to retain and retrain the artists. Take the example of "the girls," six experienced painters in their fifties responsible for filling in the line drawings with color. None of these women was accustomed to working on a computer, but all received instruction in the new techniques. Retraining these workers made more sense than replacing them. "It's easier to teach someone a new step than it is to train a new person to understand how animation works, explain all the steps, impart all the history," observed Alba. "These experienced painters can spot problems that only a trained eye can see. They lend artistic value. We didn't want to lose their experience."

These and other seasoned artists appear to have adapted to the new mode of production. Ana Cruz has worked in the Animation Studio for nearly forty years. Describing the process of coloring in the cells, she notes that working with pen and ink in the past "was magic." Yet, she insists that this "sensation has not been lost with the computer." Dagmar Lorenzo has also worked in film for a long time, first with Cuba's ICRT and now with ICAIC animation. She agrees that even with new technology, the magic continues. "The computer helps you see results immediately," she notes. "Before we had to film everything and send it to the lab. With this machine, you can do anything from a zoom . . . to camera movements." Lorenzo sums up by remarking, "It's a marvel."[31] Through the years, the Animation Studio—like all branches of the film institute—has invested time in training its employees. The commitment to building human capacity among artists and support staff has undoubtedly helped develop a formidable film industry.

The shift to new technology has predictably yielded changes in the production process. José Eduardo García, a twenty-five-year-old animation artist, stresses that the new technology has not made animation work any easier. What it has done, however, is streamline and speed up the process. Whereas it was once necessary to wait for the laboratory to complete processing in order to check the results, this can now be done at a computer. Filters also provide shortcuts; rather than developing two different color palettes, one for day and one for night, a filter can accomplish the change. Various effects — rain, snow, stars — can now be achieved with relative ease. And the up-to-date technology permits changes. "If you make a mistake, you can turn back," García explained to me. "Before, you'd have to throw out the work and start over." Alba agrees that computer animation can be done more quickly than hand drawing. Yet, he notes a paradox: The new technology creates an immediacy that fosters perfectionism. With the traditional mode, the artists did not participate in the editing phase. Now they do, and they tend to pick out subtle defects that might otherwise go unnoticed. So while their input can yield a superior product, it also adds hours to the process.

The greatest challenge in migrating to computer animation for the studio, according to Alba, has to do with changing the way people think. Even though the technology exists, some directors and artists do not understand how to conceptualize a project in new ways. They do not understand the concept of libraries of movement, stock images that can be used time and time again. They do not appreciate the range of possibilities. Alba cites the example of a senior director who assigns someone to create a fire sequence by hand when there are numerous fire options available, all far superior to what can be developed using paint and ink. In reflecting on the challenges of migrating to computer animation, Juan Padrón agrees that the difference lies not in the technology per se, but in knowing how to utilize it. As he explained to Joel del Río Fuentes:

> The computer is a tool. Imagine the difference between making a sculpture out of rock with a jackhammer rather than with a hammer and chisel. Or writing with an electric typewriter instead of with a goose quill. The problem lies with the people. Early on, because the visual effects (lights, rain, snow, reflections, shadows . . .) were so easy to make and control, the young people wanted to stick all of

this in the film. Sometimes [the films] seemed like catalogs of effects rather than film animation. They got carried away. With time and experience, the quality of the image has continued to improve, and the results are now better.[32]

From the perspective of animation artists and producers, ICAIC's studio appears to have overcome challenges and migrated to computer animation with aplomb. In the Animation Studio, artistic innovation coexists with politically charged production.

In 2000, the operation renewed its commitment to supporting the political agenda of the state. Esther Hirzel Galarza, director of ICAIC's Animation Studio at the time, articulated the goals as follows: "Our mission today is immense: increase the minutes of animation and continue discovering all the possibilities of the new technologies. We learn with practice, because it's the only way to keep our promise to Cuban children and to Fidel. Yes, it's a lot of work, but we're always happy. This is the only way to achieve love and quality. Our flag is happiness."[33] The political fervor evident in her statement, along with the concerted effort to step up production, begs a series of questions. Can artistic innovation coexist with politically charged production? Is a goal of increased production compatible with the aesthetic concerns that have been a hallmark of Cuba's revolutionary animation? The varied content and diverse styles of recent films, coupled with their positive reception at home and abroad, suggest that both questions can be answered in the affirmative, as some examples of recent work will demonstrate. *Para curiosos* (*For the Curious*), directed by Ernesto Padrón, was developed for the purpose of teaching and entertaining Cuba's youth. Based on a series first published in the magazine *Zunzún*, each of the thirty-second didactic pieces answers a question, explaining the intricacies of animals (*About Elephants, Animals with Four Knees and with the Largest Spinal Column in the World* and *About the Fastest Animals*); natural phenomena (*About the Movements of the Planet Earth, Explanation of Stars*, and *Tides*); the body (*About Eyes, the Most Active Muscle of the Human Body* and *The Relation between Balance and the Inner Ear*); and technology (*History of Things: The Computer*). The first ten shorts in the series were completed in 2001, and each of the following years saw the production of an additional ten. Despite their didactic purpose, these shorts are anything but dull. One explains how the fork was invented, but not before the misdirected tines from one utensil catch the hem of a dress, revealing one woman's underwear. Another heralds the advent of the outhouse, depicting a patron in action to demonstrate its usefulness. Children may be the audience targeted to learn from these lessons, but viewers of all ages chuckle at the facts imparted with the studio's signature humor.

In stark contrast to these fun facts is a series denouncing terrorism. Three politically charged shorts cast Uncle Sam as a promoter of terrorism for harboring those who carry out destructive acts. The fifty-two-second *Fuga homicida* (*Homicide Fugue*, Mario Rivas and Daniel Rivas, 2005) portrays Luis Posada Carriles, the man widely alleged to be responsible for blowing up a Cuban airliner over Barbados in 1976; he was imprisoned in both Venezuela and Panama before being pardoned and offered asylum in the United States. Sporting a Nazi swastika on his black beret, the figure of the villain remains stationary, with only the label of the prison bars changing from "Venezuela" to "Panama." All the while Posada Carriles smiles; it's as if he foresaw his future—and the final sequence of this animated clip, when he is depicted as a free man sailing into the Miami harbor. *Los terroristas no tienen cueva* (*The Terrorists Don't Have a Hideout*, Ernesto Padrón and Mario Rivas, 2005), eighty-nine seconds in duration, features George W. Bush as a cowboy decked out in jeans held up by a bullet belt and topped with a bright yellow fringed shirt and red neckerchief. If the message failed to come through in the caricature, it would be delivered in the lyrics of the theme song: "The terrorists have a hideout; the Yankee boss created one for them." This animated piece satirizes the antiterrorist rhetoric of the U.S. president, given his close connections with perpetrators of violence against Cuba. The third work in this series, *La patata ardente: Opera de Bushini* (*Hot Potato: Bushini's Opera*, Ernesto Padrón, 2005), devotes a half-minute to underscoring George W. Bush's propensity to protect terrorists. The artwork is straightforward and the musical score is appealing. These shorts were linked to the Cuba vs. Terrorism website denouncing "the terrorists Posada Carriles, Orlando Bosch and other criminals on the loose in Miami," a site maintained by Cuba's Ministry of Foreign Affairs (Ministerio de Relaciones Exteriores, or MINREX).[34] Although none of the sequences conclude with credits, all were produced in ICAIC's Animation Studio. Armando Alba explained that MINREX contacted the studio with the request for animation that would highlight the

U.S. contradictory approach to terrorism—that of denouncing it on one hand and embracing known terrorists on the other. The studio took on the project despite a very short window of time in which to produce the pieces. A small team was assigned the work and labored around the clock to meet the deadline. The speed with which these films were created is evident in their simplicity: Drawings are basic, figures and backgrounds are recycled, and story lines are straightforward. Yet they achieve their primary goal in communicating Cuba's stance on terrorism to a wide audience.

The ICAIC Animation Studio reached a major milestone in 2003 when the first computer-animated feature-length film premiered. With *Más vampiros en La Habana* (*More Vampires in Havana*, Juan Padrón), the studio returned to a tale that had delighted audiences nearly twenty years earlier. The eighty-six-minute sequel provides a unique opportunity to compare the same characters and similar narratives, albeit created in vastly different ways. In coproduction with Spain's Estudios Iskra, *More Vampires* was made with a much smaller team than its predecessor. A broader range of colors is employed with greater consistency, thus enhancing the images. And the backgrounds exhibit far more complexity. With 35 millimeter, the maximum number of layers is four; by the fifth, the image becomes opaque and details are lost. Optical sound yields a better mediation of voices. While *More Vampires* trumps its predecessor in terms of image and sound quality, most viewers—including ICAIC's animations artists—find it less satisfying overall. The first *Vampires* benefited from a superior script, as well as from the novelty of the characters and their antics. *More Vampires* illustrates that in Cuba, as in film markets around the world, a sequel rarely measures up to the original. It demonstrates, moreover, that digital technology does not guarantee blockbuster results; good ideas and strong scripts create compelling stories.

ICAIC's Animation Studio has made a tremendous recovery. In one decade, it has reaffirmed its commitment to Cuban youth and to its mission of serving the Revolution, garnered new resources, retrained and expanded the workforce, and migrated to computer-generated images. Perhaps most astonishing is that while accomplishing all of this, the studio managed to increase significantly its output. In 2002, 150 minutes of animation footage were completed. In 2003, the level rose to 181 minutes. In 2004, output increased once again to 267 minutes. By 2005, production had reached 330 minutes, more than twice as many minutes as only three years earlier.[35] Production indicators from recent years indicate that Cuba's animation operation is thriving.

Promoting Cuban Animation Abroad: Increased and Expanded Markets

Cuba's Animation Studio announces that it "has gained a new dimension, opening itself to the world." With "modern facilities and equipment" and "other possibilities in the creative and technological spectrum," the organization "ensures success" in creating digital cinema.[36] The website promotes a variety of services, including special effects, coproduction, specialized workshops, graphic design, and publicity campaigns. While the advertisement might imply Cuba's animation operation has shifted its focus from serving local audiences to garnering global capital, this is not the case. Tight finances might have compelled the operation to rely more heavily on revenue from beyond the island, but in fact the state has multiplied its investment. Funding from the national coffers remains essential. Paco Prats asserts, "If the state didn't provide support, we wouldn't exist." Armando Alba concurs, commenting, "I don't work for a market. I don't work to sell a product. The purpose of the work I do is to give pleasure to Cuban children. I'm more interested in giving away my work than selling it." He qualifies his statement by adding, "provided the state can continue to support the Animation Studio." State subvention, then, continues to be critical for the studio's survival and growth. While the entity does indeed generate revenue to support its operations, Cuba's subsidy has ensured that the studio will not "sell out" to the global marketplace.

Cuba has stepped up its role as an animation service provider for international clients. This has not, however, been at the expense of programming for Cuban children. Alba notes that the studio actually turns away business sometimes. It has more offers for work than it can accept if it is also to satisfy local demands. While working on *Más vampiros*, for example, the studio had to reduce the hours it logged for Spain's Neptuno Films. The studio has made a commitment to increase output for Cuban consumption. "We had no production quotas for many years," explains Alba, "but in 2003 we made a promise to Fidel that we would increase our production levels for Cuban children."[37]

Production quotas increase yields, but they can also invite shoddy workmanship and shortcuts. The emphasis on quantity can diminish quality. Thus far, however, it appears that high quality has been maintained. Recent pieces reveal original scripts and careful crafting. *El frijol viajero* (*The Traveling Bean*, Rainer Valdés, 2004) is a three-minute short featuring a unique (and easy-to-draw) protagonist; an adventurous bean escapes from the cooking pot and sets out to explore the city. *Sueño* (*Dream*, Nelson Serrano, 2004) combines black-and-white with color sequences to move a little boy from a crowded, contaminated city into the realm of make-believe using a storybook trope. *El güije enamorado* (*The Love-Struck Monster*, Homero Montoya, 2005) depicts a grunting monster, one recurrent in Cuban folklore, whose affection for a fair maiden smooths his rough edges. *El negrito cimarrón y la seda del marqués* (*The Little Black Runaway Slave and the Marquis's Silk*, Tulio Raggi, 2004) narrates another humorous episode in this popular series featuring a crafty hero.

The aforementioned works and numerous others have circulated widely on and beyond the island—broadcast over television, exhibited in schools, and screened as part of festivals and cultural events. The International Festival of New Latin American Cinema remains an important venue for ICAIC animation. In 2004, animation directors and artists appeared alongside feature and documentary filmmakers on the panel devoted to Cuba's cinema. During the event, they expressed their pleasure at having been included among the directors for the first time in the festival's history. They understand the importance of asserting themselves in the nation's film scene, for only by increasing their visibility will they begin to change the perception of animation as a second-class mode of filmmaking lagging behind feature and documentary. The Muestra Nacional de Nuevos Realizadores (National Exhibit of New Filmmakers), featured in Chapter 7, also constitutes an important showcase on the island. The February 2006 installment included five animation films— two made within ICAIC's Animation Studio, two created under the auspices of the ICRT, and one done independently by a student enrolled at the ISA.[38]

The Animation Studio has channeled more energy into placing its production in international festivals. In 2005, for example, six works competed in the Prix Jeunesse Iberoamericano Festival in Chile. Three of these garnered prizes, including Alexander Rodríguez's *opera prima* titled *Nené Traviesa* (2003); *El árbol de la vida* (*Tree of Life*, Mario Rivas, 2002); and *Para curiosos 7–8* (*For the Curious 7–8*, Ernesto Padrón, 2004). In 2005, a program of Latin American animation at the Havana Film Festival in New York included several works from Cuba. The following year, upon concluding the presentation of a series of Cuban "Street" films I curated for this same event, members of the audience applauded the animated shorts, expressed their enthusiasm for the works, and congregated outside the auditorium afterward to hear more about Cuban animation. The high quality of the studio's output has translated into its increased prominence at Cuban and international festivals and cultural events.

The studio has taken the lead in creating a film event of its own. ICAIC's Animation Studio was instrumental in establishing the Festival Internacional del Audiovisual para la Niñez y la Adolescencia (International Audiovisual Festival for Youth and Adolescence) in Havana, an event designed to "promote networks of exchange and audiovisual production and stimulate thematic, aesthetic and cultural diversity in a globalized world context."[39] Juan Padrón presides over the festival along with Cuban theater director Carlos Alberto Cremata Malberti and U.S. philanthropist Julie Belafonte. For this event, the ICAIC has partnered with various Cuban governmental and nongovernmental agencies as well as international organizations.[40]

The first installment was held in June 2004; the second, in June 2006; and the third, in September 2008. Entries are accepted not only for animation but also for fiction films and documentaries.[41] Running concurrently with the screenings are workshops, exhibits, retrospectives, and special programs organized by the Cinemateca de Cuba and other entities. The event provides yet another space for showcasing Cuban animation and putting its creators in touch with artists and films from diverse national traditions. It also serves local audiences; in June 2006, a special screening arranged for children with disabilities was followed by a street carnival.

Cuban animation has indeed earned accolades. In fact, Cuba has taken its place as the most accomplished producer of animation in Latin America. By 2006, the studio had made seven feature-length animation films: *Elpidio Valdés*, *Elpidio Valdés contra dólar y cañón*, *Vampiros en La Habana*, *Contra el águila y el león*, *Más vampiros en La Habana*, and *Meñique* (Ernesto Padrón). Whereas the total number may appear modest,

Cuba is the only country in all of Latin America to have produced this many full-length animation films. Cuba's animation has garnered more than seventy major awards at international festivals in Canada, Chile, France, Portugal, the former Soviet Union, Spain, and the United States as well as at film events on the island.

The studio has focused on the local context while stepping up engagement with the global sphere. Animation has taken great strides in opening itself up to international artists and audiences. Cuban film fans, filmmakers included, have had increasing access to animation from beyond the island, with these works being screened in the theaters, on television, at video clubs, and in schools. Numerous films from Cuba, Japan, the United States, and other leading animation producers are available though the island's extensive network of video rentals—both authorized and unauthorized. The availability of materials from beyond the island must, however, be accompanied by greater opportunities for the artists to interact with international partners. In citing directions in which they believe the studio should move, the producers are particularly committed to engaging even more with international animation artists and audiences. Alba would like to see more collaboration with Latin American countries, in particular Venezuela and Argentina. Prats underscores the need to step up communication and interaction with the outside. "We have to open ourselves to the world, participate in more festivals." Both Prats and Alba believe it is important for Cuban children *and* animation artists to gain familiarity with animation from diverse traditions. "They should see Mickey Mouse. They should watch Bugs Bunny. They need to ask, 'What do those cartoons have that make me laugh?'" Exposure to other traditions can inspire Cuban animation artists, offering opportunities to draw from diverse images in order to make their own.

Embracing Homemade Efforts: Digital Technology Alters the Animation Landscape

It has become even easier, given present-day technologies, for a range of artists and filmmakers to try their hand at animation. It is not unusual for these entrepreneurial efforts to be promoted through the ICAIC and the ICRT. Some seasoned filmmakers are beginning to experiment with animation. Inserted in *Viva Cuba* (2005), a feature film to be discussed

Image from "We Are All Champions," a publicity spot by Karel Ducases Manzano created for the ICRT. Courtesy of the ICRT.

in Chapter 4, are several animated sequences; this highly popular road movie demonstrates the successful use of animation to augment fiction film techniques. Emerging artists submit their work to contests organized through the ICAIC and the ICRT, and winning filmmakers sometimes earn the use of the state's production facilities. When I toured the ICRT animation operation in March 2008, I was struck by the interconnectedness of Street and state projects. Karel Ducases Manzano, a talented animation artist who also directed the award-winning documentary *Zona de silencio* (*Zone of Silence*, 2007), introduced me to his colleagues and collaborators; virtually all were simultaneously working on projects commissioned by international clients and state agencies as well as on endeavors more personal in nature.

Given the technology of computer-generated images, it is now possible for young artists working outside state institutes to make their films. The past few years have witnessed a dramatic increase in the number of "homemade" works created by self-starters. Among these are *Guitarra 1* (2003) and *Cardinales de la ciudad* (*Cardinal Points of the City*, 2004), both by Felipe Álvarez; *Yo, ustedes, el viaje* (*Me, You, the Trip*, 2004), by Harold

Rensoli; *Serie homenaje* (2004), by Yunior Acosta; and *Jurassik Cube* (2006) and *Hombres verdes* (*Green Men*, 2006), both by Yimit R. González. These artists demonstrate a familiarity with international animation traditions, a mastery of computer-generated images, and the passion to produce animation.

One exceedingly impressive short is *Horizontes* (*Horizons*, 2004), a stop-action work by Yemelí Cruz Rivero and Adanoe Lima Cruz. In the three-minute piece, two protagonists communicate their very different dreams from a rooftop. One figure holds fast to his hammer, going about the business of repairing the building. Another wields a quill, writing poetry and creating birds out of folded pages. No dialogue is necessary to appreciate their divergent approaches to life—and to present-day Cuba, conjured through the unmistakable visual references to Havana's skyline. When the androgynous figure falls or jumps or perhaps even flies off the roof, we hear a visceral moan uttered by the man left behind, and we share his loss. But when the paper/feather flits onto the rooftop, suddenly transforming into a bird soaring against a sky of pastel blue and peach, we feel inspired. To distance ourselves from the familiar is to relinquish something; at the same time, though, moving into an unknown space brings its rewards. *Horizontes* and other recent animated films impress for the newness of their ideas and their technical mastery. Stop-action animation is also being utilized in the ICRT, where Yurina Luis Naranjo creates public-interest shorts. Resources appear to be far more limited here than in the ICAIC studio; during my visit, I noticed that the camera had been retrofitted with a makeshift lens—the housing crafted from cardboard.

Another innovative work of animation is Ernesto Piña's award-winning *eMe-5* (*M-5*, 2004). *M-5* demonstrates the familiarity of these young artists with international cultural traditions. This piece is an interesting take on the popular Japanese animated film *Voltus 5* (Tadao Nagahama, 1983); it features an electromagnetic machine, commanded by five skilled pilots, that resists repeated attacks by evildoers from the distant planet of Boazan. In Piña's version, the sleek machine is transformed into a lumbering *camello*, or camel, one of Cuba's distinctive semitractors pulling large bus-trailers that transport *habaneros*. These beasts, with the characteristic humps from which they take their name, are always crammed. Passengers line the sidewalks along Havana's main routes, waiting to mount

"Family Violence" publicity spot, stop-motion animation by Yurina Luis Naranjo. Courtesy of the ICRT.

the camel and ride to their destination. Piña drew from his firsthand experience in crafting this clever work, for he rides a *camello* back and forth between his remote Havana neighborhood and the city center. By the time he completed his degree at the ISA in 2007, he had already created several award-winning animated films. *Excursión* (2003), *Todo por Carlitos* (*Everything for Carlitos*, 2005), and *Erpiromundo* (2006) appeal for their intertextuality and originality; they "quote" other films and develop innovative story lines. All nod to the Japanese *manga* tradition, apparent in the figures' oversize eyes and diminutive L-shaped noses.[42] Piña's work resonates for Cuban viewers, particularly those of his generation who are well-versed in Japanese anime.

Like many of his peers, this artist relies on a network of friends and relatives to implement his creative vision. In the summer of 2006, I met Ernesto Piña in Havana, and over lunch we discussed his projects and Cuba's animation tradition. Later, I joined him at the ICAIC, where he was gathering several friends and relatives—many of those who had helped with his films—to screen his completed work and discuss another one still in progress. All of the dozen people around the table expressed plea-

Ernesto Piña Rodríguez flanked by two of his creations. Courtesy of the artist.

El Propietario by Ernesto Piña Rodríguez and Wilber Noguel. Courtesy of the artists.

sure at having collaborated with the young artist. Despite the fact that none had earned so much as a peso for innumerable hours of work, the voice actors, writer, musician, and others expressed enthusiasm over helping their friend make each of his films.

The momentum is strong among animation artists and filmmakers, whether they work in national institutes or at home computers. Technological advancements, namely the widespread adoption of computer-generated images and the flexibility it affords, unite these creators in their common endeavor. The ICAIC has been instrumental in fostering collaboration among those creating within and outside the state-sponsored institute. Ernesto Piña, for example, continues to work on projects independently, but he is also directing an animated film for the state studio. The producers in the ICAIC's animation operation understand the creative process. Aware that some artists benefit from guidance and deadlines whereas others require space and autonomy, they willingly accommodate a variety of styles. And they understand that if animation is to thrive on the island, it makes sense to help realize the potential of the artists—regardless of whether they are on the ICAIC payroll or working from a home computer. They concur that the technological mastery and talent of every artist can and should contribute to island animation. As a result of this productive cross-fertilization between the industry and the "independents," ideas are exchanged, expertise is shared, and resources are maximized. This healthy relationship, evident in the animation sphere, would be reproduced—albeit more slowly—in Cuba's film world as a whole. With the development of Street Filmmaking modes of production and dissemination, the state-independent dichotomy would continue to erode.

Reflections on Change—and Continuity

Cuba's animation operation is impressive. Once considered less important than other forms of filmmaking in Cuba, it now enjoys status as ICAIC's poster child. The synergy of animation and the island's other filmmaking enterprises has been key to achieving this result. As we have seen throughout the institute's history, animation artists and other ICAIC filmmakers and producers welcome opportunities to engage with one another. They recognize the value of sharing strategies and refining ideas. And they understand that they and their colleagues—whether making features, documentaries, or animated films—have together built a national cinema worthy of international acclaim. It is also significant that the studio is on firm financial footing, with state support promised and revenue from foreign sources increasing steadily. The most ambitious investment of resources—to renovate the new building and install the necessary hardware and software—has already been made. Equipment will have to be upgraded, but the cost of doing so does not compare with the expenses incurred in purchasing paint, ink, paper, film, and the other materials needed previously. Without a doubt, these two ingredients—the momentum of the national industry and the firm economic footing—have contributed to the survival and growth of Cuban animation.

Yet, this is not an easy time for animation in Cuba, or anywhere for that matter. Prats contends that the worldwide crisis in filmmaking is particularly acute in animation. A few decades ago, impressive animation work was being done by the Czechs, Poles, French, Hungarians, Russians, and others. "It seems we have gone back in time," he laments, noting that with the exception of Disney and Hollywood studios, only the Japanese continue working with the form to any significant degree. He finds their products unsatisfactory, however, deeming them to be "cheap" and "commercial." The real problem for Prats has to do with the complicated world in which we live. "What can you say to the children of today that interests them, that has artistic value?" he wonders. "Children bump up against a challenging reality. They can't be isolated from daily life, the quotidian reality in which their parents struggle to get food on the table, secure adequate housing, and seek decent living conditions." Prats believes that "the challenge for animation filmmakers is that the children's dreams begin to escape. Children in Africa and Iraq can't dream."

Despite these overarching difficulties, Prats considers the studio's future quite promising. He notes that there are lots of young animation artists with the talent and infrastructure to create great works. And at present they have the space in which to exercise their creative visions. "It's up to them," he emphasizes. It's not about their politics—"*no tienen que ser militantes*"—but about their artistic ability. Whereas one's political stance may have influenced professional possibilities and promotions

at other times, now all members of the studio team have the same opportunities regardless of their politics. "This is the reality in this country at
the moment," asserts Prats.

Virtually everyone with whom I spoke in the Animation Studio expressed satisfaction with the department's momentum, a willingness to
meet challenges head-on, and a desire to improve. Animation artists of
all ages are proud of and invested in their nation's animation tradition. It
is with pride that José Eduardo García enumerates the qualities that distinguish Cuban animation: the spark, the humor, the style of movement,
the colors, and the elaborate backgrounds. It is with pleasure that Paco
Prats shared his experiences from more than four decades in the Studio;
as he was preparing to celebrate his sixty-second birthday in January
2006, Prats had just finished producing his 531st animated film. This does
not count the 31 documentary and fiction films he helped bring to the
screen, works directed by such acclaimed filmmakers as Enrique Colina,
Rigoberto López, Oscar Valdés, and Mayra Vilasís. Nor does it include the
works he produced in London, working at the BBC from 1987 to 1989. I
expressed amazement at the statistic and asked whether he knew of
any other producer—not only in Cuba but anywhere in the world—with
that kind of record. With his usual modesty, the prolific producer speculated that there must be one out there. Rather than play up his accomplishments, he opted to reflect on his good fortune. "I feel privileged," he
stated. "I'm working in something that I've always loved. And at the same
time I'm doing something for my country, contributing to its culture."[43]
In an industry characterized by rapid transformation the world over, it is
nothing short of remarkable that Cuba has thus far managed to balance
change and continuity. The commitment of those who have dedicated
their life to this art form, and to fomenting their country's culture, has
clearly produced results.

Animation in Revolutionary Cuba has adapted in response to the nation's evolving needs. The artists have demonstrated a willingness to learn
as they go, testing new modes and methods and—recalling the attitude
of Hernán Henríquez—converting mistakes into effects or, at the very
least, into lessons for the future. Perhaps most significantly, they have
embraced new technology, employing it to enter the global marketplace
so as to sustain their local industry. This move into new terrain was anything but safe; occurring as it did during a period of extreme scarcity and

widespread uncertainty on the island, it could have meant the demise of Cuban animation. But it did not. On the contrary, it signaled a new beginning. The studio forged relationships beyond the island and mobilized them to further consolidate its mission. Cuba's cultural agenda benefited from these local-global partnerships, then, and from the foray into unfamiliar technological terrain. In a few years time, this modus operandi would inform a new generation of Street Filmmakers who would emulate the studio's example—exhibiting artistic adaptation, technological innovation, and a reliance on partnerships at home and around the world. The formula for the success of this state culture organization would be replicated by the island's next generation of filmmakers.

A recent experience in Cuba's Animation Studio inspired confidence that the animation workers—artists, producers, and others—will see to it that the equilibrium between home and the world and between tradition and innovation is maintained. As I was leaving the studio during my January 2006 visit, I asked Armando Alba about the antiquated animation equipment. What had become of that old camera I had seen and heard about more than a decade ago? Had it been discarded or lost in the shuffle, rendering traditional animation extinct in Cuba? The young associate producer gathered up several portfolios from the shelves behind his desk. He wheeled around in his chair to show me page after page of exquisite drawings, material sufficient for several animated films. As he demonstrated how the figure of a gladiator could be manipulated, repositioning its arms and legs, he mused, "I'm dying to set up the 35-millimeter camera and to get a roll of film from someone." It is clear that in the Animation Studio, change and continuity coexist. New modes and technologies have been adopted without discarding the tried-and-true ones. Subsequent chapters will reveal that Street Filmmakers benefited from this lesson; they would embrace the new without erasing the old and draw upon their local cultural traditions so as to move in new directions.

CLOSE-UP

I believe that a revolutionary is
someone who re-evolves.

—Juan Carlos Cremata Malberti

Opening New Roads

JUAN CARLOS CREMATA MALBERTI

REDEFINES REVOLUTIONARY FILMMAKING

A made-in-Cuba road movie competed in the 2005 Cannes
International Film Festival. And it met with remarkable success. *Viva Cuba* came away with the Grand Prix Ecrans Juniors,
marking the first time a Cuban film had obtained an award at
this prestigious event.[1] Upon collecting the coveted prize, director Juan
Carlos Cremata received a phone call from Cuba. It was the president's
office at the ICAIC congratulating him and wanting to discuss plans for
distributing the film on the island. Such a gesture may seem pro forma.
But it actually constituted a bold move, given the institute's earlier rejection of Cremata Malberti's proposal. The ICAIC had opted not to produce
Candela, an elaborate musical the filmmaker envisioned bringing to the
screen. Moreover, at the 2004 installment of the International Festival
of New Latin American Cinema in Havana, Cremata Malberti had been

notably absent from an industry-organized panel featuring Cuban directors with films in progress. When a member of the audience asked why this director had not participated, even though he was working on *Viva Cuba* at the time, the ICAIC spokesperson replied, "I don't know what Cremata's up to. What I do know is that he's not making a film with us." It appeared that only those working within and relying on the ICAIC could be considered "Cuban" filmmakers at that time. That may have been the case at one point, but *Viva Cuba* demonstrates that times have changed.

Juan Carlos Cremata Malberti was one of the first cineastes to cross the line and make films inside and outside the state-supported film institute. By constructing his identity as an auteur, Cremata Malberti effectively positioned himself as both a "Cuban" filmmaker working to enhance the island's national culture and a transnational auteur engaged with global cinema practices. In deftly managing his dual identity, this forty-something director set a precedent that would help redefine film production in Cuba and insert a new brand of Cuban films into the international marketplace.

The training Cremata Malberti received was a principal factor shaping his trajectory. In 1987, he was selected to enroll in the newly founded EICTV (discussed in Chapter 1). As one of fifty students from nearly twenty countries—only six Cubans in all—he had the unique opportunity to learn to make films from a cadre of international professionals and to work alongside peers from countries as diverse as Mozambique, Guineau, Brazil, and Puerto Rico. The aspiring filmmaker thrived at the school and earned his degree in 1990. This experience was transformative, exposing Cremata Malberti to a century's worth of films and traditions from around the world; empowering him to experiment with the medium, tackle new technologies, and learn "on the fly"; and affording him access to an extensive network of international film professionals and agencies. At the EICTV Cremata Malberti became adept at negotiating transnational markets, multinational finances, and global communications networks. His conception of audiovisual praxis as part and parcel of the multidirectional flows of culture and capital has, without a doubt, positioned him in the forefront of Cuba's film world today.

Juan Carlos Cremata Malberti is held up as a model for other self-starting filmmakers. If a door on the island is closed to him, this director does not stand knocking. Instead, he pounds the pavement, circulating his ideas and mobilizing his contacts in an effort to garner support from elsewhere. Cremata Malberti's vision is innovative, his list of awards is lengthy, and his Rolodex is expansive. He knows what he wants and has figured out how to get it. A border-crosser, he comfortably straddles art forms, film traditions, ideologies, and geopolitical territories. Whereas some shy away from these crossroads—contested zones that provoke clashes and produce collisions—here Cremata Malberti feels most at home. The savoir faire and entrepreneurial approach of this cineaste have inspired many of his contemporaries as well as filmmakers of the next generation.

This chapter tracks Juan Carlos Cremata Malberti over nearly twenty years to illustrate the evolution of one of the most renowned Cuban auteurs of his generation. His success emanates from his unique authorial identity, engendered by his eccentric behavior and compounded by the press, by the markers of "Cubanness" he fashions to please audiences at home and abroad, and by the low-budget digital mode that enhances his appeal to foreign producers. It is not surprising, then, that this cineaste serves as a cultural and commercial negotiator between Cuba and the international film arena.

Pounding the Pavement: *Viva Cuba* Marks a Series of Firsts

Cuba's film and video activity has changed significantly in recent years. As already mentioned, the collapse of the Soviet Union and the tightening of the U.S. blockade propelled the island into an economic free fall. Whereas previous generations of graduates had been virtually guaranteed employment in Cuba's state structure, this ceased to be the case during the Special Period, when professional positions in the cultural realm were exceedingly limited. Aspiring filmmakers at the time found themselves not under one of the many governmental roofs but, rather, walking the streets in search of opportunities.

At the same time, during the late 1980s and early 1990s, a century-long cinema tradition was coming to a close. A new audiovisual era was dawning the world over. This technological revolution—particularly the introduction of hand-held cameras, video, personal computers, and the Internet—meant that films could be made and circulated in vastly different ways. No longer was the infrastructure of an industry necessary.

Instead, one or two audiovisual artists with access to a video camera and a PC could create and reproduce copies of a film.

The landscape for filmmakers in Cuba—as for media-makers around the world—has changed dramatically in recent years. As we have seen in previous chapters, new technologies are permitting greater access to the medium, new partnerships among individuals and organizations are fostering coproduction and other transnational audiovisual activities, and increasing connectedness is reshaping national culture. Filmmakers in Cuba are taking advantage of this unique panorama to experiment and innovate. More and more emerging artists pick up cameras and head out to film. Juan Carlos Cremata Malberti is one of these Street Filmmakers who is revolutionizing the nation's cinema.

Cremata Malberti never set out to make a film outside Cuba's industry. Nor, for that matter, had he initially envisioned a road movie. It was actually a full-blown musical he had in mind, with elaborate costumes, extensive sets, and hundreds of participants. Cremata Malberti anticipated that the large scale of this production, titled *Candela*, would make securing industry financing difficult. And he was right. The ICAIC reviewed his proposal and turned it down. During tight economic times, the institute deemed such a project far too costly. Besides, seasoned filmmakers like Manolo Pérez and Jorge Luis Sánchez had been waiting far longer than Cremata Malberti for their turn to make a film. The entrenched system designed to ensure equality—allocating funds on a rotation basis so as to give everyone a turn—worked fairly effectively during the era of Soviet subsidies. But during tough economic times, the waiting period between films grew dramatically, sometimes to more than a decade. Directors had trouble sustaining their enthusiasm and creative impulse, and this showed in their artistic output. Many of the films, produced from stale scripts, were bland at best.[2]

The industry's unwillingness to support *Candela* did not, however, deter the entrepreneurial Cremata Malberti. Rather than wait for the green light from the ICAIC, he began seeking support through other channels. "I'm intuitive by nature," he notes. "I follow my nose. . . . Even if I come upon some dead ends, I keep going. I always say that for every door that closes, two more open." Under the auspices of the artistic production group he cofounded with Inti Herrera, Cremata Malberti set out to develop a project that could be tackled without the institute. Their group

is named El Ingenio, which, in Cuba, denotes both a sugar mill and ingenuity. Aware of the need to have some state institution backing him—it's
particularly useful, as one Street Filmmaker has noted, if you want to put
up a pseudo stoplight on a major street and reroute traffic during rush
hour—he identified other partners on the island. The TVC Casa Productora, a division within the ICRT, signed on. This would be their first feature
film; previously, they had produced only *telenovelas* and other programs
for domestic consumption. And La Colmenita, the acclaimed children's
theater troupe, agreed to participate. With these two respected organizations on board, Cremata Malberti had little trouble attracting other
island-based partners including the EICTV, the Fundación del Nuevo Cine
Latinoamericano (Foundation of New Latin American Cinema, or FNCL),
Martin Luther King Jr. Center, Audiovisual Universe of Latin American
Children (a UNESCO project), and several state entities promoting tourism (Gran Caribe, Palmares, Los Portales, and Transtur, among others).
The director also secured collaboration from beyond the island. France's
Quad Productions provided financing, the camera, and postproduction
facilities; DDC Films LLC, in the United States, contributed editing hardware and software; and Costa Rica–based Cinergia (Fondo de Fomento
al Audiovisual de Centroamérica y Cuba) funded part of the computer
animation and postproduction work.[3] *Viva Cuba* (2005), produced outside
Cuba's national film institute, marks a rupture in the island's revolutionary cinema tradition; until this time, the ICAIC had produced nearly every
feature made on the island by Cuban directors.

In making this film dedicated to all the children in Cuba and also to his
parents, Juan Carlos Cremata Malberti drew inspiration and support from
his own family, a cadre of talented artists immersed throughout Cuba's
cultural sphere. This project was a family affair. His mother, Iraida Malberti Cabrera, is known for her success in working with child actors and
artists and also codirected this film. Other relatives who participated are
Guillermo Ramírez Malberti (director of art design), Alejandro Pérez (photographer), Manolito Rodríguez (co-scriptwriter), and Amaury Ramírez
Malberti (music). The director's grandmother, Sara Cabrera, appears as
Malú's grandmother. And all the young actors and actresses hail from
La Colmenita (The Little Beehive), a theater troupe under the direction of
his brother, Carlos Alberto "Tin" Cremata Malberti. Street Filmmaking is
indeed a family enterprise. As we will see, virtually all audiovisual artists

undertaking projects outside the industry rely on the goodwill and collaboration of family members and friends.

Viva Cuba is a road movie in which young protagonists Jorgito (Jorge Miló) and Malú (Malú Tarrau) escape from their homes in Havana and head toward the island's easternmost point. Behind, they leave their parents: Malú's frustrated mother (Larisa Vega), whose plans to emigrate with her daughter spark the children's desire to flee, and Jorgito's bickering father (Albertico Pujol) and mother (Luisa María Jiménez), who struggle against the pressures of work and daily life. What ensues is a series of adventures—sometimes amusing, sometimes poignant—that permit a glimpse into life in present-day Cuba. When the children reach their destination, they stand facing the open sea.[4] The horizon is as expansive as their futures are uncertain, but their final embrace suggests that their friendship will endure.

In keeping with the road movie genre, the principal protagonists in *Viva Cuba* mature during their travels. Their journey across the island—by train, bus, car, oxcart, and motorcycle, and on foot—parallels their transition from childhood to adolescence. As they move eastward, Malú and Jorgito struggle to understand whether God exists, why stars shine, and what happens after death. The two rely on each other, and their friendship deepens: When the girl tires, the boy lugs her backpack; when the boy shivers from a fever, the girl hugs him tightly. At one point, weary and frustrated, they begin to bicker. After blurting out that they no longer wish to be friends, they refuse to talk to each other and go along in silence. Soon, however, they are reminded by a Che-like figure that "*sin amigos, no se va a ningún lado*" ("without friends, you don't get very far"). Indeed, it is precisely because of their friendship that Jorgito and Malú manage to overcome obstacles and reach their destination.

They are also accompanied on their journey by Elegguá, a deity in the Yoruba-based tradition of Santería. In the syncretic faith developed by the descendants of enslaved West Africans in the Americas and adhered to widely in Cuba, Elegguá is an orisha, one of the most respected deities. Serving as the god of children and of roads—crossroads in particular—he protects travelers. From the very first mention of Elegguá, in the film's opening sequence, it becomes clear to viewers familiar with the Santería tradition that this deity will play a significant role in this on-screen journey—across the island and from childhood into adolescence.

Cremata Malberti explores the tensions that prevail in present-day Cuba—between rootedness and mobility, past and future, national and transnational. The road movie genre proffers encounters with the unfamiliar, so that the protagonists in *Viva Cuba*—and viewers—grapple with the plurality of identities. This work provides a frame for encountering the ongoing process of imagining the national community in twenty-first-century Cuba. At the same time, it attests to the careful interplay between local iconographies and practices—markers of a particular nation—and the transnational production and circulation of films.

Although Cremata Malberti sought to create a work meaningful for children, he insists that *Viva Cuba* is relevant for viewers of all ages. The film's affirmation of friendship and human solidarity resonates widely. *Viva Cuba* is accessible to spectators not only across generations but across national boundaries as well. The director achieved this, in part, by highlighting human emotions: Malú's intense sadness when her beloved grandmother dies, Jorgito's deep concern upon learning that his best friend might be taken away forever, the mothers' total desperation when the young boy and girl disappear, the children's unfettered exuberance as they romp in the waves, and their utter serenity as they fall asleep under the stars. Audiences in Cuba and the world over can relate to the sentiments in this coming-of-age story. *Variety* reviewer Robert Koehler picked up on the director's self-conscious efforts to code the film for local and international viewing publics, but he predicted—incorrectly—that it would fall short for many non-Cuban audiences. He considers *Viva Cuba* to be "a slight slice of childhood life that feels calculated as a work to make Cuban cinema accessible to the fest circuit. Designed to appeal to families . . . played too broadly for sophisticated auds, but should do lusty local biz."[5]

Cremata Malberti and his contemporaries acknowledge the need to generate widespread appeal. Particularly in small countries with limited local markets, it is essential to target the film for a global audience. It is not easy to create works that resemble the international competition while retaining markers of difference. Yet, Juan Carlos Cremata Malberti manages to do so with *Viva Cuba*. This road movie contains explicit references to the national setting while relying on a formula and aesthetics that have become recognizably homogenized. Cremata Malberti understands that films "mean" differently in different contexts, and he is keenly aware of the need to code films with local *and* more universal references to reach the broadest market. National iconography abounds in *Viva Cuba*: patriotic symbols such as the flag and the national anthem, and images of heroes including Che Guevara, Camilo Cienfuegos, and José Martí; native fauna including the *zunzún* and the *tocororo*; and popular music like the *danzón* and the *guanche*. In reflecting on his self-conscious employment of autochthonous elements, the Cuban filmmaker states, "I'm interested in transmitting the singularities of this unique country. . . . It wouldn't be very savvy for me to make a film similar to those made in the rest of the world. What's interesting is that there be different kinds of films. And Cuba is a different country. That's why I insist on and try to offer *cubanía* [a sense of Cubanness] above all."[6] The distinctive "Cuban" elements provide the backdrop for the more universal experiences of Malú and Jorgito; paramount are the children's struggles with intolerance, separation, death, family strife, and other predicaments faced by young people the world over.

Notably absent from the film's dialogue are the words "revolution," "Fidel," "United States," and "Miami." The director acknowledges his self-conscious avoidance of these terms and the polemics they invoke, saying, "I'm not interested in talking about the Revolution. I'm an artist and I'm interested in the effect of these processes on people rather than in the processes per se." Besides, he explains, "for a French or German child, the Cuban Revolution doesn't mean anything." So while evidence of the Cuban Revolutionary context is evident throughout the film, at no point does it upstage or interfere with the more universal tale of human experience. The film can be viewed both as a travelogue that explores existential concerns and plays with the conventions of the road movie genre and as a serious critical examination of Cuba's current transformation.

The road movie provides the ideal framework for Cremata Malberti's exploration of the human desire to place one's self, in general, and, more specifically, the struggle for rootedness facing Cubans today. The two young protagonists set out on their journey and, in doing so, step away from their families and friends. This dislocation projects them into an unfamiliar space proffering a new perspective and permitting fresh insights. In his study of the road movie genre, Timothy Corrigan associates this trope of separation with progress toward a change in perception: "The familiar is left behind or transformed through the protagonist's movement through space and time, and the confrontations and obstacles that he encounters generally lead . . . to a wiser individual and often a more stable spiritual or social state." Within the frame of the road movie, the past is fleeting, while the future has yet to be mapped. Boundaries and borders recede and, along with them, "the sanctions, securities, and structures of a family tradition."[7] In *Viva Cuba*, the protagonists' physical journey invites a reflection on the concept of Cuban identity. In this era characterized by movement and migration, traditional notions of *cubanía* have shifted and, along with them, notions of the imagined revolutionary community. The nation proffered by *Viva Cuba* is not unlike that represented in Cuban films of the 1990s; Desiree Díaz observes the trope of the journey revealing a nation marked by "isolation, insularity and ambivalence" rather than by "national plenitude and self-sufficiency."[8] Cubanness, at this juncture, has less to do with one's presence on the island or ideological position than with one's relationships. What now defines the films' protagonists — and Cubans by extension — is their emotional connectedness.

In the *Viva Cuba* narrative, locating oneself has nothing to do with choosing sides — electing to be for or against, here or there. Instead, it entails establishing relationships. In a carefully filmed and artfully edited sequence, Malú and Jorgito kneel against an expansive sky, sharing the frame with a single solitary tree. Cut to a close-up of their hands burying the tin box holding their pledge of friendship, and then to a shot depicting the two children and the container from above. The Cuban soil in which the nearby tree grows is not what nurtures them; rather, they are sustained by their connection to each other, rooted by their mutual devotion and lifelong solidarity. It is this friendship that generates Malú's desire to stay in Cuba; conversely, her mother's relationship with a man (referred to only as a "foreigner") is the force compelling her to leave. Rather than condoning or condemning the characters' choice of place, the filmmaker explores their desires to locate themselves.

This quest for community resonates for viewers everywhere in this age of movement and transition. But it is particularly poignant on this Caribbean island characterized by centuries of migration and *mestizaje* where virtually everyone is connected to a family member or friend or neighbor or colleague living elsewhere. The director attributes his interest in the theme of emigration to the fact that he lived in various countries outside Cuba for eight years. During this time, he felt the "necessity" of expressing himself "as a Cuban." This experience revealed his desire to make films in Cuba. Cremata Malberti reflects on this outcome, saying, "Perhaps this is why my films, up until now, deal with being here or there, with staying or leaving."

This film attests to the fact that Cubans, like people the world over, are shaped by diverse experiences. Cuba is not populated by a monolithic mass but, rather, by individuals who view their homeland and the world in complex and nuanced ways. Island identity is multifaceted, and the island's inhabitants enact it in different ways. At the entrance to Jorgito's home hangs a picture of Fidel Castro; at the entrance to Malú's, an illustrated crucifix. Both images are accompanied by the words, *"Esta casa es su casa"* ("This house is your house"). The vastly different images bearing the same assertion remind us of the heterogeneity of Cuban attitudes and experiences, the diverse political positions, religious affiliations, historical interpretations, and cultural traditions. *Viva Cuba* challenges the myth of a single revolutionary ideology, instead highlighting plurality and the multiple ways in which Cubans imagine themselves and their national community.

Deftly edited parallel montages illustrate the complexity of Cubanness. The difference in the protagonists' socioeconomic status, for example, is made exceedingly clear: Malú soaks in a bubble-filled bathtub, whereas Jorgito washes himself by dipping a cup into a water-filled bucket; Malú's lunch plate holds a large, colorful salad, its ingredients purchased with convertible pesos, while Jorgito's holds more simple fare from *la libreta* (the ration book), a fried egg covering some rice; and Malú can select volumes from a bookshelf of leather-bound tomes, while Jorgito is limited to reading the *Granma* newspaper or his schoolbooks. "The Cuban Revolution has many readings and many readers," contends the director. "It's not black and white." For this reason, he avoids taking a stand either for or against the Revolution. Instead, he reveals the plurality of the Revolutionary experience through the diverse lives of his protagonists.

Cremata Malberti enacts his "revolutionary" identity with the goal of "remaking" the world around him. In his words,

> I'm an avid defender of difference, of tolerance. In my personal life I
> try to be different, to avoid being cubby-holed. Because I think that

revolutionaries are those who re-evolve, the ones who get up each day and seek to change everything, including what they have accomplished. I think that re-evolution isn't about the satisfaction of having accomplished something, but about the joy of re-creating, re-making, re-inventing, re-discovering in a new way, in a better way, over and over again. Some have cubby-holed me as "experimental" or "postmodern." I believe in the desire and vocation of remaking the world in which I live. That's why I seek out situations that are alive ... [and] unique.

Viva Cuba demonstrates the filmmaker's commitment to "re-evolution," marking a "first" in many ways. It is the first Cuban film to be made both for children and with children, the first film to depict some of the island's most remote landscapes, the first feature film to be made under the auspices of the TVC Casa Productora, the first Cuban feature made independently of the ICAIC and yet distributed by this entity on the island, and the first Cuban film to earn a prize at Cannes. Perhaps more significant for this study is the director's own "re-evolution"; simultaneously constructing himself as a national filmmaker committed to continuing Cuba's cinema tradition and an auteur versed in transnational techniques and practices, Cremata Malberti has opened new roads for audiovisual artists on the island.

A New Mode for a New Generation: Street Filmmakers Employ Digital Technology and Invent Solutions

In leaving Havana and traversing the island, *Viva Cuba* revealed the beauty of the island's landscape and the diversity of its people; Cremata Malberti also piloted a new production mode. More island locales appear in this film than in any other in the nation's history. This Street Filmmaker relied on conventions of the road movie, and although the genre was employed earlier with *Guantanamera* (Tomás Gutiérrez Alea and Juan Carlos Tabío, 1995), *Viva Cuba* stops off at far more destinations. The protagonists travel eastward from Havana to Matanzas, on to Varadero, into Trinidad, through Sancti Spiritus, past Camagüey, and all the way to Punta Maisí. Along the way, the landscape varies from pristine beaches and expansive swamps to wide rivers and cloud-filled forests. For many viewers—including most Cubans—this film marks the first opportunity to glimpse these sites.

Executive producer Inti Herrera reflects on the genesis of this film. (Both Herrera and Cremata Malberti studied filmmaking at the EICTV, graduating "a few" years apart; Herrera, with a smile, opts to keeps to himself just how many years for fear of offending his friend and collaborator.) The two had often talked about working together, and finally an opportunity presented itself. Cremata Malberti approached Herrera, saying he had come up with a small amount of money for a very simple project. All the filming would be done in Havana in two weeks with a small Handy cam. Later, they'd seek financing for the blowup to 35 millimeter. "We began working, little by little," recounts Herrera, "and we began to see the possibilities afforded by the script—that the story really lent itself to presenting Cuba in a broader way, that it could be a journey of initiation for the children, and that it made sense to go beyond Havana." It was then that they began to develop plans to realize these more ambitious goals.[9]

The absence of industry backing compelled Cremata Malberti to experiment with new ways of making a film. The filmmaker believes strongly in the power of experimentation. "Lots of people are afraid of trying something new," he says. "But if Christopher Columbus hadn't experimented, he wouldn't have discovered America." And this experimentation—undertaken with photographer Alejandro Pérez, editor Angélica Salvador, executive producer Inti Herrera, and other members of the team—engendered a new mode of production. This itinerant approach to making a movie would have been far too cumbersome for the ICAIC. An industry feature can employ hundreds and require several truckloads of equipment. *Viva Cuba*, in contrast, was filmed with a team of fifteen and a small digital camera.[10] The moderate group size and portable equipment afforded flexibility that would not have been possible with a project filmed in the traditional manner.

The new technology has contributed to "massifying" film production. More aspiring directors than ever before can launch projects. But the ease of access should not be confused with effortless production. This new mode of filmmaking—and the constant renovation in technology—requires that audiovisual artists keep abreast of rapid changes. For Street Filmmaking to yield positive outcomes, directors and photographers and other members of the production team must plan carefully and be aware

Filming the Varadero Beach scene for *Viva Cuba*. Pictured are director Juan Carlos Cremata Malberti (standing in background), photographer Alejandro Pérez, and actors Jorge Miló and Malú Tarrau. Courtesy of Alejandro Pérez.

of the potential afforded by the rapidly evolving digital medium. The pre- and postproduction stages are critical if filming is to proceed smoothly and efficiently. In the words of Pérez, "You can't count on working anything out 'on the fly' during filming." Locations must be scouted, conditions must be created, and the entire production team must be fully engaged before the director ever gives the signal.

Of equal importance to this careful planning is developing a thorough understanding of the possibilities afforded by the technology. Cuban directors, photographers, and editors who first learned the analog mode must constantly adapt their existing skills and master new concepts. This adaptability and know-how was crucial during the filming of a key sequence in *Viva Cuba*. Dubbed "The Great Decision" by the crew, this turning point in the film, when the two children make up their minds to leave Havana and venture forth together, required a particular light. Pérez and Cremata Malberti had envisioned a soft sunset illumination to create the atmosphere in which Malú and Jorgito, seated on a rooftop against the Havana skyline, come to their decision. But on the afternoon they were preparing to film this sequence, a gray sky enveloped the city. The mood produced was far too menacing. And yet, postponing the filming was out of the question; the *Viva Cuba* team had to adhere to a very tight schedule. So, aware of the enhancements that could be made to the image during the postproduction phase, Pérez went ahead and filmed. He could proceed with confidence, because he knew the possibilities afforded to him by the digital medium. And indeed, the result is powerful: In a single take, Perez's camera captures the children and the cityscape behind them against the pastel sky. Had the photographer been unaware of options for adjusting color and contrast, he—in conjunction with the director and editor—might not have produced such a compelling image.

Street Filmmaking requires constant troubleshooting and inventing. The ability to problem-solve is crucial. Because money is tight in Street Filmmaking, solutions must be economical and appropriate for the circumstances.[11] A "fix" in postproduction costs far less than one in production, and this is how the *Viva Cuba* team managed to create another key sequence. "The Night in the Boat" depicts the children falling asleep in a wooden dingy on the beach, rocked by gentle waves and lulled by strains of the popular lullaby "Duerme Negrito." There was no budget for elaborate lighting—illumination can be among the most expensive elements of a film—and so the impression of night and darkness had to be created some other way. An obsolete Hollywood technique was resurrected. The "American Night" approach, also known as "Day for Night," simulates night scenes. To avoid costly and technically challenging night filming, the scenes were shot during the day instead; special blue filters and underexposed film created the illusion of darkness or moonlight. (Common to early B-movies and westerns, this practice is now virtually extinct.) This approach can be risky, for rarely does it succeed in producing a "realistic" night scene. But the *Viva Cuba* team decided to give it a try, rendering the starry-skied night scene by filming at nine o'clock in the morning on a sun-saturated beach. Later, in the editing studio using Photoshop, the sun was converted into the moon and the sunlight shimmering on the water became moonbeams. Whimsical touches, added with animation, permitted the children to move the stars around by pointing a finger. The result is a night more magical than realistic, but one perfectly suited to the narrative and artistic design. Low-budget filmmaking requires constant innovation; fixes like these are only possible with extensive knowl-

The day-for-night sequence in *Viva Cuba* produced with editing software.
Courtesy of Alejandro Pérez.

edge of digital filming and editing and a willingness to *resolver*, or make do. Street Filmmakers are adept at communicating through audiovisual media in ways compatible with global technologies *and* local circumstances.

Street Filmmakers must constantly develop cost-saving strategies so that inexpensively made films give the impression of their large-scale counterparts. *Viva Cuba* once again proffers an example in the sequence in which the children run frightened through the woods. An industry filmmaker would have used a dolly shot in which the camera moves horizontally across the scene. But that would have required laying tracks and mounting a camera on a platform. Renting or purchasing these items, assuming they were even available on the island, would have been costly, and their installation time-consuming. So a different approach had to be devised. The photographer located an ideal spot in the woods, a clearing surrounded by trees. Next, he positioned the camera in the center and traced a circle around it on the ground. The children were then instructed to run around the circle while the camera rolled. It would be difficult for a viewer to distinguish this shot from one made using the far more costly industry approach. And that is how virtually all of Cuba's Street Filmmakers measure success in making low-budget films. Pérez sums up by saying, "You have to create an image that doesn't show the real cost, one that appears to be a grand production."

In reflecting on *Viva Cuba*, Juan Carlos Cremata Malberti acknowledges that with this film, his art has moved in a new direction. The lack of opportunity within the industry compelled him to develop a new kind of production mode—one relying on a small team, one employing cutting-edge technology and requiring experimentation, and one bringing together partners from nearby and far away. He credits the EICTV with preparing him for this kind of project, saying, "At the EICTV we learned to make a movie with all the means used by the industry, but we also learned to make it with very few people, 'with just three cats,' as the saying goes. The digital technology allows us more movement, more speed, fewer constraints and a greater degree of concentration in our work with the children."[12]

The director explained to me his intentions to continue employing this style of filmmaking: "The fact that I couldn't make *Candela* with the ICAIC generated this encounter with a mode of production that I intend to continue. I've left the industry schema behind. I'm more interested in small-scale production. My confrontation with the industry isn't political—although in the end everything's political; rather, it's a confrontation with the industry mode of production. This in no way implies a confrontation with official discourse or government discourse." With the opportunities afforded by digital technology and his positive experience making *Viva Cuba*, Cremata Malberti doubts he will film again in 35 millimeter. (He qualifies this statement by adding, "unless I have all the money in the world.") The greatest struggle now, not only in Cuba but in all of Latin America, is adopting a kind of production that is "more in tune with the new generations, more appropriate for the conditions in our countries, more compatible with the direction in which technology is heading." With *Viva Cuba*, Juan Carlos Cremata Malberti has proffered a production model for Street Filmmakers in Cuba. They admire his tenacity and talent. Esteban Insausti characterizes Cremata Malberti as "an insatiable creator," an artist from whom he draws inspiration. The success of Cremata Malberti's approach has compelled others to work in similar ways.

Cremata Malberti's unique production mode was accompanied by an innovative dissemination strategy. The first audience to watch *Viva Cuba* on the big screen was not Cuban but French. When the Cannes children's jury prize was bestowed on *Viva Cuba* in France, there were repercussions on the island. Despite the fact that Cremata Malberti had produced the film without ICAIC support, Cuba's state industry moved to align itself with the project. International accolades undoubtedly helped pique the interest of Cuba's national film institute and paved the way for the film's success at home. *Viva Cuba*'s trajectory reveals the complexity of cultural flows in this era of new technologies and increasingly connected communications networks.

This road movie premiered in Havana in July 2006 and became an instant hit. Contributing to the favorable domestic reception was the director's framing of the film in terms consistent with Cuba's revolutionary discourse at the time. This youth-centered film appeared on the island precisely when Cuba was focusing attention on its children. The refusal of the United States to turn Elián González over to his natural father in Cuba and the impulse generated for Cuba's youth by the Batalla de Ideas were foremost in people's minds. Juan Carlos Cremata Malberti did not set out to take advantage of this moment in which young Cubans featured prominently, but it was within this context that *Viva Cuba* emerged. The inaugural screening was an invitation-only event for those who had helped make the director's dream a reality. As a part of that audience, invited by the filmmaker and accompanied by Esteban Insausti and Angélica Salvador, I watched Cremata Malberti step up to the microphone and listened to his impassioned speech. He positioned *Viva Cuba* as being for youth, against terrorism, and quintessentially Cuban through a moving discourse in which he recalled his own childhood encounter with terrorism. At the age of fifteen, "Juanqui" learned that his father, who worked for Cubana Airlines, had perished in an airplane explosion over Barbados. Carlos Cremata Trujillo and seventy-two others died as the result of a terrorist act in 1976; the bombing left Juan Carlos and his siblings fatherless and hundreds of others mourning the loss of their loved ones.[13] The audience listened intently, deeply touched by the fact that the artist before them had suffered such a loss—so violent, so senseless, so unconscionable—at such a tender age. When the filmmaker concluded his remarks, he raised his right hand in a fist and shouted, "Viva Cuba!" The slogan—most often followed by "Viva la Revolución, Viva Fidel, Viva!"—is a familiar one for Cubans. They employ it to voice their opposition to imperialism, to demonstrate their commitment to the Revolution, and to underscore their love for their homeland. When the cries subsided, Cremata Malberti continued, linking his personal childhood experience with the political panorama of that moment:

> Right now, not only in our country but in the whole world, there's a battle taking place against terrorism. . . . [We] can shout out loud "Viva Cuba," which is exactly what wasn't wanted by those who attacked us, and those who supported and financed them. . . . This is what I want to say with the film: "Long live Cuba! Long live children! Long live parents! Long live cinema! Long live television!" But above all, I want Cubans, wherever they may be, to remember the film and feel that it belongs to them, to have the chance to repeat time and time again, together with the children and adults of the entire world: "Viva Cuba!" And that they understand that this country is different because of its authentic character. A unique country that has the right and responsibility to live.

This politically charged (and politically correct) speech placed *Viva Cuba* *with* international efforts to counter terrorism, *against* terror and violence, and *for* families and film.[14] What was not to like? The audience joined in the rally, raising their fists and shouting in unison, "Viva Cuba!" In doing so, they affirmed their—and the film's—Cuban identity. So whereas a feature film made outside the state institute might have been accorded a cold reception on the island, Cremata Malberti's eminently "Cuban" film was warmly embraced. The director's discursive positioning of the work undoubtedly contributed to its favorable reception at home. *Viva Cuba* permits us to see the active role Street Filmmakers play in launching their films. With no industry infrastructure on which to rely, they participate fully in promoting their work.

Cremata Malberti's behavior also reveals the increased tendency among young audiovisual artists to assert their identities as auteurs, creating their public personas and influencing audience reception. A few days later, the filmmaker emphasized his youthfulness by appearing at the cinema dressed in the *pionero* outfit typically worn by schoolchildren—maroon shorts, white shirt, and red neckerchief. He carried his signature strand of jingle bells, shaking them to announce his arrival and to elicit applause during his remarks. This "intentional and authorial agency," as Timothy Corrigan has noted, produces "a kind of brand-name vision that precedes and succeeds the film."[15] Cremata Malberti and other emerging filmmakers self-consciously flaunt their status as auteurs, then, as a strategy for eliciting favorable responses among moviegoers.

Cuban viewers of all ages flocked to see the film in the eleven cinemas where it was showing. The director had insisted repeatedly that each adult coming to see *Viva Cuba* be accompanied by a child, and most fans heeded his request. The cinemas were packed day after day.[16] Film aficionados outside Havana also had access to *Viva Cuba*; copies were circulated to 125 movie theaters and video clubs across the island in what was the ICAIC's—and Cuba's—most massive film distribution initiative to date. Digital technology facilitated *Viva Cuba*'s immediate and widespread dissemination; the inexpensive, lightweight, and reproducible format permitted the movement of the film on DVD around the island—and also overseas. This marked a stark contrast to Cremata Malberti's previous film, *Nada*, which required that the filmmaker lug five heavy canisters, pay excess baggage fees, and struggle with customs officers. This time around, the director could simply tuck a few DVDs in his small backpack. The digital technology that had proved advantageous during the production process—albeit with its share of challenges—also afforded new possibilities for the film's circulation.

And circulate widely it did. The road movie story reasserted itself in the film's exhibition trajectory as *Viva Cuba* crisscrossed the globe. In the year following its premiere, *Viva Cuba* earned more than a dozen prizes at various festivals around the world.[17] Momentum continued for quite some time. In the summer of 2007, I received an email from Cremata Malberti sharing the news of a prize at the Festival des Mureaux, in Paris; by then *Viva Cuba* had had earned three dozen awards.

The director expresses surprise at the widespread impact of what he calls his "little film dealing with little people." He is very pleased—satisfied to have contributed to his nation's film tradition and hopeful for new opportunities to come his way. But the greatest reward for this filmmaker is observing the reactions of the young spectators: "It moves me tremendously to walk into a cinema and hear the children reciting the dialogues." When I interviewed him in Havana in June 2006, he recalled the impact when he learned that for some Cuban children, *Viva Cuba* marked their first moviegoing experience. Cremata Malberti was moved

Juan Carlos Cremata Malberti (center), flanked by renowned colleagues director Orlando Rojas and actress Daisy Granados, during the Havana Film Festival in New York City (2003). Courtesy of the festival.

to learn that his efforts had introduced these young people to the magic of cinema.

I had an opportunity to experience this magic firsthand, not only in Havana but also in New York, at a screening of *Viva Cuba* during the Havana Film Festival held there in April 2006. A class of fifth graders entered the theater, exhilarated at being away from school for a couple of hours. Their whispering and squirming subsided almost immediately, however, as they became captivated by the film. They laughed, sighed, and cried along with the on-screen children their same age. The fact that Spanish-language dialogues required them to read English-language subtitles did not diminish their enjoyment or understanding of the film. Afterward, festival director Carole Rosenberg introduced one of the producers, John della Penna, who moderated a discussion. (The filmmaker's request for a U.S. entry visa to participate in the New York event had been denied.) It was clear from comments and questions that the Cuban film had resonated for these English-speaking children in the United States. With *Viva Cuba*, Cremata Malberti created a work committed to communicating—a work taking root in common experiences rather than taking sides.

Forming a Filmmaker

Juan Carlos Cremata Malberti credits his formal training and family background as key to his creative trajectory. Born in Cuba in 1961, he grew up surrounded by culture. From an early age, he enjoyed dance performances, plays, concerts, and films. Before long, he was collaborating with his mother, choreographer-director Iraida Malberti Cabrera, on television programming for children. Among the notable programs is *Cuando yo sea grande (When I Grow Up)*, designed to enable children to develop their imagination and creativity. This experience convinced Cremata Malberti that "the function of cinema is first and foremost to entertain the viewer; only then can it achieve any educational purpose."

After earning his degree in theater and dramaturgy at Havana's ISA in 1986, he enrolled in the newly inaugurated EICTV. His three years there would shape his artistic expression and influence his production style for years to come. And as already noted in Chapter 1, his thesis project, *Oscuros rinocerontes enjaulados (muy a la moda)* (*Dark Jailed Rhinoceroses [Very Much in Style]*), is often cited and circulated as proof of the innovative vision characterizing EICTV students and graduates. More than a decade after graduating from the EICTV, Cremata Malberti still acknowledges the school's impact on his professional and personal development. There, he contends, he was "reborn." Immersed in the enriching setting, Cremata Malberti exchanged ideas with artists his own age and seasoned professionals in the media industry. He worked alongside renowned filmmakers, foremost among them Fernando Birri, a man Cremata Malberti considers his principal mentor and a special friend. He broadened his repertoire on world music, literature, and art. And he gained a greater appreciation of international films and of Cuba's film tradition.[18] With people from around the world he was able to compare notes on how cinema functioned in Cuba with its workings in other countries. New relationships were forged and contacts were developed that would endure to the present day.

This formal training differentiates Street Filmmakers from earlier generations of Cuban directors. Cremata Malberti—along with Miguel Coyula, Pavel Giroud, Léster Hamlet, Dania Ileasástegui, Esteban Insausti, Luis Leonel León, Humberto Padrón, Ian Padrón, Ernesto Piña, Arturo Sotto, and numerous others—has had the opportunity to pursue formal programs of study or, at the very least, to complete some filmmaking courses and workshops. Unlike their predecessors, then, Street Filmmakers have not had to learn by doing. The majority of Cubans who entered the ICAIC in the 1960s, 1970s, and 1980s learned to make films on the job, mentored by experienced professionals.[19] To become a director required a great deal of patience, for apprentices moved up the ranks from second assistant to first assistant, and only then were they permitted to try their hand at directing a newsreel or documentary. After more practice and the passing of more years, they might earn the right to undertake a feature-length film. For many, including some of the industry's most talented filmmakers, this privilege was not accorded until after two decades of working in the ICAIC, often after they turned forty or sometimes even fifty years old.[20] That the early generations of island directors mastered their art through on-the-job training in no way implies a lack of formal education. On the contrary, they were encouraged to pursue university degrees; the ICAIC supported them in furthering their studies by providing release time as well as a salary and benefits. But as there was no program in film production and aesthetics per se, they specialized in related areas such as literature, music, journalism, and political science.[21] The generation of audiovisual artists that began to emerge in the 1990s, in contrast, approached the industry as trained professionals and, in some cases, managed to make a feature film while still in their thirties.

Juan Carlos Cremata Malberti affirms the importance of his training and acknowledges the ways in which he and his peers differ from earlier Cuban cineastes. "The new generation of filmmakers has a lot more information and knowledge than those working in the 1960s," he asserts, "because of their formation in the Escuela Internacional de Cine y Televisión, the Instituto Superior de Arte, and other institutions." Despite this difference in their formation, however, he contends that present-day filmmakers share the commitment of their predecessors. They, too, seek to document their unique reality just as the founders of Cuba's revolutionary cinema did some fifty years ago. "We have the same desire to make films as did cineastes from the 1960s," affirms Cremata Malberti, "to make a cinema of our own. Why?" he asks. "Because it signifies our vision of the world at this time. It's important for us to make films—as it was for the filmmakers in the 1960s—that reflect new people and new themes, ones that haven't been treated." Cremata Malberti and his contemporaries have a great deal to say, and they are skilled at transmitting their message. Their formal training has positioned them to communicate effectively through the audiovisual medium.

Unique learning experiences like the one afforded this director are critical to the evolution of Cuba's new generation of Street Filmmakers. Through their education, they have familiarized themselves with the century-plus tradition of world cinema and developed the skills to create compelling films. They have gained the confidence to defend their ideas, take risks, and experiment with new techniques. And they have been conditioned to look at home and abroad for inspiration, potential partners, and viewing audiences. Many Street Filmmakers, Cremata Malberti among them, have worked outside their home countries.[22] Regardless of the number of stamps in their passports, all have been introduced to a range of cultures, traditions, and "ways of seeing" through their formal training. This common experience informs their work and influences their career trajectories. It provides a window through which they view their surroundings with greater complexity and transmit that vision to audiences.

Following his graduation from the EICTV, Cremata Malberti continued nurturing his creativity and expanding his cultural knowledge. A grant from the John Simon Guggenheim Memorial Foundation permitted him to spend a year in New York City. There Cremata Malberti immersed himself in a plethora of cultural offerings: He became a regular at Barnes and Noble and acquired tomes of all sizes and amassed a large collection of CDs; he frequently lined up for student rush tickets to plays on Broadway or concerts at Lincoln Center and Carnegie Hall; he walked up one side of Manhattan and down the other admiring the architecture and cityscape; and he visited with the other artists at the National Arts Club where he stayed. He also accepted invitations to present his work to university audiences. At the College of William and Mary in Virginia, he impressed my Hispanic studies and film students with his lively short *Dark Caged Rhinoceroses* and his unique vision. (At that time the young cineaste was very interested in the relationship between the film medium and the spectator. Cremata Malberti discussed his interest in experimenting with celluloid and also with the screen. He was intrigued by the fact that Norman McLaren's technique rendered each copy an "original," thereby challenging the notion of film as a reproducible form of cultural expression, and he wondered if the screen might also be manipulated so as to recuperate the cinema-as-spectacle experience.) The year 1996 was a special one for the Cuban filmmaker: He recharged his creative batteries; he enhanced his understanding of the entire world, gleaning from the cosmopolitan microcosm of Manhattan; and he was able to regard his homeland from a distance, reflecting on its importance for his work. So formative was this experience for the filmmaker that he vowed to list the Guggenheim Foundation in the credits of every film he ever makes.

And indeed, when his next work premiered in 1999, the foundation's name once again featured prominently in the credits. This experimental short, titled *La época, el encanto, y el fin del siglo* (*The Epoch, Enchantment, and the End of the Century*) probes life in Havana within an innovative structure. Each of the three components of the title corresponds to a department store in pre-Revolutionary Cuba. With this trope, the director moves deftly between 1959 and 1999, creating slippage between the material abundance evident in shop windows back then and the scarcity of the present noted by the Havana informants. Innovative camera work, impressive graphic design (by Pavel Giroud), and effective editing demonstrate the filmmaker's preparedness to tackle a feature. And, in fact, only two years would transpire before Cremata Malberti brought his *opera prima* to the screen.

Nada (*Nothing*, 2001) is a ninety-two-minute feature that continues the director's interest in experimenting with cinematic techniques, thereby proving his engagement with international cinema language and global filmmaking practices. The style is reminiscent of French New Wave; the narrative focuses on the theme of emigration; and funding from four countries—France, Spain, Italy, and Cuba—underwrote the production. In this film, a bored postal worker embellishes some of the letters that pass through her hands; in doing so, she livens up the lives of others as well as her own as she waits for a visa to emigrate. The unique artistic design relies on black-and-white images and high-contrast lighting. Interestingly, *Nada* pleased international audiences more than Cremata Malberti's compatriots. With this film, the director's concessions to the international market may have impeded communication with local viewers. Cremata Malberti had envisioned *Nada* as part of a trilogy and hoped its success would attract a producer for the other two installments. He shared these hopes, strategically, at festivals and in media appearances. But, as he laments playfully, nobody (*nadie*) ever (*nunca*) appeared to finance *Nadie* and *Nunca*. Fortunately, *Viva Cuba* afforded other opportunities. With that film, Cremata Malberti struck the right balance. In doing so, he took his place among Cuba's most accomplished industry directors while effectively modeling the Street Filmmaking approach.

Cremata Malberti plans to continue working on his own, making films through his production label El Ingenio. He has several projects under way. In addition to those mentioned earlier—*Candela*, *Nadie*, and *Nunca*—he is working on a screen adaptation of Héctor Quintero's play *El premio flaco* (*The Smallest Prize*). The energetic director is seeking to create a film based on the testimonial novel *Hombres sin mujer* (*Men without Women*), by Carlos Montenegro; a filmed version of three tales written by Cuban women called *Alguien tiene que llorar* (*Someone Must Weep*); another children's project titled *La esperanza del mundo* (*The World's Hope*); and some more theatrical performances. The filmmaker acknowledges his readiness to tackle any one of these—or something else altogether. By his admission, he is "always looking around for new projects."

Whereas Cremata Malberti's ingenuity may seem unique, he insists that it is not. "There are lots of young people who do business with a camera here and an editing space there," he says. "They're doing it—lots of it. In fact, they're creating more than what's being produced in the industry." For Cremata Malberti, the work of these individuals more than that of the industry professionals lends richness to Cuban film events like the National Exhibit of New Filmmakers (Muestra Nacional de Nuevos Realizadores) and the No-Budget Film Festival (Cine Pobre). "The new generation has a great deal to say." What accounts for the intensive audio-visual momentum on the island? One factor is the greater access to the medium that new technologies have spurred. He explains: "What's happening in Cuba is completely sui géneris; you don't see it anywhere else in the world. Access to a tremendous amount of information with this avalanche of media technology and the force of digital video are offering many more people the possibility of creating. It's increasingly democratizing the modes of production." This effervescence in Cuba's audiovisual realm also has to do with the fervent desire among young artists to transform their ideas into images and sounds. "Come hell or high water, we are going to make films," insists Cremata. The director likens this strong commitment to the early years of the Revolution. "The triumph of the Revolution generated a powerful force creating the urgency to communicate, to express, to show new phenomena. And it was from that strong desire that Cuba erupted on screens for the first time." Like most of the Street Filmmakers, Cremata Malberti finds parallels between those working inside and those working outside the industry, and between present-day audiovisual artists and their predecessors.

The times have changed. And so have the modes of moviemaking on the island and around the world. This transformation in no way signals the demise of Cuba's Revolutionary cinema. On the contrary, Cremata Malberti and other Street Filmmakers like him express a commitment to building on their nation's cinema. Their efforts call to mind the words of Cuban writer Senel Paz, who asserts, "Art is revolutionary when it renews, discovers, opens doors, but not when it revolves around its own advances."[23] For helping forge a new mode of film production on the island, these audiovisual artists are moving a once concertedly national film tradition onto transnational terrain. By self-identifying as both a Cuban cultural worker and an international audiovisual artist, Cremata Malberti is helping expand the scope and reach of the island's production. We will now turn to two more Street Filmmakers, Pavel Giroud and Esteban Insausti, to continue our examination of how a generation of audiovisual artists has helped alter the course of filmmaking in Cuba.

The great sin of Cuban cinema is to have been so uniform.
I'm not saying that the existing Cuban films shouldn't have
been made. What I'm saying is that other kinds of films should
also be produced. Cuba's cinema offerings should be more
popularized so as to extend to all levels of the public.
—Pavel Giroud

Promoting Popular Genres

PAVEL GIROUD REVISES

CONCEPTIONS OF CUBAN CINEMA

It is customary for Cuban filmmakers working in the
industry to get feedback from their peers while developing their projects. This exchange of ideas takes place
informally, for the most part, but the ICAIC generally
presents each new film in progress at some stage and facilitates a discussion afterward. When a rough cut of Pavel Giroud's first feature-
length film, *La edad de la peseta* (*The Awkward Age*, also translated as
The Silly Age, 2005), was screened at the film institute, it impressed the
filmmakers and other industry professionals in attendance. Some, however, expressed concern that the work did not seem to be sufficiently
Cuban. They asserted that the way the film was made—particularly its
tempo—aligned it more closely with European cinema traditions than

with Cuba's. Might this unfamiliar aesthetic in an island film alienate local viewers? they wondered. And might the "foreign" feel impede the work's sale abroad, disappointing international audiences accustomed to seeing certain kinds of films from Cuba? These concerns left the film-maker nonplussed. "To be honest," he admitted, "I never analyzed this during the process of creating this film. I've been shaped by lots of differ-ent influences, and it's likely that every one of these—some Cuban and others not—have marked the development of my work."[1]

Precisely what constitutes a "Cuban" film or filmmaker at this junc-ture is a key issue underlying this study. The concept of national cinema has been interrogated by critics working in various geopolitical contexts. They tend to concur that national films rely on government funding to some extent, are aimed primarily at domestic audiences, develop stories that represent the history and traditions of a specific nation, and employ a language peculiar to a particular locale.[2] The convergence of nation and cinema is particularly relevant in Cuba, given the deliberate employment of the medium to disseminate the Revolutionary consciousness. During the early years of the Revolution, immediately following the ICAIC's in-ception, artists in Cuba grappled with the challenge of creating autoch-thonous forms to communicate authentically Cuban content. The quest to inscribe and invent *cubanía*, or Cubanness, has been a hallmark of the island's national culture for more than a half-century. As noted in the Introduction, the ICAIC was founded with the explicit purpose of foment-ing a concertedly national cinema.

Over the years, Cuba's film industry has had to respond increasingly to global forces, and coproduction became the prevalent mode for financ-ing films.[3] The island industry began to team up with a series of interna-tional partners in order to raise capital, procure equipment, and reach larger audiences. Most films produced by island filmmakers during the 1990s resulted from this border-crossing mode. A sampling of production partners from this decade reveals the broad range of collaboration: Tele-visión Española, Telemadrid, Canal Plus, Wanda Vision, Ibermedia, Torna-sol, and SGAE in Spain; IMCINE, Tabasco Films, Estudios Churubusco, and Producciones Amarantha in Mexico; FONCINE and ALTER Producciones Cinematográficas in Venezuela; Pandora Cinema and DMBV in France; Kinowelt Gluckaf Film and ARD Degeto in Germany; Yalta Films in the Soviet Union; Promotora de Inversiones y Financimiento in Nicaragua;

and Channel 4 in England.[4] The case of Pavel Giroud permits us to examine precisely how this transnational mode is contributing to and challenging notions of national cinema. We will observe a correlation between the increasing reliance on coproduction and the need to craft and circulate markers of autochthonous culture. Street Filmmakers like Giroud seek to transform the markers of *cubanía* into cultural currency in the global marketplace; they blend carefully coded "national" elements with transnational signs in order to reach worldwide viewers. And they position themselves as auteurs in order to negotiate between local and global contexts. Marvin D'Lugo has aptly deemed national cinema in Latin America to be "much less a sacrosanct expression of national culture than a particularized discursive formation, the product of a local film culture intended to represent that culture commercially not only within, but also beyond its own borders."[5] We will see how this applies to the Cuban context in the pages that follow.

Pavel Giroud is not intent on fitting into existing categories. This Street Filmmaker resists the "sociological emphasis" of some Cuban films that depict problems facing the island nation. Instead, this avid fan of popular films consistently integrates elements from thrillers, comedies, and dramas. He has tackled a host of projects, working both within and outside the industry. Giroud understands the business of filmmaking—identifying coproduction partners and negotiating agreements, casting international actors so as to enhance market potential, and undertaking a particular project as a strategy for tackling another. This is not to say he eschews the art of cinema but, rather, that his approach is eminently pragmatic. It is also highly effective, for at age thirty-five, Giroud was the youngest Cuban filmmaker of his generation to have made a feature. In embracing popular genres, employing a variety of production modes, and attracting capital and consumers from beyond the island, this Street Filmmaker is indeed expanding the rubric of "Cuban cinema."

From Action Movies and tv to Design and Film:
Fashioning an Audiovisual Artist

Pavel Giroud's introduction to film was anything but highbrow. He grew up in Havana's humble Jesús María neighborhood, just around the corner from the Patria cinema. Whenever he could, he would slip out of the house and into the theater for the movie matinee. In the small screening room there, with only a ceiling fan to circulate the air on even the hottest summer afternoons, the young Giroud watched action films starring Charles Bronson, Bruce Lee, and others. He credits these films—particularly their solid structure and treatment of suspense—as having influenced his work. Giroud came to appreciate "art films" much later. He explains: "I would love to be able to tell the story that I was walking along Twenty-third Street one day and, with nothing better to do, stepped into the Cinemateca. The screening was of Tarkovsky's *The Mirror*. I watched it and my life changed from that moment on. But that's not the way it happened." Giroud admits to being seduced by the action and adventure movies; these popular works would influence his creative trajectory.

Cuban television also shaped Giroud's artistic vision. For many years, Enrique Colina hosted the weekly program *Veinte-cuatro por segundo* (*Twenty-Four Frames per Second*), guiding viewers in understanding the language of cinema. His frame-by-frame analysis of international films trained Giroud—and many would-be filmmakers—to identify the process through which sequences were constructed. Giroud notes his debt to Colina for introducing him to suspense as a dramatic element. He recalls seeing Alfred Hitchcock's *Psycho* on Colina's program when he was about eight years old. For quite some time thereafter, he was afraid—panicked even—at having to get in the shower. When he realized that the person who had made the film was "a chubby old man with the face of a kind old grandpa," Giroud figured he'd like to try his hand at filmmaking, too. He credits Hitchcock with teaching him valuable lessons. "As I matured as an individual and developed as a professional," recalls Giroud, "I began to realize that cinema was so much more. And that's when I began discovering other filmmakers. I even came across Tarkovsky and eventually grew to like his films—but it was a process."

This young Cuban auteur is "fanatical" about Asian cinema, believing the greatest innovations in filmmaking are taking place there. And he is "in love" with French film, preferring French thrillers over their North American counterparts. (Giroud observes that the great North American thrillers have often been made by Europeans, as in the case of his revered Hitchcock films.) "Hitchcock is a cineaste who has greatly influenced me," acknowledges Giroud, who then adds with a smile, "My films don't come out quite as good as his do." In addition to Hitchcock, Giroud credits Michelangelo Antonioni, Francis Ford Coppola, Brian De Palma, Billy Wilder, Pedro Almodóvar, Martin Scorsese, Francois Truffaut, Jean Luc Godard, and F. W. Murnau as contributing to his "sublime obsession" with cinema.

This Cuban cineaste confesses that his island's films are not among his favorites. There are exceptions, however, like the "populist cinema of the 1980s" that he enjoyed a great deal as a boy. "It was the era in which I began to discover films like *Los pájaros tirándole a la escopeta* and *Se permuta*," he recalls. "Today these films are brushed off as 'populist,' but they were indispensable to my formation." So, too, were a handful of other Cuban films far more complex in nature: *Madagascar* and *Suite Habana*, by Fernando Pérez; *Memorias del subdesarrollo* (*Memories of Underdevelopment*) and *Hasta cierto punto* (*Up to a Certain Point*), by Tomás Gutiérrez Alea; and *Papeles secundarios* (*Supporting Roles*), by Orlando Rojas. "There are Cuban films here and there that contributed to my development," he acquiesces, "but I've never been—I say this with absolute honesty—a big fan of Cuban cinema."

What Giroud considers to be lacking in his nation's cinema is "the plurality of genres and aesthetics." It's rare to see a thriller, for example. In this director's mind, the uniformity of Cuban films has yielded a "subgenre. All the films are alike and, well, either you like that genre or you don't. Kind of like the musical . . ." He would love to see the "specter of national cinema" open widely to accommodate all kinds of genres. "A great leap" will occur, for Giroud, when Cuba's cinema is comprised of a multitude of styles. And indeed, his efforts and those of other Street Filmmakers are already bringing this about.

Pavel Giroud studied design at the Instituto Superior del Diseño. Although he hoped to pursue graphic design, he claims his poor grades forced him to study costume design instead, something he never liked and for which he purports to have had no talent. To get by, he painted, made collages, and created artworks using elements from fashion. In this way, he developed from a costume designer into a fashion illustrator and managed to complete his graduation requirements. Then he began to paint, featuring his own "brand" in these images. Along the lines of Giorgio Armani, he created Giroud jeans, Giroud suits, and other Giroud items. These components of his "Giroud Emporium" made their way into his first works of video art, a series of 30-second spots done between 1998 and 2000, when Giroud's talent as an audiovisual artist became apparent. Shortly thereafter, he undertook a video clip. *Arráncame la vida* (2001) re-creates for viewers the golden age of the Orquesta Sensación, in the 1950s. Giroud achieved this with only a television, a curtain, a couple of actors, and a good musical number. It was from the fine arts, then, that Giroud entered the audiovisual world.[6]

Giroud wanted to make a work of video art, but one that integrated elements of narrative cinema. So one day, when the well-known artist Raúl Cordero returned from a trip and showed Giroud a toy pistol he had brought back, Giroud decided he and his friend would make a video. "I picked out a suit for him to wear and we spent the afternoon filming in his house with a Hi-8 camera. Later, Pedro Suarez edited the piece in the ICAIC and that's how this short came about." The three-minute *Ring* (1998) unfolds in three sections, each labeled with an intertitle. The introduction sets up the conflict; a ringing telephone gives way to a male voice say-ing, "Hello, it's me, the detective. Your wife is being unfaithful to you—in your own bed." Part 2, "The Body," resembles an advertisement for a sports car. Takes of a speeding roadster are interspersed with close-up shots of wheels on pavement. The final sequence, "The Ending," reveals the detec-tive—his pop art shirt collar protruding from his fashionable suit, eyes concealed by trendy sunglasses—as he listens at a closed door. Moan-ing sounds come from within. With gun in hand, the man bursts into the room. Cut to the face of a stunned woman. The frame then reveals a second figure and freezes on the image of a blonde-haired woman. The telephone voice wraps up the sequence; "It's me, the detective. I caught your wife in bed with someone else." A text bubble captures his thoughts, adding, "But there are certain things a man can forgive." *Ring* borrows from the detective genre and then exaggerates those conventions—the detective is a little too slick, the car is a bit too sporty, and the gender roles are a bit too contrived. Overall, the film succeeds in generating suspense and entertaining viewers.

Giroud considered *Ring* a work of video art and was surprised to find that others deemed it a work of fiction. This assessment and the short's success on the festival circuit was all it took for Giroud to try his hand at making narrative cinema. So he set down his paint and brushes and picked up a camera. The artist enrolled in a program in screenwriting at the EICTV and received training that strengthened his filmmaking skills.

Giroud believes his formation as a designer contributed to his development as a media artist. "Making a film is like creating an object," he explains. "You keep peeling away the extra layers until you get to the true essence. The process of creating film scripts and production designs isn't very different from that."

Eminently pragmatic, Pavel Giroud understands that in order to undertake the films he wants to make, he must work on projects that pay the bills. He values each experience as a lesson that will serve him later. He has made commercials and promotional videos for a number of agencies at home and abroad, with clients ranging from Bucanero and Cristal Beer and Cubana Airlines to the Casa de las Américas, HBO Family, the International Festival of New Latin American Cinema, and the Spanish Cultural Center. Under the auspices of the Cuban BIS Music Publishing label, promoted through the art export society of Artex, he has directed more than a dozen music videos. This practice is increasingly common among Cuba's Street Filmmakers. In fact, as audiovisual artists attest, their principal income comes from what are called "video clips" in Cuba—spots, commercials, and music videos. With earnings from these shorts, they can then turn to projects that are less lucrative and more personal. The cycle works like this: An individual or group wishes to promote a "product," be that a brand of whiskey, a cultural event, a music group, or a public welfare campaign. They contract a Street Filmmaker to create the video clip and then sell this to a television network interested in the content—most often in Cuba, Spain, Mexico, or Venezuela. In this way, the investor benefits from increased visibility, the television network procures content at a reasonable cost, and the Street Filmmakers test new ideas and approaches while earning money for subsequent projects.[7]

Whereas some media artists express disdain for this kind of contract work, Giroud welcomes it. Not only do these projects yield a modest stream of income; they also provide opportunities "to practice without taking great risks." In answer to the question of why he makes video clips, put to him by José Luis Estrada Betancourt, Giroud replied, "Do you want the truth? To live. And yet video has helped me a lot; it's been my best training camp. Many of the elements that are in my films I've tested out first in my videos. But I should clarify that the video clip is eminently commercial in its character. You must satisfy the expectations of a particular party who is at the same time respecting the norms of a particular record company. So the video ends up having very little of you in it. Even when I've had the opportunity to put a lot of myself into them, video clips never cease to be hired works."[8]

At one point, Giroud's frustration with analog video led him to move away from it. "I couldn't get the kind of image that a form like that required." The texture struck him as more appropriate for a newsreel than for a work of art. The filmmaker recalls that with analog video, the harder he tried to "perfect the image," the less satisfied he was with the results. The arrival of digital technology has made a huge difference for Giroud.

The young filmmaker purports to have become "addicted" very quickly to digital technology. "Whenever I have limited resources," confesses Giroud, "I prefer an 'indie' aesthetic rather than trying to 'sophisticate the unsophisticatable.'" His first experience using a digital camera was for a documentary contracted with Skyline Community. HBO Family in New York had commissioned the group to offer a summer documentary workshop for students at an inner-city school. Giroud recalls the project as an interesting one, in great part because the subject grew out of the interests of workshop participants. They decided to make a short examining the lives of Latino children growing up in homes without a father. The workshop's executive producer traveled from the United States to Cuba and asked Giroud to "give form" to the material in order to transform it into a documentary. Although the short was filmed with a Betacam SP, Giroud requested an auxiliary camera, and that's how a Sony VX 1000 "fell into his hands." He was enthusiastic over the camera's potential at that time and still values the texture it imparts. "I had the camera in my hands long enough to realize the enormous possibilities."

Giroud's first work using digital technology was *Manzanita.com* in 2001. He deems this a transitional film, an "audiovisual experiment" that brought together "various demons" he would later exorcize. Giroud describes the film:

> It's a short with elements of genre films. . . . There's constant talk of a serial killer, lots of irony, a play with graphic design elements as well as great emphasis on the inability to communicate and the decline of interpersonal relations. I made it at a time when the Internet still wasn't widely available to the public in Cuba. . . . The premise had to do with the Internet and all the modes that decrease the distance be-

tween people, but at the same time result in a loss of the warmth of letters from bygone days . . . something like the cost of development.

The project is flawed, in Giroud's estimation, but he acknowledges its importance to his development as a filmmaker. With the experience of making *Manzanita.com*, his "soul returned to [his] body," for he realized the infinite possibilities afforded by this new and accessible technology.

This director believes that one's creative production emanates from lived experience. "Tarantino makes the films he makes because he worked in a video rental shop. Visconti made his films in tune with the cultural development he had." To have studied design, then, and to have invested time in making commercials and music videos have undoubtedly shaped his art. So, too, has his training at the EICTV. Pavel Giroud works exceedingly hard—a fact acknowledged by virtually all of his friends and associates. His filmography lists an average of five projects per year since he began filming in 1997. The prolific Cuban director considers filmmaking a privilege. "I think all of us who dream of making films should be aware that there's a high probability we won't be able to do it," he says. "It's like playing Russian roulette."

Strategizing to Enter the Industry: *Todo por ella*

In 2002, Giroud created his own production group called Guagua & Co. The name is a play on words: "Guagua" is a distinctively Cuban term for a bus, and "Guaguancó" is a typical Cuban rhythm, a rumba beat. The creation of a "production company" with a catchy name is common among Street Filmmakers. Giroud explains this "game" of making up fictitious companies to denote the "two or three friends who get together to work on a project." The production companies are "fictitious" because they are not recognized legally and have no official status. For Giroud, Guagua & Co. is a "philosophy," a way of saying that "you're capable of telling a story in audiovisual terms."

Guagua & Co. grew out of Giroud's collaboration with Léster Hamlet. The two decided to join together in a creative partnership in which each would pursue his own audiovisual projects but share ideas with and offer support to the other. "Working with friends who are also excellent professionals is a luxury," acknowledges the director. The composition of this production group changes according to the comings and goings of its members. Among the collaborators are Luis Najmías as photographer, Alberto Ciokler and Danielito Díaz in production, and Vivian del Valle and others as direction and production assistants. This group created video clips, short works of fiction, and documentaries. The members of Guagua & Co. pool their talent to support one another and other filmmakers working on their own. Giroud has edited several works, including *Utopía* and *El intruso* (*The Intruder*), both directed by Arturo Infante, and *Cualquier mujer* (*Any Woman*), by Tamara Morales. "I don't consider myself an editor," he confesses, "but I've worked on these projects to help move them forward." This attitude characterizes Cuba's Street Filmmakers. They understand that collaboration is the most effective way to achieve their goals. By combining their talent and resources to support one another, they manage to complete their projects. The lengthy credit sequences of these films, many of which bear the same names, attest to the spirit of solidarity.

Most Street Filmmakers list their artistic production group in the credits of their films. Esteban Insausti acknowledges Sincover (Without Cover) in his work; Juan Carlos Cremata Malberti cites El Ingenio (Sugar Mill, Ingenuity); Eduardo del Llano credits Sex Machine; Ian Padrón offers Achepé (H.P.) and Tostones Pitchors (Fried Plantain Pictures/Pitchers); Ernesto Piña Rodríguez uses Erpirostudios (a combination of the first two letters in his names); Luis Gárciga Romay lists Recursos Propios (Own Resources); Aram Vidal references Kastalia Producciones; Carlos Díaz Lechuga notes Producciones de Carne y Huevos (literally, "productions from meat and eggs," but understood in slang as "flesh and balls"); and Jeffrey Puente García employs Delirio (meaning both "delirium" and "out of ire"). Even though these "companies" are not recognized by Cuban law, they do serve an important function for emerging filmmakers. The naming of entities like these has been essential to the momentum of Street Filmmaking. Through their affiliation with such production "labels," these up-and-coming artists share ideas and resources. The camaraderie and entrepreneurial spirit propels them forward. Perhaps most importantly, to team up with one or more of these groups is to identify with emerging artists in Cuba's audiovisual world. Such an alliance marks an important step in enacting one's identity as a filmmaker.

Whereas all of Giroud's earlier works either had some link to the

ICAIC or were contracted by agencies and individuals, the young director assumed complete responsibility for producing his next film, *Todo por ella* (*Everything for Her*, 2002). The narrative centers on Sergio, an ideal student-turned-misfit. We follow his descent into Havana's murky underground and witness his encounters with drugs, sex, prostitution, and even murder. The film is set in a precise time and place; it is the summer of 2002, and "the city of Havana is not what many people think." This film aims not so much to analyze youth culture and expose social problems in Cuba's capital as to employ a plethora of film techniques—synchronous and asynchronous sound, panning and close-ups, jump cuts and freeze frames, soft focus and filtered images, and so on. Indeed, the mastery of these conventions was precisely the story the director sought to tell.

Giroud explains how this particular short came about: "I had been working for two years without a break, completing projects that I was contracted to do. I had the idea of making a film about an ideal boy who had a dark side, but never managed to develop it because I always had to be doing something else at the same time. I needed to film. I needed to demonstrate that with a few bucks you could make a dignified film. I wanted to get past that point of seeing a low-budget film and saying, 'It's a good idea but if only there had been more resources.'" By this time, Giroud had a project approved by the ICAIC, but there were no resources to make the film. Instead of waiting for the funding to appear, he mobilized his Guagua & Co. team and set out to make a different film without industry support. This pragmatism, rather than a burning artistic desire, engendered *Todo por ella* and propelled Giroud into the industry.

When I interviewed Pavel Giroud, he recounted the genesis of this film. "I'm going to be absolutely frank—I've never told this to anyone. This film was strategic. Strategic. In Cuba's independent cinema, you'd find very good stories, . . . excellent ideas, but too often the results were crushed by poor-quality image and sound. People filmed with a little light bulb, with an analog camera, and then they edited in any way they could. The result is that these poor-quality formal elements lacerated the work. So I got my friends together—there were five of us—and I said, 'We're going to make a film that's very good on a formal level.'" At this time, Giroud didn't yet know what the story line would be. He reviewed some of the projects he had written and took stock of his finances. From the work he had been hired to do "on the street," he had saved up a little money.

Although *Todo por ella* was perhaps "the worst" project among them, in Giroud's estimation, it was the one that could be made with his small budget and a team of five. In explaining the financing of this film, Giroud begins by saying, "You know how budgets work here. One thing is the cash you invest and another is the true cost. I took about $300 dollars out of my pocket, money I had saved up. But if you count the number of people who worked for free and the facilities and services provided at no charge, the actual cost would have been about $3,000 dollars."

Within these tight financial constraints, he was committed to creating a film that not only told a story but did so with top-quality image and sound. The premise of *Todo por ella*, recalled Giroud, "was that it be well-made, that the photography be high quality, that the sound be dignified. (Sound is the element of a low-budget film most often found to be lacking in quality.) And then, that it be a little bit uncomfortable." The director's desire to make an "uncomfortable film" corresponded to a clear objective: He wanted the people in charge of cinema in Cuba to "see that a film made in the streets could be provocative." Thus, he sought from the outset to design a project that would impress upon the ICAIC producers the possibility of making high-quality films with low budgets outside the industry. And he wanted to demonstrate that these films could capture the public's attention. The director confesses that this film does not "move" him, but he acknowledges that it did fulfill his objectives.

Part of the success of *Todo por ella* can be attributed to the tremendous marketing effort on the part of Giroud and company. They made a short trailer and disseminated it widely over e-mail. A poster was designed with the intent of attracting the attention of even more potential viewers. On it, the slogan "an independent Cuban short film" appeared in letters almost as large as the title, just under the words "Havana isn't the city that many imagine it to be." Accompanying this provocative text was the image of a young man behind bars. This publicity campaign "created certain expectations," observes Giroud. He hung the poster in the Cine Chaplin, advertising that *Todo por ella* would be shown during the International Festival of New Latin American Cinema. On the scheduled screening date, viewers packed the theater, and even though another film was programmed along with the short, Giroud recalls people confessing that they came out to see *Todo por ella* because "it seemed out of the ordinary." The film, a hit among Cuban audiences, also had repercussions beyond the island.[9] Edginess appeals in present-day Cuba—and elsewhere. The marketing of this film testifies to the street smarts of these audio-visual artists; Street Filmmakers understand the correlation between careful promotion and the positive reception of their work. What pleases Giroud about *Todo por ella* is not so much the story it tells but where it led him. Thanks to this work, Giroud and two other filmmakers secured a producer for their next projects.

Piloting a New Production Mode: *Tres veces dos*

Pavel Giroud's independently made film showcased the high quality of a work made "on the streets." It also opened the door for what would be the first feature to result from the formal collaboration of the industry and the independents. Upon seeing *Todo por ella*, the ICAIC's vice president for production, Camilo Vives, contacted the entrepreneurial filmmaker. Together they explored the possibility of combining this Street mode using digital technology with support from the industry to make a feature-length film. Giroud insisted that it could be done and offered to prove it. The pressure was on for this director, for if the state-street collaboration did not work out, he and two other emerging filmmakers would suffer the consequences. A failed experiment would limit his opportunities to work in the industry in the future; it would jeopardize the chance for others like himself to try their hand at making a film; and it would squander resources that the industry simply could not spare. Giroud need not have worried, though, for he successfully completed his story. And within a month's time, two other Street Filmmakers were working on segments of their own, all three of which would be combined to create *Tres veces dos* (3 × 2 [*Three Times Two*], 2004).

The island's economic crisis and the industrywide tendency toward coproduction had resulted in a decline in the number of films financed exclusively by the ICAIC in recent years. It was time for the national institute to produce a film on its own. This was feasible, in part, because of the increasing momentum toward digital filmmaking. The relative low cost and ease of use of this technology had already made it a standard in Cuba's foremost audiovisual training programs and among emerging artists. That the ICAIC would be able to see the finished product before investing in the costly transfer to 35 millimeter was an additional advantage. In

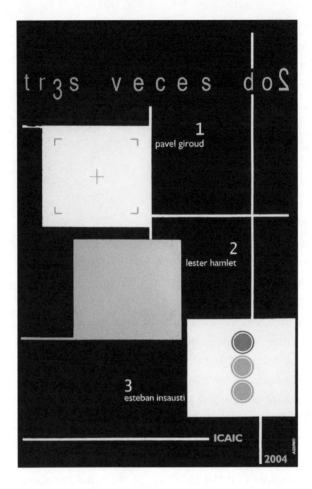

tr3s veces do2

1
pavel giroud

2
lester hamlet

3
esteban insausti

ICAIC

2004

Tres veces dos poster
by Aquino. Courtesy
of the ICAIC.

the past, when filmmakers captured images directly on the expensive celluloid, their backers took a gamble. Resources had to be allocated with no
guarantee of a successful product. In this case, however, the feature could
be made using digital technology and then, if it were deemed worthy of
35 millimeter, the costly transfer could be undertaken.

Industry decision makers recognized the talent of numerous young
audiovisual artists and wanted to support their development. They also
understood the limited exhibition possibilities for short films, which generally compete in only a handful of festivals specifically designated for
this kind of work. Feature films, in contrast, can travel more widely. So the
plan took shape to create a showcase featuring three young filmmakers,
each making a short to be combined into a single feature-length film. A

sum of $30,000 was allocated for the project, to be divided in three ways. The competition was announced.

All three winning filmmakers—Léster Hamlet, Esteban Insausti, and Giroud—had already demonstrated their audiovisual efforts at the Muestra Nacional de Nuevos Realizadores (National Exhibit of New Filmmakers). With input from a seasoned scriptwriter on salary at the ICAIC, Senel Paz, they polished their scripts and prepared to film. ICAIC resources including cameras, editing equipment, and a sound studio were placed at their disposal. All three recall being encouraged to work with a great deal of autonomy; they determined who would comprise their team, where they would shoot, what story they would tell, and how they would go about doing so. When all these shorts were completed, the ICAIC merged *Flash*, *Lila*, and *Luz roja* to create *Tres veces dos*. The ninety-minute film, narrating three distinct love stories in three unique styles, showcased the abilities of this trio of up-and-coming directors.

Although this was not the first time several filmmakers worked on disparate projects that were combined into a feature film,[10] this production mode marked a new direction. For the first time in the history of Cuba's revolutionary cinema, filmmakers trained in film schools and working outside the industry were awarded ICAIC funds to make a film. Esteban Insausti elaborates on the significance of this shift: "In all generations there are opportunists, conformists, fighters, irreverent people, heretics—but my generation is unique in that we've come in off the streets with formal training. We've learned in film schools. We're skilled. We have strong theoretical backgrounds. . . . It is up to us to demonstrate what we're capable of doing."[11] These three filmmakers did not work their way up the ranks within the industry as did their predecessors. Instead, they came in off the street, stepping to the front of the line to make a feature.

Each filmmaker pursued his project independently, but the segments addressed similar themes. The conditions of loneliness, unfulfilled desires, and sadness predominate in *Tres veces dos*, serving to unify the work. Giroud's short leads off the trilogy. *Flash* is the story of a young Havana photographer who is preparing for an important exhibition that has the potential to propel his career forward. As he is taking pictures for the show, he keeps confronting strange apparitions. Viewers learn, at the end of the film, that the ghostly image is a woman who was burned in a department store fire years earlier.[12] Reflections on the act of representing, the power of memory, and the resilience of the past are proffered through an artistic design informed by advertising. Images in *Flash* seem to have originated on the pages of a 1950s fashion magazine, so effective are they at re-creating the atmosphere and aesthetics of a bygone era.[13] The second segment of *Tres veces dos* moves back and forth from pre-revolutionary times to the present. In *Lila*, Léster Hamlet deconstructs the myth of the infallible revolutionary hero through a series of flashbacks. The memories of his protagonist, from whom the short takes its name, introduce viewers to the rather ordinary young man whom she grew to love and her disappointment at his betrayal. In having Lila sing her story, Hamlet employs the musical, a genre heretofore used sparingly by Cuban filmmakers.[14] The third part, to be discussed at length in the next chapter, extends even further beyond the film tradition out of which it grows. *Luz roja* (*Red Light*) conjoins fantasy and reality through montages that merge a series of opposites—inside/outside, light/shadow, vision/blindness, stop/go. In doing so, it blurs the boundary between imagined and lived experiences. What results is an impressionistic film that can be read as an intimate tale about interpersonal relationships as well as an allegory of the challenges facing present-day Cubans.

In showcasing the talent of these three filmmakers, this collective project illuminated the potential of Cuba's emerging generation of Street Filmmakers. The diversity of the segments comprising *Tres veces dos* displeased an occasional critic. Most, however, lauded its stylistic innovation and proclaimed the ICAIC and the island's cinema to be back on track. This film demonstrated that Cuba was engaging with new technologies, for all three sequences were filmed with digital cameras and edited on personal computers. It showed that island cineastes were experimenting with a new style, merging disparate experimental shorts into a feature-length film. And it revealed a commitment to fostering the creativity of emerging artists, despite the fact that they were not on the industry payroll. All of this, it seemed, the ICAIC had accomplished with aplomb.

The film was selected to inaugurate the International Festival of New Latin American Cinema in Havana in December 2004, an honor generally reserved for an outstanding new work by a well-known director. (Alea's *Fresa y chocolate* [*Strawberry and Chocolate*], for example, had opened the festival a few years earlier.) Fernando Pérez introduced the film and the young directors in a subsequent screening at the Cine Chaplin. I recall the enthusiasm of the three filmmakers at appearing in this prestigious venue and sharing the stage with a director as highly regarded and well loved as Pérez. And I remember the seriousness with which Pérez underscored the "independent" genesis of this work, telling the audience—and presumably his colleagues in the ICAIC as well—"we don't need to fear the efforts of these young people who have gotten their start outside the industry." And indeed, *Tres veces dos* would demonstrate that a film made with a low budget by directors working outside the institute need not pose a threat. Such works could, in fact, bring greater glory to Cuba's cinema tradition.

By the time of its Havana premiere, the three-part film had already garnered festival prizes including the Silver Zenith (second place) in the Opera Prima category at Montreal's World Film Festival. With the success of *Tres veces dos*—for the industry, for the Street Filmmakers, and for the island's cinema—everyone expected that similar projects would soon follow. At a cost of $30,000 dollars, *Tres veces dos* is the least expensive feature-length film to have been made in the history of Cuban cinema, and it yielded concrete results. So it appeared likely that subsequent industry endeavors would employ this mode, showcasing more work by new directors. Cuba's Street Filmmakers were energized, believing they, too, might be awarded the resources necessary to try their hand at making a modest film within the industry. As Giroud explained to me, "Havana is full of people working on projects with cameras. I thought several films like *Tres veces dos* would appear because they can be made so economically." Three years would pass before the industry tackled the next such project. In 2007, the ICAIC selected several filmmakers whose work had met with success in the Muestra Nacional de Nuevos Realizadores. Aram Vidal, Alina Rodríguez, Daniel Vera, and Beny Ray were invited to create distinct short films examining literacy in various Latin American countries. These sequences were then compiled into a single feature-length work titled *La dimensión de las palabras* (*Dimensions of the Word*, 2008).

Giroud would like to see the ICAIC produce one film each year along these lines, and he believes they are equipped to do so. The precedent has been set, he observes. A similar process could be employed providing guidance to the filmmakers through each stage, from the conception of the idea through script development, pre-production work, filming, and postproduction. It is the industry's unwillingness to pursue more films

Pavel Giroud accepts a prize at the International Festival of New Latin American Cinema. Courtesy of Adonirán Fuentes.

made this way rather than its inability, Giroud believes. At the same time, he acknowledges that the institution is facing some very real challenges. For one thing, the ICAIC's equipment is outdated and must be upgraded. Giroud contends that they cannot keep making films with programs that are "*crackeados*" ("pirated" or "hacked") and hardware that is obsolete. He finds it "absurd," in fact, that industry filmmakers must work with the same equipment used by some of the media artists working independently in their homes. Another problem that needs addressing is that of artistic property rights. This challenge faces not only filmmakers but all artists who work in Cuba.

Although regulations have been modified to give artists greater control over their production, the water is muddied when works emanate from joint ventures between state entities and individuals. Ariana Hernández-Reguant provides an in-depth analysis of artistic property rights in Cuba during recent years in her essay titled "Copyrighting Che." Her outline of the progression of art from a "communal effort" to "an individual and independent enterprise" and the concomitant clashes certainly resonate for this study. When independent audiovisual artists team up with the industry, both parties seek exclusive ownership. Predictably, tensions and misunderstandings result. I inadvertently contributed to one such clash. While in Havana, I attended a special screening of *Luz roja*, the third short comprising *Tres veces dos*. Esteban Insausti had benefited from the use of editing equipment at the FLC, so when he was asked to present *Luz roja* to a group of U.S. university students the FLC was hosting, he obliged. The screening took place in the ICAIC. Insausti introduced the film and then, together with several members of the production team—among them actress Zulema Clares, actor Alexis Díaz de Villegas, and editor Angélica Salvador—participated in a discussion afterward. The students were thrilled with the sneak preview and enthusiastic about the unique opportunity to meet the artists. So when the subject of the film came up the following day at a meeting in the ICAIC, I congratulated the vice president of production and expressed my appreciation for Insausti's film. Where had I seen it? came the question. How was it possible that this work had been shown independently of the other two segments, and without the authorization or even knowledge of its producer? I had unwittingly fueled the fire of an ongoing polemic. Esteban Insausti and other Street Filmmakers like him perceive themselves as having complete control over the exhibition trajectory of their artistic production. After all, the works emanate from their ideas and creative vision. But ICAIC administrators believe they should be in charge. They have allocated funding for the projects and are responsible for promoting them at local and international festivals, the latter with severe constraints on previous exhibition.

In reflecting on challenges like these, Pavel Giroud observes problems on both sides—within the film institute and "on the streets"—that need attention. Despite his diplomatic stance, he aligns himself squarely with the Street Filmmakers. "I'm not an industry filmmaker," insists Giroud. "I work with the industry, but I continue considering myself a filmmaker on the streets." This self-proclaimed Street Filmmaker would next undertake a very different kind of project, a high-budget 35-milimeter feature to be coproduced by Spain's Mediapro and Cuba's ICAIC.

Tackling an Industry Coproduction: *La edad de la peseta*

It was a script written by someone else that would engender Giroud's first feature-length film. Arturo Infante, a graduate of the EICTV and director of the acclaimed short *Utopía* (2004), prepared the script for *La edad de la peseta* (*The Awkward Age*, 2005). He submitted his text for the script competition at the International Festival of New Latin American Cinema in Havana and came away with the highly coveted first prize. According to the terms of the competition, each of the award-winning scripts is to be made into a film underwritten by the industry of the writer's home country. This award, then, essentially guaranteed the project's production. Cuba bore primary responsibility, and Spain and Venezuela stepped up to participate as coproducers. All that remained was to identify a director for the project.

Infante invited Giroud to read the script, which had by this time been refined in a series of workshops—one offered by Gabriel García Márquez at the EICTV, another hosted by the Sundance Institute, and yet another sponsored by the Fundación Toscano in Mexico. "I always thought that if called to direct a film based on someone else's script," reflects Giroud, "the genre would be a thriller." Instead, it was a coming-of-age story involving a Cuban boy living with his mother and grandmother in 1950s Havana.

Giroud found the project appealing for two reasons. First, it would permit him to try something new. Until this time, his work relied heavily on elements of suspense. His next film was to have been a thriller, and even though he would have manipulated the conventions somewhat, it would have still adhered to that genre. His previous film had also been a thriller: The first sequence of *Tres veces dos*, *Flash*, is characterized by its maker as a thriller, albeit a "mild" one. So the opportunity to tackle something different appealed to him. The element of suspense would be nearly absent from this film. (Before *La edad* was ever completed, Giroud announced, "It's my duty to inform you that my goal with this film isn't to scare people but to make them cry.") Like his Street Filmmaker counterparts, Giroud is eager to experiment and take risks with the medium. "I've always thought that cineastes like Polanski, Wilder, and Coppola will leave this world knowing they were capable of making every kind of film. I'm ready to encounter for the first time children, cats, foreign actors, and full industry support. Rather than scaring me, this gives me the urge to call out, 'lights, camera, action!'"

This project also appealed to him because of the era in which the story takes place. What impressed Giroud most was not the story per se but the potential it afforded to create a particular atmosphere. He recalls being passionate about 1950s styling from the time he studied design. "I wanted

Samuel (Iván Alberto Carreira Lamothe) observes as his grandmother (Mercedes Sampietro) works on her photographs in *La edad de la peseta*. Courtesy of the ICAIC.

to make a film capturing that atmosphere, that tempo—one that would be 1950s through and through." And, indeed, he achieved it. Giroud drew inspiration from period photographs and advertisements, particularly their flat, static quality and "postcard" feel. He chose a pastel palette with shades of pink, aqua, green, and yellow. Whether walls or furnishings, clothing or accessories, each detail contributes to the aesthetic. And he utilized filters to further intensify the colors and soften the silhouettes; a pink tone, for example, distinguishes the darkroom sequences and sets them off from the other interiors in the film. Absent are the intense tropical hues that characterize many recent Cuban films.

The fact that Art Deco architecture and design pervade *La edad* is not surprising, given the film's temporal framework and Havana's preeminence among cosmopolitan centers exhibiting this style. Many of the sequences were filmed in the renowned López Serrano apartment building in the capital's Vedado district, and others feature the recently restored Bacardí building in Old Havana. Recognizable, too, is the distinctive Columbus Cemetery, where massive funereal monuments and wide avenues create a stately outdoor sculpture garden. Although the Havana locale contributes to the film's atmosphere, Giroud insists the story could be set anywhere in the world. In his filmmaking approach, he privileges the text over the context. "What's important is the dramatic conflict and that should be universal," he insists. "The local should serve as a backdrop.

What's bad is when the local becomes transformed into the essence of the dramatic conflict. And that's what bothers critics about Cuban cinema—when the spectator lacks the information necessary to follow the narrative and gets tangled up in symbols and *criollo* codes." Here Giroud is referring to films from the late 1980s and 1990s that seemed stuck in a rut. A series of feature films develop along similar story lines, reproduce Cuban street speech, and employ almost interchangeable stock characters—the curvaceous *mulata*, the adventure-seeking foreigner, and the fast-talking *jinetero*. The formula became so entrenched that one Spanish producer purportedly announced his refusal to read even one more script with a voluptuous *mulata* who dabbled in prostitution, so overused was the convention.

Giroud understands the need to select carefully the locally coded ingredients that will create an internationally palatable product. In avoiding the mistakes of some of his industry counterparts, he typifies the successful film authors that have emerged in Latin America in recent years. Marvin D'Lugo sums up their contributions: "Struggling to survive creatively, compelled by circumstance to serve as mediators between the business and art of Latin American film, they find themselves forced to negotiate their own political and artistic visions in accordance with the commercial demands of global film finance arrangements."[15] Giroud and other Street Filmmakers like him are managing to succeed at this momentous task. And most often, they welcome the challenge. In reflecting on the success of his film, Giroud emphasized that for a coproduction to succeed, the story must take precedence over the locale. That said, the artist acquiesced that Havana did indeed made a great "sauce" to flavor his film.

Giroud invested a great deal of time in preparing to make *La edad de la peseta*. When the start date for shooting was delayed nearly a year, he used the extra months to refine each sequence. The filmmaker's creative process is very systematic. In conceptualizing a film, he often seeks an image or object that "synthesizes" the story he wants to tell. For this project, he came up with a photo that his grandfather had taken; it depicts his father's worn-out boots from when he was about five years old. Giroud shared this image with Infante, who was inspired to change the script and add sequences in response to the poignant image. Giroud generally draws the frames, one by one, and memorizes each of them. The story board serves as his map, guiding him as the film moves forward; only rarely does he deviate from the drawings.

This careful planning with La edad comes through in the final product. The photography is indeed noteworthy; Luis Najmías achieves a sense of stasis through the camera's constant motion. In one sequence, Alicia, the daughter and mother in the film, is fitting shoes on a male client. The camera captures her from above; the viewer's gaze parallels that of Ramón, her boss and suitor who watches over the scene from the mezzanine. A relentless roving camera effectively evokes Ramon's panic as he sees his beloved brushing her hand across the foot of a dashing young man. Giroud also worked extensively with the actors—Mercedes Sampietro as the grandmother, Susana Tejera as Samuel's mother,[16] and Iván Alberto Carreira Lamothe as the young Samuel. Lacking experience in directing a young actor, Giroud pressured himself to get it right. He invested countless hours in working with the young boy to communicate his expectations and desired outcomes. This project provided Giroud with the support of a larger team and the luxury of greater resources. He did not have to spread himself as thinly as he had previously, nor did he have to make do with so little. Giroud enjoyed the benefits afforded by his first industry production.

This film marked a turning point for Pavel Giroud. People commented that La edad seemed unlike his earlier films. To that he would respond, "Well, let's hope that every film I make is that different from the others." In a sense, the coming of age of young Samuel in the film parallels Giroud's own development, for the process of making this film was new to him. The thirty-something director is exceedingly pleased to have had this experience. In his words, "What started out as a film-for-hire has turned out to be the love of my life as a creator."

He has also developed a greater respect for filmmakers. In an essay published in Cine Cubano shortly after the film's release, Giroud confesses his awareness of filmmaking as risky business. La edad de la peseta "has enabled me to grow and it increased my respect for every director who manages just to finish a film. It's an exhausting process where you constantly straddle the border between good and bad. Any false step can destroy the film, so you have to give yourself over completely to it and concentrate fully. I've recently come to understand why great masters have flawed works. You can only grasp this once you've experienced the crazy adventure of making a movie."[17] Viewers share Giroud's fondness for this film. Audiences as well as festival juries have responded favorably to *La edad*. Shortly after its completion, the film came away with prizes from both the International Festival of New Latin American Cinema in Havana and the Cartagena Festival in Colombia. As it began its sojourn on the circuit of international festivals, it appeared that this director's first feature would launch him into the film world beyond Cuba. Less than a year later, in June 2007, Giroud commented to Pedro de la Hoz, "I never thought my first feature film would travel around so much. Really," he continued with his customary modesty, "my hope was that people would say, 'Caramba, this guy isn't so bad. He deserves to continue telling his stories on the screen.'"[18]

Extracting the Formula for Success: Partnerships and Persistence

The opportunity to make a large-budget film during tight economic times, when even wizened industry filmmakers continue to wait their turn, might breed jealously among Giroud's counterparts. And the fact that his uncle, Iván Giroud, directs the International Festival of New Latin American Cinema, an event that has yielded some of the young Giroud's awards, might provoke critical comments. But Cuba's Street Filmmakers are, by and large, proud of their friend and colleague and impressed by his accomplishments. They consistently commend "Pavel" for his hard work and perseverance and hold him up as proof of what can happen when filmmakers working on the streets join forces with the industry.

Even before finishing *La edad de la peseta* in 2005, Giroud had lined up his next project. This genre film titled *Omertá* (*Code of Silence*) centers around a bodyguard to one of Havana's most famous gangsters in the 1950s who, forty years after his career heroics, has another chance to be the tough guy he once was. The plot advances with three men and a woman locked inside a house that is surrounded by the police. Giroud classifies this work as a dramatic comedy, a thriller in the style of the Coen brothers, combining theatrical with cinematic elements. The script won the prize for best unfilmed script at the 2005 International Festival of New Latin American Cinema. This award compelled and in fact obligated the ICAIC to earmark resources for the film. A Spanish coproducer has stepped in, thereby offering a further guarantee that the film will be made. "It's a coproduction," notes Giroud, "but it's my story and my film. That someone showed up willing to gamble on it is great, but it's the script I wrote and the film I'm going to make." Giroud emphasizes once again that undertaking a coproduction in no way implies giving up control of the project.

To understand this filmmaker's repeated defense of coproduction as a viable mode, one need only consider historical antecedents in Cuba, and in the region. Coproductions made with Cuban directors in the 1980s and 1990s often resulted from scripts that seemed contrived, designed as they were to integrate at least one non-Cuban actor with the goal of reaching a wider market. Box office disasters ensued, as did accusations of directors and producers "selling out," relinquishing creative control in order to garner funding. Worse yet, some of the early coproductions—not so much in Cuba but elsewhere in Latin America where the nascent industries had less experience upon which to draw—proved disastrous for the host country.

Coproduction does run certain risks. It has, at times, been deemed the destroyer of local cinema. The argument against coproduction goes like this: Intervention from outside the country waters down, taints, homogenizes, and leaves films devoid of "authentic" or "local" qualities; economic imbalances are reproduced in that the rich get richer off the labor and talent of the poorer counterpart; eventually, the fledgling home industry can be eroded. And, in fact, these dangers are very real. The case of the film *El dorado* remains, even a decade after I initially wrote about it, one of the more compelling examples of what can go wrong.[19] Well-known Spanish filmmaker Carlos Saura was preparing to make a film about 1492, the encounter of the Old and New Worlds. He negotiated a coproduction agreement with Costa Rica that should have been of mutual benefit. This was not the result, however, for events surrounding the making of that film actually parallel the conquest depicted in it. When the filming was completed in the Caribbean coast of this Central American country, the Spanish team cleared out. What they left behind were months of unpaid hotel bills, scores of uncompensated actors and technicians, and a local film institute lacking even a copy of the film. Most egregious of all, the Spaniards purportedly made off with a gold crucifix lent to them by a local church in the country's impoverished Limón province. This experience demonstrates that coproduction can indeed make the rich richer and the poor poorer.

But, as the case of Cuba proves, it can also be a lifeline. Given the island's ongoing economic crisis, state funding alone would not have permitted the creation of films. Outside investment has been essential for Cuban cineastes to make films and witness their circulation beyond the island. One of Cuba's preeminent directors, Humberto Solás, elaborates on the necessity of transnational collaboration for the island's industry: "There is no longer an economic base for film production.... For established filmmakers there is not a single cent for production. We are obliged to seek co-productions. If a film project is not co-produced, it will not be made. Cuban filmmaking could very well disappear if not for co-productions. So, if I, Humberto Solás, want to make a film, it must be co-produced, and if I don't secure sponsors outside of Cuba, I will be unable to make the film."[20] Without foreign capital and coproduction agreements, Cuban filmmaking would have slowed dramatically and likely come to a standstill.

Longtime cinematographer Raul Pérez Ureta reiterates the importance of coproduction in his country. Filmmaking is a very resource-intensive enterprise, he reminds us. So as Cuba's economic crisis worsened, particularly during the Special Period, a new approach was needed. Filmmakers and industry professionals sought to reduce costs without sacrificing the quality and essence of Cuba's cinema. And one strategy was to turn to coproduction. This mode ensured the continuation of Cuba's cinema despite the dramatic decrease in resources available through the ICAIC. Pérez Ureta finds it remarkable that, given the circumstances, Cuban films have continued to be made. Perhaps they are not created exactly as he and his colleagues would like, but at least they continue to be made. "I believe that as films continue becoming more costly, not only in Cuba but around the world, especially in poor countries, if we don't want to close our industries, we have to cooperate, to join together and combine resources to film."[21] Pérez Ureta contends that this transnational mode is here to stay.

How has this move away from exclusively Cuba-produced films toward coproduction affected the filmmakers and the industry? Perspectives vary. Solás contends that "foreign investors in co-productions want to

Ana Victoria "Bebé" Pérez contemplates the future in *La vida es silbar*, a coproduction directed by Fernando Pérez and filmed by Raúl Pérez Ureta. Courtesy of Fernando Pérez.

either impose their conception of our reality or promote themes and narratives that are openly critical of Cuba." He goes on to say that "with a few notable exceptions, it is very difficult to find a producer who wants to invest in a film about the Cuban reality and not tell the director what point of view to take." For Solás, this predicament leaves Cuban filmmakers "on very difficult terrain."[22] Yet, he acknowledges his good fortune in having made, by the time of this interview, two coproductions that entailed no compromises whatsoever.

Pérez Ureta advises that care be taken with these cooperative ventures. He believes that Cuba's film institute has proceeded thoughtfully, seeking coproduction projects that take aesthetics into account and respect the island's film tradition. In his words, "I think that looking for coproducers that pay attention to these needs has been a very intelligent move on the part of ICAIC, that is to say, that [coproducers] don't come to make cheap commercial cinema but rather that they respect and support the cultural character of our cinema . . . that it be not only an economic enterprise but also a cultural one. And for those of us who make films, it's important that this balance has been achieved."[23]

The reflections of another established industry filmmaker, Fernando Pérez, shed further light on the practical implications of coproduction. In response to my question about the challenges of this transnational mode, Pérez replied,

> Initially I was very biased against coproductions, but with Wanda Visión and José María Morales I have found a coproducer interested in much more than business. He is a creative coproducer who wants to make a different kind of cinema. And as far as I know, my colleagues haven't felt pressured by other coproducers. I feel that Juan Carlos Tabío, Daniel Díaz Torres, Orlando Rojas and other filmmakers have made the type of films they've wanted to make. Some of them have aimed to address the masses using comedy, a tradition in Cuban cinema and Cuban culture in general. Naturally the works have been of varying quality, but I don't feel that a certain cinema has been imposed upon them.[24]

Humberto Solás, Raúl Pérez Ureta, Fernando Pérez, Pavel Giroud, and most other Cuban cineastes working today consider coproduction to be indispensable for making films—that is, in the absence of a blank check or bottomless savings account.

Giroud insists that the art and business of filmmaking need not be contradictory. There are rules and requirements to which the director must adhere. But they are not necessarily incompatible with one's creative goals. "What's important about coproduction," he explains, "is that you get the resources you need to develop your project. But if the requirements are such that they would diminish the quality of your work, then you would have to abandon that producer. You can always negotiate, though; as you sail along, you guide the boat where you want it to go."

So while coproduction does require a filmmaker to comply with certain norms, Giroud does not see this as necessarily restrictive. With *La edad de la peseta*, for example, the director was under no pressure to reserve one of the principal slots for a Spanish actor. "I could have given a role to any Spanish character appearing on screen two or three times," he explains. Yet, he had intended from the outset for Violeta to be "the typical *Gallega* grandmother," and he was pleased at the opportunity to cast Mercedes Sampietro in that role. Having envisioned this character as Spanish all along, he was thrilled when the accomplished Spanish actress signed on to the project. With his foray into coproduction, Giroud purports to having enjoyed absolute liberty in terms of both content and form. He acknowledges, of course, that every member of the team—from scriptwriter and photographer to editor and producer—made suggestions along the way. But for him, this input was not limiting in the least; on the contrary, it constituted part of the "logical creative process" for the "collective art" of cinema.

The practice of coproduction is expanding the range of films made by Cuban directors. Giroud is encouraged that the industry is sponsoring a genre film. His interest in genre films has been a liability of sorts, for these kinds of formulaic works have been made infrequently in Cuba. Of the seven proposals Giroud submitted to the ICAIC over the years—all of them for genre films—none was selected. He recalls getting positive feedback on one of the projects, but it was ultimately rejected because of his inexperience as a director and its high production cost. *Omertá*, in fact, was initially turned down by the ICAIC selection committee. But believing in the project, Giroud put it in front of other producers. He submitted it for the Havana festival script competition and came away with the prize. In 2007, this Street Filmmaker began filming what would be his second feature film and second coproduction. Giroud considers himself lucky to have won the script competition and fortunate to be working more or less full time on film projects. But it is not luck alone that has propelled him forward. This director attributes the award and his coproduction agreements to lots of labor and persistence; this entry marked the tenth consecutive year he had prepared something for this competition. So while it never hurts to "be in the right place at the right time," Giroud believes that "luck comes your way if you've worked to attract it." He sums up, saying, "I've worked hard. I've worked like a crazy man—without sleeping much—for years and years."

Pavel Giroud deems it a privilege to work as a filmmaker and feels fortunate to be making a living doing what he enjoys. Despite the opportunities he has had, he does not consider himself that different from other Street Filmmakers. "I'll tell you one thing," he confided to me, "if it weren't for *La edad de la peseta* and *Omertá*, I'd be in the same boat with everyone else. Maybe I would have made something independently that turned out even better than this other work," he muses. "You never know. But what I do know is that I wasn't going to stand around waiting. I've always said that if the industry doesn't give me the opportunity, I'll look for it myself." Like virtually all Street Filmmakers, Giroud is eager to film and far too impatient to stand in line waiting his turn.

Another film project Giroud dreams of undertaking is *Emporio Habana* (*Havana Emporium*). The script he wrote for this film, like the case of *Omertá*, was a finalist in the script competition at the International Festival in Havana. And like *Omertá*, it is set in the gangster world. Giroud confesses to finding the topic of the Mafia to be seductive. This love story between Lucky Luciano and a glamorous woman takes place in the historic Hotel Nacional; Meyer Lansky is another prominent figure in the tale. Because of the project's estimated cost, and because of the additional complication in needing to cast English-speaking actors, plans for making the film are on hold. Conditions in Cuba's industry at the moment are not right for undertaking this project, Giroud explains. The ICAIC may be unable or unwilling to support this project at the moment. But given its crossover appeal—with its familiar genre conventions, English language dialogue, and transnational plot—it may well attract the attention of an international producer.

Pavel Giroud believes in magic, particularly the kind one brings about. "You have to make magic all the time," he remarks. "Sometimes it's possible to work magic with few resources; other times it's not. But I believe a filmmaker is like a magician. He must seduce the public, leaving viewers in a limbo of sorts, so they don't escape your tricks and later they applaud you." Giroud is full of plans and has lots of ideas for future projects. "Those I can get moving with support from the industry will follow that path," he notes. "The others I'll make happen through sweat—or magic. Not a single one will be tucked away in a drawer."

From the trajectory of the filmmaker examined in this chapter, it is apparent that the body of films considered under the rubric of "Cuban cinema" is changing. Given the economic situation in present-day Cuba, it is understandable that material conditions of production differ from those of past times. Collaborative financing has become the norm now that the ICAIC can no longer bankroll films on its own. The stories being told on film have also changed as up-and-coming filmmakers employ popular forms and tackle genre films with greater frequency. Viewers at home on the island, in the countries backing the film, and elsewhere welcome this new brand of cinema. Given that Cuban currency no longer finances films made on the island, and that elements from multiple contexts make their way into the film texts and their trajectories, Ana M. López is accurate in saying that we can no longer "conceive of the force field of 'Cuban cinema' as delimited by the frontiers of the nation."[25] Both "Cuba" and "cinema" are decidedly unbounded.

My subject will always be humans and
the mystery implicit in existing.
—Esteban Insausti

6 Filming in the Margins

ESTEBAN INSAUSTI EXPLORES
LIFE AND ART AMIDST CHAOS

In the summer of 2006, a Florida television program aired a short film made in Cuba. Miami viewers tuned in, as did the scores of Havana residents with access to one of the many unauthorized satellite dishes. This transnational audience heard the commentator frame the film *Existen* (*They Exist*, 2005) as counterrevolutionary and its maker as anti-Castrista. Having seen the experimental short only a few months earlier in Havana and having known the filmmaker, Esteban Insausti, for several years by this time, I was intrigued by this assessment.

Existen premiered in December 2005 at the FLC, a nongovernmental organization located in Havana. And, as already mentioned in Chapter 1, viewers applauded the work. The audience commended the innovative

filming and editing techniques, the respect accorded to the filmed subjects, and the homage it paid to Cuba's avant-garde cinema tradition.
How can we explain the incongruent perspectives, the divergent readings of this film by Miami and Havana audiences? Films, like virtually all
works of expressive culture, lend themselves to interpretation. And the
position from which we view—the place where we stand—shapes and
influences our vision. In other words, precise circumstances contribute to
determining our particular ways of seeing. And the image of the island
has, to a great extent, corresponded to the geopolitical location of the
viewer over the past half-century. Residents of Cuba and of south Florida
"see" the island in vastly different ways. They have, in fact, built a wall
between their divergent perspectives—loving Fidel or hating Castro, supporting the liberating Revolution or opposing the oppressive dictatorship,
condemning the blockade or defending the trade embargo, and so on. In
actual fact, many individuals in both sites occupy a far more nuanced
position. But that fact has not eroded the barriers, symbolic as well as
tangible. So it should come as no surprise that the film meant something
different on opposite shores of the Straits of Florida. The fact that this
work could be co-opted by Miami Cubans for its purportedly anti-Castro
stance and simultaneously embraced by Cubans on the island for its revolutionary form and content demonstrates the skill of Street Filmmakers
at eliding dichotomies. Insausti and his counterparts situate their films
not in a bounded national frame but, rather, in a broad field of cultural
meaning where many discourses intersect. Insausti's twenty-five-minute
experimental film refuses to take sides; it resists dichotomies and rejects
absolutes. In conjoining as it does past and present, aesthetics and politics, here and elsewhere, and "us" and "them," *Existen* yields a poignant
reflection on the complex times in which we live.

  This chapter will examine the work of Esteban Insausti, a Street Filmmaker who strives to craft a unique film language appropriate for his
explorations of the human condition. Drawing on video art, advertising, and avant-garde cinema, the young auteur creates complex works
capable of producing multiple meanings. Unlike the avant-garde revolutionary filmmakers from whom he draws inspiration, Insausti uses digital technology. He works sometimes with and sometimes without industry infrastructure. From this in-between position where many of Cuba's

Street Filmmakers find themselves, this director probes the meaning of life and role of art in our chaotic world, experiments with the audiovisual medium, and calls into question extant histories and truth claims.

Exploring Craziness in Havana — and in the World: *Existen*

In *Existen*, Esteban Insausti takes to the streets of Havana and focuses on people suffering from some degree of dementia. The filmmaker locates these individuals in an urban setting, within the context of their everyday lives, and permits them to speak. Framed in extreme close-ups, they share their unique visions on the present state of Cuba and the world. By casting those who "exist" as active agents in narrating their stories, Insausti embraces their idiosyncrasies and diverse experiences. *Existen* portrays its protagonists with dignity and respect.

Compiling the stories of Havana residents considered crazy by some was no easy task. The filmmaker pedaled around the Cuban capital on a bicycle with a borrowed camera, seeking informants whose perspectives could be integrated into this film. Most days, serendipity rather than scheduling determined where and when and with whom interviews took place. Informants were not "called" to a filming location, then, but instead were identified as Insausti made his way through the city. When he came upon someone who appeared interesting for the project, he would get off his bicycle and begin a conversation. These exchanges often led to the filming of an interview. This spontaneity allows the voice and vision of the subjects to dominate the narrative of *Existen*; Insausti permits his informants to occupy the foreground.

In amassing interview footage, the filmmaker recalls an unexpected pattern emerging. He explains:

> The greatest surprise I've had with this material is the coherence of these people who appear to be — or in most cases are — sick. Behind all these chaotic responses and strange logic there's always coherence. Deep down there's something surprising, a perspective that can be more lucid than many of the options that aren't official, that aren't orthodox in the etymological sense of the word. Among these "*locos*" I've found incredible people — a physics professor, an ex-fighter pilot, a twenty-six-year-old crack addict. You see it all. And behind all these

Existen poster by Samuel Riera. Courtesy of the artist.

threads that create the web of craziness, there's coherence. That's what surprised me most.

Upon observing the coherence in the positions and perspectives of these individuals deemed "crazy," Insausti felt compelled to reformulate the project. He grew increasingly aware of the need to treat the topic and his subjects with respect. It was critical, he determined, to avoid making a film that could be interpreted as poking fun at these people or provoking laughs at their expense. Indeed, as Insausti was developing the project, he referred to it in shorthand as "Los locos." Eventually, the title became "Existen," a masterful change that resulted in embracing rather than distancing the subjects. Whereas "Los locos" would have ascribed them a fixed identity, "Existen" leaves space for their actions. Rather than telling us what or who they *are* and thereby containing them in a precise definition, then, this film gives them voice to tell us what they *do*. The approach of this auteur echoes the formulation of Ella Shohat and Robert Stam in *Unthinking Eurocentrism*; he is "less interested in identity as something one 'has,' than in identification as something one 'does.'"[1] Instead of branding these individuals as victims, dismissing them as strange, or treating them as objects of ridicule, the film accords them agency. These protagonists play an active role in articulating their impressions and experiences.

Existen produces information overload through a barrage of details, a collage of confusion. In a brilliantly edited rapid-fire montage, newsreel clips bombard us with facts and figures. Pig-breeding is on the rise; "by the end of next year there will be 300,000 sows." There are twenty stockyards in a citrus-producing area where "the young bulls come in weighing around 120 kilograms and in less than a year they reach 400 kilograms. There are already 20,000 head of cattle and the number is expected to reach 30,000 in the 36 fattening centers." An old crane factory has been transformed into a producer of farm implements; "the result of a single day of production in this agricultural equipment factory is 30 plows." And "despite all the work done, there are still 1,150,000 metric tons of sugar cane to be cut on the whole island in the final stage." These statistics hark back to the early years of the Revolution and the documentaries recording that time, when increasing production was touted as the route to greater autonomy. These opening sequences seem to suggest the film will adopt a critical stance opposed to revolutionary ideology. But almost immediately, it becomes clear that *Existen* refuses to take sides.

Insausti's film elides easy dichotomies and never aligns itself with or against the Revolution.[2] For Insausti, like others of his generation, notions of nation and revolution and utopia have become empty signifiers through oversaturation. Intent on exposing contradictions, deconstructing myths, and resisting dogmatism, Insausti takes in his surroundings with an ironic gaze. To identify as Cuban or to adopt affiliation with any national tradition, for that matter, is exceedingly complex. So, too, are the problems plaguing the island—and our world. For one informant, "to be Cuban is completely the back part of what is the fourth third ninth of the ideological causes that have to do with the procession of the third part of the intensification of nature." This convoluted statement captures the elusiveness of identity. How exactly do we construct our sense of home and community? How do we imagine our relationships to one another, to nation-states, and to the greater globe? The concept of Cuban identity is complicated further by the incorporation of "Manolito's" perspective. He notes that some Cubans are well-mannered, and others are not. "There are those who work and those who don't want to work, and those who are lazier than the workers." And then "there are Cubans who are anti-Cuban," those "who don't belong to the Mafia, but they say bad things about Cuba." "That's not right," he interjects; "they are anti-Cuban, like the CIA Mafia and they are counterrevolutionary. They are not showing any love for Cuba." Manolito adds that this is "punished, definitely punished." His reflections suggest a spectrum of Cubans' identification with Revolutionary ideology. At one extreme are those who say "bad things" about the country; at the other are those so intolerant of hearing "bad things" they advocate punishing the perpetrators. Multiple voices, rather than a single one, articulate the evolving conceptions of Cuban identity.

This protagonist shares his feelings in an apostrophe to Cuba's commander in chief: "Sometimes one . . . fails, once, not all the time, but don't do it again. I love you very much and the Cuban people too . . . and all of Cuba and the Third World. I love you very much Fidel, I appreciate, I esteem you, I appreciate you and love you, always, as if you were my father, because I love you more than just a friend, like a father. That's all." Even this emphatic statement, proffered as it is by one of Havana's more notable "crazies," remains ambiguous. *Existen* defies containment within a singular ideological position or geopolitical locale. The craziness treated is not unique to Cuba. Even though the subjects speak with an unmistakable Cuban dialect, their articulations suggest that craziness is a phenomenon growing out of and connected to issues affecting people the world over.

The discourse indeed evokes Cuba's Revolutionary rhetoric, but it also calls to mind global news broadcasts and the capitalist forces promoting consumption. Cuba has 375,000 shops, reports one protagonist. But in order for the island to become a "total capital," it needs about 490,000 more shopping centers. And it needs to join its land with that of some other country—who knows which one—but a large area, like Japan or North America. *Existen* demonstrates the toll taken by the barrage of information assaulting us. It affects our thought processes and shapes our perspectives. The juxtapositions in quick succession produce a sensation of disorder, chaos, and frenzy, connecting the overload of information with the condition of confusion. Interspersed among these statistics are allusions to the increase in psychoses; the incidence of schizophrenia rose by 45 percent between 1985 and 2000, and between 20 and 30 percent of the world's population suffers from some sort of mental illness during their lifetime. The result, evoking the rapid montage style of video clips, provides a glimpse into the protagonists' thought processes and mental states. It also compels viewers to acknowledge the chaos of our contemporary world, the irrationality of war, the incomprehensibility of decisions made by political leaders, the violence emanating from dehumanization, and so on. The interweaving of facts and statistics and impressions reminds us that we all experience moments of emotional confusion and vulnerability, that to some extent we all live on the edge. In *Existen*, Esteban Insausti contextualizes craziness as part of our twenty-first-century lives.

The boundary between "them" and "us," between the "crazies" and the "sane ones," becomes increasingly blurred. In one sequence, a forty-something male stands in Central Park surrounded by a group of *habaneros* and tourists. His monologue culminates in his reciting—backwards—of the alphabet. "Z, Y, X, W, V, U, T . . . ," he rattles off, and then he asks onlookers and film viewers, "Can you do that?" We can't. Perhaps we've never even thought to try. But he can. And he does. Those gathered around him stand mesmerized and amused. Insausti's camera captures all of this, rolling until the man, upon arriving at "A," holds his hand out for a few coins. The film never distances the filmed subjects from others in their midst or from off-screen viewers. We are all implicated in the craziness. This work transforms emotional instability from a personal phenomenon into a collective condition; craziness affects many people in diverse places for a variety of reasons. The object of inquiry isn't "the crazies," then, but, rather, their encounter with a world that is incomprehensible—to them and, increasingly, to all of us.

Existen does not proffer answers so much as it provokes questions: To what extent are we all affected by "*la locura*," or craziness? Might craziness be the most logical reaction to the illogical world we inhabit? What would be appropriate responses to such heinous acts as the 11 March bombings in Madrid and those of 11 September in New York? To the U.S. unprovoked military intervention in Iraq and the Bay of Pigs invasion? To the torture and disappearance of thousands of Argentines and Chileans in the 1970s and 1980s? To the intentional bombing of the Cuban passenger plane that killed seventy-three people? *Existen* implores us to ask the question, To what extent can any of us live in today's world—amidst escalating violence, environmental degradation, and rampant poverty—without going insane? The film, like the title, provokes a constant questioning and insists that spectators locate themselves vis-à-vis the subjects, the issues they address, and the world they portray. *Existen* avoids delineating those deemed crazy from those considered sane; it jettisons dichotomies and didacticism. Insausti is not interested in producing a "pamphlet."[3] "I'm looking for answers in the craziness," he explains, "and I'm finding them every day in this city that is as crazy as these people are. ... That's what this film is about." The weaving together of these people's experiences and impressions provokes a solemn reflection.

Insausti's film took three years to complete, and in the time that transpired from beginning to end, film technology changed dramatically. The filmmaker began with a Hi8 format, which more or less ceased to exist by the time he finished the project. As a result, much of the early material could not be used; partway through the project, he had to start filming all over again. Eventually, he combined sequences filmed on mini-DV, Hi8, and Betacam with material filmed on 35 millimeter from ICAIC archives. For this director, however, the greatest challenge is not the rapidly changing technology but, rather, "filming in disastrous conditions without support."[4] Even this obstacle he does not find to be insurmountable: "I make most of my films this way." And indeed, each of the works preceding *Existen* emanated from the director's passion to explore the mystery of human existence, irrespective of the challenging conditions. Like other Street Filmmakers, Insausti is willing to forge his products out of the materials and equipment at hand.[5]

Making Films in Cuba—and Making Do

By the time Insausti tackled *Existen*, he had already completed several films working both with the industry and on his own. Like most of Cuba's Street Filmmakers, Esteban Insausti pursued a formal training program in film. He earned his degree in film, radio, and television direction in 2000, just before his thirtieth birthday.[6] Insausti's films reveal traces of his varied academic and professional trajectory. In addition to training as a film director, he pursued advanced studies in music history and performance. Insausti worked as a scriptwriter for Cuban television from 1991 to 1997 and served as a media consultant with Cinema Satélite in Mexico. He has directed spots, commercials, and trailers and has been engaged as a producer and art director of music events. The aesthetics of these varied forms is evident in his work, as is his voracious appetite for culture.

The mediaphile watches classic films, popular soap operas, video clips, international experimental works, Hollywood genre films, and almost everything he comes across. This mélange provides fodder for the films he makes and the unique audiovisual language he creates. Part of this technical mastery results from the director's concerted efforts—what Insausti terms his "obsession"—to develop an aesthetic framework appropriate for each film: "It's the obsession with saying something in the most authentic way possible. This artistic preoccupation is always with me—how to say something in a way that's different and yet artistically rigorous. I don't believe in pamphlets . . . nor am I an educator. I'm a communicator and so my films all reveal the same obsession—my obsession with saying something through art in a way that's different but that people understand." Insausti consistently strives to forge a film language appropriate for reflecting on the human condition and the role of the artist in that endeavor. His films explore not only stories, then, but the act of storytelling as well. They reveal his quest for crafting an artistic form appropriate for his existential ruminations.

All of Insausti's films explore the mystery of life, and all do so by employing cinematic techniques in innovative ways. *Las manos y el ángel* (*The Hands and the Angel*, 2002) treats the now-deceased jazz musician Emiliano Salvador. In portraying the life and work of this outstanding artist, Insausti communicates through jazz-inflected representational techniques. Jazz piano and voice-over commentary accompany a variety of diverse images—close-ups of fingers running over piano keys, footage from concerts, still photos of the musician's childhood, and talking heads. Interspersed throughout are graphic designs and fragments of text. Words and phrases move across the screen; sometimes bits of the narrative are shared by the interviewees, and other times by quotes from music magazines such as *Rolling Stone* and *Billboard*. In a stunning sequence introduced simply as "*el solo*," a frenetic jazz improvisation propels a rapid montage depicting Havana's harried streets. The urban atmosphere envelops viewers who are at once caught up in the hustle and bustle and mesmerized by the jazz-inspired technique. The polyrhythm of the jazz score—that is, the simultaneous sounding of two or more independent rhythms—parallels the textured cityscape created by overlaying a series of images. Insausti succeeds in creating a unique language for this work honoring Emiliano Salvador, one appropriating the very musical form the film addresses. Rather than merely recycling the language employed by other filmmakers, Insausti experiments here to create a form well suited to the content. He succeeds with *Las manos* in honoring this world-acclaimed artist who was not appreciated fully during his short life. Insausti's innovative approach pays tribute to one of the island's underrepresented composers and performers by inserting him into Cuba's music history.[7]

Sometimes the resultant techniques are serendipitous; they emanate from the need to *resolver*—to "get by" or "make do." The framing in *Las manos y el ángel* serves as an example. At times the jazz musician or the talking heads take up the entire frame, but just as often they appear in a reduced frame within the film frame. Insausti explained how his reliance on archival footage influenced the project. While he would have welcomed the opportunity to interview the jazz musician and incorporate that material into this project, Emiliano had died years earlier. Insausti did film interviews with several people close to the musician—including Emiliano's daughter, Angélica Salvador, who is also the director's *compañera* and professional collaborator—but for the most part, he mined archives for footage and still images. Some material did turn up, but many of the available images were in poor condition. The recovered footage and photos could not be included in screen-size dimensions, for their reproduction at this scale would have diminished the quality to such an extent as to have obliterated the image. An added complication was that the filming had taken place at different times during a lengthy period, and in varying formats, with whatever camera Insausti could borrow. The frame-within-a-frame technique emerged as a strategy for salvaging and reproducing some of the damaged archival material and integrating the footage filmed in various formats. "What's important is what you have to say, not the format you use in filming," insists Insausti. If format alone mattered, this director believes he would be the "champion." Referring to *Las manos*, he remarked, "I think I'm the only filmmaker who has made a documentary using six different formats." Insausti's films, like those of his Street Filmmaking cohorts, exhibit traces of the context in which they are made. Precise circumstances on the island—local conditions—converge with global forces to yield products forged out of a specific moment.

By the time Insausti completed *Las manos y el ángel*, he had made significant progress developing his next project, a short work of fiction to be produced with industry support. As outlined in the preceding chapter, the ICAIC sought proposals for three short films to be made by the island's emerging filmmakers. The plan was to combine these into a single feature. Insausti's *Luz roja* (*Red Light*, 2003) was among the winning scripts; it would, upon completion, come to constitute the third segment of *Tres veces dos* (*Three Times Two*). *Luz roja* presents a psychiatrist and a radio announcer whose professions have positioned them as conduits for all kinds of emotions and experiences. In counseling and advising sessions, whether offered in person or over the radio, these two protagonists encounter problems similar to their own—a pervasive loneliness and an inability to establish meaningful relationships. They meet on the street by chance during a drenching downpour. A traffic light is stuck on red. He is seated inside a car; she stands outside under an umbrella. From his position in the driver's seat, he rolls down the window and invites her to

Image from *Luz roja*, directed by Esteban Insausti. Courtesy of Insausti.

get into the car. She hesitates and then quickly moves toward the vehicle as the rain pounds down. Once seated side by side, each fantasizes—first caressing the other, then kissing, and then making love. These erotic sequences of shared pleasure are intercut with the street scene. In the same way that the car is impeded from going forward because of the broken semaphore, so their desire for love and intimacy is impeded by their inability to communicate and connect. The artistic design intensifies the protagonists' loneliness and alienation; gray tones produce a cold, metallic, inhospitable atmosphere.

"Red light" connotes the semaphore stopping traffic and alludes to the protagonists' inability to move forward together in a relationship. It also permits a reading of life in present-day Cuba. On a metaphorical level, "red light" conjures an urban district where prostitution, gambling, drug dealing, and other underground activities take place, and it also evokes stasis. It is this state in which many Cubans find themselves. They are stalled out. Like the couple in the car at the red light, they have come to a stop. And like the protagonists, they are unable to develop relationships that might move them forward. With their windows fogged and vision occluded, they are blinded to the future. They wait. And hope. And fantasize. That the film opens and closes with an image of the male protagonist masturbating—a pleasurable yet ultimately unproductive act—further underscores the pervasive alienation and isolation. It is a condition lived by these two protagonists and by present-day Cubans who share their plight. The film was made in Cuba, and its outdoor scenes depict Havana's streets; but the allegory extends to individuals the world over who find themselves alone and alienated.

Insausti made this film with backing from the industry, but he had to devise ingenious solutions to keep costs down. The production budget of $10,000 was exceedingly small for the type of film Insausti had envisioned, so he sought to minimize expenditures wherever he could. The director employed a small team of inexperienced actors who were more interested in the opportunity than in earning top wages. Both Zulema Clares and Alexis Díaz de Villegas made their film debuts in *Luz roja*, contributing extraordinary performances. And Insausti limited severely the number of *llamadas*, or "call days," when the team was expected to show up for work. All the filming was done in the short span of six days; this meant they worked more or less around the clock. Insausti recalls the difficulty of filming the sequences that take place during the downpour. It was summer in Havana, the driest time of year. So he and the photographer, Alejandro Pérez, prepared to create the effects for a handful of takes outdoors and the remainder in a studio.

The outdoor sequence, in particular, required careful planning and innovation. It also posed some risks. The low-budget production could not afford the time it would take to secure official permission. So, proceeding without papers, Insausti and team arranged to create a rainstorm on Galiano, one of Havana's busiest streets. A fake traffic light was installed, and water hoses were connected to spigots on the rooftops of buildings lining the streets. Officers in the area had agreed to cooperate, rerouting traffic as necessary. When everything was ready, four cars belonging to members of the production crew moved crossways into the avenue, blocking any other vehicles from entering. As horns blared from frustrated drivers, the unauthorized filming commenced; water sprayed down from the buildings, and the camera rolled. Some passersby, caught unawares in the drenching "storm," shouted curses at the production crew. The uniformed police did what they could to divert more cars from entering while the team worked quickly. As soon as the crew had the nec-

Photographer Alejandro Pérez and director Esteban Insausti (right) consult with each other while filming *Luz roja*. Courtesy of Pérez.

Esteban Insausti (left) and Alejandro Pérez filming a street scene for *Luz roja*. Courtesy of Pérez.

essary takes, the water ceased to rain down and the automobile barricade dispersed.

The remainder of this sequence was filmed in a studio. How did they create the effect of pouring rain at minimal cost? Once again, the solution required ingenuity. Barrels punched full of holes were placed on top of the car. Water channeled into the large drums flowed out through the holes and covered the vehicle, thereby simulating a downpour. One car door was removed to allow Pérez to film the couple from that side and capture the conversation taking place inside. That door was then replaced, and the other was removed. All the while, Insausti and other members of the crew ran around the car to simulate the passing of pedestrians on the street.

During this portion of the project, the *Red Light* team worked double shifts, and then some. After all that time laboring in sopping clothes under the staged downpour, it is not surprising that the performance of Zulema Clares—her weariness as she enters the car, the trembling of her fingers as she folds up her cane, the chattering of her teeth between words—is convincing. She produces an extraordinary rendition of the young blind woman whose voice soothes the listeners tuning in to her radio program. The experience was an exceedingly positive one for this actress. Despite the intensive and laborious job of acting in the low-budget *Luz roja*, Clares would like to work on another project with Insausti. During the Havana Film Festival of New York in 2006, after a screening of Insausti's latest film, *Existen*, she shared with me her aspiration to team up with this director in the future. It was the role of Ana in Insausti's project devoted to Ana Mendieta that most interested her at that point. Despite her temporary location in New York, where she was attempting to make inroads as an actress, she sought to keep the door open to return to Cuba. Just two years after I spoke with Clares in New York, she was back in Havana working with Insausti. Clares was cast in the lead female role in *Larga distancia* (*Long Distance*, 2009). So while collaborating on *Luz roja* had indeed been challenging, Clares deemed the experience worth repeating.

Insausti recalls the experience of working on this film as both exhilarating and exhausting. On the sixth and final day, after more than twenty hours of filming, he asked the photographer how a particular take had come out. There was no response. Alejandro Pérez had fallen asleep while filming. "I had to look down at the camera to check," admits the photographer. In reflecting on the conditions under which the team worked, Insausti shakes his head from side to side. "We did seventy takes in one day. In terms of training, I suppose that's fine. But not every film can be made that way. It hurts the work immensely. And it takes its toll on the director and on everyone else. You start to feel drained." Despite the tight budget and challenging conditions, the director is pleased with the outcome. *Red Light* permitted him to work closely with artists he deems to be among Cuba's finest. It consolidated his position among the new generation of Street Filmmakers. And it demonstrated the potential afforded by digital technology.

His short as well as the other two comprising *Tres veces dos* proves, for Insausti, that the use of digital technology need not limit a director's artistic potential. He explains: "It's a cliché to assume that digital technology presupposes a documentary-style film language—a 'dirty' camera, illumination that lacks subtlety, an emphasis on the actors. . . . For me, these features don't necessarily emanate from digital technology; they have more to do with Neorealism." Insausti and his team developed the film keeping in mind the story rather than the format they were using. In other words, it is the quality and character of a film and not the technology used that determine the outcome for Insausti. He believes it's all too common to "divorce" film and video, aligning certain characteristics with each. This need not be the case; Insausti cites *Suite Habana* as a film that is "so powerful and done in such a cinematic way" despite having been filmed with a digital video camera. Yet, the director is quick to add that filming in digital is not and should not be the only way to go. He notes that digital technology "is considered to be the future, the hope," and he sees it as a valid option for making films. Still, the formats should coexist, he contends. "Who among us doesn't dream of holding an Arriflex [a camera favored among industry directors around the world]?" he asks. "It's a dream so far-fetched that I don't worry about filming on celluloid. But when the day comes, I'll do what it takes to adapt my project to that format." Once again, Insausti eschews dichotomies. It is not a matter of choosing one format over another; instead, he advocates relying on and even combining a variety of options.

Tres veces dos alluded to the potential of Cuba's emerging generation and showcased the talent of these Street Filmmakers. "No one can say that there's a lack of faith in us," affirmed Insausti, referring to Pavel

Giroud, Léster Hamlet, and himself, the creators of this three-part film. "We entered the industry generating revenue, so if we're talking in terms of capital and concrete results, this film made by the three of us proves it." As noted in the previous chapter, *Tres veces dos* left Cuba's Street Filmmakers energized, believing that they, too, might team up with the industry to make a modest film. Still, they did not remain idle while awaiting the green light. Instead, they continued to forge ahead with their work.

This director stands with one foot in the state industry and the other outside: He is not on the ICAIC payroll, but he does collaborate closely with his counterparts in the organization; the film institute produced one of his films and purchased the rights to distribute another, but he has made the majority without their support. He has developed numerous alliances. On the island, he feels at home with the ICAIC, the FLC, the UNEAC, and the ISA; he is a member of Spain's SGAE. In addition, he collaborates with individuals and organizations in Mexico, teamed up with my Cuban Cinema Classics initiative in the United States, and joined me in Canada at a session and screening I organized as part of a Latin American Studies Association annual meeting. Connected to a variety of organizations on and beyond the island, Insausti activates contacts and taps resources essential for making his films. The entrepreneurial director seeks opportunities wherever he can, whether by submitting his films to festivals; soliciting grants (from the Sundance Institute, Cinergia, and other organizations); or spreading the word about his creative aspirations.

Esteban Insausti demonstrates that making films outside the industry in Cuba is not synonymous with working against it. The inside-versus-outside paradigm is much too simplistic. His reflections reveal that there is a great deal of synergy between the ICAIC and Street Filmmakers: "The difference between previous generations of Cuban filmmakers and my generation is that we're not going to wait. We've decided to make films without the national film institute, and we're doing it. . . . When I entered ICAIC, it was like getting into Metro Goldwyn Mayer; it was the ultimate aspiration for every filmmaker. I tell you that today my ultimate aspiration is to make my films. It's not about belonging to an institution. Not any more." Working within the industry is no longer the "end-all" for young filmmakers. Fortunately, they need not choose whether to craft their films inside or outside the state-sponsored institute. In a marked move from past times, the ICAIC has developed new ways to support and promote island filmmaking. State actors and Cuban entrepreneurs are working together. The trajectory of Esteban Insausti illuminates this space where many of Cuba's Street Filmmakers find themselves.

Continuing Cuba's Revolutionary Film Tradition—from the Streets

All of Insausti's work pays homage to Cuba's revolutionary film tradition and continues the original mission of the ICAIC, that of forging a new film language appropriate for the ever-changing nation. Although this film-maker works "in the streets," for the most part, he consistently expresses his debt to the revolutionary filmmakers whose tradition he inherited. Insausti describes himself as an "eternal apprentice" to Cuban cinema. Among the cineastes he most admires, those who have pushed the limits in depicting the island's changing reality, are Sara Gómez, Santiago Álvarez, Jorge Luis Sánchez, and Juan Carlos Cremata Malberti. Insausti credits Tomás Gutiérrez Alea, in particular, with inspiring his own artistic vision. "Titón [Alea] is someone I discover every day, every single day of my life," he explains. "Not a month goes by when I don't take another look at a sequence of *Memorias del subdesarrollo* [*Memories of Underdevelopment*, 1968]. That film is always teaching me something new." It is Fernando Pérez, however, who most impresses this "apprentice" of his island's film tradition: "I consider Fernando Pérez the most important cinema *auteur* alive in this country. And I would say that more than a filmmaker, he's an auteur. He's a man with a very particular sensibility, of pain reflected in his work through the medium of art. It's not just harshness for the sake of it; Fernando is someone who has known how to combine feelings with artistic rigor. For me, he's like a demigod." And indeed, there are some nods to Pérez in *Existen*: the predominance of exterior shots of urban street life, the treatment of the capital's disenfranchised sectors, and the personalizing of the protagonists by naming them and stating the causes of their precarious emotional states. Insausti, like Pérez, perceives the labor of a filmmaker as one of process. It is a constant quest to experiment with the film medium so as to tell a story in the most powerful way possible.

The work of yet another ICAIC director served as a source of inspiration for *Existen*; Nicolasito Guillén Landrián is the Cuban auteur to whom the work is dedicated. "When I watch his films, I still cannot conceive how, in his era, he managed to develop a language, a form that didn't contradict his message," notes Insausti. "What generally happens [with films like these] is that there's an elitism which results in incommunication and a distancing from the people. But in the case of Nicolasito, with rudimentary tools—a Moviola and a little bit of film—he turns a political pamphlet into a work of art." During his brief career at the ICAIC, spanning the decade from 1962 to 1972, Guillén Landrián made several documentaries. Among these are *El Morro* (1963), *En un barrio viejo* (1963), *Ociel del Toa* (1965), *Coffea arábiga* (1968), *Taller de Línea y 18* (1971) and *Nosotros en el Cuyaguateje* (1972). While the often-cited *Coffea arábiga* is indeed impressive, with its rapid montage and the textured effect produced from scratchings on the celluloid, I also find compelling *Ociel del Toa* and *En un barrio viejo*. The former, already mentioned in Chapter 2, portrays the daily life—arduous and monotonous—in rural Cuba during the early years of the Revolution. The latter, also filmed in black and white, captures poignantly the deterioration of Old Havana and the destitution of its inhabitants. In long, languid takes, the camera lingers on a small boy only partially covered by tattered clothing. The viewer watches him gaze, motionless, at the camera. No commentary is provided—and none is needed—to communicate the plight of this child and others like him for whom the Revolution was fought and won. Life on the fringe is made all the more compelling due to the artistic rendering.

In an era when official discourse emphasized the Revolution's progress, this filmmaker highlighted social ills and shortcomings. Predictably, this approach generated discord between the filmmaker and the state. It culminated, in the early 1970s, in Guillén Landrián's expulsion from the ICAIC. Feeling confined and unable to express his creative vision, the filmmaker emigrated in 1989. Guillén Landrián lived in Miami until his death in 2003. After leaving Cuba, he never made another film.[8] Insausti emulates the Cuban filmmakers he most admires, all of whom can be considered auteurs. What these filmmakers have in common is the attention they pay to the margins of society, their commitment to probing existential questions, and their penchant for experimentation. These same concerns inform Insausti's creative output.

While Esteban Insausti admires his nation's moving picture tradition, he expresses disappointment with the national film institute. Recent experiences have left him disillusioned. After devoting half a decade to

Angélica Salvador and Esteban Insausti in Havana. Photo by the author.

preparing the material for *Las manos y el ángel*, he presented the preliminary project to the institute, saying, "Look, I have this and need only three days' worth of AVID post-production from you and then I'll give you the documentary." The director's request was considered, but his proposal didn't pass the selection committee; they turned down the project. He went on to complete the documentary with support from the SGAE, initially arranging to pay the ICAIC to use their equipment. Later in the process, the ICAIC permitted him to use their facilities free of charge. Insausti expresses gratitude to ICAIC president Omar González for making the decision. "It was incongruent to be charging for work on a documentary about Emiliano [Salvador], to be charging someone like me who was affiliated with the ICAIC and who had gotten this far on the project working on my own."

Insausti and his partner Angélica Salvador devised an effective exhibition strategy. They arranged to premiere the work as part of a larger music event honoring Emiliano Salvador. The screening and concert in the Sala Covarubias in the Teatro Nacional was a hit. At that point, the ICAIC approached the director with a contract offering to buy the distribution rights for Cuba. Insausti set a precedent; by signing on the dotted line, he became the first Cuban filmmaker to have made a film on his own and then received a stipend from the ICAIC in exchange for the rights to island distribution. The arrangement suited the young director, who was eager for his documentary to circulate widely. When a high-ranking administrator from the national film institute later expressed disbelief at having turned down this project and asked how it was possible that the ICAIC had failed to produce *Las manos*, Insausti replied with candor, "It's because of your myopia." He then added, "I don't want to know what you're producing. I'd like to know what you've got tucked away in a drawer."

Whereas finances are always a factor in considering the number and kinds of films that can be produced through the ICAIC, *Las manos* would not have cost anything. How, then, can we explain its rejection? Might the subject of Emiliano Salvador have been deemed too hot to handle?[9] Or had the music genre run its course, with several dozen documentaries already devoted to singers and musicians? Both of these scenarios seem unlikely. After all, the music of this jazz artist is now widely available in Cuba and even comprises part of the curriculum in the country's most prestigious art schools. Regarding the music documentary genre, Cubans are credited with having invented the music video (with Santiago Álvarez's *NOW!*) and, with their impressive oeuvre, having set the standards for this filmmaking form.[10] If the rejection cannot be attributed to ideological difference or budgetary constraints, how can we account for it? Insausti remains perplexed. "I can't explain why no one in this country was interested in having a film made about Emiliano Salvador," he notes. "I can't understand how erratic a commission can be. And the fact that it wasn't going to cost anything—that's the craziest part. Then once it's made, they're interested and want to buy it." For Insausti, "this proves that commissions make mistakes." He insists that "these errors translate into lost opportunities." *Las manos* went on to earn numerous national and international prizes, garnering twenty-nine awards in a single year. "You don't work for prizes," asserts the filmmaker, "but I've asked myself, 'Can so many people be wrong?'"

Insausti identifies shortcomings within the state-sponsored institute and advocates an overhaul. A key problem is that the ICAIC has not moved quickly enough to integrate younger filmmakers. The institute could be doing more to support the up-and-coming audiovisual artists. Over the past decade, young directors have made relatively few films within the industry. "The years go by and we continue working on our own," explains Insausti. "The industry has to sharpen its edge, refine its approach. Decisions are made far too erratically." It is hard for Insausti to understand how the industry could "lose" an artist like Juan Carlos Cremata Malberti, for example, leaving him to make his film on his own. Or how a filmmaker as talented as Jorge Luis Sánchez had to wait ten years to make his first feature, a treatment of Benny Moré nonetheless, one of Cuba's preeminent musicians. Insausti insists that the process for selecting projects be improved. Only when decision making becomes more democratic will funds be invested in the nation's top talent. And only then will the overall quality of Cuban films increase. Furthermore, he believes that coproduction should matter less in selecting potential projects; ICAIC financing should not be allocated according to whether someone has outside funding or not. To require as a condition the garnering of outside funding is to give short shrift to local talent and ideas, according to Insausti. Channeling scarce resources into a project because some producer is interested will not necessarily help Cuba advance in the film world. Summing up his impressions of the ICAIC, Insausti states, "A lot of things have to change there. A lot of minds have to change. The real world moves at another speed and ICAIC has fallen behind, way behind."

Despite his conviction that the ICAIC needs to be overhauled, Insausti never advocates driving a wedge between those working within and those working outside Cuba's film industry, or between present-day endeavors and earlier efforts. On the contrary, he maintains that collaboration among filmmakers across generations is essential. And he hopes to continue working with the industry as well as on his own. So while acknowledging the difficulties of making films in Cuba and the shortcomings of this state-sponsored entity, he insists that filmmakers working in the industry and those working "on the streets" focus on their common mission and their shared heritage. "You have to really want to make films to do so under current conditions. This is living *for* cinema, not living *from* cinema. . . . I think we have to interact [with previous generations of filmmakers] because without a doubt, it's *our* cinema, the cinema of this country; it's not some other cinema in Bangladesh or New York. It's Cuban cinema. We share the same history." It will require the effort of all of Cuba's filmmakers—regardless of whether or not they are on the

ICAIC payroll—to continue moving the island's filmmaking enterprise onto firmer footing.

And Insausti is doing his part. He is a staunch advocate of his nation's cinema, participating fully in island and international activities showcasing Cuban films. During the annual International Festival of New Latin American Cinema, Insausti attends screenings, debates, press conferences, and a variety of events. During the National Exhibit of New Filmmakers, he supports the efforts of the organizers, offers thoughtful critiques to participants, shares contacts and information on opportunities, and has served as a member of the jury. The director frequently takes the initiative in creating opportunities to disseminate his films and those of his compatriots. In December 2006, Insausti helped bring to Mexican audiences some of Cuba's most celebrated films from the past forty years. The Primera Muestra de Cine Alternativo de México (First Exhibit of Alternative Cinema in Mexico), held in San Francisco de Campeche, programmed a long list of internationally acclaimed experimental films from Cuba: Santiago Álvarez's powerful exposé of racism in the United States (*NOW!*, 1965); Nicolasito Guillén Landrián's experimental record of coffee production in Cuba (*Coffea arábiga*, 1968); Sara Gómez's poignant examination of gender, race, and representation in the Revolution (*De cierta manera*, 1972); and Juan Carlos Cremata Malberti's award-winning short (*Oscuros rinocerantes enjaulados [muy a la moda]*, 1990), among a host of others. The four-day event attracted filmmakers, students, and aficionados. It enjoyed top billing, running as it did as part of the celebration of the tenth anniversary of Campeche's Cultural Institute, a celebration underwritten by such high-profile sponsors as Delta Airlines and Corona Beer. Esteban Insausti curated the film program and, with his Mexican collaborator and friend Carlos Sánchez Gamboa, masterminded the event. The two have plans to transform this into an annual festival in Mexico and to expand it to other locations across the country. As a participant in the Muestra in Campeche, I was struck by Insausti's commitment to circulating Cuba's cinema. It was not merely the opportunity to showcase his own work that appealed, but the possibility of sharing his island's rich cinematic tradition. Insausti, like other Street Filmmakers, participates in promoting his films and assumes responsibility for disseminating Cuba's cinema. And regardless of where he assumes this role, he speaks knowledgeably and passionately about his country's film tradition, never

Balkanizing the artistic endeavors of his colleagues according to whether they work inside or outside the industry.

Dreaming to the Very End: A Passion for Making Films in Cuba

There is no shortage of projects on Insausti's to-be-filmed list. One of his works in progress, which he has been developing for more than a decade, is devoted to Ana Mendieta, a Cuban American artist whose enigmatic death remains mysterious. And then there is a drama about Charlie Parker, Emiliano Salvador, and Jaco Pastorius, three musicians whose lives Insausti considers to be "as complex as jazz itself."

Insausti experiences difficulties—as a Street Filmmaker working without institutional backing, as an ICAIC affiliate having to adapt to the institute's idiosyncrasies, and as a Havana resident during trying times. A major challenge for Cuba's Street Filmmakers is finding ways to circulate their films. Successful distribution requires contacts and capital, two elements in short supply for island directors—and for independent filmmakers around the world. Insausti finds it hard to establish alliances with would-be producers and distributors. He and his *compañera* and professional collaborator, Angélica, have been waiting several years for a telephone to be installed in their one-bedroom apartment. In the meantime, they make do by routing calls to the home of a family member and then checking in there to retrieve messages. They do have e-mail accounts, but the lack of a phone line at home limits their ability to access electronic messages. Communicating with local and international film colleagues is difficult, to say the least.

Despite these challenges, this director is adamant about staying put. In Havana, he works long days on projects that matter to him. In the evening, he works out at a nearby gym, listens to music from his extensive CD collection, and relaxes with Angélica. He has a network of friends, among them Juan Carlos Cremata Malberti, Léster Hamlet, Alejandro Pérez, and Jorge Luis Sánchez. He attends concerts, art exhibits, film screenings, and an array of cultural events. On Sundays, he gathers with his family to enjoy a meal over leisurely conversation. And he has opportunities to travel frequently, participating in international film festivals. Immersed in his local context, Insausti is committed to making films in his home country. I recall his frustration when, one evening at an event hosted by

Esteban Insausti and Angélica Salvador at home reviewing their archive of filmed material (2008). Photo by the author.

the FLC, a foreign invitee asked him why he stayed in Cuba. "I'm Cuban," he mentioned to me later with exasperation. "Where would I go? What would I do? This is my country and this is my reality." Insausti confided his impatience with the assumption—all too common among visitors to the island, especially those from the United States—that all or even most Cubans want to leave the island.

This connection to his reality and his fervent desire to continue making films in his own way compelled Insausti to decline an invitation to work in the United States. In 2005, a producer from Los Angeles proposed that the talented young Cuban cineaste come to Hollywood to direct a series of horror films. Insausti reflects on declining the offer: "It was a decision that I made without having to do much thinking. I simply don't have what it takes to do that. Sometimes you say, 'Well, maybe by making those films I can accomplish what I want to.' But I need time to think, to develop my films. Right now I'm not focused on budgets or specific markets. . . . I'm thinking about the films I want to make. Besides, I have to be coherent with my context. Away from here, I don't think I could say the same thing." This artist's seriousness of purpose and clarity of vision compelled him to stay on track. Rather than deviating from the course he had charted, he would continue making the films he envisions on his own terms.

Esteban Insausti seems aware of the adage that all that glitters is not gold. This is evidenced by his comments:

> Generally, when those kinds of producers approach you, they're not interested in your artistic ideas or your film language. They're interested in having you produce a film in a certain amount of time. And being Latino—Cuban, and young besides—means they're interested in paying much less than the going rate. That doesn't interest me. I'd have to leave behind everything I've struggled for in my life. It would be like betraying myself. It goes beyond ideology and all that. It has to do with coherence in my life; developing a body of filmed work is my obsession. Doing it the way I dream of doing it. It's not that you say "Hollywood . . . no." In fact, lots of people, myself included, dream of someday making a film there. Why not? It's part of your career as an artist. But that's one thing, and another is becoming a mercenary—and that's what it would be, working for money. That's not what motivates me in life. I prefer to dedicate myself to developing a concept, refining my ideas, writing my own scripts, and looking for financing instead of letting myself be pulled every which way by a world I don't even know. The only place these kinds of siren songs take you is to money. And money's not my main objective right now. That's the truth.

For Insausti, at home in Cuba is where he is able to dream. "Dreaming is the force that motivates me every day, the source of my energy. My dreams are my life and, well, struggling to achieve them. I don't think I'll die dream-less. I'm going to be dreaming up to the very end—dreaming about doing something, no matter what. That's what's important." Smiling, he confesses, "My spirit is sort of feisty."

Roughly two years after turning down the offer to work in Hollywood, early in 2007, Insausti was ready to begin his first feature. *Larga distancia* takes on the theme of emigration. Rather than dealing with the experiences of the person who leaves Cuba and then returns to visit—as have films such as *Miel para Oshún* (*Honey for Oshún*, Humberto Solás) and *Rey y reina* (*King and Queen*, Julio García Espinosa, 1994)—Insausti's film addresses what happens to those who stay. *Larga distancia* explores what it is like to confront the pervasive loss of friends and family members who have moved away from the island.

The first step in the prefilming process would be to scout locations. On that day, producer Luis Lago carried an official letter from the national film institute sanctioning the project; this would help open doors. Procuring the letter had not been easy. He and Insausti had visited the ICAIC numerous times, met with several individuals, and completed stacks of forms. And despite having gotten the go-ahead, obstacles still abounded. For the scouting trip, the challenge had been procuring the necessary gasoline. Among the information required by the ICAIC in order to provide a gas card were the numbers of the drivers' *carnets*, or identification cards, the numbers of their licenses, the autos' registration numbers, the numbers of the cars' engines, and the numbers of the cars' chassis. These details and corresponding documentation had been submitted, as had a list of the potential locations to be visited. It seemed, though, that gas was in short supply. Lago had gone to the institute several days in a row, each time leaving with nothing more than words of encouragement to try again the following day. Meanwhile, precious time was being lost, and frustration was mounting. So, after several unproductive attempts at procuring the necessary fuel, a member of the film team stepped in. Photographer Alejandro Pérez proposed that he fill the tank using his own funds, money he had earned from filming a video clip. If the gas card ever materialized, he would welcome a refill. And if it did not, at least *Larga distancia* would be *encaminado*, on its way.

Insausti invited me to join him and members of his team in scouting locations. So on a sunny day early in March 2007, eight of us set out in two cars. We spent the entire day traversing Havana. Our list of destinations included a museum that might serve as the interior of one home, a nightclub under consideration for a discotheque sequence, and a former yacht club that could be transformed into a hospital. The ICAIC letter of support permitted us access to some—but not all—of the places we wished to visit. At times we were welcomed and were allowed to film as much and for as long as we wished; at other times we were turned away. In one instance, the person designated to meet with us had not come to work; in another, we had arrived too early—the building was not scheduled to open for another half-hour. One memorable stop on our route was the

ICAIC production studio in Cubanacán, an expansive enclave with storage for furniture, costumes, and props as well as lights, cameras, and equipment. An enormous shed on the property, large enough to accommodate several sets at one time, contains a sizable pool that, when the metal covers are removed, holds several boats.

Two impressions of that day predominate. First, I was struck by the sense of camaraderie among the group—including director, photographer, producer, and artistic designer.[11] Sometimes all would agree immediately that a space was ideal for the film. At other times, however, opinions would vary. In these cases, a discussion would ensue with hands gesturing and voices raised. Before the argument would get too heated, though, one member of the group would call a truce saying, "Let's think it over. We've got footage of the space and we'll line that up against other options and then see." They operated as a team, more intent on advancing the collective project than on forwarding individual agendas. The other impression that remains with me is just how much fun they had working together. Like high school students on a field trip, they teased and cajoled and pulled pranks on one another. Having struggled for so long to get to this stage, they were elated to be moving their project forward.

This turned out to be a decisive day for *Larga distancia*. During our visit to the ICAIC studios, Luis Lago received a call on his cell phone. He did not talk long, for the massive structure interfered with the signal and the connection faded. But later that day, we learned that a foreign producer had decided to invest in *Larga distancia*. The very individual who had invited Insausti to work in Hollywood two years earlier was now expressing interest in coproducing the film. This support from beyond the island, coupled with that of Cuba's film institute, would permit Insausti to make his next film. It appeared that the locations we had identified that day would indeed make their way onto the screen.

JUMP CUT

Cuban cinema has earned the respect of
the population because we have spoken
with sincerity about our reality.
—Humberto Solás

7 Making Space for New Interventions

A MONTAGE FROM THE NATIONAL
EXHIBIT OF NEW FILMMAKERS

"You have arrived in the capital that belongs to all Cubans."
An image of a billboard displaying these words opens *Bus-cándote Havana* (*Searching for You, Havana*, 2006), a poi-gnant documentary juxtaposing hope with harsh reality. In
this work Alina Rodríguez Abreu zooms in on Cuban campesinos who
make their way to Havana. She investigates the challenges faced by these
internal migrants seeking nothing more than a job and a dwelling in order
to improve their lot in life. They recount the difficulties of being "undocu-mented" within their own country. Their lack of a legal address in the capi-tal impedes them from procuring employment, and the resultant poverty
leaves them without food to feed their families. Their desperation is com-pounded by the discrimination they experience. This testimony is inter-spersed with images of their homes and environs. As "María" tells about

fashioning her dwelling, the camera guides us through the swimming pool in which she lives; as "Fidel" introduces his family of four crowded into a tiny room, we learn the baby is named "Elián" to honor the Cuban boy held in Miami against the will of his father—and the entire island. With respect and rigor, the twenty-something Street Filmmaker probes the precarious spaces occupied by these transplanted islanders.

Given the difficulty of their situation, these Cubans might express bitterness. They might take a stance critical of the Revolution, their comrades, or their leader. Indeed, they do express frustration over the hardships endured and injustices experienced, and yet they never relinquish their dream of becoming "at home" in Cuba. What these disenfranchised islanders seek above all is to locate themselves. Rather than shunning or abandoning their nation, they are seeking to make sense of its transformation. Their physical journey across the island, then, parallels their desire to move from confusion to clarity and to create a community capable of accommodating them and others on the margins.

This portrait of islanders living on edge and seeking to be "at home" in Havana serves as a metaphor—both for the island nation in transition and for a new generation of audiovisual artists. As we have seen thus far in *On Location*, Cuba's Street Filmmakers are also seeking to place themselves. As they document their rapidly changing reality and explore what it means to be "Cuban" in the twenty-first century, they struggle to locate themselves vis-á-vis Cuba's film tradition, the shifting role of the state, *and* larger culture markets.

More pragmatic than idealistic, Street Filmmakers are indeed invested in the here and now. Gustavo Arcos—critic, professor, and avid supporter of young artists—challenges those who criticize this generation for being self-absorbed, immersed in their own environs, and invested in their own preoccupations. How can we expect these young people to be committed to Revolutionary paradigms, he asks, when all the sacrifices made by their parents have only left this "future generation" worse off than the preceding one? And how can we expect their adherence to Revolutionary dogma when they have grown up in a world where practically all the myths have been shattered—"heroes have been taken down from their pedestals, systems have failed—and . . . everything that was is no longer?"[1] For Arcos and others, the unique circumstances during which this generation came of age go a long way toward explaining their personal concerns and artistic approaches. This is not, however, to suggest they are disengaged from their local context. On the contrary, Street Filmmakers express disillusionment with their milieu but go on to envision alternatives and strive to bring them into being.

Audiovisual artists on the island today recognize the potential of their work to effect change. Like Cuba's revolutionary filmmakers of the 1960s, 1970s, and 1980s, these young cineastes acknowledge the link between representation and transformation. The camera is indeed a tool and can be used to challenge, provoke, and construct. Although the concept of the Cuban nation has evolved a great deal over the past half-century, island filmmakers regard their changing circumstances with an attitude similar to that of their predecessors. The reflections of José Massip, written in 1968, still resonate today. For this founding ICAIC filmmaker, revolutionary cinema was "inconceivable" without constant "searching" and "experimentation." New cineastes had to venture into the unknown, hurl themselves into the void, and expose themselves to failure "like the guerrilla who takes the path made by the strokes of his own machete."[2] Street Filmmakers working today find themselves engaged in a similar quest. More and more films are being created by increasing numbers of young audiovisual artists. And as they strive to represent in new ways, they are depicting their environs with greater diversity. Their cameras frequently focus on the here and now, and their viewfinders seek glimpses of the island's disenfranchised. With an eye toward redressing social ills and injustices, they employ the medium to reveal that not all have benefited equally from the Revolutionary project. They are not afraid to speak out. As Danae C. Diéguez observed, "These kids know how to tell it like it is."[3] By focusing on the margins, illuminating issues and individuals previously ignored by state institutions, they are broadening the scope of public discourse.

The activist stance of these culture workers has positioned them to engage in polemics and intervene in politics. This chapter revolves around the Muestra Nacional de Nuevos Realizadores (National Exhibit of New Filmmakers), a state-supported event designed to showcase the work of young filmmakers. This venue is undoubtedly important for the role it plays in promoting recent audiovisual material. More significant, how-

ever, is the space it provides for state actors to come together with artists working on their own; the ensuing dialogue and negotiation engages
them in reshaping the state's hegemonic project. Guided more by individual motivation than by some industry agenda or political manifesto,
Street Filmmakers are agents of change in present-day Cuba.

Creating a Forum for New Filmmakers: The ICAIC Establishes the Muestra

The Muestra Nacional de Nuevos Realizadores was established in 2000.
What began as a modest series of screenings has grown into a multiday workshop designed to serve the country's audiovisual artists under
age thirty-five. The Muestra invites young filmmakers to come together
and exchange ideas, establish contacts, screen contemporary and classic
works, and engage with their industry counterparts. Although emerging filmmakers are at the center of the Muestra, their more experienced
counterparts also participate. Special sessions like master classes, carried
out by renowned professionals—whether directors, scriptwriters, editors, or actors—provide opportunities for cross-generational interaction.
"I tried to design the Muestra so that the influences would move back and
forth," explains Jorge Luis Sánchez, a founder of the event who has also
served as its president. "That's what makes it dynamic: I receive from you
and you receive from me."[4] With its workshops, retrospectives, and competition, the exhibit has become a must for up-and-coming filmmakers
in Cuba. Most of Cuba's emerging audiovisual artists get their start here.
Attracting scores of young creators from across the island, the Muestra
Nacional de Nuevos Realizadores has come to define "who's who" among
Cuba's new media-makers.

The event is designed to promote the work of emerging cineastes on
the island. Virtually all of these young people—whether they are making
documentaries, animated shorts, music videos, promotional spots, or
feature films—undertake their creative projects with the explicit goal of
communicating with a wide audience. They intend for their film to be
seen by others. This is no easy task for emerging filmmakers anywhere;
film dissemination is decidedly complex the world over. To circulate a
film requires developing marketing strategies, making contacts, prepar-

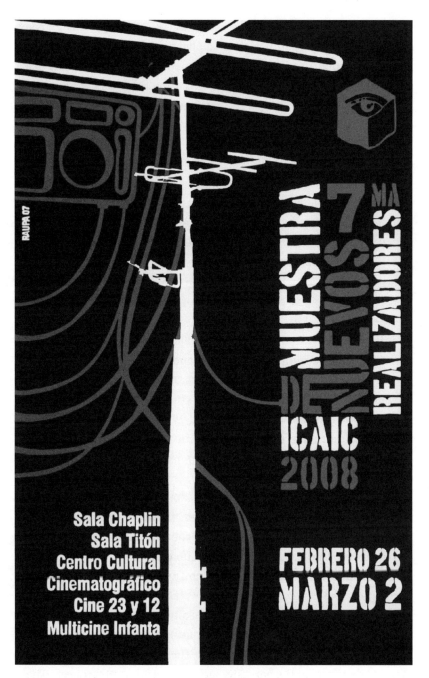

Publicity poster from the Muestra Nacional de Nuevos Realizadores.
Courtesy of the ICAIC.

ing publicity materials, adding subtitles, securing permissions for copyrighted material, preparing festival applications, attracting the attention of critics, negotiating distribution agreements, and a host of other tasks. If this process proves challenging for full-time producers working with renowned directors in major studios, imagine how daunting it can be for Cuba's Street Filmmakers, many of whom have never traveled outside the country, have no training in business or marketing, and do not have savings accounts or a credit card.[5] Until recently, most have not even carried a cell phone.[6] The Muestra supports these artists in getting their films in front of viewers and critics. For many, it has also stimulated their creative agenda; in fact, several filmmakers remark that the Muestra inspired them to begin conceptualizing their first film.

The event has also been vital to rejuvenating the state-supported film industry. While inside the ICAIC headquarters, I generally run into people in their fifties, sixties, and seventies. But during the Muestra Nacional de Nuevos Realizadores, the demographics shift. People in their thirties, twenties, and even teens make up the majority. Every February in recent years has found dozens of young men and women filling the building. Sporting casual dress, carrying backpacks, and chatting animatedly with one another, they resemble university students the world over. In the same way that the presence of these artists changed the look and feel of the ICAIC during my recent visits, so, too, are their films—emanating from a vision unique to their generation—enhancing the texture of the island's cinema. Cuban Revolutionary cinema grew out of a resistance to extant paradigms and a questioning of past histories and present practices. It was a cinema of challenge, one designed, above all, to effect change. In the "clips" that follow, we will recognize the restlessness and wariness of the status quo that have characterized Cuban filmmaking for more than a half-century. In addition to this continuity, we will observe a significant disjunction. The expressly political is not the overarching concern. Early filmmakers opposed imperialism, especially in the form of Hollywood's cultural domination. Present-day filmmakers focus on their context and personal preoccupations. They insist on the human need for a dignified life. And they lament the pervasive lack of hope among their peers. These Street Filmmakers are intent on broaching subjects the national industry has shied away from. That they do so within the framework of a state-sponsored event demonstrates the interplay between state actors and artists working outside governmental structures. The Muestra Nacional de Nuevos Realizadores, founded and sustained by the ICAIC, permits us to appreciate both the state's alignment with alternative—even oppositional—representations for purposes of enhancing its credibility and renewing its output, and the association of Street Filmmakers with the state in order to further their artistic objectives and participate in shaping the creative climate in which they work.

Provoking Reflection: Aram Vidal Promotes Human Values and Social Justice

It was the Muestra Nacional de Nuevos Realizadores that inspired Aram Vidal to venture into filmmaking. He got involved with this event during its second installment, in 2002, and has attended every year since then. "I identify with many of the materials projected there," Vidal notes. The knowledge that his work could be exhibited in this forum motivated him to make his first film, *Calle G* (*G Street*). Vidal believes his experience is common among young audiovisual artists; the Muestra is the impetus behind a lot of first-time projects. "We young filmmakers have great affection for the Muestra," he acknowledges, "and for all those who defend that space." There are other venues in the country for showcasing materials made by Cuba's up-and-coming audiovisual artists—Cine Pobre (Gibara), Cine Plaza (Havana), Por Primera Vez (Holguín), Festival Internacional del Documental Santiago Álvarez in Memoriam (Santiago de Cuba), Festival Cine de la Montaña (various sites)—but the Muestra is the longest running and unique in that it focuses specifically on Cuba's emerging filmmakers. For them, big-screen projections in the capital's cinemas are exceedingly important. So, too, are the opportunities to meet with reporters, be interviewed, and have their films reviewed in the national and international press. In Vidal's mind, the Muestra has been a decisive force not only in exhibiting new work but also in promoting audiovisual production by young Cuban artists.[7]

This audiovisual artist takes learning seriously—both formal education and personal enrichment. After earning a degree in social communication, and with it the intellectual preparation he considers essential for any creative profession, he continued to refine his filmmaking knowledge and polish his technical skills. Vidal studied scriptwriting for a year in a workshop directed by Enrique Pineda Barnet.[8] He spent another year honing his scriptwriting skills in the Onelio Jorge Cardoso Center, enrolled in a program devoted to literary narrative techniques.[9] (Vidal also writes fiction.) More recently, he participated in a workshop offered by Gabriel García Márquez at the EICTV in San Antonio de los Baños. In addition to these formal *talleres*, Vidal has learned by doing—and by watching lots of films.

The work of Aram Vidal has met with favorable reviews at the Muestra. *De generación* (*Degeneration; From/Of the Generation*, 2006) compiles the fears and dreams of Cuba's youth. Reviewer Maylin Alonso Chiano described the film as "a collective exercise of psychoanalysis."[10] The testimony of a handful of young people, all twenty-somethings born in the 1980s, structures the film. Their assertions reveal their vision of the world as well as of their immediate surroundings. Addressed either explicitly or implicitly in *De generación* are issues foremost in the minds of young people in many places—relationships, the future, drugs, music, identity, and so on. The group of *habaneros* in this twenty-minute documentary proffers a collective portrait of Cuba's youth today.

Vidal had formulated the idea behind this project during his student days at the University of Havana. It struck him that when he conversed with friends his age, they would turn to the same subjects, provoking the same reflections and doubts. This compelled him to create a documentary chronicling the perceptions of some young people in Cuba at the time. He had hoped to develop this material into his thesis, but his program required the culminating project to be in written form. Two years later, he took up the idea again and managed to make *De generación*. The wait ended up being productive, notes Vidal, for it permitted him to try his hand at some other projects first, thereby refining techniques that would be useful later.

Because so few avenues exist for disseminating their work, Street Filmmakers take charge of getting their material in front of viewers. "Distribution in Cuba is interesting" notes Vidal, "in that the filmmakers don't mind having their work pirated. In fact, we participate in the pirating," he admits, explaining that he and his counterparts give copies to anybody requesting them. "And we even ask that they show it to their family and friends." In this way, films are passed from hand to hand and computer to computer. Another common practice, notes Vidal, is that of arranging screenings in private homes. Because of the filmmakers' efforts, "a significant number of people have seen a range of these films" despite the fact that only rarely are they projected in the cinema or shown on television.

Like other Street Filmmakers, Vidal relies on "invention" to create his work—using lamps designed for household lighting, making do with computer microphones rather than specialized ones, transforming a piece of white foam rubber into a light reflector, jerry-rigging an editing workstation with components belonging to different people, using a borrowed cart as a dolly, and so on. As for software, it's all downloaded from the Internet. "We pirate the software," elaborates the director, "because nobody has the money to pay for the licenses. They're really expensive." Summing up, Vidal states, "We invent everything."

This constant need to devise creative solutions certainly poses challenges. But Vidal chooses to look on the bright side. "I've had to deal with all kinds of problems. But this also makes you more creative, and it prepares you." He echoes the sentiments of other filmmakers who contend that overcoming obstacles strengthens their resolve and contributes to sharpening their skills. "The day I make a real film, with all the necessary equipment and technicians, I'm going to feel strange," he confided to me in 2007. "But I definitely intend to work with the industry. This artisan independent mode gives you a lot, but in the end, if you want to make a more serious film of a technical quality sophisticated enough to be distributed through traditional channels, you can't turn your back on the industry."

A year later, Vidal would have the opportunity to work on an ICAIC project. He and four other young filmmakers—Carlos Machado, Benny Rey, Alina Rodríguez, and Daniel Vera—were invited to collaborate on a documentary examining literacy in Latin America. Gustavo Arcos deems this "a surprising strategic move" on the part of the industry. He goes on to speculate as to the ICAIC's motives. Is "the center" seeking to capture this young talent for its own purposes? Or is it merely giving them an opportunity? The answer will lie in what happens after projects like this one—whether they follow their own artistic instincts or become part of official discourse, "reproducing without questioning" dominant modes.[11] *La dimensión de las palabras* (*Dimensions of the Word*, 2008) narrates five stories related to the "Sí yo puedo" ("Yes I Can") literacy project under way in Bolivia, Honduras, Guatemala, and Venezuela.[12] The documentary's protagonists, ranging in age and living in different contexts, share their experience of learning to read and write. Despite their adverse circumstances, the testimony of these informants reveals their collective belief that these new skills will enhance their lives.

At the same time he was working on this industry project, Vidal tackled another. In *xxxx años después* (*40 Years Later*, 2007), he revisits the assassination of Ernesto "Che" Guevara four decades after the fact. The camera moves along the streets of Valle Grande and La Higuera, revealing both the persistence of memory and the pervasive tendency to forget. That the ICAIC is listed as coproducer of this project, with Vidal's own Kastalia, indicates once again the synergy between the state and the streets. This Street Filmmaker expressed enthusiasm for working on an ICAIC production. "The advantages of having the support of the industry are great," he notes. That said, he will likely continue making some films independently, particularly works he deems more personal in nature. "But if the institutions decide to support me, I won't say no. All I ask is that they respect me as a creator, that they respect my decisions." And thus far Vidal has found this to be the case. "They've been very respectful," he asserts, referring to the ICAIC. "They've treated us with a great deal of professional trust."

In thinking more broadly about industry and Street modes of filmmaking, Vidal expresses a hope that young filmmakers have channels open to them both inside and outside the industry. His sense is that in recent years the ICAIC has changed its stance—for the better. Instead of ignoring those working on their own, the industry, in Vidal's view, is trying to assist them. This artist expresses hope that the industry will continue supporting young filmmakers, as in the case of *Tres veces dos* and this recent project, *La dimensión de las palabras*. At the same time, he underscores the benefit of having multiple spaces in which to make films. "Diversity is positive for a society," asserts Vidal, "and the fact that there isn't only one center for film and video production means that more kinds of projects can be developed. Topics the ICAIC wouldn't be interested in financing may appeal to other producers. The development of alternative cinema represents greater liberty, and this is very positive from a societal point of view."

For Vidal, the matter of working within or without the industry concerns him far less than the question of how to employ the audiovisual medium to promote human values. Shortly after returning from Guatemala, where he worked on *La dimensión*, Vidal reflected on his affirmed commitment to social justice—around the world and at home. "What's most important is to defend human values wherever they may be," he noted. "We believe that teaching people to read and write is of great value. The sensibility that allows us to see the good things accomplished by the revolution permits us to oppose all kinds of injustice; it makes us recognize the positive aspects of our revolutionary project, and criticize to the end all the negatives we see within it."[13] Vidal's films have grown out of his conviction that cinema can provoke a reflection leading to action. "Cinema is a way to see yourself," he explains. "It's a way to reflect on that which is too close to observe, that which you need to watch on screen in order to think about." The filmmaker does not believe his documentary *De generación* says anything that young people aren't thinking on their own. "But upon seeing their vision in the cinema," he explains, "viewers experience a catharsis; they identify with the speaking subjects and know there are many others who share their perspective. So cinema can bring like-minded people together and encourage them think and act." And indeed, this is a significant achievement of the Muestra Nacional de Nuevos Realizadores. In convening young artists—providing them with a space to create, critique, and criticize—it has helped forge a community of audiovisual artists committed to their individual and collective futures. The Muestra has engaged these filmmakers in articulating precisely what matters most, as the words of Vidal reveal: "Despite the rapid transformation characterizing the world of today, or perhaps because of it, you have to continue preserving the most simple and essential human values, the best human intentions of each era. Ideologies change—drastically sometimes—but ethics and humanity and a sensibility to defend that which is worthwhile have to continue existing and have to be valued even more." In summing up, Aram Vidal expresses a desire "to keep on dreaming, without running out of steam, without losing the light." Vidal and other Street Filmmakers, brought together by the Muestra, strengthen their commitment to "preserving human values."

Bridging Worlds: Gustavo Pérez Seeks to Awaken Emotions and Effect Transformation

The Muestra regularly includes collateral programs, among them screenings of films that are not in the competition. Here Gustavo Pérez, born in 1962, no longer qualifies as a "young" director, so his films are ineligible for the competition that is reserved for the under-thirty-five set. It is in these parallel screenings, then, that Pérez finds space for his films. This self-taught filmmaker is also a poet with four collections published and a photographer specializing in black-and-white images. He earns his living by working in Televisión Camagüey, a TV station in the provincial capital where he makes his home. During off hours, he nurtures his passion for creating documentaries. Although it is not easy for this director to travel from his home in Camagüey to the capital, a seven-hour bus ride each way, Pérez has participated in nearly every Muestra since its inception. He finds the event exceedingly worthwhile, affording him opportunities to screen new and classic films from Cuba as well as from other countries and to meet with directors working inside the industry and on their own. It also provides feedback from Havana audiences and Muestra participants.

The Camagüey director began filming during the Special Period, and in 1994 he completed a documentary around a subject relevant at the time. The title, *Amigos del mal* (*Friends of Evil*), which is a play on words with *amigos del mar* (friends of the sea), alludes to its controversial subject matter. At the time, beach resorts and hotels became sites of contestation. The island was developing its tourist infrastructure, and policies were established that limited Cubans' access to tourist centers. Not surprisingly, islanders resented finding themselves turned away from places they had once enjoyed. The exclusivity afforded tourists went against the grain of such basic Revolutionary principles as equality and solidarity. Two other films followed—*Buscando a Céline Dion* (*Looking for Céline Dion*, 1996) and *Sola: La extensa realidad* (*Alone: Extensive Reality*, 2003)— before Pérez completed the project that would earn a prize at the Cine Pobre Festival in Gibara. *Despertando a Quan Tri* (*Awakening Quan Tri*, 2005) is about this city in Vietnam that, like so many others, was wiped out by U.S. military operations during the war and then hastily rebuilt later. In this documentary, the testimony of inhabitants reveals their lack

An image from *Despertando a Quan Tri*, directed by Gustavo Pérez.
Courtesy of the director.

of connection to the place where they live. Surrounded by impersonal concrete structures, they feel alienated from this site and devoid of any sense of home. A constant in Pérez's films is a concern for social themes. This director explores ways in which life in Cuba and elsewhere can be improved.

It is often by probing transnational topics—the coming together of individuals from diverse geopolitical territories—that this filmmaker communicates his message. In *Todas iban a ser reinas* (*All Were Going to be Queens*, 2006), Pérez treats emigration. But whereas emigration often conjures images of Cubans leaving the island, in this fifty-four-minute documentary it refers to women leaving the former Soviet Union destined for Cuba. Pérez records the perspectives and experiences of six Russian women, all of whom fell in love with Cuban men visiting their native country, and all of whom subsequently emigrated so as to live with their husbands on the island. The years have passed, and with them any possibility of a fairy-tale ending for these border crossers. This documentary, like all works by this filmmaker, probes quotidian life—with an eye toward effecting positive transformation. "I'm not interested in repeating what's being said in the media," Pérez notes, "but rather in being faithful to my reality." In Pérez's condition as a "poor filmmaker," he believes it essential to be honest with his context. Two Cuban filmmakers have influenced him in this regard: Nicolasito Guillén Landrián, in terms of point of view, and Santiago Álvarez, for the clarity of his narrative style.[14]

How did this young man from the provinces break into Havana's audiovisual world? It was not easy, recalls Pérez. He grew up in a sugar mill town, the Central Azucarera Violeta. An asthma sufferer, he traveled regularly to Havana for medical care from the time he can remember. While going back and forth as a young boy, he glimpsed images of the countryside, the city, and the spaces in between. "I have the ability to observe," he explains, "to visualize and to record in my head what I see." The practice of describing these different worlds to his friends turned him into a storyteller. And the brief visits to the capital gave him just enough confidence to pursue audiovisual avenues there. Opening doors into the Havana film world is never easy, but for out-of-towners, the challenge is compounded. Pérez has managed to do so, however, and lends a hand to others seeking to do the same. Situated in Camagüey, Pérez is well positioned to help link the capital and the eastern provinces. He takes seriously his responsibility as a bridge, helping to move people, ideas, and projects back and forth between Havana and Santiago de Cuba. Pérez's audiovisual accomplishments and commitment illustrate a variety of features prominent to Street Filmmaking and underscored in this study: First, many of these entrepreneurial filmmakers have some formal link to Cuba's state culture apparatus, whether working in the ICAIC, the ICRT, or some regional entity (here, the provincial Televisión Camagüey). Second, while the capital continues to play a key role in audiovisual production on the island, it is by no means the exclusive purveyor of images. Finally, these artists value collaboration, connecting the forward momentum of their peers with their own progress.

Pérez considers the Muestra Nacional de Nuevos Realizadores to mark "an interesting opening." The ICAIC had to acknowledge the young filmmakers working outside the industry and come to terms with the fact that its own filmmakers were getting older. Now, he notes, you don't have to be inside the industry in order to collaborate with it. The ICAIC recognizes and accepts the fact that new expressions are coming from outside. "Diversity is always important," Pérez asserts, "the diversity of the gaze.

Gustavo Pérez self-
portrait. Courtesy
of the artist.

A country has to be seen from a variety of perspectives, not just the official ones." What's needed is a questioning of reality rather than a "trium-
phalist" discourse, contends Pérez, for in this way people can formulate
opinions and take action to solve problems.

The advent of digital technology means more people can develop their
ideas, make their films, and communicate their visions. Digital filming
and editing have certainly been important for Pérez, whose projects are
modest in scale. He works with a small digital camera and an aging computer, constantly "making do" and "inventing." His team generally consists of no more than four, himself included; on his most recent film, for
example, three friends collaborated—a photographer, a sound specialist,
and an editor. What does it take to be a filmmaker in present-day Cuba?
"Ability, a sense of wonder, tenderness, and sensitivity," enumerates
Pérez. In order to be a filmmaker, one must "be human and work on be-
half of others." This Camagüey-based artist intends to keep making films.
"I have lots of questions I ask myself. I have a strong desire to do lots of
things. I'm a poet and I work with images." He intends to continue work-

ing toward his dream, creating films that "awaken emotions and elicit questions compelling people to become better."

Revisiting the Classics: Carlos Barba Mines
Revolutionary Cinema for Material

Throughout this study, Street Filmmakers express their admiration for Cuba's film tradition. For one young artist, Cuba's revolutionary cinema is absolutely essential to his creative expression. Carlos Barba draws upon classic island films for virtually all of his documentaries. From his base in Santiago de Cuba, this Street Filmmaker works as a promoter of his island's cinema. He helps organize film screenings and events; serves as a point person bringing together local, regional, and national organizations; and paves the way for ICAIC teams coming to town to film. Barba has helped coordinate the restoration of several blocks in preparation for a period film, for example, and often is called on to help local officials and agencies understand the importance of attracting such projects. Las Gallegas, the family restaurant operated by his aunts, has become a favorite meeting spot for industry directors, actors, and technicians when visiting this provincial capital.

Barba was born in 1978, and even before reaching his thirtieth birthday, he had made several documentaries. The bulk of his audiovisual output chronicles Cuban filmmaking. Barba's first work, *Ecos de un final* (*Echoes of an End*, 2002), proffers testimony by some of the nonprofessional actors who participated in the final sequence of Humberto Solás's *Miel para Oshún* (*Honey for Oshún*). Another, titled *Memorias de Lucía* (2003), compiles reflections by the actresses in Solás's legendary film, *Lucía* (1968), nearly forty years after its making. Yet another, *Mujer que espera* (*Woman Who Waits*, 2005), is devoted to the renowned screen actress Isabel Santos. Barba's admiration for this talented artist is evident in this homage to her. More recently, he completed *Canción para Rachel* (*A Song for Rachel*, 2008), an eighty-minute collective reflection on the musical *La bella del Alhambra* (*The Belle of the Alhambra Theater*, 1990), by Enrique Pineda Barnet. In my conversation with Carlos Barba shortly after he completed the film, I was fascinated by his ingenuity. He managed to compile interview footage of all the key participants, despite the fact that they now lived in four different countries. It was easy enough to film the testimony of the Cuba-based director Pineda Barnet, actress Verónica Lynn, photographer Raúl Rodríguez Cabrera, and actor Jorge Martínez. More complicated, though, was documenting the impressions of actress Beatriz Valdés in Venezuela, actress Isabel Moreno and editor Jorge Abello in Miami, and composer-conductor Gonzalo Romeo in Mexico. Committed to including the perspectives of these *Bella* participants despite the distances separating them, Barba devised the following solution: He got in touch with each of them via e-mail to request their assistance. Would they be willing to address a series of questions he would provide, and do so in front of a camera? And could they then send him a mini-DV with the filmed interview? He also supplied some details about preferred framing and artistic design. All agreed to collaborate, and thus Barba was able to move forward with the project as he had envisioned it. The result, in the words of Pineda Barnet, is "very moving, beautiful and intelligent."[15] It is also proof that Cuban Street Filmmakers are not reluctant to engage with individuals—including Cubans—in locales far from home.

In addition to making films that record Cuba's cinema tradition and promoting Santiago de Cuba as a site for audiovisual endeavors, Barba is also a film critic. He frequently contributes interviews and essays to the ICAIC's *Cine Cubano*, the Editorial Oriente's *Revista SIC*, the festival bulletin *Cine Pobre Hoy*, and several other publications in Spain. And Barba publicizes developments in Cuba's film world; his e-mail distribution lists circulate information to friends and film fans across the island and overseas.

The experiences of this Santiago-based media artist enable us to appreciate the effervescence in audiovisual activity beyond Cuba's capital. Barba and other filmmakers in the provinces connect with one another and with a variety of cultural organizations so as to achieve their audiovisual production goals. Oftentimes, it is at the Muestra Nacional where they first meet and establish contacts useful in opening doors to other opportunities. Some display their films at the Festival Documental Santiago Álvarez in Memoriam, held each March in Santiago de Cuba. Founded by Lázara Herrera, Álvarez's widow and president of the Santiago Álvarez Office in the ICAIC, this venue has grown from a small regional festival to a respectable international event. Others participate in the Cine Pobre Festival, scheduled for every other April in the picturesque town of

Carlos Barba during the filming of *Ciudad en rojo* with director Rebeca Chávez (second from left) and actresses Yoraisi Gómez and María Teresa García. Courtesy of Barba.

Gibara. Conceptualized and presided over by Humberto Solás, this festival is also instrumental in linking Cubans—some working within and others outside the state apparatus—to their international counterparts.

Carlos Barba has effectively mined the island's revolutionary cinema for raw material to create his documentaries. His efforts, undertaken as many of the founding fathers retire and still others pass away, are helping to preserve the memory of Cuban cinema. Through film projects, Carlos Barba and other Street Filmmakers like him are creating a visual record of the island's rich film tradition and keeping alive the stories of its protagonists. Barba is undoubtedly making a meaningful contribution to Cuba's cultural patrimony; at the same time, his selection of subject matter is eminently pragmatic. By choosing topics of interest to the national film institute and by rubbing shoulders with industry professionals, Barba has been able to hone his skills and garner new opportunities. He was invited to assist Rebeca Chávez on the ICAIC film *Ciudad en rojo* (*City in Red*, 2007) and take care of some casting for Fernando Pérez's film about José Martí.

Establishing Alliances: Alejandro Brugués and
Inti Herrera Team Up on a Feature

As might be expected in an event showcasing the talent of young cine-astes, the majority of the films presented each year during the Muestra are short documentaries. Increasing numbers of animated and fiction films compete too, however, as filmmakers expand their skills and ex-periment with narrative modes. Predictably, the projects tend to be of short duration. Of the nearly three dozen fiction films participating in the seventh Muestra, only one exceeded twenty minutes in length.

It is notable, then, that the sixth Muestra featured a ninety-eight-minute fiction film titled *Personal Belongings* (Alejandro Brugués, 2006). A love story provides the impetus for approaching universal experiences like the desire to belong, the disintegration of the family, and the ten-dency of humans—even those who care for one another—to cause suf-fering. At the center is a couple, a young woman and man who begin to fall for each other. Their relationship is destined to fail, however, because she insists on staying put and he is intent on emigrating. Major turning points are heralded by a particular object framed in close-up; a series of "personal belongings" structures the narrative and makes for a compel-ling story.

Personal Belongings played to a full house in the expansive Cine Chap-lin. Audience members applauded the film, which was also received favor-ably by the local press. Reviewer Gabriel Caparó affirmed the emerging director's talent and potential, stating, "Alejandro Brugués demonstrates, with this *opera prima*, excellent credentials as the orchestrator of a dis-course that's coherent, effective in its narration, [and] adept at playing with subtlety."[16] I had interviewed the director and the producer, Alejan-dro Brugués and Inti Herrera, respectively, only a few months earlier. At that time, hearing about the feature they were filming, I never imagined it would premiere only a few months later. They, like other Street Film-makers, do not wait around.[17]

Both Brugués and Herrera are trained in filmmaking, having completed programs of study at the EICTV; both move comfortably in domestic and international film circles; and both believe that when it comes to captur-ing their ideas on film, sooner is better. So when the two developed what they thought was a compelling story, they were determined to film it. To make a successful film, according to Brugués, you only need two things: a good story that everyone believes in and (he adds with a smile) good food. Herrera agrees that the content of a film—the story being told—is paramount. "What's important continues to be what has mattered since men were in caves—beginning with the words, 'Once upon a time . . . .' What's important is the story. Tell me a story. The form in which you do that can be novel. . . . But if you have an interesting story, it's going to get my attention." Contemporary Cuban filmmakers do not excel at story-telling, in Herrera's estimation. "We're not making films that tell stories. Instead, we're glossing over the top of stories to address a certain topic. Or we're thinking, 'I'm going to talk about this and be brave, because no one has broached this subject.' But this is definitely not what's important. . . . I believe that good stories are lacking in films made in the industry in Cuba—and outside the industry as well." Herrera contends that the new generation of filmmakers has inherited this ineffective mode of story-telling.

These two audiovisual artists exhibit the Street Filmmaking spirit. They believe in their projects and in their ability to realize them. They willingly pound the pavement to move their films forward. "We were born into an alternative process," explains Herrera. "We disseminate our ideas in an alternative way. We seek spaces that take this into account—whether through personal contacts or the Internet or whatever—but always thinking of some way outside of the known protocol to get what we need. Either they give it to us, or we take it." Brugués echoes the sentiment of his colleague and friend. In making *Personal Belongings*, they garnered the backing they needed from outside Cuba, without the industry's help. He acknowledges that support from the ICAIC is useful—"a guarantee of credibility, an endorsement." That said, they have managed to accomplish a great deal on their own. "Without ICAIC we've gotten as far as the U.S. studios, talking to people there. You find a way, you know. If you have something interesting to say, people are going to listen to you." Through their know-how and perseverance, Alejandro Brugués and Inti Herrera have succeeded in making their movies.

Both young cineastes are reluctant to deem their work and that of their peers as "independent." It is easier to talk about working independently in the case of painters and composers, contends Herrera, than in the case

The protagonists in *Personal Belongings*, directed by Alejandro Brugués, ponder their competing desires. Courtesy of the Muestra Nacional de Nuevos Realizadores, ICAIC.

of filmmakers. Cinema is an "industry art" and, as such, relies on collaboration—for the production of films and for their dissemination. "I think the word 'independent' is a bit of an overstatement for filmmaking," he cautions. "Instead, I think in terms of the process, of filmmaking as an activity carried out in an independent manner." Herrera goes on to explain, "Let's say I have an idea as a producer, or a director comes to me with an idea. Together we determine how to finance the film and select actors and set the schedule. There's a series of things to talk about."

For Herrera, the process does not begin with any conscious decision to make an independent film. Rather, it starts from an idea that then gets developed in a series of conversations. In other words, it grows out of an artistic sensibility and a practical approach. "I have the need to express myself in a certain way, using what's at hand right now," he notes. Take, for example, the matter of genre films. Herrera and Brugués have just completed a love story. Their next film might be radically different. It might be a genre film, a kind of project rarely seen emanating from within the industry, notes Herrera. "At the moment, we're thinking about a zombie film. I can't imagine the ICAIC making a film about zombies. I wish it would . . . because genre films have a large following and there are good films in this genre." Summing up, Herrera states, "It's like saying, 'I want to express myself in this way right now.' That's my point of departure. That's the first step."

Brugués shares this sentiment. He does not believe in the concept of an independent cinema, nor does he see himself helping to create a new movement. What motivates him is the need to express himself through his art. "I see things simply: I have a story to tell," he explains. "I believe in it, and I don't want to wait for the industry to make it because the industry here—here and everywhere—can be a long road. It takes a lot of work to get a project approved, and even once it's accepted, there are always slowdowns. So the mode we're using to make films is simply one of not waiting. We have stories to tell, we have the desire to tell them, and we want to do it now. For me, that doesn't translate into 'independent' or 'alternative' cinema."

When they're going to make a film, Brugués and Herrera give free rein to their ideas. Avoiding thoughts of making "an independent film with a low budget" gives them greater latitude, permitting new discoveries and fostering creativity. If they envision a particular sequence, they develop it for the project. It's not about imposing limitations due to economic constraints but, rather, about achieving the desired results. Having the ability to proceed in this way corresponds to a unique moment for Cuban filmmakers. "Right now, you can pick up a project and hold it in your hand, whereas at other times you would have had to depend on a series of things. I think it's a lot easier today for someone with training in a film school to enter the film world saying, 'Okay, I believe in my story and I believe I have what it takes to tell it in a modest yet dignified way. I can access mechanisms for financing that will permit me—with others— to put together my film and make it digitally, perhaps blowing it up to 35 millimeter afterwards.'" This is not to suggest that it's easy to make films without industry backing. On the contrary, difficulties abound. Working as a producer of films made outside the industry, Herrera constantly confronts obstacles—at the creation stages and in the distribution phase. Securing permission to film is common practice the world over, and this can be difficult in Cuba for a street-style production. Even when permission has been granted, there is no guarantee that everything will proceed as planned. "It's not uncommon for the producer to have to tell the entire team, just when everyone is ready for action, 'Take ten. We're going to look for a new location and we'll be right back,'" notes Herrera.

These production challenges, while stressful, can actually contribute to creating an esprit de corps. With *Personal Belongings*, for example, they wanted to film a sequence on the beach. But the fee to film at the exclusive Varadero resort was prohibitive, given their modest budget. So they decided to proceed without permission, relying instead on discretion. Brugués and Herrera instructed the group to keep a low profile, saying, "We can't do anything that draws attention to ourselves." Everyone concurred. One member of the team took to heart the instructions—and entertained the film team at the same time. Herrera recalls his amusement upon seeing the sound technician walk by completely covered with leaves and branches; both man and microphone were camouflaged. But a discreet demeanor is hard to sustain. On the last day of the filming, about fifteen members of the team were lugging the bags and equipment and boxes needed for filming the final takes. When a couple of bikini-clad female tourists strolled by, the males in the group began whistling and shouting. "That was not keeping a low profile!" Herrera says with agitation. "Thinking back now, a year later, we can laugh," he adds, "but at the time it was pretty stressful." This sense of camaraderie, characteristic of Street Filmmaking, provides a contrast to industry productions. Herrera offers an explanation: "I think that when you take away the figure of the industry, people relax. They have a greater awareness of the problems and the fact that they're working for themselves." In situations like these, the "union mentality" recedes, leaving only the artists trying to help one another. Street Filmmaking accords ownership of the creative process to the participants in it.

Once the film is made, the director and producer face another major hurdle: disseminating the work. As has been noted throughout this study, Street Filmmakers must develop strategies to get their films in front of audiences. Given the ways in which the film market operates, this is no easy task. For one thing, it can be difficult for emerging filmmakers to break into the festival circuit. Participation in domestic and international festivals is critical for showcasing new work. But making the cut can be exceedingly difficult. For one thing, festivals rely heavily on favorable reviews in determining their selections. Positive critical reception is arguably the most important factor in getting a film noticed by festival organizers and programmers. So the difficulty becomes one of getting noticed by critics. That poses challenges of its own, since film journals prefer to dedicate their pages to works that have already had play at festivals or secured distribution. In effect, film critics are discouraged from treating films with no reception history, particularly when they have been made by unknown directors. It is exceedingly difficult for young Cuban artists to break into this closed circle.[18]

Street Filmmakers working with low budgets and without industry infrastructure must rely on their ingenuity and contacts—and also on serendipity. With *Personal Belongings*, Brugués and Herrera were fortunate to have all three. Their film premiered soon after a new Cuba-based Internet portal was created. María Caridad Cumaná, film critic and historian at the FNCL, recognized the need for a space that would coordinate and disseminate information on Cuban and Latin American cinema. Under her leadership, the portal came into being. In order to generate content for the site and feature the young audiovisual artists on the island, Cumaná dispatches reporters to cover screenings and related events at the annual Muestra Nacional de Nuevos Realizadores. Film reviews, interviews, photos, and accompanying information are then uploaded to the site. So when Brugués and Herrera submitted *Personal Belongings* to the Works-in-Progress section of the Berlin Festival, they directed members of the selection committee to the portal to access reviews of their film. *Personal Belongings* was accepted, making it the *only* film from Latin America selected for that event. Brugués and Herrera acknowledge the efforts of Cumaná and the portal in helping them get a foothold in the international film world.

As the seventh Muestra was getting under way in February 2008, Alejandro Brugués accompanied his film first to the United States for the Miami International Film Festival and then on to Mexico for the Guadalajara International Film Festival, where it garnered the Emilio García Riera prize. (A dual passport facilitates his border-crossings.) He and Herrera had contracted the Mexico-based agency Latinofusion to promote their film. Their decision had been a sound one, given that *Personal Belongings* was indeed traveling on the international festival circuit.

What lies ahead for these two Street Filmmakers? Shortly after completing *Personal Belongings*, Herrera was looking forward to a time when all that is occurring now in "alternative sectors" will be transformed into the normal way of making films. "I dream that our way of making films becomes as valid as the industry mode that existed in Cuba until just a few years ago. That it cease to be framed as a problem, and instead be seen as a solution." A year later, Herrera was participating in the Muestra; he shared his expertise on a panel devoted to audiovisual production in Cuba. The seminar attracted emerging filmmakers and seasoned professionals hailing from virtually all of the film and art schools, the ICAIC and the ICRT, several NGOs, regional television, and the streets. The exchange of ideas among a producer relatively new to the audiovisual arena (Inti Herrera), an industry veteran and vice president of ICAIC production (Camilo Vives), and a former director of Televisión Serrana, currently working in the ICAIC's documentary division and advising students at the EICTV (Daniel Diez Castrillo), is highly significant. The presence of producers from various sectors demonstrates how quickly the island's audiovisual landscape has changed. Such a session would have been unthinkable only a few years earlier. Without a doubt, the boundaries between Street Filmmaking and industry endeavors have blurred. Individuals working outside and within state structures acknowledge the importance of collaboration; combining their respective strengths is key to making and marketing Cuban films.

Revisiting the ICAIC's Past:
Images—and Injustices—from Bygone Days

Whereas the Muestra exists in great part to showcase the work of contemporary artists and to provide a forum for debating issues affecting their individual and collective futures, each year it includes activities that take participants back in time. Through displays of film posters, exhibitions of photos, and programs of "classic" films, participants are invited to experience the ICAIC of the 1960s, 1970s, and 1980s. Retrospectives featuring the work of accomplished Cuban directors serve a number of functions within the Muestra. Most obviously, they constitute spaces for honoring Cuba's legendary filmmakers. Previous installments have paid tribute to Manuel Octavio Gómez, Tomás Gutiérrez Alea, Jorge Herrera, Belkis Vega, Pastor Vega, and others. Besides rendering homage, the retrospectives constitute an important vehicle for returning to moments—some uncomfortable, others painful—in the film institute's past.

Such was the case with "The Polemical 1960s" and the homages to Nicolasito Guillén Landrián and Oscar Valdés. The former gathered some thirty films by fifteen filmmakers depicting the Revolution's tumultuous first decade. In programming "The Polemical 1960s," the ICAIC did not shy away from controversy. Among the works shown were the highly charged *P.M.—Pasado Meridiano* (Sabá Cabrera Infante, 1961), the film that instigated Fidel Castro's legendary "Words to the Intellectuals" in June 1961. Several documentaries by Nicolasito Guillén Landrián—*Coffea arábiga* (1968), *Desde La Habana 1969* (*From Havana 1969*, 1972), and *En un barrio viejo* (*In an Old Neighborhood*, 1963)—also contributed to this program. As noted in the preceding chapter, this filmmaker is being recovered by young artists who credit his vision and technique with fostering their own creativity. Recently, material by this revolutionary auteur has been programmed as part of the National Exhibit of New Filmmakers, in events hosted by the FLC, for screenings at various video clubs on the island, and at international film festivals.[19] Documentaries by this filmmaker, in fact, were selected by Esteban Insausti for the program of Cuban avant-garde he curated for the Primera Muestra de Cine Alternativo in Campeche, Mexico. Nicolasito Guillén Landrián is experiencing a comeback. Some thirty years after he emigrated, his portrait was added to the filmmaker's gallery in the national film institute; Guillén Landrián has, posthumously, taken his place alongside his industry counterparts. The efforts of the nation's emerging filmmakers—their affinity with this misunderstood auteur—have contributed to the resurgence of interest in his life and work.

During the sixth Muestra, a photo display in the lobby of the Cine Chaplin introduced visitors to another controversial filmmaker: Oscar Valdés. Born in 1919, this acclaimed documentarian entered the ICAIC shortly after the establishment of the institute in 1961. He first worked as an assistant on didactic shorts and segments for the newsreel series Noticiero ICAIC Latinoamericano (ICAIC Latin American Newsreel). In the early 1960s, he collaborated with Humberto Solás to direct two short fiction pieces, *Minerva traduce el mar* (*Minerva Translates the Sea*, 1962) and *El Retrato* (*The Portrait*, 1963), and by the middle of the decade, he had made what is now considered his best work, *Vaqueros del Cauto* (*Cowboys of the Cauto River Region*, 1965), already mentioned in Chapter 2.

Early in the 1970s, Valdés produced a series of films that would remain among his best known, including *Escenas de los muelles* (*Scenes from the Docks*, 1970); *Muerte y vida en El Morrillo* (*Life and Death in Morrillo*, 1971); and *El extraño caso de Rachel K.* (*The Strange Case of Rachel K.*, 1973). The latter, constituting this director's first and only feature, is notable not so much for its quality but, rather, for the polemic it generated. Alberto Ramos has examined the film's mixed reception in his essay "*Rachel K.*"; the director's attempt to blend two discourses, one rooted in historical narrative and the other in the film noir structure, collided with the paradigm of *cine imperfecto* that predominated in the ICAIC during this time. Film critic Mercedes Santos Moray contends that this difficult moment left an indelible mark on Valdés. "This experience was painful for the artist and the man in the midst of incomprehension, ignorance, and also injustice, three I's that are difficult to digest, especially knowing that with each work, regardless of aesthetic outcome, a creator gives himself over entirely, up until his last breath, as was the case with this filmmaker."[20]

And indeed, more than thirty years after Valdés made the film, his reflections on the project still revealed disappointment and a desire to distance himself from it. "I don't like the end result," he confessed to Pedro Noa in an interview. "It's not the film I had imagined. There were lots of problems: limited resources for a period film, difficulties in the casting of actors, some discrepancies with the production team, and serious problems with the script. Overall, it left me feeling somewhat disillusioned." Although Valdés never directed another feature, he did continue to make documentaries at a steady pace—completing four or even five some years. His subject matter and style took a major turn, however. During the 1980s, Valdés focused on Cuba's music and art traditions. He made *Rita* (1980), *Lecuona* (1983), *María Teresa* (1984), and *Roldán y Caturla* (1985). Many viewers and critics deemed these documentaries to be less compelling than his earlier work. Alberto Ramos assesses the results of this shift as more "complacent," "simplistic," and "didactic." This negative industry experience in the 1970s affected Oscar Valdés until his death in 1990. Without a doubt, curtailing the efforts of this talented filmmaker had caused him suffering and had also hurt Cuban cinema. In highlighting the tensions and misunderstandings that plagued this director, the Muestra turned the gaze backward to revisit an industry misstep.[21]

Candid portraits of industry filmmakers—particularly controversial auteurs—serve as the impetus for reopening chapters of the institute's history. By permitting and indeed encouraging such a reflection, the ICAIC is demonstrating a willingness to take ownership of its mistakes. To acknowledge past injustices is to minimize the likelihood of their repetition. It also bodes well for the future, for as young filmmakers are exposed to the glories and shortcomings of the island's revolutionary film tradition—and a Cuban state institution—they will be better equipped to make their own contributions and interventions.

Building Capacity: Seminars and Workshops Empower Young Artists

The principal goal of the Muestra is to showcase the work of young audiovisual artists. But concerted efforts are made to help these future filmmakers develop their skills and advance their projects. To that end, master classes and workshops are offered by established industry professionals. Ambrosio Fornet shared his experiences as the scriptwriter for *Retrato de Teresa* (*Portrait of Teresa*, Pastor Vega, 1979). Julio García Espinosa and José Massip recalled learning and working alongside participants in the Italian Neorealist movement in Rome. And director Fernando Pérez, actress Isabel Santos, and actor Luis Alberto García reflected on working together some twenty years earlier on *Clandestinos* (*The Clandestine Ones*, 1987); they addressed the concerns of listeners packed into the auditorium—how to elicit the best performances from actors and how to make do with endings that result from unforeseen circumstances. Sessions like these tend to be preceded or followed by film screenings that illustrate and enrich the interventions of these ICAIC notables.

In February 2007 Enrique Colina offered a multiday workshop on documentary filmmaking, a *taller* that held great interest for the young filmmakers. The instructor was familiar to them—as an accomplished director, as the host of a long-running (but now discontinued) television program devoted to international film, and as a teacher and mentor at the EICTV. The sessions were "sold out"; not all emerging filmmakers who sought admittance were allowed to participate. Widening the gap between those accepted and those left out was a constraint imposed by the instructor; Colina insisted on a workshop format rather than lecture-style sessions. An experienced pedagogue, he recognized the correlation between modest class size and potential for learning. Priority was given to audiovisual artists who had already completed a film. Even with this condition, bodies far outnumbered seats in the screening room.

The workshop covered a lot of ground. Colina shared his impressions of documentary filmmaking in general and Cuba's tradition in particular. Cuban documentaries are important, he noted, and aspiring filmmakers should study them. But they present only a limited panorama, so work from a variety of national traditions must be examined. Colina showed clips from several documentaries and occasionally projected an entire film. Following these screenings, interspersed throughout the sessions, he facilitated discussions about the medium. The instructor integrated the students' observations and questions, encouraging them to learn from their own experiences—especially their errors. He also referred to works in this year's competition, effectively connecting theory with practice. At one point, Colina applauded a Muestra film for its unique point of departure. In *Bunker* (2006), Renier Quer Figueredo probes an elderly man's Revolutionary zeal that has endured for nearly a half-century. With a handheld camera, the filmmaker follows this protagonist around his minuscule dwelling—inside a monument. It is the unique residence that, for Colina, propels the narrative forward and renders effective this work. Key qualities for documentary filmmaking, according to Colina, are curiosity, human sensitivity, and the ability to listen and connect with people. But, above all, the activity requires modesty; otherwise, there is no chance of learning from one's mistakes.

Colina practiced what he preached by bringing in two of his own shorts. Both had defects, he explained, and were intended not as perfect examples but, rather, as vehicles for discussing what worked as planned and what the filmmaker might have done differently. By way of context, he noted that in the 1970s and 1980s, some of the Revolution's shortcomings were becoming apparent; many filmmakers, Colina included, treated these in their works. In Colina's case, he adopted a humorous tone and sought to create irony. *Chapuserías* (1986) exposes the problem of shoddy workmanship and probes its impact, with a light tone. *El rey de la selva* (*King of the Jungle*, 1991) tackles the challenges of the Special Period—the scarcity of adequate housing; the proliferation of a *doble moral*, or double standards; and the massive emigration. This short is, in my estimation, an exceedingly valuable commentary on a decisive moment in Cuba's recent history.[22] Colina, however, sees room for improvement. He confesses that if he could make it all over again (and he would like to), he would cast the lion protagonist not as a common fellow but, rather, as an aristocrat. These works launched a discussion on the importance of creating interest—the need for documentary filmmakers to find something unusual, original, or attractive to catch and sustain viewers' attention.

For Enrique Colina, the function of a documentary is to reveal that which is invisible. The trick as a documentary filmmaker is "to take what you feel and make it visible to others." Whereas fiction filmmakers construct the drama, documentary filmmakers extract the drama from reality. The structure of a documentary is a key factor in accomplishing this. All documentaries need a focus of conflict, "something explosive that moves the narrative."[23] He shared numerous documentaries from several countries both to illustrate his contentions and to provoke analysis and discussion. Among those included were *Lift* (Alrick Riley, 2000, U.K.); *Nada con nadie* (*Nothing to Do with Anyone*, Marcos Pimentel, 2005, Brazil); *Daughter from Danang* (Gail Dolgin and Vicente France, 2002, U.S.); *Radio Belén* (Gianfranco Annichini, 2005, Peru); *Roger and Me* (Michael Moore, 1989, U.S.); and *American Pimp* (Albert and Allen Hughes, 1999, U.S.), as well as some newsreels from Nazi Germany. His choice of illustrations was dictated by the works to which he had access. While teaching in France and at the EICTV in Cuba, he acquired some materials from colleagues and students. Others he picked up along the way. The lack of Spanish subtitles on an English-language documentary did not deter Colina from sharing it with the audience; he provided simultaneous translation of the soundtrack for the duration of one thirty-minute piece. At these four-hour sessions, Colina demonstrated his passion for documentary filmmaking *and* for imparting ideas. Whether analyzing a sequence, providing context, eliciting experiences from students, or running back to the projection booth, he exuded enthusiasm.

By all barometers, Colina's documentary workshop was a hit. A brief break was scheduled partway through each session, providing participants with a chance to sip coffee and get acquainted. We would stand in the reception area adjoining the screening room and continue the discussion. The consensus was that the *taller* was informative and inspiring. Invariably, this would lead to the same assertion: There was a need

Enrique Colina shares his
opinion with a gathering of
film specialists in Havana.
Photo by the author.

for more learning opportunities like this one. The Muestra should be expanded from once annually to several times per year. And the workshops
should be ongoing, convening participants monthly or quarterly at the
very least. In addition, they should contain a production component,
some hands-on application of the theories and techniques discussed. No
one disagreed. This sentiment, expressed by the emerging filmmakers,
was reiterated by the instructor and by the directors of the ICAIC-
sponsored Muestra. All recognized the value of providing practical
training for the island's up-and-coming audiovisual artists. And no one
doubted that this was best accomplished through collaboration.[24]

Moviendo Ideas: Audiovisual Artists Take On State Television

Among the activities comprising the Muestra Nacional is a series of
Moviendo Ideas (Moving Ideas) sessions attracting young filmmakers,
reporters, and a variety of people aligned with the television and film
worlds. These debates begin with a screening of several works sharing
common themes or aesthetic concerns and then engage the filmmakers
in a dialogue with viewers. Invariably, the conversation posits artistic cre-

ation within the present-day context. During the seventh Muestra, for example, one such session was devoted to works of fiction exploring violence—among them the Hilda Elena Vega's prizewinning *La bestia* (*The Beast*), Llaned Marcoleta's innovative *Domingo del Pez*, and the eleven-minute short *La guerra de las canicas* (Wilbert Noguel and Adrián Ricardo Hartill). Discussion ranged from the persistence of machismo and domestic violence in Cuba to the increasing appeal of genre conventions among young media-makers.

Another session tackled sexuality. Audience members screened *Ella trabaja* (*She Works*, 2007), in which Jesús Miguel Hernández Bachs portrays the experiences of several transvestites. By emphasizing their desire to join the workforce—and the success of those who have managed to do so—he casts them not as Other but, rather, as productive contributors to Cuban society. We also viewed *Sexo, historias, y cintas de video* (*Sex, Stories, and Videotapes*, 2007), Ricardo Figueredo's exploration of sexuality and prostitution. Multiple informants ranging from prostitutes to sociologists and psychologists share their experiences. This testimony is inserted into the context of Cuba's political history by the montage of Fidel Castro in a newsreel denouncing prostitution and other forms of aberration. Both films, observed the moderator following the screening, signaled a call to examine our consciences. How do we treat Others in Cuba? In the ensuing discussion, audience members emphasized the need for greater tolerance of these and other Cubans living in the margins. They concurred that only by engaging with them and seeking to understand their experiences would prostitutes, transvestites, transsexuals, and numerous others be integrated into the nation's social fabric.

Yet another Moviendo Ideas program highlighted social problems with a screening of five documentaries. Two of the most impressive— *Como construir un barco* (*How to Build a Boat*, 2007) and *Patria* (*Homeland*, 2007)—were made by the same filmmaker. In both, Susana Barriga probes social ills through the sensitive portrayal of individuals who are disillusioned with their lot in life and disenfranchised from Revolutionary Cuba. A frustrated boat builder has been unable to obtain the permit necessary to repair his craft or construct another; a toiling laborer has been working to repair the same road for four years. The languid takes, minimal dialogue, and deftly constructed montages are reminiscent of Nicolasito Guillén Landrián's work several decades earlier. In fact, *Como construir un barco* makes explicit its debt to *Ociel del Toa*, a film addressed in Chapter 2. The discussion following this session underscored the exhaustion of islanders accustomed to facing one obstacle after another. The Moviendo Ideas gatherings, whether measured by the number of participants or the length of the animated discussions, undoubtedly succeed in generating debate and fostering dialogue. They also serve to create community among Cuba's Street Filmmakers, mobilizing them to voice opposition and pressure for change.

One session during the sixth Muestra featured three filmmakers — Sandra Gómez Jiménez, Jeffrey Puente García, and Daniel Vera — whose documentaries grew out of their personal experiences. *Las camas solas* (*Lonely Beds*, Sandra Gómez, 2006) centers on a dilapidated tenement near Havana's Capitolio building, where the filmmaker had visited a friend on occasion. When Hurricane Iván was approaching, as residents began to evacuate, she entered the building with her camera to compile testimony from residents and catalog images of the precarious structure. The recurrent observations by a woman with mental disabilities, who insists that the beds are lonely, constitute an effective unifying device for the documentary. *Protectoras* (*Protectors*, Daniel Vera, 2006) portrays a grassroots initiative in Havana. A few devoted animal-lovers, the filmmaker's grandmother among them, have tackled the problem of stray dogs in the city. Vera's documentary probes the motivation behind their itinerant sterilization efforts while pondering why the government has failed to address this public health issue. *Setenta y dos horas* (*Seventy-two Hours*, Jeffrey Puente García, 2006) takes as its point of departure the annual carnival in the media-maker's hometown of Candelaria. The three-day event constitutes the framework in which Puente probes the difficulty of making ends meet, the resilience of cultural and religious traditions, and the strength of the human spirit. All these projects emphasize the difficulties facing the filmed subjects and, in doing so, provoke a reflection on present-day life in Cuba. None was executed with technical perfection, yet all demonstrated their maker's commitment to rendering visible that which is not apparent. Taken together, the three constitute a collage of the underside of island life.

Candid interventions propelled the discussion. Filmmakers were called on to explain and defend particular components of their projects. They responded, noting some of the constraints within which they worked.

The hurricane was imminent, recalled Gómez, and she had to wrap up quickly in order to get to her home in a distant suburb before it struck. They had to film with a single camera, explained Puente, and the ambient noise from the carnival was intrusive regardless of the hour. The sterilization operations were shut down, lamented Vera, so additional footage could not be obtained. At times, these three filmmakers asked follow-up questions and expressed their gratitude for new information gleaned. For example, Gómez was describing the filming she did in a building she knew as "the old Regina Hotel," when a member of the audience added that this structure was also called "La Isla de Cuba" ("The Island of Cuba"). This discovery buoyed Gomez's project, enhancing the structure's significance as a metaphor for Cuba.[25] The Moviendo Ideas session undoubtedly furthered the goals of the Muestra—both in introducing film fans to the work of young filmmakers and in providing the emerging audiovisual artists the opportunity to debate, reflect on, and refine their craft.

The discussion of the films developed into a larger conversation about the challenges facing media-makers and many Cubans at the moment. These young people articulated the need for changes—some small and some sweeping. But one stood out above all. They needed to have expanded venues for exhibiting their work. Possibilities for circulating their films—even on the island—were few and far between. The Muestra constitutes an important space, they agreed, but it is exceedingly limited. It takes place only once each year in Havana and lasts only a few days. Why can't the films selected for the annual event be programmed in cinemas across the entire island, rather than just in Havana, and be shown all year, rather than for a few days? And the most pressing question of all is Why can't or won't national television broadcast these works for the country's TV viewers to see?

Fingers were pointed at both the national film and television institutes. It was time for the state to step up its efforts to support emerging directors in more ways. Muestra participants asserted that the ICAIC can and must work to expand the programming in the island's cinemas and cultural spaces. And it must do more to foment audiovisual art among up-and-coming filmmakers. Industry decision makers have to acknowledge that their function is changing. "Their role," asserted Léster Hamlet, "should be to do less production and more distribution." In this way they would "catch up" with audiovisual activity on the island and actually serve the area in greatest need. Such a shift, the young artists agreed, would empower them in concrete ways.

State television has also been remiss, according to Muestra participants, for neglecting to show many films made by Cuban directors. The list of ICAIC films that had yet to be programmed on Cuban television was long.[26] Even features that had enjoyed worldwide acclaim—such as *Strawberry and Chocolate, Guantanamera, Suite Habana,* and *Páginas del diario de Mauricio*—had never been shown over television. Why had the ICRT refused to exhibit these works? And why doesn't it televise more material featured in the Muestra? Some of the young filmmakers criticized state television for seeking to show only triumphant representations and rejecting less-than-flattering portraits of Cuba and its inhabitants. They insisted that the ICRT proffer a nuanced vision of the country. It cannot present only positive images of Cuban society but must depict the problems as well and highlight areas that need improving. One audiovisual artist deemed it "ridiculous" for this work not to be televised, noting that it was going to circulate anyway.

The ICAIC and ICRT representatives in attendance—whether onstage moderating the panel or in the audience—tended to agree. It was time for a change. A conversation ensued about the respective institutions and their roles in promoting and producing audiovisual material. The observation that television was traditionally driven more by ideology and cinema more by artistic concerns was offered as one explanation of why the ICAIC filmmakers tended to enjoy greater creative license and why films produced and exhibited by the industry are not disseminated on television. Individuals—regardless of whether they worked in the film industry, for national television, or on the streets—concurred that change was desperately needed. It was not enough to point fingers at the state. "Let's be honest," intervened one moderator from the ICRT, "people make up the institutions." It was up to individuals working in state agencies as well as in the public sphere to effect transformation.

Flashing Back to the Quinquenio Gris: A 1970s Polemic Sets the Tone

The politically charged Moviendo Ideas session discussed above coincided with and gained momentum from a cultural polemic. In January 2007, Cubans got an unwelcome "blast from the past." Appearing on state television was the former president of the Consejo Nacional de Cultura (National Council of Culture, or CNC). It was not his discourse that provoked outrage—in fact, he had praised the island's cultural achievements and celebrated the work of Cuba's artists and writers—but, rather, what was left unsaid. No mention was made of the fact that during Luis Pavón Tamayo's tenure as CNC president, the council had imposed strictures limiting expression and enforcing censorship. In the five-year period commencing in 1971, Pavón led the charge that effectively marginalized a host of writers and artists, homosexuals foremost among them. Many of those under scrutiny lost their jobs—and with them their professional identities and personal sense of well-being. Others were demoted, relegated to out-of-the-way places far from the public eye. As a result, several opted for exile. The exodus of these talented artists, teachers, and other intellectuals left significant gaps. Cuba's cultural sphere suffered immeasurably. The period was an excruciatingly painful one; reverberations were felt across the island and beyond—by those deemed to be unfit to train and influence the island's youth, by their families and friends and colleagues affected by their suffering, by artists and writers and teachers and intellectuals across the island who felt their ground was eroding, by the Cuban people who had valued their progress in reducing discrimination based on gender and race, and by intellectuals in other countries who had, until this time, aligned themselves with Cuba's Revolutionary agenda. The CNC campaign to weed out gay, outspoken, and otherwise "undesirable" teachers, writers, and artists—all those perceived as threatening to the nation's youth—was nothing short of devastating.

Memories of Pavón and his damaging edicts remained etched in the minds of Cubans in general and intellectuals in particular. That is why they deemed it unconscionable for the ICRT to have invited him to be a guest on the *Impronta* program and audacious that no mention whatsoever was made of the "witch hunt" he had instigated in Cuba some thirty years earlier. Writers and artists were outraged: Lives had been destroyed because of the censors' interventions, and Cuba's culture had suffered irreparable damage. Those facts could not be forgotten. Cuba's intellectuals mobilized to ensure that past ills be acknowledged and that their perpetrators be held accountable. The past could not and would not reassert itself in the present, a time of uncertainty given the lingering legacy of the Special Period and the declining health of the aging commander in chief. The protesters mounted a massive media campaign, circulating messages in print on the island and throughout cyberspace.

Bombarded by e-mails, the UNEAC expressed its own indignation and asserted that the censorship practiced in the past would not be repeated. Perhaps, as an Associated Press reporter speculated, the UNEAC was "emboldened" by Acting President Raúl Castro, who was "encouraging young people to honestly debate Cuba's realities—though within the government structure."[27] Whatever the motivation, the assurance from this official entity was highly significant. So, too, was the fact that other state cultural organizations quickly chimed in.

The Criterios Cultural Theory Center intervened, offering to address the polemic in its series Cultural Politics of the Revolutionary Period: Memory and Reflection. One of Cuba's leading intellectuals, Ambrosio Fornet, was invited to share reflections on that dark moment in the 1970s he had termed El Quinquenio Gris (The Five-Year Gray Period). His lecture would serve as the point of departure for a collective discussion of the issues facing culture workers—then as well as now. Other renowned specialists would join him on the panel, including architect Mario Coyula, philosopher Fernando Martínez Heredia, writer Eduardo Heras León, theater specialist Raquel Carrió, and essayist Arturo Arango.

The event was initially scheduled to be held in a meeting room in the film institute headquarters, but it became apparent immediately that interest far exceeded space. The venue was changed to the Casa de las Américas. In no time at all, that auditorium had also become inadequate for the burgeoning numbers. Due to such widespread interest, the decision was made to control admission, reserving space for those most directly affected by these issues. An e-mail circulated explaining that a ticket would be required for admission; these would be divided up among various culture organizations—the Casa de las Américas, the UNEAC, the ICAIC, and so on—and distributed in the workplace ahead of time. This announcement provoked another outcry: What about those who did not report to work at one of the island's state culture institutions? The proposed solution had unintentionally created another problem. Rather than making equitable the allocation of tickets and ensuring that those most affected by the discussion could participate, it had locked out scores of culture workers, including a disproportionate number of young people who, in the lingering legacy of the Special Period, had yet to gain a position in the nation's culture infrastructure. So another solution had to be devised. A second installment of the event was scheduled; Fornet would repeat his interventions on the Quinquenio Gris and facilitate a second debate. This time the venue would be the ISA, a highly regarded school where Cuba's young artists—many of them students and alumni—felt very much at home.

At both installments of the debate, Fornet's reflections on this period and on Cuba's cultural politics held attendees captive. "It seemed that the nightmare was something from the distant past," Fornet began, "but what's certain is that when we awoke the dinosaur, it was still there." In his remarks, he deftly identified antecedents leading up to the repressive Quinquenio Gris and analyzed the implications of that moment. Fornet deemed the five-year period to be a turning point for Cuban artists and intellectuals:

> In '71, to our detriment, the equilibrium we had enjoyed until that time shattered and with it, the consensus on which cultural politics had been based. It was a clear situation of *before* and *after*: A period during which everything was done through consultation and discussion—even though everyone didn't always agree—gave way to one of Ukases: a cultural politics imposed by decree and another complementary one, of exclusion and marginalization, that converted the intellectual terrain into a barren wasteland (at least for the carriers of the virus of ideological divergence, and for the young people prone to extravagance, that is to say, fans of long hair, the Beatles and tight pants as well as those of gospels and scapulars).

Throughout his presentation, Fornet foregrounded the fact that his own experiences had shaped his perspective on this time, situated the past in the present, and framed the young intellectuals as central architects of the island's cultural future.[28]

Predictably, this polemic set the tone for the Muestra Nacional de Nuevos Realizadores. Street Filmmakers were intent on discussing a host of questions: How would injustices of the past be treated? Who could be embraced within Cuba's cultural sphere? Where should artistic and political visions converge—and how could the inevitable collisions be managed? What forms should and could comprise revolutionary culture? How should expressive culture be exhibited and disseminated? These questions engaged Muestra participants in a collective reflection on their identities as creators *and* as Cubans.

Effecting Change: Emerging Audiovisual Artists Help Shape the Future

From the filmmakers and films addressed herein, it is apparent that there is no one way to make a film in Cuba. Nor is there a single subject or style. A variety of films are being made—harsh social critiques, tender love stories, self-reflexive animated shorts. Young cineastes, in Havana as well as across the island, are transforming their artistic visions into moving images. The Muestra has created a space effective in convening aspiring and established filmmakers, putting them in touch with one another and with several of the country's cultural organizations. Because of this annual event, new works have been produced and new filmmakers trained. Old histories have been revisited—and mined for meaning. It seems fitting, in light of all these accomplishments, that the event should close with a celebration. Following the presentation of awards and final screening, participants in the sixth Muestra made their way to the *clausura*. The gatherings that wrap up many Cuban cultural events generally reflect the tastes and preferences of participants—and this was no exception. In the Teatro Nacional, adjacent to the expansive Plaza de la Revolución, strobe lights flashed and rock beats pounded. Energetic dancers filled the floor, occasionally taking a break to nibble a sandwich and sip a rum-filled Cuba libre. The festive spirit was fueled by satisfaction over prizes earned and the successful completion of another installment. The moment was undoubtedly one to be savored—and, in 2007, the best was yet to come.

A few weeks after the event had ended, the challenge Muestra participants and others posed to the ICRT was met. Their lobbying for more Cuban films to be exhibited over state television paid off. Two recent films that had yet to be seen on TV, *Páginas del diario de Mauricio* (*Pages from Mauricio's Diary*, Manuel Pérez, 2006) and *Suite Habana* (Fernando Pérez, 2003), were broadcast. Both can be interpreted as critical takes on contemporary Cuba, expressing as they do—albeit in very different ways— the challenges of getting by on the island. Not long thereafter, in May 2007, Cuba's educational channel programmed *Fresa y chocolate* (*Strawberry and Chocolate*). Viewers across the island tuned in to this poignant and arguably critical reflection on Cubans' schematized perceptions and the intolerance of homosexuality. That this film was shown in Cuba on prime-time television after fourteen years of theater-only dissemination was highly significant.

Apparently, the scandal provoked by the appearance of Pavón on state television and the ICRT's unwillingness to tackle the censorship issue head-on required that amends be made. The current director of Cuba's national television institute, Ernesto López, had to respond to accusations that the ICRT had not only buried past injustices but also continued the repressive practices. In dialogue with the minister of culture, Abel Prieto, the ICRT director agreed to televise films previously banned from TV. Cubans would be able to watch, on local television, a host of films heretofore exhibited only on theater screens. The intellectuals had clearly scored a victory. Industry filmmaker Juan Carlos Tabío exclaimed that their efforts had made the intransigent ICRT "open its doors" to Cuban films that were previously banned from television.[29] Spain's *El País* heralded the "opening of the air" in Havana; reporter Mauricio Vicent announced that a new era was dawning for Cuban intellectuals. The broadcasting of these films deemed "complicated" or "incompatible" with Revolutionary aims was only one of the results of the "email hurricane," according to this correspondent. He believed the campaign had accomplished a great deal more: "The mobilization of the intellectuals has served, above all, to open spaces of debate that Cuban creators have been attempting to reclaim for a long time." Its significance, for Vicent, goes beyond denouncing past repression to actually "change the reality of today."[30] Exclusionary politics on the island, such as the ICRT's refusal to give credence to films presenting Cuba through a critical lens, were being resisted and redressed. A victory had been won by those insisting that the ICRT broaden its programming. The pressure applied by artists and writers and intellectuals had pushed the television institute to alter its practices. Cuba's artists and intellectuals—those employed by the state and those working on their own—were indeed helping to shape their nation's cultural politics and determine the reach of the state's power.

That the resurgence of this "nightmare" set the stage for the 2007 Muestra Nacional de Nuevos Realizadores is instructive. It reminds us that in Cuba—like virtually everywhere—culture is produced and consumed within precise circumstances. It is linked with political, economic, social, and other forces, all of which are tied to particular places and periods. Artists—including the young Muestra participants—do not create in a vacuum; their work resists and responds to larger forces in their midst. Another lesson learned from this convergence is that the past continues to inform the present and the future. The "dinosaurs" are still with us, to paraphrase Fornet, and occasionally we awaken them. The past cannot and should not be buried. To do so is to risk repeating past mistakes and perpetuating painful legacies. Only by excavating injustices from earlier years can future generations avoid the errors of their predecessors. The output of this new generation of Cuban intellectuals and artists—Street Filmmakers among them—is in constant dialogue with attitudes, actions, and aesthetics from earlier times.

As we have seen herein, young people working outside Cuba's state culture apparatus are claiming their space. They expect to participate and be taken into account. They see themselves as active agents shaping Cuba's culture and the nation's future. Invested in their community and their work, they refuse to stand by while residue from "dirtier" times is swept under the rug. They are exceedingly committed to protecting the space within which they exercise their creativity and enact their identities. Because of this, they expect to be accorded legitimacy as Cuban artists and intellectuals. And, for the most part, they are. The Cuban state respects their vision and has reserved a place for them. Street Filmmakers and others working outside official government channels have teamed up with their "insider" counterparts. They are not debating who's "in" and who is "on the streets," nor are they drawing lines to divide the generations. Instead, they are joining forces to usher in a new era. These critical debates and discussions, then, serve to integrate newly emerging values such as tolerance, social justice, and individual development into a political vision.

As we have witnessed in this montage of films, filmmakers, and cultural polemics, the Muestra is a significant forum. It fosters solidarity and creates a sense of community—not through a movement, per se, but, rather, from a vision shared by artists. It is not the revolutionary community proffered by the ICAIC of the 1960s, 1970s, and 1980s, one founded with a specific agenda placing culture at the service of the Revolution. Instead, it is a growing public space in which to express ideas, identify common concerns, lobby for change, and develop tactics of intervention.

The collective voice of Cuba's culture workers is making itself heard—and making a difference. Audiovisual artists from across the island, connected to one another through the Muestra, are willing to challenge the status quo. These individuals are exercising their influence and participating in effecting changes. As the twenty-two-year-old filmmaker Alina Rodríguez Abreu remarked, "When there are so many of us expressing something, something is happening."[31] And indeed, as we have seen throughout this study, Cuba's culture workers—audiovisual artists foremost among them—are contributing in concrete ways to transforming the world in which they live and work.

Every day I'm more convinced
that the existence of a film
industry in Cuba is a miracle.
—Esteban Insausti

Reflections on Cuba, Filmmaking, and the Times Ahead

Before taking leave of this generation of Cuban culture workers, it is worth our while to reflect on the island's audiovisual future. In the preceding pages, we witnessed the transformation of "Cuban cinema"; what is connoted by the category has shifted dramatically over the past twenty years. The endeavor of filmmaking, once confined within a concertedly national paradigm—emphasizing autochthonous cultural production designated principally for domestic consumption—is now increasingly propelled by transnational linkages and responsive to global forces. The boundaries of "cinema" have been pushed outward as well. The accessibility and ease of digital media and communications networks have expanded the forms of expressive culture considered under the rubric of "cinema" well beyond 35-millimeter films projected in theaters.

For Cuba's culture workers, the past two decades of accelerated change have been both arduous and exhilarating, due to the convergence of an economic crisis, new media technologies, and an entrepreneurial generation of new cineastes. Industry filmmakers once wary of these developments now express hope for the island's audiovisual future. "It would be great if I could spend the last years of my life watching films by young people and hearing what they have to say, filmmakers whose aspirations are not to have a villa or a castle with a swimming pool," mused Humberto Solás not long ago. "Fortunately, before I die it seems that I will see the reemergence of the avant-garde."[1] Indeed, it appears that the efforts of filmmakers like those treated herein—as well as many others—have helped revive the island's fledging film field and transform it into a robust audiovisual terrain.

It bears remembering, though, that the future of Cuba's cinema is not guaranteed. In fact, several pressing problems persist. Cuban filmmakers, producers, and others face a series of challenges at this juncture. Foremost among them is distribution. New audiovisual technologies have increased access to production but have not necessarily expanded distribution channels. Filmmakers the world over struggle to get their films before audiences, and Street Filmmakers are no exception. While they have developed strategies for making films without the industry apparatus, they have yet to figure out how to disseminate them to significant numbers of viewers on and beyond the island. This poses a serious impediment even for experienced auteurs. Juan Carlos Cremata Malberti decided to return to the ICAIC for his next feature after the highly successful *Viva Cuba*. Despite having devised a new filmmaking mode consistent with the Cuban context—one relying on low budgets, a small team, and modest resources—he remains dependent upon the industry's distribution network. The key factor motivating Cremata Malberti's decision to team up with the national film institute on another project was distribution; the ICAIC's infrastructure would increase the odds of this film reaching a broad audience. This experience and others like it beg the question, To what extent can innovative efforts flourish if the state apparatus is needed to successfully penetrate the international market? A key challenge for Cuba-based artists—and those of virtually every small nation with limited domestic audiences—is that of reaching worldwide consumers. Street Filmmakers have cleared the production hurdle only to find that the next one they face, that of distribution, appears even more imposing.

This new generation of Cuban filmmakers is connected to global communications networks; they rely extensively on YouTube and other sites for uploading their work and communicate with their counterparts around the world via e-mail, in chat rooms, and over Internet telephone. But new communications technologies have not mitigated the problem of distribution. The Internet can proffer access, it's true. But the widespread nature of this access poses another problem. Because virtually every artist who is connected can upload audiovisual material, visitors to the site encounter a plethora of options. The work by young Cuban artists who have not yet made a name for themselves often goes unnoticed. Given the barrage of material—an amount growing exponentially—it is unlikely that the work of any individual or group will stand out and reach large numbers of viewers. So although Street Filmmakers do take advantage of the Internet, this has not and likely will not replace the importance of cinemas, festivals, and television for circulating their films. Nor will it permit them to recoup even a small part of their investment. Besides, like emerging cineastes the world over, one dream of most Cuban filmmakers is to see their name on the marquis of a cinema and view their work on the big screen. The next few years remain critical to Cuba's audiovisual future; solutions will have to be devised to ensure that Street Filmmakers succeed in reaching the global marketplace. Their accomplishments with production will have to be paralleled by considerable progress with distribution.

Another critical problem facing Cuba's audiovisual sphere at this juncture grows out of the increasing decentralization of the state apparatus. Whereas the opening of greater space for new artists has generated creative momentum and yielded an impressive array of cultural products, this has come at a cost. The position of the state film institute is more precarious than ever. Coproduction agreements help the institute produce films, but they do not replenish Cuba's coffers; even successful films rarely yield domestic dividends, for profits generally go to international distributors rather than producers. At present, the ICAIC struggles to keep coproduction promises; sometimes, as a recent example will illustrate, it cannot bankroll its share of a film even when the Cuban contribution is a fraction of the total production cost. In 2007, Esteban Insausti managed to garner a $200,000 commitment from a foreign producer, an amount admittedly paltry by international standards but more than sufficient to get *Larga distancia* off the ground. Nevertheless, the project stalled because the ICAIC lagged behind in coming up with its share. Partnerships have indeed provided Cuban filmmakers with greater resources, but external funding is no panacea for this cash-strapped national film institute.

The dire economic straits have translated into the obsolescence of equipment and deterioration of films and related documents. Island film facilities are inadequate and equipment is in disrepair. ICAIC filmmakers must make do with outdated cameras, lighting, and sound equipment—that is, when they are fortunate enough to be granted access to the dwindling supply. Many industry filmmakers in Cuba work with equipment that is several generations behind that of both the worldwide industry and their counterparts working in the streets. The vehicles for scouting locations and transporting equipment and crews are dilapidated. Computers are outdated, and printers and photocopy machines, more often than not, lack toner cartridges and paper. There is simply not enough of anything—equipment, supplies, staff—to go around. So while the ICAIC has been able to proffer some support for Street Filmmakers thus far—most notably in the form of the Muestra Nacional—its future contributions appear limited at best. For the state film institute to continue fomenting audiovisual activity outside its walls, it will have to establish clear priorities, identify new sources of capital, and scrutinize the process through which scarce resources are allocated.

The inadequacy of production facilities is paralleled in screening venues. Many—if not most—of the island's theaters are in disrepair. Across the island, these structures suffer from lack of routine maintenance and harsh climatic conditions: In lobbies, light fixtures are broken and cracked window glass is covered with tape and plastic; in screening auditoriums, upholstery is torn, seat cushions are missing, and the subflooring shows through the worn carpet; in the lavatories, fixtures are broken and plumbing is inoperable. The filmgoing experience suffers as a result. During the International Festival of New Latin American Cinema, moviegoers monitor the programming carefully so as to catch a particular film in one of the better theaters. In-the-know *habaneros* avoid Actualidades, for example, a once grand but now dilapidated cinema across the street from the Bacardí Building. They are reluctant to perch on broken seats, struggle to discern dialogues from the static in the sound system, and suffer the consequences of backed-up toilets and broken pipes. Routine maintenance has fallen woefully behind; it will take a major influx of human and financial resources to repair these once magnificent venues. Compounding these problems is the severe damage wreaked by recent hurricanes. The destruction in the wake of Gustav and Ike, in September 2008, was staggering.[2]

Another serious problem has to do with archiving—of both the "classic" Revolutionary films and the body of new material being produced. In Cuba, conditions for preserving films are exceedingly precarious. Already some of the nation's cultural patrimony has been lost due to harsh climatic conditions, insect damage, and mishandling. For this project, I screened hundreds of documentaries, newsreels, features, and animation films. In most instances, I viewed the original 35-millimeter copy. While certainly ideal from a research standpoint, it was problematic from a preservation point of view. Each time the brittle celluloid passed through the projector, it became increasingly susceptible to scratching and breakage. Over the years, the ICAIC has lacked the resources necessary to create multiple copies on film and transfer 35-millimeter masters to video. An apparatus permitting the creation of video copies was purchased, but the secondhand Telecine has never functioned properly. The originals have continued to suffer from wear and tear and sometimes lack of care. Although efforts are currently under way to preserve some films by digitizing and reissuing them on DVD, this important step has been taken too late to save all the materials. Significant damage has already been done.[3]

While carrying out research in the ICAIC, I was dismayed to find that several films I had hoped to screen were no longer available. In some cases, they had simply disintegrated, the archivist would open a canister to find a reel with dust and bits of celluloid rather than film. Air conditioning units are old, inefficient, and unreliable. Frequent blackouts during the Special Period and ensuing years have only exacerbated the damage done by heat, humidity, and the tropical conditions. On one occasion, I was told that a particular newsreel documenting the establishment of the ICAIC in 1960 had been lost. The staff member communicated with regret that Noticiero 49 (Newsreel 49) had been lent to an overseas festival and was never returned to the archive. Recalling that I had first seen the newsreel in a documentary about Latin American cinema, I set out to locate a copy. I succeeded in doing so and created a digitized version to comprise part of the first volume of my Cuban Cinema Classics initiative. In this way, I could return it to the ICAIC. While I was pleased to have helped recover this historic newsreel, I was dismayed by the inferior quality resulting from having to rely on a video copy rather than the 35-millimeter master. On another occasion, I arrived at the screening room before the projectionist had reported to work. There on the floor outside the projection booth were several canisters containing films. The janitor had placed a wet rag on top of the stack; dirty water dripped down the sides. On yet another occasion, while screening of one of Cuba's first revolutionary films as part of a Muestra session, I watched as the deteriorated celluloid broke repeatedly and was rethreaded through the projector only to tear again. The other members of the audience and I never did manage to see the ending; the projectionist later confirmed that those of us in the screening room that day were the last people who would see this work, for this had been this film's final exhibition.

Friends and colleagues in Cuba have shared experiences of their own. One audiovisual artist recalls requesting scrap footage to be attached to his film for winding it onto the reel; when he looked over the piece handed to him, he discovered it was a classic short by one of the maestros. The desire to provide what was needed, despite the lack of materials, had compelled one ICAIC employee to *resolver*. Unfortunately, this solution to this filmmaker's problem risked the integrity of the film archive. (Fortunately, the filmmaker recognized the valuable footage he was given and reported the incident as he handed back the strip.) The ICAIC faces a formidable challenge; the paucity of resources is such that maintaining the archive—much less taking steps to reverse the damage already done—poses a monumental task. It is already too late to preserve *all* the material filmed on celluloid. Yet, if conservation is deemed a priority and international partners assist, there may still be time to save the bulk of this cultural patrimony.

Given the ease with which digital material can be reproduced and stored, it may seem that preservation has become a problem of the past. In fact, this is not the case. The rapid proliferation of media-making among Cuba's young audiovisual artists has generated a wealth of material, but as of yet, there is no centralized system for storing and proffering easy access to it. Each filmmaker takes responsibility for his or her own works. Under ideal circumstances—in which each filmmaker had a reliable computer with a large hard drive and extensive external memory for backing up media—this could be effective. But circumstances are far from ideal: Many filmmakers work on a computer belonging to a friend or family member or state institution, and some operate on a budget so tight that the cost of even a single DVD can be prohibitive. While most manage to *resolver* through the solidarity of individuals and institutions on the island, there is a pressing need for a central clearinghouse to archive and manage this material. Staff members of the Muestra Nacional office, located in the ICAIC, have been exceedingly helpful in collecting and cataloging new digital material. Other organizations have also pitched in—the FLC, the EICTV, the FNCL, and the SGAE, among others. But a more concerted effort is required if Street Filmmakers are to have guaranteed access to their own work as well as that of their counterparts, and if related promotional material is to be made available in a systematic way for producers, distributors, and scholars.

Archiving and preserving a half-century's worth of filmed material is not the only challenge. The island has no lab, which means that films must be sent elsewhere for postproduction. Facilities in Spain and Mexico have proved useful over the years. More recently, the ICAIC sought assistance from its ally Venezuela. The master copy of Pavel Giroud's first feature was dispatched to Caracas for completion. But once again, there was no guarantee of a positive outcome. *La edad de la peseta* was damaged in a Venezuelan processing lab and salvaged—according to the version told to me by a third party—only because the director was willing to cover up the mishap, and the missing parts, by making changes to the completed work. Clearly, the lack of adequate facilities on the island poses a significant risk to Cuban films and their makers.

The U.S. trade embargo exacerbates many of the difficulties facing Cuban filmmakers and ICAIC specialists. The United States is an international leader in manufacturing audiovisual equipment and supplies, so the fact that Cubans cannot purchase from U.S. sources or from companies that do business with the United States limits significantly the range of suppliers while increasing transportation costs. ICAIC vice president Luis González Nieto explains that "the list of material resources the blockade denies us is long: spare parts and equipment, raw stock, chemicals, accessories for film equipment." The Cuban film world is adversely affected by this U.S. policy, in regard to both preserving existing materials and producing new ones. González Nieto estimates that the raw stock and chemicals necessary to "rescue" Cuba's "film heritage" would cost about 40 percent less if it were not for the embargo. Similarly, scarce production funds could be stretched farther if Cubans had the opportunity to do business with U.S. vendors. The industry vice president shares an example: In 2006, the ICAIC paid some $85,000 for six video cameras outfitted with accessories. Only two of them were high definition, a number woefully inadequate to satisfy their needs. The money would have gone much farther if the equipment could have been purchased in the United States. "We cannot buy Kodak directly," observes González Nieto, and so transactions take place in Europe and elsewhere; costs increase dramatically, given currency exchange rates and the reliance on a "middle man." Similarly, the United States holds the Dolby sound permit, and this fact also poses a hardship. Dolby sound is essential for the international marketing of Cuban production, but as González Nieto explains, "although Cuba has sound labs meeting the requirements for the permit, they are denied it, so the only form of obtaining the permits is through . . . the participation of third parties in our productions. [In 2006], dozens of thousands of dollars had to be spent additionally for having six of our films meet this requirement." The United States also serves as an important conduit for accessing international distribution channels, and for this reason, the U.S. practice of denying visas for these artists and industry professionals to enter the country signifies a major obstacle. Cuban producers cannot attend such commercial events as the American Film Market, and filmmakers are blocked from accepting invitations to festivals and conferences where they might promote their work.[4] It is clear, then, that the field of Cuban filmmaking is replete with obstacles.

For the ICAIC to continue serving as a producer, it will have to consider making a sizable investment in replacing obsolete equipment, creating a processing lab or identifying a foolproof partner, and upgrading neglected facilities. Alternately, industry leaders may deem it more effective—and indeed more lucrative—to scale back on production in order to enhance the ICAIC's role as a distributor. By continuing to reconfigure its mission as one of supporting Street Filmmakers—serving as an advocate and ally for audiovisual artists working on a variety of projects—the institute will ensure its ongoing relevance while helping to guarantee the continuation of Cuba's rich cinematic tradition.

Making films in present-day Cuba continues to be a precarious undertaking. As one filmmaker confided to me, referring to the obstacles facing him and his colleagues, "We're at a juncture where Cuban cinema saves itself or is screwed" ("Estamos en el momento en que el cine cubano se salva o se joda"). Challenges persist. Problems proliferate. And yet, I remain hopeful that Cuban cinema will survive. Cuba's audiovisual artists, with their knack at *resolviendo*, will likely continue propelling their culture forward. I am encouraged by the development of more partnerships beyond the island with producers, distributors, festivals, cultural organizations, and educational institutions. I am impressed by the increase in audiovisual creation and circulation outside Havana. I am buoyed by the proliferation of new spaces for viewing films on the island—in video clubs, in festivals, in schools, in special screenings hosted by state and nongovernmental organizations, and in historic theaters such as Santiago's Cine Cuba—that have been restored. But what inspires most confidence in the island's audiovisual outlook are the filmmakers themselves. Artists in their forties, thirties, twenties, and even teens—those treated herein as well as dozens or perhaps even hundreds of others—are, I believe, just hitting their stride. Cameras in hand, they are defining the future of their nation.

It is fitting to give the last word to one of Cuba's Street Filmmakers who shared with me his wonder at the resilience of his island's cinema despite the less-than-ideal conditions: "In this country right now, where there are difficulties distributing gasoline and buying powdered milk, the fact that films are made is a miracle."[5]

NOTES

Introduction

1 Fornet, introduction, 11.

2 See the introduction to Stock, *Framing Latin American Cinema*. For more of Fernando Pérez's thoughts on this time, see my essay "Imagining the Future in Revolutionary Cuba."

3 Here I am, of course, referring to Benedict Anderson's seminal work, *Imagined Communities*.

4 Sheldon Hsiao-Peng Lu has examined related issues in his study of contemporary Chinese cinema; see *Transnational Chinese Cinemas*, 16–17.

5 Lievesley, *Cuban Revolution*, 160; Hernández-Reguant, "Copyrighting Che," 3.

6 Readers interested in the construction of Cubanness from late colonial times

until 1959 should consult Lou Pérez's definitive analysis of that period. In *On Becoming Cuban*, the acclaimed historian argues convincingly that the convergence of Cuban and U.S. cultures produced a fusion of "dynamic adaptation and accommodation" that yielded a unique sense of Cuban identity.

7 Martin and Paddington, "Restoration or Innovation?," 11.

8 Quoted in Resik, "Writing Is a Sort of Shipwreck," 86.

9 Gutiérrez Alea, "Respuesta a *Cine Cubano*," 103.

10 Writing in the *Cine Cubano* journal, in an essay titled "Notas para una cronología del dibujo animado," Roberto Cobas Arrate reflects on that momentous act: "With the triumph of the Revolution, the cultural sphere embraced cinema as a mode for communicating with the people. The Revolutionary government established as its first decree in the cultural realm, the creation of the national film institute. . . . From this date forward, the true Cuban cinema emerges, film that will have among its principal objectives combating ignorance, ideological and cultural underdevelopment, and recovering our traditions" (3).

11 The film that comes to mind immediately is Walter Lang's *Weekend in Havana*. In it, Carmen Miranda is the simpleminded Spanglish-speaking Cuban who falls head over heels for John Payne, a serious "American" businessman—all of this against a backdrop in which Cesar Romero strikes up colorful musical numbers.

12 Ambrosio Fornet shares these reflections in the documentary by Michael Chanan, *The Long Road*.

13 Martin and Paddington, "Restoration or Innovation?," 6.

14 For reflections by both ICAIC leaders—the outgoing Alfredo Guevara and the incoming Omar González—see issue 48 of *Cine Cubano*, particularly "Mi pasión se inspira más allá del cine," by Guevara (7–9), and "El tiempo es transparencia," by González (10–13).

15 The film world mourned the death of maestro Tomás Gutiérrez Alea in 1996, followed by Santiago Álvarez in 1998 and Pastor Vega in 2001. Directors Octavio Cortázar, Sergio Núñez, and Humberto Solás all died in 2008.

16 Fernandes, *Cuba Represent*, 3.

17 Martínez Heredia, "In the Furnace of the Nineties," 147.

18 Hernández, "Looking at Cuba," 127.

19 It would not be until the new century that rates would drop back to earlier levels: In 2000, 5.4 percent of the population was deemed "economically inactive"; in 2001, 4.1 percent; and in 2002, 3.3 percent. See Martínez Puentes, *Cuba más allá de los sueños*.

20 Convergences like these can yield exceedingly productive zones. A range of

postcolonial critics have interrogated these "crossroads" and their potential: the "Borderlands," for Gloria Anzaldúa; "Third Space," as designated by Homi Bhabha; "Cultural Reconversion," according to Nestor García Canclini; and "Contact Zones," in the words of Mary Louise Pratt, to name only a few. Their work builds on earlier formulations by Fernando Ortiz; the concepts of "transculturation" and "mestizaje" forwarded by this Cuban anthropologist are central to understanding the coming together of diverse cultures.

21 Students from other countries studying filmmaking at the EICTV outside Havana have also honed in on the challenges facing Cubans. In *No te acuestes* (*Don't Lie Down*, 2005), Giovanni Federico's camera follows a young man going about the business of making ends meet. When the entrepreneur in the film is inspired to create a Pink Panther doll to sell at a crafts market in Havana, his challenge becomes one of finding enough foam cushions to meet the increased demand for his product. The poignant work of this young Italian-born artist demonstrates his keen awareness of the context in which he was living and studying.

22 *Video de familia* earned more than a dozen awards at national and international festivals, including the first prize (Coral) for short fiction at the International Festival of New Latin American Cinema and the same prize in the same category at the Latino Film Festival in Los Angeles. Propelled by this momentum, Padrón went on to make the feature-length film *Frutas en el Café* in 2005.

23 Jorge Fornet has examined the phenomenon he describes as the "dehistoricization" of history among young intellectuals. Although he limits his study to literature, it has relevance for audiovisual expression as well.

24 This beloved Cuban baseball player left the country on a boat in December 1997. He established residency in Costa Rica and, a few months later, signed on as a pitcher with the New York Yankees.

25 In Caparó, "La era, la apertura," 10.

26 Hall, "Cultural Identity," 220.

27 The term "Cine Pobre" must also be considered here. Acclaimed Cuban filmmaker Humberto Solás founded a festival by this name. While the term does designate low-budget films, a feature shared with Street Films, it is more expansive in embracing films the world over made with minimal resources and new technologies. "Cine Pobre," then, refers to international filmmaking efforts rather than to ones specific to Cuba during a precise moment. The festival has come to attract filmmakers and sponsors from numerous countries.

28 Quoted in Caparó, "La era, la apertura," 16, 18. Another young filmmaker,

Tupac Pinilla, follows suit. In advocating for more flexibility in the island's audiovisual world, he articulates his desire to avoid "a divorce between the institution [ICAIC] and the creators *on the street*" (21) (emphasis mine).

29 Galeano, preface to *Memory of Fire*, xv.

30 See, for example, those drafted by Alfredo Guevara: *Revolución es lucidéz* (1998); *Un sueño compartido* (with Glauber Rocha, 2002); *Ese diamantino corazón de la verdad* (with Cesare Zavattini, 2002); and *Tiempo de Fundación* (with Cesare Zavattini, 2003). See also *Tomás Gutiérrez Alea: Volver sobre mis pasos*, ed. Mirtha Ibarra (Madrid: Ediciones Autor, 2007).

31 Among these are Fornet's *Alea*, Évora's *Tomás Gutiérrez Alea*, Labaki's *El ojo de la Revolución*, Fowler's *Conversaciones con un cineasta incómodo*, Flores Gonzalez's *Tras la huella de Solás*, and Caballero's *A solas con Solás*.

32 Principal among these are *El cine silente en Cuba*, by Raúl Rodríguez, and *La tienda negra*, by María Eulalia Douglas.

33 Juan Antonio García Borrero deals with recent fiction films in his *Guía crítica de cine cubano de ficción*.

34 See, for example, Fornet, *Bridging Enigma*; Kirk and Fuentes, *Culture and the Cuban Revolution*; and Castillo, *Con la locura de los sentidos*.

35 García Borrero, "El cine submergido."

36 MacCannell, *Empty Meeting Grounds*, 9.

37 Ambrosio Fornet acknowledges some of the many ways in which Cuban traditions are connected to the United States. In the introduction to *Bridging Enigma*, he writes, "American films, literature, and popular music—not to mention, baseball and hot dogs—are part of our collective imaginary and everyday life.... Cuba is no doubt one of the countries that knows the *americanos* best—for better or worse" (4).

38 Hernández, "Looking at Cuba," 124.

39 Galeano, preface to *Memory of Fire*, xv.

Chapter 1

1 See Douglas, Vega, and Sarría, *Producciones del Instituto Cubano*.

2 The Centro Memorial Dr. Martin Luther King Jr. has also supported audiovisual projects. Hosted by the Ebenezer Baptist Church, this organization was established in 1987 in honor of the social justice activist and spiritual leader from whom it takes its name. Its purpose is "to accompany the Cuban people and their churches in creating the formation for popular participation."

3 This is not to suggest that video was altogether absent from the ICAIC. Some

industry filmmakers did indeed turn to video in order to continue working. Their efforts yielded documentaries on video including the following: *La virgen del Cobre* (Félix de la Nuez, 1994); *Del otro lado del cristal* (Guillermo Centeno, Marina Ochoa, Manuel Pérez, y Mercedes Arce, 1995); *El cine y la vida: Nelson Rodríguez y Humberto Solás* (Manuel Iglesias, 1995); *Y me gasto la vida* (Jorge Luis Sánchez, 1997); and *Identidad* (1999) and *De mi alma, recuerdos* (2002), both by Lourdes de los Santos.

4   EICTV website.

5   Brugués interview. In keeping with this emphasis on practical training, the school has been directed by an internationally renowned filmmaker from its inception. These include Fernando Birri from Argentina (1986–90), Orlando Senna from Brazil (1991–94), Lisandro Duque Naranjo from Colombia (1994–96), Alberto García Ferrer (1996–2000) and Edmundo Aray (2000–2002) from Venezuela, Julio García Espinosa from Cuba (2002–6), and Tanya Vallete from the Dominican Republic (2007–9).

6   During this time, the Cuban director accepted my invitation to meet with students and colleagues and share his recent work. When we conversed in Williamsburg, Virginia, during his 1996 visit to the College of William and Mary, Cremata Malberti impressed us with the range of his interests—in music, literature, art, theater, dance, and film—and also with his passion for each of these areas.

7   I am grateful to Enrique Colina for introducing me to these materials. Colina served as an adviser on both documentary projects and presented them as part of a workshop he gave during the Muestra Nacional de Nuevos Realizadores in February 2007.

8   The Serie Taller de Cine, directed by Gabriel García Márquez, stands out as one of the most notable. Proceedings from this series were published under the title *Así de simple* by Editorial Voluntad (Santafé de Bogotá, Colombia) in 1995.

9   The press seized the moment, and the EICTV was featured in writing and on film around the world. A CNN reporter visited the school, his report comprised the web stream titled "CNN's Morgan Neill Visits a Film School in Cuba That's Reportedly Uncensored" that was disseminated over CNN.com. In response to the journalist's question about freedom of expression, the academic director and Argentine filmmaker Rolando Pardo emphasizes the students' autonomy in choosing their topics. Permission has to be requested for filming on location, as is the case virtually everywhere in the world, he explains, but he insists that the school enjoys academic freedom. In the report, San

Antonio de los Baños was featured as the most filmed city in Cuba, a theme that was reiterated in events leading up to the anniversary celebration.

10 "Escuela Internacional de Cine y Televisión de San Antonio de los Baños (Cuba) celebrará 20 años."

11 The history of these brothers is available over the AHS website: In August 1957 they planned a celebration in their home province of Pinar del Río to observe the birthday of Fidel Castro. Before leaving home, they purportedly told their mother not to worry and promised that someday their actions would make her proud. Minutes later, they were gunned down. See <http://www.nnc.cubaweb.cu/historia/historia45.htm>.

12 Julián del Casal, born in Havana in 1863, is considered to be one of the precursors of Modernism in Latin America. His best-known works are *Hojas al viento* (1890), *Nieve* (1892), and *Bustos y Rimas* (1893). Del Casal died of a brain aneurism in 1893.

13 Shortly after *Un pedazo de mí* and *El fanguito* appeared, Pérez would take up the alienation of Cuba's youth in his renowned Special Period film, *Madagascar*, and Díaz Torres would treat a similar subject in his controversial *Alicia en el pueblo de Maravillas* (*Alice in Wondertown*, 1990). More than a decade later, Esteban Insausti would nod to Sánchez in *Existen* (*They Exist*, 2005), an exploration of another of Havana's disenfranchised sectors—those people deemed to be crazy.

14 The director position was set up on a rotation; film critic Juan Antonio García Borrero led the first installment, and Sánchez later took his turn.

15 Other accolades were forthcoming for Sánchez—several prizes during the Havana event as well as awards in Switzerland, Dominican Republic, Spain, Paraguay, and Mexico.

16 For more details regarding early use of video in Cuba, particularly in education, see Reyes Rodríguez and Acosta, "Una aproximación a la evolución de la técnica del video." To examine the role of video in documentary production, see Naito López, "El documental cubano desde sus orígenes hasta nuestros días."

17 Film practices of developing countries that call into question colonialism and imperialism have been understood as part of the Third Cinema movement. Teshome H. Gabriel has outlined the aims of Third Cinema to be decolonizing minds, contributing to the development of a "radical consciousness," provoking a revolutionary transformation of society, and developing a new film language (*Third Cinema in the Third World*, 3). Adherents to Third Cinema have produced a wide variety of films from within distinct national contexts on several continents. Despite the divergent subject matter and varied styles of

these films, some common features can be identified: These works often treat themes related to oppression (class antagonism, racial and ethnic struggle, armed conflict, the emancipation of women); they frequently include some call to action; a particular national reality is often evident (issues of local import); and the filmmakers tend to jettison Hollywood-style representation for a style more consistent with the particular contexts in which they work. It is not surprising, then, that the images and ideas of Latin American film theorists and practitioners—Fernando Birri, Julio García Espinosa, Octavio Getino, Glauber Rocha, Fernando Solanas, and Jorge Sanjinés among them—are considered germane to Third Cinema. Key texts on Third Cinema and on the films from various contexts comprising this movement include Pines and Willemen, *Questions of Third Cinema*; Armes, *Third World Film Making and the West*; Downing, *Film and Politics in the Third World*; and Guneratne and Dissanayake, *Rethinking Third Cinema*.

18   Belkis Vega is credited as one of the pioneers of video within the ICAIC. She was honored during the first installment of the Muestra Nacional de Nuevos Realizadores for her efforts in fomenting the production and dissemination of this medium. From the time of her initial foray into video in 1998—serving as assistant director on the series titled *La botija*, consisting of twenty-one installments lasting twenty-seven minutes each—she has carried out an impressive production program. During the 1990s alone, she made some three dozen works, including fiction, documentary, and publicity spots. Although she deals increasingly with video, two of her projects from this time—*Una gota en el mar* (*A Drop in the Sea*, 1990) and *Canción de gesta* (*Gesture Song*, 1991)—were made using 35 millimeter.

19   The armed forces had, as early as 1959, created didactic films, documentaries, and newsreels. This activity continued within the Film Section of the Revolutionary Armed Forces (Sección Fílmica de las Fuerzas Armadas Revolucionarias, or ECIFAR), established in 1961. The education sector provides another example where filmmaking formed part of their mission. The year 1972 witnessed the founding of the Department of Educational Cinema (Departamento de Cinematografía Educativa, or CINED).

20   Unless otherwise noted, all quotes from this filmmaker and information about her career come from my interview with her in Havana on 23 Dec. 2005.

21   Rolando dedicates *Oggún* to her mother, grandmother, and "African ancestors." An epigram by the Haitian James Stephen Alexis—"Africa does not leave the Negro in peace, no matter from which country he is, the place from where he comes or goes"—underscores the centrality of African traditions

in the Caribbean, in Cuba, and in this documentary. Afro-Cuban composer Pablo Milanés has arranged the musical themes, and members of the Conjunto Folklórico Nacional de Cuba perform the dances. The filming and editing are stunning at times. Occasionally, however, the choreography approximates cliché for me (as when a languid female caresses her nude body in the forest as a machete-wielding male looks on). Nevertheless, *Oggún* serves as a formidable ethnographic document, one that manages to teach tradition through poetic evocation rather than didacticism.

22   The theme of Afro-Cuban identity has been treated extensively in Cuba's revolutionary cinema by Sara Gómez, Rigoberto López, and numerous others. Among the works with Afro-Cuban history and culture are *El otro Francisco* (*The Other Francisco*, 1974); *Buscando a Chano Pozo* (*Looking for Chano Pozo*, 1987); *Omara* (1983); *Roble de Olor* (2003); and *El Benny* (2006).

23   Minh-ha, *Woman, Native, Other*, 141–51.

24   See <http://www.afrocubaweb.com/wiwc.htm>.

25   Established by Karen Ranucci, with support from the Rockefeller Foundation, the Latin American Video Archive was envisioned to disseminate Latin American films to U.S. audiences. For more than a decade the organization flourished. University professors and students invested hundreds of hours in translating scripts to facilitate subtitling in English. The organization closed its doors in 2005.

26   Sáez Carvajal and Benítez Muñoz, "Ludwig Foundation of Cuba," 2.

27   The first foundation established in revolutionary Cuba was the Fundación del Nuevo Cine Latinoamericano (<http://www.cinelatinoamericano.org>), created in 1985. This entity, founded through the efforts of Armando Hart, the minister of culture at that time, would pave the way for several more foundations to appear during the 1990s. Among these NGOs devoted to culture are the Fundación Nicolás Guillén (<http://www.fguillen.cult.cu>), founded in 1991; the Fundación Alejo Carpentier, the FLC, and the Fundación Antonio Nuñez Jiménez de la Naturaleza y el Hombre (<http://www.fnh.cult .cu>), all in 1994; and the Fundación Fernando Ortiz (<http://www.fundacion fernandoortiz.org>) and the Fundación Caguayo para las Artes Monumentales y Aplicadas, both in 1995.

28   The foundation president's words are cited in the report prepared by Sáez Carvajal and Benítez Muñoz, "Ludwig Foundation of Cuba."

29   Helmo Hernández and Wilfredo Benítez shared contacts, helped open doors, and put their staff and facilities at my disposal. One FLC specialist, Luis Enrique Prieto Armas, invested countless hours in assisting me with everything from conducting research and transcribing filmed interviews to shuttling me to

meetings and events. The FLC served as my base for filming interviews with directors on several occasions. Access to this well-equipped facility and the added bonus of a welcoming atmosphere and professional attention helped advance this project. During virtually every one of my visits to the FLC, I have met scholars and artists and educators—from Cuba, Europe, Canada, the United States, and elsewhere—all benefiting from the foundation's commitment to cultural exchange.

Chapter 2

1. The founding director of TVS, Daniel Diez Castrillo, shared his experiences during the seventh Muestra Nacional de Nuevos Realizadores and in e-mail correspondence with the author. Unless otherwise noted, citations come from these exchanges, which were enriched by the Cuban television program *Pantalla Documental* and the UNESCO "Making Waves" report.

2. Among the festivals in Cuba where TVS documentaries have been projected are the Festival de Cine de la Montaña (various rural locales), Cine Pobre (Gibara), Festival Documental de Santiago Álvarez in Memoriam (Santiago de Cuba), Muestra Nacional de Nuevos Realizadores (Havana), and the Festival Internacional del Nuevo Cine Latinoamericano (Havana).

3. Gumucio-Dagrón, *Sustainability of Community Media*, 1.

4. Yúdice, *Expediency of Culture*, 83.

5. UNESCO Havana, "Conmemoran década de la TV Serrana."

6. See "Making Waves" on the Communication Initiative website for more details on development in the region.

7. Chanan, *Cuban Cinema*, 29.

8. Louise Spence and Robert Stam have analyzed the process whereby colonial relationships are reproduced through film and television. See their seminal essay, "Colonialism, Racism, and Representation."

9. This documentary as well as several other experimental works by Nicolás Guillén Landrián are available on DVD, subtitled in English, from Cuban Cinema Classics <www.cubancinemaclassics.org>.

10. Other notable works that embrace rural settings and the people who labor there include *Y me hice maestro* (*And I Became a Teacher*, Jorge Fraga, 1961), and *Madera* (*Wood*, Daniel Díaz Torres, 1980).

11. Díaz Torres, "Más allá de La Habana."

12. "Making Waves."

13. Among these are the Concurso Caracol of the UNEAC; the Premio Abril of the Unión de Jóvenes Comunistas; the Premio Vitral, the prize for the best

documentary in the Encuentro Iberoamericano y Caribeno; and the Premio de Mérito de las Televisoras del Caribe. See UNESCO Havana, "Conmemoran década de la TV Serrana." Prizes in international competitions have come from the Caribbean Broadcasting Union (for Daniel Diez Castrillo's *Un cariño poderoso* in 1996), the International Festival of New Latin American Cinema (for Waldo Ramírez's *La chivichana*), and the encounter of youth cinema in Venezuela (for Marcos Bedoya's *Tocar la alegría* in 2001). See "Festejan aniversario."

14 UNESCO Havana, "Conmemoran década de la TV Serrana."

15 Intergovernmental Council, "Evaluation Summaries of 100 Terminated Projects."

16 Gumucio-Dagrón, *Sustainability of Community Media*, 11.

17 For more than twenty-five years Adalberto Alvarez has been involved in creating and developing Cuba's foremost musical form, the *son*. Building on the tradition of his legendary compatriots—Arsenio Rodríguez, Miguel Matamoros, and the great Cuban troubadours—Alvarez founded the *Son 14* ensemble in Santiago de Cuba. The prolific Cuban composer recorded a compact disc for release in the United States titled *Jugando con candela* (*Playing with Fire*) on the Atlantic Records "Havana Caliente" imprint. His compositions have been recorded by such Latin music heavyweights as El Gran Combo, Oscar De León, Sonora Poncena, Juan Luis Guerra, and many others in the United States and Europe. The *New York Times* describes Alvarez and his groups as "one of Cuba's great bands"; The *Miami Herald* warns that when listening to his music, "You won't be able to sit still for long" (<http://www.ritmoartists.com/Alvarez/alvarez.htm>, accessed 18 Oct. 2005).

18 Televised over Tele Rebelde on 8 June 2005.

19 Díaz Torres, "Más allá de La Habana."

20 Across the world, there are at least a few other examples of state support: the Indigenous National Institute in Mexico, Radio Kiritimati in the Pacific island nation of Kiritimati, and Radio Kothmale in Sri Lanka.

Chapter 3

1 Mario Rivas made this comment during a conversation with the author in Havana on 3 January 2006. Most studies of Cuba's film tradition give short shrift to animation, but a handful of critics have paid the art form some attention. For the most comprehensive history of animation in Cuba, see Douglas, *La tienda negra*, and Douglas, Vega, and Sarría, *Producciones del Instituto Cubano del Arte e Industria Cinematográficos*. Roberto Cobas Arrate

("Notas para una cronología del dibujo animado" and "El dibujo animado en Cuba o la verdadera historia de Quijotes y Sanchos") and Giannalberto Bendazzi (*Cartoons*) have also addressed this subject in their respective studies. Cuban film critics Joel del Río Fuentes and Dean Luis Reyes have also treated the island's animation.

2   Cuba's first two animated films were created in 1937 by different teams. The earlier, *Napoleón, el faraón de los sinsabores* (*Napoleon, the Pharaoh of Troubles*), was based on the comic strips of the same title published in the Sunday edition of the newspaper *El país gráfico*. Cartoonist Manolo Alonso and several associates created this two-minute black-and-white piece, filmed in 35 millimeter. The latter, appearing almost simultaneously, was created by Manuel Roseñada y Silvio and featured the character Masabí. Although these works met with positive reception, animated shorts were not in great demand. Production costs could not be recovered, so their makers stopped after these first attempts. Nearly a decade later, animation initiatives emerged in two other island locales. In Guantánamo, Luis Castillo attempted to set up an animation shop. There he convened other artists and, relying on material sent from the Walt Disney studios as a guide, created *Coctél musical* (*Musical Cocktail*) in 1946. Paradoxically, this animated film about music was silent. The piece apparently did not meet with great success, nor did the group's subsequent work titled *El jíbaro y el cerdito* (*The Farmer and the Little Pig*, 1947). Still further to the east, in Santiago de Cuba, another animated film was produced in 1946. The brothers César and Mario Cruz Barrios set up a modest studio in their father's garage. With the help of a group of family members and friends, they created *Restituto el detective* (*Return of the Detective*). Shortly thereafter they produced *El gato con botas* (*Puss in Boots*) and *El tesoro de todos* (*Everyone's Treasure*). Motivated by their success, and believing that making animated films in Cuba could yield dividends, this group invested their own capital to establish the Productora Nacional de Películas de Santiago de Cuba. They produced the island's first 35-millimeter animated film made in color, *El hijo de la ciencia* (*Son of Science*, 1947). Although a first for Cuba, it was the last for this company. With local film circuits controlled by U.S. distributors, it was nearly impossible to get the film exhibited. *El hijo de la ciencia* never recovered its production costs. The loss compelled the company to discontinue animation and turn instead to newsreels, publicity documentaries promoting tourism, and fiction films featuring local actors.

3   The creation of Cuba's animation department has been traced back to various moments between 1959 and 1963. Even official sources differ as to the founding date: The website of Cuba's national film institute reports 1960 (<http://

www.cubacine.cu/boletin/noticias.html#aniv>), and that of the Animation Studio notes 1963 (<http://www.cubacine.cu/dibujosanimados/index .htm>). I find most compelling the testimony of two insiders who pinpoint the studio's origin in 1959. Hernán Henríquez recalls teaming up with Jesús de Armas and Eduardo Muñoz Bachs and beginning work in the ICAIC late that year. Paco Prats, a producer who joined the Animation Studio in 1963, reasons that with 1960 being the year in which the first two animated films were released, it is highly likely that work on them had begun the previous year. There was no laboratory in Cuba at this time, and the films were dispatched to California for processing—a fact that further supports Prats's contention. Later, many films were sent to Czechoslovakia for developing; Roberto Cobas Arrate notes that it was not at all unusual for the turnaround time to take six months (see "Notas para una cronología del dibujo animado," 4). Colleagues from the time concur with Prats that the studio was established late in 1959. See del Río Fuentes, "Diálogo con Juan Padrón."

4 Hernán Henríquez's testimony in this chapter comes from Léa Zagury's interview with him in *Animation World Magazine*.

5 Del Río Fuentes, "La historia contada por un testigo cómplice," 26.

6 Del Río Fuentes, "Diálogo con Juan Padrón," 26.

7 Bendazzi, *Cartoons*, 386.

8 Cobas Arrate, "Notas para una cronología del dibujo animado," 7.

9 This organization is comprised of more than 2 million Cuban children and adolescents, more than 98 percent of the island's primary and secondary school students. Founded in 1961, the organization has engaged Cuban youth in educational and cultural activities, recreation, and sports. Some 200 facilities on the island—parks, summer camps, explorer camps (similar to scouts), and clubs designed around areas of professional interest—are available to the young Pioneers.

10 Feedback from children would continue to be valued for years to come. Experienced animation director Mario Rivas underscored the importance of communication between animation filmmakers and their audiences in an essay published in *Cine Cubano* in 2001. He calls for even more contact, noting that "although meetings have taken place with girls and boys, and they've been successful, there's a feedback deficit between the creators and the small spectator for whom the work is destined" ("Niñas, niños, y nuestro dibujo animado," 66–67).

11 Other renowned animation artists in Cuba treat this conflict in their projects. Mario Rivas filmed a short work about Máximo Gómez and Antonio Maceo and their 1895 invasion. Tulio Raggi devoted an animated short to José Martí

in New York. And in Mario Rivas's *El bohío* (*The Palm Hut*, 1984), presenting various moments of Cuba's history, a brief sequence addresses the War of 1898. For information on other films treating this conflict—from Cuba as well as from France, Spain, and the United States—see Alejandro Pizarrozco Quintero's "Guerra, Cine, e Historia: La Guerra de 1898 en el cine," in *Historia y Comunicación Social*, no. 3 (1998): 143–62.

12   Reloba, "Juan Padrón."

13   In Spanish the lyrics are,

> Para Elpidio Valdés, patriota sin igual,
> no hay gaito que lo pueda espantar.
> En el combate es enérgico y vivaz,
> a las balas el pecho siempre da. Él no cree en nadie,
> ni en esto ni en lo otro,
> ni en lo de más allá.
> Él no cree en nadie
> a la hora de buscar la libertad.

14   See del Río Fuentes, "Diálogo con Juan Padrón," 27.

15   Dean Luis Reyes analyzes this film in "El etnocentrismo blando."

16   Chanan, *Cuban Cinema*, 358–59.

17   Douglas, *La tienda negra*, 292.

18   Cobas Arrate, "Notas para una cronología del dibujo animado."
      Yeyín is a twelve-year-old girl, and the tale revolves around her adventures with her friends of the Cosmo Palace of Intergalactic Pioneers. Ernesto Padrón introduced a female protagonist as a counterpart to all the male characters in Cuban animation at the time. In *Yeyín* as well as in his other work, Padrón gravitates toward themes of diversity, tolerance, and human solidarity. See Chávez Spinola, "Ernesto Padrón Blanco," for more details about this artist and his creation.

19   See Reloba, "Juan Padrón."

20   These figures were provided by Luis González Nieto during my interview with him in Havana.

21   Del Río Fuentes, "Diálogo con Juan Padrón."

22   Douglas, *La tienda negra*, 216.

23   Alba Noguera interview. All quotes by this producer and information about his career come from this interview.

24   Prats interview. All quotes by this producer and information about his career come from this interview, unless otherwise noted.
      Others have noted how ingenuity has sustained ICAIC filmmaking, in-

cluding animation, during difficult periods. The observations of Cesar Coehlo, Brazilian animator and codirector of the Anima Mundi animation festival, are illustrative. He writes, "Whatever they lack in resources and technology, Cubans compensate for with improvisation and creativity. In the entire animation studio, I only saw one computer which was used for pencil texts. However, after using an Oxbury camera for the first time, technicians from the ICAIC constructed a second one utilizing parts designed from the first" ("Havana Connection").

25 Aja Díaz, "La emigración cubana." By this time, Hernán Henríquez had already been gone for a decade. In a 2005 interview with Ivette Leyva Martínez in the Spanish edition of the *Miami Herald*, *El Nuevo Herald*, the Cuban animation artist discussed his reasons for leaving Cuba. "From the time I was a little boy, my aspiration was to come to the United States and work in animation. My father lived here, and my mother and brothers and sisters had emigrated. . . . I hadn't been able to go with them." As the 1970s were ending, Henríquez requested permission to leave the country in order to reunite with other members of his family. While waiting for his request to be granted, he and his wife and two children, living near the Peruvian embassy at the time, took advantage of the Mariel Boat Lift in 1980.

26 The impact of this initiative extended beyond Cuba's borders through Operación Milagro (Operation Miracle), in which Cuban doctors performed eye surgery at no cost to their Latin American and Caribbean neighbors suffering from impaired vision or total blindness. See *Granma* [Havana], 4 Jan. 2006, 3–4; <http://embacu.cubaminrex.cu/Default.aspx?tabid=2111>.

27 Cultural critics have analyzed the imperialist ideology proffered by Disney. *How to Read Donald Duck*, by Armand Mattelart and Ariel Dorfman, remains the touchstone; it became the best-selling collection of essays among Spanish-language readers in the 1970s. Kevin Shortsleeve provides a comprehensive review of the literature by "Disney detractors" in "The Wonderful World of the Depression: Disney, Despotism, and the 1930s; Or, Why Disney Scares Us," *The Lion and the Unicorn* 28 (2004): 1–30.

28 De la Hoz, "Hay Elpidio Valdés."

29 Nilza González Peña provided these figures to the author during an interview.

30 In 2003, the Ministry of Culture announced the development of animation as a new area of specialization at the country's premiere fine arts school, the ISA.

31 Estrada Betancourt, "Tengo Elpidio Valdés," 4.

32 Del Río Fuentes, "Diálogo con Juan Padrón."

33   Estrada Betancourt, "Nuestra bandera," 4.

34   <www.cubavsterrorismo.cu>.

35   I am grateful to Luis González Nieto for providing these figures during our conversation in Havana.

36   <www.cubacine.cu>.

37   Initial projections were ambitious. The time frame and hoped-for number of minutes proved unrealistic, given the need to procure and install new hardware and software, train existing staff and hire new team members, and move the operation to a building undergoing renovation. Still, 2000 saw the creation of the first films done using video-Betacam, and the following year saw the introduction of a new series.

38   Titles include, from the ICAIC, *El güije enamorado* (Homero Montoya) and *El lápiz* (Ulises de Jesús Ramos); from the ICRT, *El libro* (Liván Rodríguez) and *Solución fácil* (Yurina Luis Naranjo); and from Erpiro Studios & Musimagestudios, *Todo por Carlitos* (Ernesto Piña Rodríguez).

39   See <http://www.cubacine.cu/dibujosanimados/festival/convoca.htm>.

40   Island partners include the ICRT, Cuba's educational television and education channels; the Universo Audiovisual del Niño Latinoamericano network, a nonprofit organization comprised of individuals and institutions committed to projects that support the development of media for children from the earliest ages and the creation of active, critical, and participatory spectators; the EICTV in San Antonio de los Baños; and UNICEF. International partners, principally but not exclusively from the Spanish-speaking world, include CEFOCINE (Ecuador); University Film Club of Maracaibo, Cinema Department of the University of los Andes, and FUNDACIN (Venezuela); the Centro de Estudios e Investigaciones sobre la Infancia (Argentina); ACIPAZ (Perú); the Movimiento Nacional de Meninos y Meninas de Rua, the School of Communication and Library Science at the Universidad Federal de Goias, and the Núcleo de Educación y Comunicación de la Escuela de Comunicación y Arte at the Universidad de Sao Paulo (Brazil); Producciones Nicobis and Centro de Arte Audiovisual (Bolivia); Centro de Investigación de la Comunicación (Mexico); Departamento de Periodismo y Comunicación Audiovisual of the Pompeu Fabra University and the Facultad de Ciencias Sociales y de la Comunicación of the University of el País Vasco (Spain); and Kinderfilmfest in Marl and Kinderkino Munich (Germany) (<http://www.habanafilm festival.com/universo/index_noticias_amplia.php3?ord=10> [accessed 5 Nov. 2005]).

41   The films can have been produced for cinema or television and need not adhere to any specific duration parameters. Other requirements include their

being directed at children and adolescents and being understandable to Spanish-language audiences (whether originally in Spanish, dubbed into that language, or understandable without any language). Prizes are awarded by three juries—one comprised of children, another made up of adolescents, and a third involving five international (including Cuban) filmmakers or specialists.

42 *Manga* refers to Japanese comic books and graphic novels. Whereas Japanese *manga* takes a range of forms, the term outside Japan generally conjures the "moe" style of animation featuring characters with large eyes and a simple L-shaped nose.

43 Prats's career has been the subject of a documentary by Aram Vidal titled *Paco* (2005). This affectionate portrait pays homage to the man who, for more than forty years, has helped build Cuban animation into one of the nation's preeminent cultural forms.

Chapter 4

1 Cuban films had previously participated in this prestigious event, but no other Cuban feature had ever earned a prize.

Unless otherwise noted, all quotes from Juan Carlos Cremata Malberti are taken from my interview with him in Havana on 30 June 2006. Quotes from Alejandro Pérez are taken from conversations and my interview with him during the Primera Muestra de Cine Alternativo en México in Campeche in December 2006. For discussing with me their experiences collaborating on *Viva Cuba*, I am grateful to Angélica Salvador, John Della Penna, Esteban Insausti, Inti Herrera, and Sandra Vigil Fonseca.

2 As a result, morale among the filmmakers plummeted. Orlando Rojas, in fact, attributes this uncertainty over when he might next be able to film to his decision to emigrate in 2003. It likely had to do with his disillusionment when "Closed for Renovations," a project on hold for more than a decade, was shut down after his first day of filming. The blow was devastating, Rojas confided to me. He now makes his home in Miami.

3 Cinergia was founded in 2004 by María Lourdes Cortés, Central American cinema specialist and former director of the Centro Costarricense de Producción Cinematográfica (CCPC) in San José. Principal sources of funding include the Ford Foundation, Hivos, and the Fundación Clementina. In Costa Rica, additional support is provided by the Universidad Veritás and the CCPC, among others.

4 This sequence calls to mind the final frames of Truffaut's *400 Blows. Viva*

Cuba differs, though, in that the children have each other. They face the sea, then each other, and then the sea in quick succession. In contrast, the solitary French boy stands before the sea alone and turns back to face the camera. Both open endings invite varied interpretations. Yet, Cremata Malberti's protagonists have the benefit of their friendship.

5 Koehler, review of *Viva Cuba*.

6 Some Cuban directors, particularly during the 1980s and 1990s, immersed themselves so fully in the island's idiosyncrasies that their films didn't resonate with international viewers. Even Cuban audiences eventually tired of these films saturated with rapid-fire slang, stock characters, and sexual innuendos.

7 Corrigan, *Cinema without Walls*, 144, 146.

8 Díaz, "El síndrome de Ulises."

9 From the author's interview with Inti Herrera.

10 Cremata Malberti's willingness to embrace the new technology offered by the French partners—a Panasonic 100 AE camera, in a PAL 25 progressive frames system—positioned him alongside other Cuban directors eager to experiment with unfamiliar equipment. Among the other films created digitally by this time are *Miel para Oshún* (Humberto Solás, 2001), *Suite Habana* (Fernando Pérez, 2003), *Tres veces dos* (Pavel Giroud, Léster Hamlet, Esteban Insausti, 2004), and *Barrio Cuba* (Humberto Solás, 2005). With each foray into digital technology, Cuban filmmakers become more adept at working with new equipment and employing new production modes.

11 To illustrate his point, Alejandro Pérez shared an anecdote with the audience at the Primera Muestra de Cine Alternativo de México (First Exhibit of Alternative Film in Mexico), in San Francisco de Campeche late in 2006. A company selling Crazy Glue contracted with film professionals in Japan and Latin America. The publicity teams were tasked with communicating the effectiveness of the product and emphasizing how quickly the glue works— it takes hold in a mere ten seconds. The Japanese group, with a huge budget, designed a superproduction in which a huge crane lifts a semitrailer; the two are connected by a single drop of glue. The Latin Americans, working with limited resources, communicated their message much more simply. A drop of glue is applied to a clock, and the second hand gets "stuck" at the ten-second mark.

12 See De la Soledad, "Exclusive Interview."

13 Ann Louise Bardach revisits this event in the November 2006 *Atlantic Monthly*. Her investigative report reveals compelling evidence suggesting that the act was indeed carried out by Orlando Bosch and Luis Posada Carriles

with support from the U.S. Central Intelligence Agency ("Twilight of the Assassins," 88). The fact that the CIA reports key records from the time to be missing in no way weakens her claim.

14 And, implicitly, against the United States, for it is still widely believed that the CIA played a role in the bombing.

15 Corrigan, *Cinema without Walls*, 102.

16 Participants in the film became instant celebrities. The young protagonists appeared on several talk shows and children's programs, Cremata Malberti was interviewed on the national news and cultural programs, and the children of La Colmenita theater troupe were whisked off to Europe for performances.

17 Among these are the International Festival of Giffoni (Italy), Festival of Films from Spain and Latin America (Belgium), Festival of Children's Film (Venezuela), International Festival of New Latin American Cinema (Cuba), International Festival of Children's Films and Television (Taiwan), Cyprus Film Days (Greece), International Festival of Film and Video CINESUL (Brazil), and Sydney Latino Film Festival (Australia). It was also Cuba's entry for the Oscars' Best Foreign Film category.

18 Cremata Malberti admires the films of many Cuban directors, including Titón (Tomás Gutiérrez Alea), Humberto Solás, Santiago Álvarez, Fernando Pérez, Juan Carlos Tabío, Orlando Rojas, Daniel Díaz Torres, Rolando Díaz, Gerardo Chijona, Manuel Herrera, Manolito Pérez, Octavio Cortázar, Idelfonso Ramos, Julio García Espinosa, Pastor Vega, and Adolfo Llauradó.

19 In "Respuesta a *Cine Cubano*," Tomás Gutiérrez Alea reflects on the "birth" of Cuba's revolutionary cinema, noting that it has come into being "in the midst of a group of young people who to some extent are related to one another and constantly exchange ideas and opinions. They are young people who have become filmmakers on the fly" (103). Alea and Julio García Espinosa are notable exceptions to the learn-by-doing style of filmmaking during the early years of the Revolution; both studied at the Centro Sperimentale di Cinematografía in Rome.

20 Fernando Pérez was in his forties when he filmed *Clandestinos* (*The Clandestine Ones*), and Jorge Luis Sánchez was forty-six years old when *El Benny* premiered. Both Enrique Colina and Rigoberto López were in their fifties when they made *Entre Ciclones* (*Between Hurricanes*) and *Roble de Olor* (*Scent of Oak*), respectively.

21 Cuban filmmakers graduated in a variety of academic disciplines: Rebeca Chávez in art history and journalism; Gerardo Chijona and Mayra Vilasís in English language and literature; Rolando Díaz in Cuban studies; Daniel Díaz

Torres, Manuel Herrera, and Rigoberto López in political science; Fernando Pérez in literature; and Orlando Rojas and Gloria Rolando in music, to mention only a few.

22 Cremata Malberti worked in Argentina; Esteban Insausti, in Mexico; and Jorge Luis Sánchez, in Venezuela.

23 Resik, "Writing Is a Sort of Shipwreck," 86.

Chapter 5

1 All quotes attributed to Pavel Giroud, unless otherwise noted, are from my interview with him in Havana on 4 July 2006 and his written answers to my follow-up questions in an e-mail dated 9 March 2007.

2 For studies of national cinema, see esp. Elsaesser, *New German Cinema*; Higson, *Waving the Flag*; Williams, *Film and Nationalism*; Hjort and Mackenzie, *Cinema and Nation*; and Crofts, "Reconceptualizing National Cinemas." Transnational cinema texts have proliferated in recent years; among them are Ezra and Rowden, *Transnational Cinema*; Nestingen and Elkington, *Transnational Cinema in a Global North*; and Lu, *Transnational Chinese Cinemas*.

3 It bears remembering that from the time when moving pictures arrived on the region's shores, more than a century ago, their creation and circulation has been transnational in nature. D'Lugo, "Authorship, Globalization, and the New Identity of Latin American Cinema," and Paranaguá, "America Latina, Europa, y Estados Unidos," remind us that these present-day collaborations and coproductions are hardly new to Latin America. Nor are they new to Cuba, as Laura Podalsky has convincingly argued in "Negotiating Differences." What differs between these earlier border-crossing initiatives and current ones is the scope. At present, it is increasingly difficult, if not impossible altogether, to find sites of "national" culture not influenced by transnational and global processes.

4 Among the films made employing the coproduction mode during the 1990s are *Adorables mentiras* (Gerardo Chijona, 1991); *Vidas paralelas* (Pastor Vega, 1992); *El siglo de las luces* (Humberto Solás, 1992); *Fresa y chocolate* (Tomás Gutiérrez Alea and Juan Carlos Tabío, 1993); *Derecho de asilo* (Octavio Cortázar, 1994); *El elefante y la bicicleta* (Juan Carlos Tabío, 1994); *Reina y Rey* (Julio García Espinosa, 1994); *Guantanamera* (Tomás Gutiérrez Alea and Juan Carlos Tabío, 1995); *Pon tu pensamiento en mí* (Arturo Sotto, 1995); *Amor vertical* (Arturo Sotto, 1997); *Kleines Tropikana* (Daniel Díaz Torres, 1997); *Un paraíso bajo las estrellas* (Gerardo Chijona, 1999); and *Las profecías de Amanda* (Pastor Vega, 1999).

5 D'Lugo, "Authorship, Globalization, and the New Identity of Latin American Cinema," 112.

6 Video art relies on moving pictures and is comprised of video and/or audio data. Yet, it differs from television and experimental cinema in significant ways. Video art may exclude actors altogether, may jettison dialogue, and may develop without any discernible plot or narrative. And whereas a principal aim of cinema is to entertain, the intentions of video artworks are more varied. Some serve to push the limits of the medium; others, to defy viewers' expectations of conventional representation. Emerging in the 1960s and 1970s, video art continues its forward momentum as technologies evolve and present new possibilities.

7 I am grateful to Alejandro Pérez and José Luis Lobata for sharing with me their production experiences as well as copies of their respective video clips.

8 Estrada Betancourt, "Soy un aprendiz."

9 The film earned awards at several Cuban festivals, including El Almacén de la Imágen, the second Muestra Nacional de Nuevos Realizadores, and the Encuentro Nacional de Video. At the Rosario film festival in Argentina, the film came away with prizes for best editing and best male actor.

10 It occurred earlier with *Mujer transparente* (*Transparent Woman*, 1990) and had been attempted in 1993 with *Madagascar* (Fernando Pérez, 1994); *Melodrama* (Rolando Díaz, 1995); and *Quiéreme y verás* (*Love Me and You Will See*, Daniel Díaz Torres, 1995). Although this short was undertaken as a collaboration that would join the three segments into a single film, that plan changed along the way. Fernando Pérez explained to me that the filmmakers took varying amounts of time to complete their respective works, and the projects grew lengthier than anticipated. Thus, it was deemed more sensible to launch each film individually as it was completed rather than to wait for the other pieces of the trilogy and risk releasing an overly long film. See my interview with him in Stock, "Imagining the Future in Revolutionary Cuba."

11 Insausti interview.

12 Giroud developed the script for this project in a writing workshop. He had always wanted to deal with the subject of a photographer who had to confront what he saw in his photos. But Senel Paz, the director of the workshop, suggested that the story be told with this element of the apparition. Giroud credits Paz with being the "motor" propelling this narrative forward and acknowledges support from two other senior colleagues in the industry, producer Camilo Vives and filmmaker Fernando Pérez.

13 Prerevolutionary popular forms, advertising included, have been overlooked by earlier generations of revolutionary filmmakers who sought their inspira-

tion elsewhere. For insight into Cuba's fashion advertising, see Hector Cruz Sandoval's documentary on Alberto Korda, best known for capturing the iconic image of Che Guevara. *Kordavision* (2005) traces the career of this renowned Cuban back to his early years as a fashion photographer in Havana.

14 *La bella del Alhambra* (*The Belle of the Alhambra Theater*), directed by Enrique Pineda Barnet in 1990, is perhaps the most significant ICAIC film employing the musical genre.

15 D'Lugo, "Authorship, Globalization, and the New Identity of Latin American Cinema," 103.

16 A graduate of the ISA, she works in theater and television as well as in cinema. Giroud cast her earlier in *Flash* as the enigmatic woman in the photographs. She also worked with Giroud on his video clip *Arráncame la vida* (2003). It is very common among Cuban directors, both industry and Street Filmmakers, to collaborate with some of the same individuals. A great deal of emphasis is placed on relationships, and when they work, they can last a lifetime. Notable partnerships are evident, for example, in Fernando Pérez's repeated collaboration with photographer Raúl Pérez Ureta, editor Julia Yip, and composer Ediseo Alberto. Laura de la Uz acted in two consecutive films of his, and Luis Alberto García has appeared in several as well.

17 Giroud, "Dejándo atrás *La edad de la peseta*."

18 De la Hoz, "Nunca pensé que mi primer largo corriera tanto."

19 A more complete version of this coproduction disaster can be found in my essay "Hollywood South?"

20 Martin and Paddington, "Restoration or Innovation?," 9.

21 Fadraga Tudela, "Cada historia lleva su luz," 18.

22 Martin and Paddington, "Restoration or Innovation?," 10.

23 Fadraga Tudela, "Cada historia lleva su luz," 18.

24 Stock, "Imagining the Future in Revolutionary Cuba," 71–72.

25 López, "Cuba."

Chapter 6

1 Shohat and Stam, *Unthinking Eurocentrism*, 346.

2 This explains, at least in part, the reaction of the director and editor to the Miami broadcast. I visited with Insausti and Angélica Salvador in their home in Havana, and they expressed their dismay and disillusionment over the film having been "hijacked" by Miami. That *Existen* was shown without their permission and without them having received any compensation seemed to matter little. The "pirating" of the film troubled them far less than its co-

option for political maneuverings. Their artwork had been reduced to a strand in the rope tugged back and forth across the Straits of Florida. For Miami television, it may have seemed benign to wield *Existen* as a political tool to widen the U.S.–Cuba rift. For the filmmaker and his production team, however, this disrespectful treatment robbed them of a unique opportunity. They were denied thoughtful criticism that might have contributed to their professional development and perhaps even facilitated the film's circulation. A television broadcast like this one in another country could have yielded a careful analysis of *Existen* as a work of art—albeit one engaged with larger social, political, and economic issues. Insausti and his team sought intellectual engagement, criticism that would stretch them as artists and demonstrate the extent to which their vision had touched viewers beyond the island. They also worried that the antirevolutionary rhetoric of the commentator could limit their options for making films later on. Many partners in Cuba, the ICAIC included, would be reluctant to fund films that could be used to further the agenda of Miami's Cuban community.

3 This director follows in the footsteps of the masters before him who managed with deftness to accomplish the same: Sara Gómez with *De cierta manera*, Orlando Rojas with *Papeles secundarios*, Jorge Luis Sánchez with *El Fanguito*, Fernando Pérez with *Madagascar* and *Suite Habana*, and Juan Carlos Cremata Malberti with *Viva Cuba*.

4 Insausti credits alternative spaces, like the FLC and El Ingenio (Cremata Malberti's independent production initiative), with providing some backing.

5 This technique of gathering bits and pieces to fashion a new work has a precedent in revolutionary cinema. The collage approach constitutes a hallmark of the politically charged work of Santiago Álvarez and Mayra Vilasís. For Álvarez, the discarded broadcast footage from U.S. news programs—with *NOW!* being one of the most compelling examples—was employed to use the language of the oppressor. Similarly, *Oración* (*Prayer for Marilyn Monroe*, Marisol Trujillo, 1984) recycles Hollywood film footage and magazine pinups of the actress to deconstruct the myth of film stardom. In both cases, the collage approach yielded results both hard-hitting and artistically stunning. While the integration of this "found" material was indeed practical, the decision to employ the collage approach was politically motivated. With Street Filmmakers, in contrast, the willingness to use whatever equipment and materials are at hand emanates more from their pragmatism rather than from some political or aesthetic agenda.

6 Insausti's first fiction short, *Más de lo mismo* (*More of the Same*, 2000), ful-

filled his graduation thesis requirement at the ISA in Havana; it was invited to participate as an official selection in the Cannes Film Festival in 2001.

7   Insausti pays homage to another talented artist from Cuba in *Sed de mirar* (*Thirst for Watching*, 2004). This film portrays the renowned cinematographer Jorge Herrera, whose contributions to the ICAIC date back to its very founding in 1959. The film ponders the genesis of his creative spirit, an exploration made more meaningful by chiaroscuro lighting evoking this man's intense desire to create the ideal image and his extreme satisfaction at getting it just right.

8   Little has been written about this early filmmaker. Those interested in the life of this Cuban auteur should consult one of the two documentaries made about him. Although rudimentary in terms of technique, they are of interest for their sequences featuring the onetime filmmaker in his Miami surroundings, the vestiges of his battle with mental illness and substance abuse dating back to his Havana days readily apparent.

9   The music of this artist was, for a time, deemed too esoteric to serve the purposes of the Revolution. Salvador and many of his contemporaries—Silvio Rodríguez and Pablo Milanés included—found numerous doors closed to them on the island; they were given space within the ICAIC, however, and comprised the highly successful Grupo de Experimentación Sonora del ICAIC. Jaime Sarusky has examined the trajectory of this group in *Una leyenda de la música cubana*.

10 Among the more notable are *Nosotros y la música* (*We are the Music*, Rogelio París, 1964); *Y tenemos sabor* (Sara Gómez, 1967); *Hablando del punto cubano* (Octavio Cortázar, 1972); *Omara* (Fernando Pérez, 1983); *Yo soy la canción que canto* (*I Am the Song I Sing*, Mayra Vilasís, 1985); and *Buscando a Chano Pozo* (*Looking for Chano Pozo*, Rebeca Chávez, 1987). The last three mentioned are available on DVD with English subtitles through Cuban Cinema Classics <www.cubancinemaclassics.org>.

11 Editor Angélica Salvador declined to participate in this phase. She explained to me her concern that scouting trips might introduce a bias into her work. When she is splicing the footage, later in the process, she does not want to know just how invested the team was in a particular locale or just how much energy went into rendering spaces appropriate for the film. She believes she will be more inclined to cut out sequences her editorial eye deems superfluous. For this same reason, she keeps as low a profile as possible during the filming and prefers not to accompany the team. See Salvador interview.

Chapter 7

1   Arcos, "Gustavo Arcos sobre el audiovisual joven en Cuba."

2   Massip, "Opina José Massip."

3   Diéguez, "La dimensión de las palabras."

4   Sánchez interview.

5   Given the deflated value of Cuba's currency, few islanders have the financial resources necessary to make any payment beyond the island—a $50-dollar festival application fee is as untenable as a $5,000-dollar permissions fee. The latter helps explain why some recent films—even award-winning works—do not circulate beyond the island. Cuban artists integrate the songs and verses and images of others into their films but cannot pay the steep fees to secure permission. The case of Waldo Ramírez with *Freddy o el sueño de Noel* was already treated in Chapter 2. Whereas one might assume that this limitation affects only those filmmakers working on the streets and not those in the industry, this is not the case. The compelling portrait of Harry Belafonte, *A veces miro mi vida* (*Sometimes I Look at My Life*, Orlando Rojas, 1981), for example, contains footage of Hollywood films for which permission has not been granted. I requested this title for inclusion in my Cuban Cinema Classics initiative; the ICAIC lawyer expressed regret at being unable to permit the reproduction and circulation of this work that, like many others, is destined to stay at home.

6   Until March 2008, Cubans could not legally have cell phones. Some entrepreneurial Street Filmmakers managed to *resolver*, however, making arrangements with foreigners residing in Cuba who had access to the service and were allowed more than one number.

7   Vidal e-mail to author.

8   This filmmaker has earned the respect of his peers in the ICAIC as well as that of the young audiovisual artists that he mentors. Pineda Barnet has directed and/or authored the scripts for more than two dozen films. In 2006, he was named recipient of the Premio Nacional de Cine, the island's most prestigious film award. His best-known film is the musical *La bella del Alhambra* (*The Belle of the Alhambra Theater*, 1989).

9   The Centro de Formación Literaria Onelio Jorge Cardoso was created in 1998 under the auspices of the Ministry of Culture, the UNEAC, and the Hivos Foundation (Netherlands), with the objective of training young writers. The center takes its name from a prominent figure in Cuba's literary landscape. Cardoso was born in 1914, and during his lifetime spanning more than seventy years he developed a reputation as one of the island's best-known short-story writers. See <http://www.centronelio.cult.cu>.

10   Chiano, "Los desafíos de una generación."

11   Arcos, "Gustavo Arcos sobre el audiovisual joven en Cuba."

12   The "Sí yo puedo" literacy initiative was developed in Cuba to help Third World countries address illiteracy. With the momentum built by the founding organization, the Instituto Pedagógico Latinoamericano y Caribeño (Latin American and Caribbean Pedagogical Institute), other partners have signed on. Several governmental and nongovernmental organizations are working together to promote literacy among impoverished and disenfranchised people in various regions.

13   Diéguez, "La dimensión de las palabras."

14   Gustavo Pérez interview.

15   Barba interview. Pineda Barnet quoted from <www.cubanews.net>.

16   Caparó, "Efectos de una mirada muy personal," 5–6.

17   Brugués interview; Inti Herrera interview. All quotes from Brugués and Herrera and information about their careers come from my interviews.

18   Even a positive festival record can be insufficient for breaking into the press, as a recent experience of mine will illustrate. I approached a well-known U.S. film journal that has often devoted space to Cuban cinema, offering to submit an interview with Juan Carlos Cremata Malberti or a review of *Viva Cuba*. I noted that his road movie was a hit on the international festival circuit and took prizes at numerous prestigious events. They replied in the negative, explaining that they only accepted essays on films being distributed in the United States. Their editorial policy precluded them from considering *Viva Cuba*'s worldwide acclaim and making concessions in light of restrictions imposed by the U.S. trade embargo limiting exchanges between Cuba and the United States.

19   Several impressive documentaries by this filmmaker are compiled in a volume in the Cuban Cinema Classics series. The English subtitles, supplementary information, and DVD format make them accessible to a wide audience. See <www.cubancinemaclassics.org>.

20   Ramos, "*Rachel K.*"; Santos Moray, "El extraño caso de Oscar Valdés."

       Julio García Espinosa earned the admiration of filmmakers and theorists across Latin America and beyond for his influential formulation of an "imperfect cinema." This film theorist-practitioner insisted on a mode of production compatible with local conditions. Like other adherents to Third Cinema and New Latin American Cinema, he warned that Hollywood could not and should not be the model for artists in "underdeveloped" nations to follow.

21   Ramos, "Oscar Valdés," 21.

22   I have included this work as well as Colina's delightful *Estética* (*Aesthetics*,

1986) in my Cuban Cinema Classics series; both have pleased film audiences at festivals as well as in the university classroom.

23 Colina interview.

24 During the 2008 installment, the Muestra added another important component. For the first time in the event's history, a session was held for select filmmakers to pitch their ideas to producers.

25 From my correspondence with Pablo Fornet, an urban geographer in the Oficina del Historiador de la Ciudad de La Habana, I learned that the Isla de Cuba and the Regina were, in fact, two different hotels. The former was located on Montes Street as early as 1900; the latter was on Águila and then Industria Street in the 1920s and 1930s, respectively.

26 Enrique Colina enumerated them in an article by Gerardo Arreola published in Mexico's *La Jornada*. Among them are *Techo de vidrio* (*Glass Roof*, 1982), by Sergio Giral; *Alicia en el pueblo de Maravillas* (1990), by Daniel Díaz Torres; *Adorables mentiras* (1991) and *Perfecto amor equivocado* (2003), both by Gerardo Chijona; *El elefante y la bicicleta* (1994) and *Lista de espera* (1999), both by Juan Carlos Tabío; *Guantanamera* (1995), by Tomás Gutiérrez Alea and Juan Carlos Tabío; *Madagascar* (1994) and *La vida es silbar* (1998), both by Fernando Pérez; *Pon tu pensamiento en mí* (1995) and *Amor vertical* (1997), both by Arturo Sotto; *La ola* (1995), by Enrique Álvarez; *Miel para Oshún* (2001) and *Barrio Cuba* (2005), both by Humberto Solás; *Nada* (2001), by Juan Carlos Cremata Malberti; and *Entre ciclones* (2003), by Enrique Colina.

27 Associated Press, "Cultural Thaw?"

28 Fornet's weighty remarks—a comprehensive assessment of Revolutionary cultural politics over the past three decades—were published in their entirety in the *Casa de las Américas* journal and in *La política cultural del período revolucionario*.

29 Juan Carlos Tabío is quoted in Vicent, "Aires de Apertura." Despite the popular reception of this director's films at the box office and on the festival circuit, many—including *El elefante y la bicicleta*, *Lista de espera*, *Aunque estés lejos*, and *Guantanamera*, the latter codirected with Tomás Gutierrez Alea—were not shown on Cuban television until after this polemic.

30 Ibid.

31 Quoted in ibid.

Epilogue

1 Martin and Paddington, "Restoration or Innovation?," 13.

2 An ICAIC report characterizes the impact of these storms as "brutal"—for

the damage to homes as well as to culture centers including theaters. Some 200 *salas de cine*, or screening venues, across the island were affected. Worse hit were those in the provinces of Holguín (where more than 60 percent of the venues were damaged); Las Tunas (where 15 of the 16 theaters suffered damage of varying degrees); Camagüey (where half of the cinemas are in a "critical state"); Pinar del Río (where 29 of 33 theaters suffered some damage); and the Isla de la Juventud (where neither of the 2 theaters that once existed remains). See "Nota informativa del ICAIC," <http://www.cubacine.cu/boletin/index.htm#presentan> (accessed 21 Sept. 2008).

3 There is also hope that the European Union will commit resources to preserving the extensive collection of the ICAIC's Latin American Newsreel; for thirty years, from 1960 to 1990, one documentary was produced each week heralding some event or informing of some issue in the region.

4 Estrada Betancourt, "Long History of Aggressions."

5 Insausti interview. This filmed interview is available on DVD; it comprises part of volume 6, "Jazz," of Cuban Cinema Classics. See <www.cuban cinemaclassics.org>.

WORKS CITED

Acosta, Dalia. "Cine-Cuba: Cámara en mano, pies en la tierra." *IPS Inter Press Service*, 6 Mar. 2008.

Aja Díaz, Antonio. "La emigración cubana hacia estados unidos a la luz de su política inmigratoria." *CEMI*, July 2000. <http://www.uh.cu/centros/ceap/emigracion.html> (accessed 4 Apr. 2006).

Alba Noguera, Armando. Interview by author. Havana, Cuba, 3 Jan. 2006.

Alonso, Nancy. Interview by author. Filmed. Havana, Cuba, 3 Mar. 2008.

Anderson, Benedict. *Imagined Communities: Reflections on the Origins and Spread of Nationalism.* 1983. London: Verso, 1989.

Arcos, Gustavo. "Gustavo Arcos sobre el audiovisual joven en Cuba." In "La pupila insomne" blog, ed. José Antonio García Borrero (31 Mar. 2007). < http://cine-cubano-la-pupila-insomne.nireblog.com/post/2007/03/31/gustavo-arcos-sobre-el-audiovisual-joven-en-cuba> (accessed 18 Sept. 2008).

Armes, Roy. *Third World Film Making and the West*. Berkeley: University of California Press, 1987.

Arreola, Gerardo. In *La Jornada* [Mexico City], 7 May 2007.

Asociación Hermanos Saíz website. <http://www.artejovencubano.cult.cu/Paginas/index.htm> (accessed 14 Nov. 2006).

Associated Press. "Cultural Thaw? Documentaries Shine Light on the Underside of Island Life." 3 Mar. 2007. <http://www.iht.com/articles/ap/2007/03/04/news/CB-FEA-GEN-Cuba-Open-To-Criticism.php> (accessed 5 Mar. 2007).

Barba, Carlos. Interview by author. Havana, Cuba, 2 Mar. 2008.

Bardach, Ann Louise. "Twilight of the Assassins." *Atlantic Monthly*, Nov. 2006, 88–101.

Bendazzi, Giannalberto. *Cartoons: One Hundred Years of Cinema Animation*, 385–88. Bloomington: Indiana University Press, 1994.

Berthier, Nancy, and Julie Amiot, eds. *Cuba: Cinéma et Révolution. La Revolución cubana a través de las películas*. Lyon, France: Le Grimh, 2006.

Brugués, Alejandro. Interview by author. Filmed. Havana, Cuba, July 2006.

Caballero, Rufo. *A solas con Solás*. Havana: Editorial Letras Cubanas, 1999.

———. *Un pez que huye: Cine latinoamericano, 1991–2003*. Havana: Editorial Arte y Literatura, 2005.

Caparó, Gabriel. "Efectos de una mirada muy personal." *El Bisiesto Cinematográfico*, 22–23 Feb. 2007, 5–6.

———. "La era, la apertura, el corazón: Acercamiento a un nuevo scenario de relación y los jóvenes realizadores." *Cine Cubano* 166 (Oct.–Dec. 2007): 2–24.

Castillo, Luciano. *A contraluz*. Santiago de Cuba: Editorial Oriente, 2005.

———. *Con la locura de los sentidos*. Buenos Aires: Colección Artesiete, 1994.

Centro Memorial Dr. Martin Luther King Jr. website. <http://www.cmlk.com/index.php?lang=es>.

Chanan, Michael. *Cuban Cinema*. 1985. Minneapolis: University of Minnesota Press, 2004.

———. *El nuevo cine latinoamericano*. Videorecording. New York: Cinema Guild, 1980.

———. *The Politics of Documentary*. London: British Film Institute, 2008.

Chávez Spinola, Gerardo. "Ernesto Padrón Blanco." *Guaicán Literario*, 16 Nov. 2003. <www.cubaliteraria.com/guaican/entrevistas/escribas/Ernesto_padron.html>.

Chiano, Maylin Alonso. "Los desafíos de una generación." *El Bisiesto Cinematográfico*, 24–25 Feb. 2007, 4.

Clares, Zulema. Interview by author. New York, N.Y., Apr. 2006.

Cobas Arrate, Roberto. "El dibujo animado en Cuba o la verdadera historia de Quijotes y Sanchos." In *A contraluz*, ed. Luciano Castillo, 122–30. Santiago de Cuba: Editorial Oriente, 2005.

———. "Notas para una cronología del dibujo animado." *Cine Cubano* 110 (1984): 1–12.

Coelho, Cesar. "The Havana Connection." Trans. Alejandro Gedeon. *Animation World Magazine*, Feb. 1998. <http://mag.awn.com/?article_no=567&1type=search> (accessed 18 Sept. 2008).

Colina, Enrique. Interview by author. Filmed. Havana, Cuba, 2 July 2006.

Corrigan, Timothy. *A Cinema without Walls: Movie and Culture after Viet Nam.* New Brunswick, N.J.: Rutgers University Press, 1991.

Cremata Malberti, Juan Carlos. E-mail to author, 7 May 2007.

———. Interview by author. Filmed. Havana, Cuba, 30 June 2006.

Crofts, Stephen. "Reconceptualizing National Cinemas." *Quarterly Review of Film & Video* 14, no. 3 (1993): 49–69.

CubaNews website. <www.cubanews.net> (accessed 17 Dec. 2007).

Cumaná, María Caridad. Conversation with author. Montreal, Canada, Sept. 2007.

———. E-mail to author, 6 Nov. 2007.

De la Fuente, Alejandro. *A Nation for All: Race, Inequality, and Politics in Twentieth-Century Cuba.* Chapel Hill: University of North Carolina Press, 2001.

De la Hoz, Pedro. "Hay Elpidio Valdés para rato! Para felicidad de los niños y de todos los cubanos." *Granma*, n.d. <www.granma.cubaweb.cu/temas4a/articulo 872.html>.

———. "Nunca pensé que mi primer largo corriera tanto," *Granma*, n.d. <http://www.granma.cubaweb.cu/2007/06/26/cultura/artico1.html> (accessed 1 July 2007).

De la Soledad, María. "An Exclusive Interview with Cuban Film Director Juan Carlos Cremata." *Progreso Weekly*, 15–21 July 2004. <http://www.progreso weekly.com/index.php?progreso=art_culture&otherweek=1089867600> (accessed 31 Oct. 2006).

Del Río Fuentes, Joel. "Diálogo con Juan Padrón: El dibujo animado es el cine en estado puro." *Miradas: Revista del Audiovisual*, 1 Nov. 2005. <http://www.eictv .co.cu/miradas/index.php?option=com_content&task=view&id=401&Itemid =99999999> (accessed 25 May 2008).

———. "La historia contada por un testigo cómplice." *Cine Cubano* 158 (2005): 24–28.

Del Valle Casals, Sandra. "Perfiles de la animación: Los caminos que Reynaud dejó." *Caimán Barbudo*, July 2005. <www.caimanbarbudo.cu/caiman329/luneta328.htm>.

Díaz, Desiree. "El síndrome de Ulises: El viaje en el cine cubano de los noventa." *La Gaceta de Cuba*, no. 6 (2000): 37–40.

Díaz Torres, Daniel. "Más allá de La Habana." *La Jiribilla* [Havana] 147 (2004). <http://www.lajiribilla.cu/2004/n147_02/147_06.html> (accessed 18 Sept. 2008).

Diéguez, Danae C. "Las cosas por su nombre." *Extramuros de la ciudad, imagen, y palabra* 19 (2006).

———. "La dimensión de las palabras: Una conversación con los jóvenes realizadores de la película sobre la alfabetización." <http://www.cubacine.cu/documentales/ladimen.htm> (accessed 15 Mar. 2008).

Diez Castrillo, Daniel. E-mail to author, 11 May 2008.

D'Lugo, Marvin. "Authorship, Globalization, and the New Identity of Latin American Cinema, from the Mexican 'Ranchera' to the Argentinian 'Exile.'" In *Rethinking Third Cinema*, ed. Anthony R. Guneratne and Wimal Dissanayake. New York: Routledge, 2003.

Douglas, María Eulalia. *La tienda negra: El cine en Cuba, 1897–1990*. Havana: Cinemateca de Cuba, 1996.

Douglas, María Eulalia, Sara Vega, and Ivo Sarría. *Producciones del Instituto Cubano del Arte e Industria Cinematográficos, 1959–2004*. Havana: Cinemateca de Cuba, 2004.

Downing, John D. H., ed. *Film and Politics in the Third World*. Brooklyn, N.Y.: Autonomedia, Inc., 1987.

Elsaesser, Thomas. *New German Cinema: A History*. New Brunswick, N.J.: Rutgers University Press, 1989.

"Escuela internacional de cine y televisión de San Antonio de los Baños (Cuba) celebrará 20 años." 13 Nov. 2006. <http://www.eltiempo.com/cultura/2006-11-13/ARTICULO-WEB-NOTA_INTERIOR-3323087.html> (accessed 16 Nov. 2006).

Estrada Betancourt, José Luis. "El día que descubrí otro mundo." *Juventud Rebelde* [Havana], 1 June 2006, 4.

———. "The Long History of Aggressions to and the Endurance of the Cuban Cinema." CubaNow.net. 31 Oct. 2007. <http://www.cubanow.net/pages/loader.php?sec=8&t=2&item=3597> (accessed 20 Sept. 2008).

———. "Nuestra bandera es la alegría." *Juventud Rebelde* [Havana], 14 Dec. 2005, 4.

———. "Los pasos agigantados de Meñique." *Juventud Rebelde* [Havana], 31 May 2006, 6.

———. "Soy un aprendiz de cineasta" *Juventud Rebelde* [Havana], 17 Dec. 2005, 6.

———. "Tengo Elpidio Valdés . . . y mucho más." *Juventud Rebelde* [Havana], 14 Dec. 2005, 4.

Évora, José Antonio. *Tomás Gutiérrez Alea*. Madrid: Cátedra, 1996.

Ezra, Elizabeth, and Terry Rowden, eds. *Transnational Cinema: The Film Reader*. New York: Routledge, 2006.

Fadraga Tudela, Lillebit. "Cada historia lleva su luz." *Revolución y cultura*, no. 2 (2000): 14–18.

Falicov, Tamara L. *The Cinematic Tango: Contemporary Argentine Cinema*. London: Wallflower Press, 2007.

Fernandes, Sujatha. *Cuba Represent: Cuban Arts, State Power, and the Making of New Revolutionary Cultures*. Durham, N.C.: Duke University Press, 2006.

"Festejan aniversario de la Televisión Serrana." *La Ventana*, 10 July 2002. <http://laventana.casa.cult.cu/modules.php?name=news&file=print&sid=297> (accessed 22 Oct. 2005).

Flores González, Luis Ernesto. *Tras la huella de Solás*. Havana: Ediciones ICAIC, 2000.

Fornet, Ambrosio. *Alea: Una retrospective crítica*. 1987. Havana: Editorial Letras Cubanas, 1998.

———. *La coartada perpetua*. Mexico City: Siglo XXI, 2002.

———. Introduction to *Bridging Enigma: Cubans on Cuba*, ed. Ambrosio Fornet. *South Atlantic Quarterly* 96, no. 1 (Winter 1997): 1–15.

———. "El Quinquenio Gris: Revisitando el término." *Casa de las Américas* 46 (Jan.–Mar. 2007): 3–16.

Fornet, Pablo. E-mail to author, 29 Jan. 2008.

Fowler Calzada, Victor. *Conversaciones con un cineasta incómodo: Julio García Espinosa*. Lincoln, R.I.: New England Latin American Film Festival, 1997.

Gabriel, Teshome H. *Third Cinema in the Third World: The Aesthetics of Liberation*. 1979. Studies in Cinema 21. Ann Arbor, Mich.: UMI Research Press, 1982.

Galeano, Eduardo. *Memory of Fire*. Trans. Cedric Belfrage. New York: Pantheon Books, 1985.

García, José Eduardo. Interview by author. Havana, Cuba, 3 Jan. 2006.

García Borrero, Juan Antonio. "El cine submergido" blog, comment posted 16 May 2007.

———. *La edad de la herejía*. Santiago de Cuba: Editorial Oriente, 2002.

———. *Guía crítica de cine cubano de ficción*. Havana: Editorial Arte y Literature, 2001.

———. *Julio García Espinosa: Las estratégias de un provocador*. Huelva, Spain: Fundación Cultural de Cine Iberoamericano de Huelva, 2001.

García Canclini, Néstor. *Hybrid Cultures: Strategies for Entering and Leaving Modernity*. Trans. Christopher L. Chiappari and Silvia L. López. Minneapolis: University of Minnesota Press, 1995.

————. "Will There Be Latin American Cinema in the Year 2000?" In *Framing Latin American Cinema: Contemporary Critical Perspectives*, ed. Ann Marie Stock, 246–58. Minneapolis: University of Minnesota Press, 1997.

García Espinosa, Julio. *Un largo camino hacia la luz*. Havana: Editorial Casa de las Américas, 2002.

García Márquez, Gabriel. *Así de simple*. Santafé de Bogotá, Colombia: Editorial Voluntad, 1995.

Getino, Octavio. *Cine iberoamericano: Los desafíos del nuevo siglo*. San José, Costa Rica: Editorial Veritas, 2006.

Giroud, Pavel. "Dejándo atrás *La edad de la peseta*." *Cine Cubano* 162 (Oct.–Dec. 2006): 42–45.

————. Interview by author. Filmed. Havana, Cuba, 4 July 2006.

González, Omar. "El tiempo es transparencia." *Cine Cubano* 48 (2000): 10–13.

González, Reynaldo. *Coordenadas del cine cubano I*. Santiago de Cuba: Editorial Oriente, 2001.

González Nieto, Luis. Interview by author. Havana, Cuba, 27 Dec. 2005.

González Peña, Nilza. Interview by author. Havana, Cuba, 15 Dec. 2005.

Guevara, Alfredo. Interview by author. Filmed. Havana, Cuba, 10 Dec. 2005.

————. "Mi pasión se inspira más allá del cine." *Cine Cubano* 48 (2000): 7–9.

————. *Revolución es lucidéz*. Havana: Ediciones ICAIC, 1998.

Guevara, Alfredo, and Glauber Rocha. *Un sueño compartido*. Madrid: Iberautor, 2002.

Guevara, Alfredo, and Cesare Zavattini. *Ese diamantino corazón de la verdad*. Madrid: Iberautor, 2002.

————. *Tiempo de Fundación*. Madrid: Iberautor, 2003.

Gumucio-Dagrón, Alfonso. *Sustainability of Community Media*. New York: Rockefeller Foundation, 2001.

Guneratne, Anthony R., and Wimal Dissanayake, eds. *Rethinking Third Cinema*. New York: Routledge, 2003.

Gutiérrez Alea, Tomás. "Respuesta a *Cine Cubano*." In *Cine y revolución en Cuba*, 99–107. Barcelona: Editorial Fontamara, 1975.

Hall, Stuart. "Cultural Identity and Cinematic Representation." In *Ex-iles: Essays on Caribbean Cinema*, ed. Mbye B. Cham, 220–36. Trenton, N.J.: Africa World Press, 1992.

Hernández, Helmo, and Fernando Sáez Carvajal. E-mail to author, 20 Sept. 2007.

Hernández, Rafael. "Looking at Cuba: Notes toward a Discussion." In *From Cuba*, a special issue of *Boundary 2: An International Journal of Literature and Culture* 29, no. 3 (Fall 2002): 123–36.

Hernández-Reguant, Ariana. "Copyrighting Che: Art and Authorship under Cuban Late Socialism." *Public Culture* 16, no. 1 (2004): 1–29.

Herrera, Inti. Interview by author. Filmed. Havana, Cuba, July 2006.

Herrera, Lázara. Interview by author. Filmed. Havana, Cuba, 26 Dec. 2005.

Herrera Ysla, Nelson. "Padrón: El humor encontrado." *Revolución y Cultura*, no. 4 (1986): 40–47.

Higson, Andrew. *Waving the Flag: Constructing a National Cinema in Britain.* Oxford: Oxford University Press, 1995.

Hjort, Mette, and Scott Mackenzie. *Cinema and Nation.* New York: Routledge, 2000.

Hjort, Mette, and Duncan Petrie. *The Cinema of Small Nations.* Edinburgh: University of Edinburgh Press, 2007.

Insausti, Esteban. Interview by author. Filmed. Havana, Cuba, 2 June 2004.

Instituto Cubano del Arte e Industria Cinematográficos (ICAIC) website. <www.cubacine.cu>.

Intergovernmental Council of the International Programme for the Development of Communication-IPDC, "Evaluation Summaries of 100 Terminated Projects" (7 Mar. 2002), 85. http://unesdoc.unesco.org/images/0012/001257/125782e.pdf (accessed 12 Oct. 2005).

Jiménez, José Antonio. Interview by author. Filmed. Havana, Cuba, 4 Jan. 2006.

Juventud Rebelde website. <http://www.juventudrebelde.cu.htm> (accessed 14 Nov. 2006).

Kirk, John M., and Leonardo Padura Fuentes. *Culture and the Cuban Revolution: Conversations in Havana.* Gainesville: University Press of Florida, 2001.

Koehler, Robert. Review of *Viva Cuba*, by Juan Carlos Cremata Malberti, *Variety*, 12 Oct. 2005. <http://www.variety.com/review/VE1117928524.html?category id=31&cs=1> (accessed 14 Nov. 2005).

Labaki, Amir. *El ojo de la Revolución: El cine urgente de Santiago Álvarez.* Trans. Lázara Herrera. São Paulo, Brazil: Iluminuras, 1994.

"Ley 169. Creación del Instituto Cubano del Arte e Industria Cinematográficos ICAIC." In *Hojas de cine: Testimonio y documentos del nuevo cine latinoamericano.* Mexico City: Fundación Mexicana de Cineastas (1988): 3:13–19.

Leyva Dehesa, Ana. "Queriendo ser ella." *El Bisiesto Cinematográfico*, 26 Feb. 2008, 3.

Leyva Martínez, Ivette. "Hernán Henríquez, dibujos con magia y suerte." *El Nuevo Herald* [Miami], 20 Nov. 2005. <http://www.miami.com/mld/elnuevo/news/special_packages/rostro_del_exito/13213199.htm?template=content Modules/printstory.jsp> (accessed 22 Jan. 2006).

Lievesley, Geraldine. *The Cuban Revolution: Past, Present, and Future Perspectives.* New York: Palgrave McMillan, 2004.

Lobata, José Luis. Interview by author. Havana, Cuba, 2 Mar. 2008.

López, Ana M. "Cuba." In *The Cinema of Small Nations*, ed. Mette Hjort and Duncan Petri, 179–96. Edinburgh: Edinburgh University Press, 2007.

Lovio Caballero, Jorge Luis. "Hablemos de Cine de Animación." *Revista Vitral* 9, no. 50 (July–Aug. 2002). <http://www2.glauco.it/vitral/vitral50/cine> (accessed 4 July 2005).

Lu, Sheldon Hsiao-Peng, ed. *Transnational Chinese Cinemas: Identity, Nationhood, Gender.* Honolulu: University of Hawaii Press, 1997.

MacCannell, Dean. *Empty Meeting Grounds: The Tourist Papers.* New York: Routledge, 1992.

"Making Waves." Communication Initiative website. <http://www.comminit .com/strategicthinking/pdsmakingwaves/sld-1884.html> (accessed 17 Oct. 2002).

Martin, Michael T., and Bruce Paddington. "Restoration or Innovation? An Interview with Humberto Solás." *Film Quarterly* 54, no. 3 (2001): 2–13.

Martín Barbero, Jesus, and Zilkia Janer. "Transformations in the Map: Identities and Culture Industries." *Latin American Perspectives* 27, no. 4 (July 2000): 27–48.

Martínez Heredia, Fernando. "In the Furnace of the Nineties: Identity and Society in Cuba Today." In *From Cuba*, a special issue of *Boundary 2: An International Journal of Literature and Culture* 29, no. 3 (Fall 2002): 137–47.

Martínez Puentes, Silvia. *Cuba más allá de los sueños.* Havana: Editorial José Martí, 2003.

Martí Pons, Bartolomé. "Extendarán la Televisión Serrana a la región central de Cuba." CHTV, 8 Apr. 2004.

Massip, José. "Opina José Massip." In *Cine y revolución en Cuba*, 81–92. Barcelona: Editorial Fontamara, 1975.

Minh-ha, Trinh T. *Woman, Native, Other: Writing Postcoloniality and Feminism.* Bloomington: Indiana University Press, 1989.

"Moviendo Ideas" session. Muestra Nacional de Nuevos Realizadores. Havana, 27 Feb. 2007.

Naficy, Hamid. "Phobic Spaces and Liminal Panics: Independent Transnational Film Genre." In *Global/Local: Cultural Production and the Transnational Imaginary*, ed. Rob Wilson and Wimal Dissanayake, 119–44. Durham, N.C.: Duke University Press, 1996.

Naito López, Mario. *Coordenadas del cine cubano 2.* Santiago de Cuba: Editorial Oriente, 2005.

————. "El documental cubano desde sus orígenes hasta nuestros días." *La jiribilla* 165 (2006). <http://www.lajiribilla.co.cu/2006/n267_06/267_01.html> (accessed Oct. 2006).

Navarro, Desiderio. "In Medias Res Publicas: On Intellectuals and Social Criticism in the Cuban Public Sphere." In *From Cuba*, a special issue of *Boundary 2: An International Journal of Literature and Culture* 29, no. 3 (Fall 2002): 187–203.

Neill, Morgan. "CNN's Morgan Neill Visits a Film School in Cuba That's Reportedly Uncensored." 11 Nov. 2006. <http://www.cnn.com/video> (accessed 16 Nov. 2006).

Nestingen, Andrew. "Aki Kaurismäki's Crossroads: National Cinema and the Road Movie." *Transnational Cinema in a Global North: Nordic Cinema in Transition*, eds. Andrew Nestingen and Trevor G. Elkington, 279–305. Detroit: Wayne State University Press, 2005.

Nestingen, Andrew, and Trevor G. Elkington, eds. *Transnational Cinema in a Global North: Nordic Cinema in Transition*. Detroit: Wayne State University Press, 2005.

Paranaguá, Paulo Antonio. "America Latina, Europa, y Estados Unidos, relaciones triangulares en la historia del cine." *Journal of Film Preservation* 62 (Apr. 2001): 9–15.

Pérez, Alejandro. Interview by author. Filmed. San Francisco de Campeche, Mexico, 2 Dec. 2006.

Pérez, Gustavo. Interview by author, Havana, Cuba, 25 Feb. 2007.

Pérez, Louis A., Jr. *On Becoming Cuban: Identity, Nationality, and Culture*. Chapel Hill: University of North Carolina Press, 1999.

Pick, Zuzana. *New Latin American Cinema: A Continental Project*. Austin: University of Texas Press, 1993.

Piña Rodríguez, Ernesto. Interview by author. Filmed. Havana, Cuba, 4 July 2006.

Pines, Jim, and Paul Willemen, eds. *Questions of Third Cinema*. London: British Film Institute, 1989.

Podalsky, Laura. "Negotiating Differences: National Cinemas and Co-productions in Prerevolutionary Cuba." *The Velvet Light Trap*, no. 34 (Fall 1994): 59–70.

Pogolotti, Graziella, ed. *Polémicas culturales de los 60*. 2006. Havana: Letras Cubanas, 2007.

Prats, Paco. Interview by author. Havana, Cuba, 3 Jan. 2006.

Ramírez, Johanhnn. Interview by author. Havana, Cuba, 3 Jan. 2006.

Ramos, Alberto. E-mail correspondence with author, Mar. 2008.

————. "Oscar Valdés." *Catalog, 6ta. Muestra Nacional de Nuevos Realizadores*, Ediciones ICAIC (Feb. 2007): 20–21.

————. "*Rachel K.*, la extraña aventura de Oscar Valdés." In *Coordenadas del cine cubano 2*, ed. Mario Naito López, 245–63. Santiago de Cuba: Editorial Oriente, 2005.

Reloba, Xenia. "Juan Padrón: Behind Elpidio's Back." *Habanera* no. 28 (2003). <http://www.walterlippmann.com/docs298.html> (accessed 22 Jan. 2006).

Resik, Magda. "Writing Is a Sort of Shipwreck: Interview with Senel Paz." In *Bridging Enigma: Cubans on Cuba*, ed. Ambrosio Fornet. *South Atlantic Quarterly* 96, no. 1 (Winter 1997): 83–93.

Reyes, Dean Luis. "El etnocentrismo blando: Mambises y vampiros como guerrilla anticolonial en el cine de Juan Padrón." *Miradas Revista del Audiovisual*, 17 Oct. 2005. <http://www.eictv.co.cu/miradas/index.php?Item id=99999999&id=401&option=com_content&task=view> (accessed 2 Nov. 2005).

Reyes Rodríguez, Marlene, and Ricardo Miranda Acosta. "Una aproximación a la evolución de la técnica del video." <http://www.varona.rimed.cu/imagenes/Revistas video/Revista%206/evolucion.htm> (accessed Oct. 2006).

Rivas, Mario. Conversation with author. Havana, Cuba, 3 Jan. 2006.

———. "Niñas, niños, y nuestro dibujo animado." *Cine Cubano* 148 (2001): 66–67.

Rodríguez, Raúl. *El cine silente en Cuba*. Havana: Letras Cubanas, 1992.

Rodríguez-Mangual, Edna M. *Lydia Cabrera and the Construction of an Afro-Cuban Cultural Identity*. Chapel Hill: University of North Carolina Press, 2004.

———. "Otras imágenes de Cuba: El cortometraje en video." "Tracking Cuba's Cinema since the Special Period," Latin American Studies Association, San Juan, Puerto Rico, Mar. 2006.

Rojas, Orlando. Interview by author. Filmed. Williamsburg, Va., 26 Apr. 2004.

Rolando, Gloria. Interview by author. Filmed. Havana, Cuba, 23 Dec. 2005.

Rolando Casamayor, Gloria Victoria. "Artist's 1998 Statement of Purpose and Biography." AfroCubaWeb website. <http://www.afrocubaweb.com> (accessed Feb. 2008).

Sáez Carvajal, Fernando, and Wilfredo Benítez Muñoz. "The Ludwig Foundation of Cuba, Almost Four Years After Its Creation." Report, 1998.

Salvador, Angélica. Interview by author. Havana, Cuba. 1 Mar. 2008.

Sánchez, Jorge Luis. Interview by author. Filmed. Havana, Cuba, 4 Jan. 2006.

Santos Moray, Mercedes. "El extraño caso de Oscar Valdés." *El Bisiesto Cinematográfico*, 20–21 Feb. 2007, 7.

———. *La vida es un silbo: Fernando Pérez*. Havana: Ediciones ICAIC, 2004.

Sarusky, Jaime. *Una leyenda de la música cubana: Grupo de Experimentación Sonora del ICAIC*. Havana: Letras Cubanas, 2005.

Shohat, Ella, and Robert Stam. *Unthinking Eurocentrism: Multiculturalism and the Media*. London: Routledge, 1994.

Soto Ricardo, Amado "Asori." Interview by author. Filmed. Havana, Cuba, 27 Feb. 2007.

Spence, Louise, and Robert Stam. "Colonialism, Racism, and Representation." *Screen* 24, no. 2 (Mar.-Apr. 1983): 2-20.

Stam, Robert. "Beyond Third Cinema: The Aesthetics of Hybridity." In *Rethinking Third Cinema*, ed. Anthony R. Guneratne and Wimal Dissanayake, 31-48. New York: Routledge, 2003.

Steinberg, Ed. Telephone interview by author. 21 July 2006.

Stock, Ann Marie. "Hollywood South? Cinema and Criticism Converge in Costa Rica." *Studies in Latin American Popular Culture* 17 (1998): 139-54.

———. "Imagining the Future in Revolutionary Cuba: An Interview with Fernando Pérez." *Film Quarterly* 60, no. 3 (2007): 68-75.

———. "Introduction: Through Other Worlds and Other Times: Critical Praxis and Latin American Cinema." In *Framing Latin American Cinema: Contemporary Critical Perspectives*, xxi-xxxv. Minneapolis: University of Minnesota Press, 1993.

TV Yumurí. "Quédate conmigo." Program transmitted over Tele Rebelde, 8 June 2005.

UNESCO Havana. "Conmemoran década de la TV Serrana, auspiciada por UNESCO." <www.unesco.org/cu/Noticias03/noticia070103.htm> (accessed 4 July 2005).

Vega, Hilda Elena. Interview by author. Filmed. Havana, 28 Feb. 2008.

Vega, Jesús. *El cartel cubano de cine*. Havana: Editorial Letras Cubanas, 1999.

Vicent, Mauricio. "Aires de apertura en La Habana." *El País* [Madrid], 7 May 2007. <http://www.elpais.com/articulo/cultura/Aires/apertura/Habana/elpepuint/20070507elpepicul_5/Tes> (accessed 8 May 2007).

Vidal, Aram. E-mail to author, 15 Mar. 2007.

Williams, Alan, ed. *Film and Nationalism*. New Brunswick, N.J.: Rutgers University Press, 2002.

Yúdice, George. *The Expediency of Culture: Uses of Culture in the Global Era*. Durham, N.C.: Duke University Press, 2003.

Zagury, Léa. "A Chat with Hernán Henríquez." Trans. Alejandro Gedeón and Léa Zagury. *Animation World Magazine*, Apr. 1999. <http://www.awn.com/mag/issue4.01/4.01pages/zaguryhenriquez.php3> (accessed 22 Jan. 2006).

INDEX

XXXX años después (40 Years Later), 246

Abello, Jorge, 253
Acosta, Aramis, 106, 123, 128
Acosta, Yunior, 139
Advertising, 181–82, 207
Afro-Cuban culture, 60–66
Alacrán, El, 62
Alba Noguera, Armando, 106, 122–25, 127, 130, 132–34, 137, 145
Al compás del pilón, 89
Alea, Tomás Gutiérrez, 7, 8 (ill.), 26, 43, 159, 179, 190, 223, 261, 290 (n. 15)

Algo más que el mar de los piratas, 60
Alguien tiene que llorar, 173
Alma trémula y sola, El, 118
Alvarez, Adalberto, 100, 298 (n. 17)
Álvarez, Felipe, 138
Álvarez, Santiago, 26, 35, 81, 223, 226, 228, 250, 253, 290 (n. 15)
Al venir a la tierra, 118
American Friends of the Ludwig Foundation of Cuba, 73
Amigos del mal, 248
Amor vertical, 47, 70
Animation, 106–45; critical assessments of, 108–9, 298–99 (n. 1); pre-

revolutionary attempts at, 109, 299 (n. 2); stop-motion, 128, 138, 140; Japanese influence in, 139–40

Animation studio, 28, 35, 76, 105–7; transformation of, 11, 107–8, 111–12, 133; establishment of, 109–12, 299–300 (n. 3); decline and precarious state of, 112, 122–23; new facility, 126–28; recovery of in wake of Special Period, 133–34

Annichini, Gianfranco, 266

Árbol de la vida, El, 135

Arcos, Gustavo, 238–39, 245

Armas, Jesús de, 109–10, 112

Arráncame la vida, 180

Artex, 65, 181

Artistic property rights, 93, 192–93

Asociación Hermanos Saíz (AHS), 27, 36, 38, 49–56

Auteurs, 13, 28, 196; Juan Carlos Cremata Malberti, 150–51, 159, 166–67; Esteban Insausti, 207; Fernando Pérez, 223; Nicolás Guillén Landrián, 223–24, 262; Oscar Valdés, 262–63

Autochthonous culture, 39, 82, 176–77, 196, 279

Avant-garde filmmaking, 18, 72, 207, 223–24

Avilés, Cecilio, 120

Barba, Carlos, 10, 24, 25 (ill.), 252–54, 254 (ill.)

Barriga, Susana, 24, 268–69

Batalla de Ideas, 113, 126, 165

Bay of Pigs invasion, 110, 213

Bedoya, Marcos, 99

Belafonte, Julie, 74, 136

Bella del Alhambra, La, 252–53

Benítez, Wilfredo, 67, 296 (n. 29)

Benny, *El*, 55

Bernaza, Luis Felipe, 83

Bestia, La, 94, 268

Birri, Fernando, 40, 169

Bohío, El, 118

Bosch, Orlando, 132

Brugués, Alejandro, 24, 41–42, 69 (ill.), 255–60

Bunker, 265

Buscando a Céline Dion, 248

Buscándote Havana, 238

Cabrera Infante, Sabá, 262

Caiozzi, Silvio, 74

Calle G, 243

Calviño, Dolores "Lola," 41

Canción para Rachel, La, 252–53

Candela, 149, 152, 164, 173

Cannes International Film Festival, 150, 159, 165

Cardinales de la ciudad, 138

Carreira Lamothe, Iván Alberto, 195 (ill.), 197

Casa de las Américas, 49, 273

Casal, Julián del, 54, 294 (n. 12)

Casals, Melchor, 40–41

Castellanos, Tamara, 70

Castro, Fidel, 30, 48, 52, 79, 81, 131, 134, 165, 268; on politics and culture, 9–10, 262; presence of in Cuban films, 45, 156, 158, 206–7, 211

Castro, Raúl, 273

Cecilín films, 120

Censorship, 272–78

Centro Martin Luther King Jr., 153, 292 (n. 2)

Centro Teórico-Cultural Criterios, 273–74

Cero, El, 114

Chacón, Rogelio, 46
Chanan, Michael, 26, 84, 116
Chapuserías, 265
Chávez, Rebeca, 254, 254 (ill.)
Chaviano, Paul, 69
Chijona, Gerardo, 18
Chivichana, La, 89–91
Cienfuegos, Camilo, 81, 156
Cine Chaplin, xxi, 42, 71, 186, 190–91, 255, 262
Cine Cubano journal, 26, 121, 197, 253
Cine de aficionados, 20
Cine Educativo (CINED), 72, 75
Cine imperfecto, 263, 313 (n. 20)
Cine Plaza festival, 243
Cine Pobre festival, 10, 173, 243, 248, 253–54, 291 (n. 27)
Cinergia, 153, 222, 304 (n. 3)
Cine submergido, 20
Cine y la memoria, El, 53
Ciokler, Alberto, 184
Ciudad en rojo, 254
Clandestinos, 264
Clares, Zulema, 193, 218, 220
Cobas Arrate, Roberto, 118
Coffea arábiga, 224, 228, 262
Colina, Enrique, 18, 42, 144, 178, 264–67, 267 (ill.)
Colmenita, La, 153
Community media, 28, 78–80; pitfalls of, 93–94; sustainability of, 102–5
Como construir un barco, 268
Como una gota de agua, 96
Computer-generated images, 28, 107, 125, 138–39
Contra el águila y el león, 136
Coppola, Francis Ford, 21, 41, 179, 194
Coproduction: as strategy for stretching limited resources, 10–11, 36, 38,
281–82; in Animation Studio, 133; as transnational media, 152, 177; partners in, 176–77; *La edad de la peseta* as, 193–98; risks and benefits in, 198–203, 281–82; list of 1990s titles, 307 (n. 4)
Copyright. *See* artistic property rights
Cornevín, Elsa, 46
Corrigan, Timothy, 156–57, 167
Cortázar, Octavio, 83–84, 98, 290 (n. 15)
Cowboy, El, 110
Coyula, Miguel, 46–47, 170
Cremata Malberti, Carlos Alberto, 136, 153
Cremata Malberti, Juan Carlos, 21, 24, 28, 149–74, 184, 223, 227, 228; training of, 43–46, 150, 161 (ill.), 164, 168 (ill.), 169–71; as auteur, 150–51, 159, 166–67; future projects of, 280. See also *Oscuros rinocerantes* and *Viva Cuba*
Cruz, Ana, 129
Cruz Rivero, Yemelí, 70, 128, 139
Cuando yo sea grande, 169
Cuatro hermanas, Las, 88–89
Cuban Cinema Classics, 222, 284, 297 (n. 9), 311 (n. 10)
Cuban Film Institute. *See* Instituto Cubano del Arte e Industria Cinematográficos
Cubanía, 6–7, 13–17, 86, 176; reconfiguration in wake of Special Period, 27–30; Afro-Cuban culture as integral to, 63–64; in animation, 117; coding of in *Viva Cuba*, 155–59
Cucarachas rojas, Las, 47
Cuchufleta, La, 89
Cuestión de fé, 47
Cumaná, Caridad, 260

Debutantes, Los, 47

De cierta manera, 228

De generación, 244, 247

Del Llano, Eduardo, 18, 184

Del Río Fuentes, Joel, 111, 121, 130

Del Tosco, 72

Desde La Habana 1969, 262

Desperando a Quan Tri, 248

Diaspora, African, 60–66

Díaz, Danielito, 22, 184

Díaz, Desiree, 157

Díaz, Rolando, 54

Díaz de Villegas, Alexis, 193, 218

Díaz Lechuga, Carlos, 184

Díaz Torres, Daniel, 18, 27, 41–42, 54, 86, 202

Diéguez, Danae C., 239

Diez Castrillo, Daniel, 79, 81–82, 82 (ill.), 86–97 passim, 95 (ill.), 103, 105, 261

Digital technology. *See* Technology, new

Dimensión de las palabras, La, 191, 245–47

Dirigible, El, 46

Disney cartoons, 9, 108, 116, 126, 137, 143

D'Lugo, Marvin, 177, 196

Doble moral, 19, 265

Domingo del Pez, 268

Donde está Casal, 54

Dorado, El, 199–200

Dotta, Pablo, 46

Ducases Manzano, Karel, 24, 138

Echevarría, Marcel, 70

Ecological concerns, 91–92

Ecos de un final, 252

Edad de la peseta, La, 175–76, 193–99, 202–3

Ella trabaja, 268

Embargo, U.S., 5, 73, 151, 285–86

EMe-5, 139–40

Emigration, 262, 302 (n. 25); during Special Period, 1–2, 68, 124, 265; in recent Cuban films, 157–59, 231–32, 249

Emporio Habana, 204

En un barrio viejo, 224, 262

Época, el encanto, y el fin del siglo, La, 172

Erpiromundo, 140

Escenas de los muelles, 263

Escuela Internacional de Cine y Televisión (EICTV), 27, 36, 38–39, 41, 70, 171, 193, 266, 285; establishment of, 40–41; partnership with TVS, 95, 105; training of filmmakers, 150, 164, 169–70, 180, 183, 194, 244, 255, 264

Esperanza del mundo, La, 173

Esta es mi alma, 60

Estrada Betancourt, José Luis, 181

Excursión, 140

Existen, 17–18, 71, 206–13

Experimentation, 68, 239; as practiced by Street Filmmakers, 15–16, 194, 224, 239; in *Viva Cuba*, 160–64; in *Tres veces dos*, 187–93; in *Existen*, 207–14

Extraño caso de Rachel K., El, 263

Eyes of the Rainbow, 62

Fanguito, El, 54

Fanon, Frantz, 57

Federico, Giovanni, 291 (n. 21)

Fernandes, Sujatha, 12, 26

Festival Cine de la Montaña, 94, 243

Festival Documental Santiago Álvarez in Memoriam, 71, 243, 253

Festival Internacional del Audiovisual para la Niñez y Adolescencia, 136

Festival Internacional del Nuevo Cine Latinoamericano, ix, 22, 38, 39, 56, 73–74, 117, 150–51, 181, 186, 190, 228, 282; as space for Street Filmmakers, 53, 57, 135, 194, 198, 203, 204

Feucha, 114

Figueredo, Ricardo, 268

Filminutos, 118–20, 122

Flash Forward, 70

Fornet, Ambrosio, 2, 9, 41, 264, 273–74, 292 (n. 37)

Freddy o el sueño de Noel, 92–93

French New Wave, 43, 172

Fresa y chocolate, 73, 190, 271, 275–76

Frijol viajero, El, 135

Frutas en el café, 291 (n. 22)

Fuera de Liga, 18

Fuga homicida, 132

Fundación del Nuevo Cine Latino-americano (FNCL), 153, 260, 285

Fundación Ludwig de Cuba (FLC), 27, 36, 38, 67–74, 193, 206, 222, 229–30, 262, 285, 296 (n. 29)

Galeano, Eduardo, 24, 32

García, José Eduardo, 130, 144

García, Luis Alberto, 264

García, María Teresa, 254 (ill.)

García, Modesto, 110

García Borrero, Juan Antonio, 27

García Espinosa, Julio, 17, 26, 35, 40–42, 48, 52, 231, 264

García Márquez, Gabriel, 40, 41, 48, 194, 244

Gárciga Romay, Luis, 184

Genre films, 203, 214, 257–58, 268; lack of in Cuban cinema, 175, 177–79;

action, 178; musical, 190, 252; thriller, 194, 198; comedy, 202; horror, 230; zombie, 257; film noir, 263

Giroud, Iván, 22, 198

Giroud, Pavel, 22, 23, 24, 28, 170, 172, 175–205, 192 (ill.), 285

Globalization, 5, 66, 104–5, 280

Gómez, Manuel Octavio, 80, 261

Gómez, Sara, 18, 223, 228

Gómez, Yoraisi, 254 (ill.)

Gómez Jiménez, Sandra, 24, 269–70

González, Elián, 30, 125–26, 165

González, Nicanor, 109

González, Nilza, 127–28

González, Omar, 11, 225

González, Yimit, 139

González Nieto, Luis, 127, 285–86

Good Bye, Lolek, 71

Granados, Daisy, 168 (ill.)

Granma, 52, 158

Guantanamera, 73, 159, 271

Guerra de las canicas, La, 268

Guevara, Alfredo, 8–9, 11, 110

Guevara, Che, 7, 81, 154, 156, 192, 246

Guevara Polanco, Luis Ángel, 89

Güije enamorado, El, 135

Guillén Landrián, Nicolás, 18, 84, 223–24, 250, 262, 268

Guitarra 1, 138

Guitarra, La, 114

Gumucio-Dagrón, Alfonso, 78, 99

Gutiérrez Alea, Tomás. *See* Alea, Tomás Gutiérrez

Habana Blues, 47

Habanaceres, 17

Haití en la memoria, 60

Hamlet, Léster, 24, 170, 183, 189–90, 222, 229, 270

Hasta cierto punto, 179
Havana Film Festival of New York, 73, 136, 168–69, 220
Henríquez, Hernán, 109–11, 113, 144, 302 (n. 25)
Hernández, Bernabé, 60
Hernández, Helmo, 68, 296 (n. 29)
Hernández, Orlando "El Duque," 18, 291 (n. 24)
Hernández, Rafael, 31
Hernández Bachs, Jesús Miguel, 268
Hernández-Reguant, Ariana, 192
Herrera, Inti, 22, 24, 69 (ill.), 152, 160, 255–60
Herrera, Jorge, 261, 311 (n. 7)
Herrera, Lázara, 253
Herrera, Manuel, 22
Hirzel Galarza, Esther, 131
Historia de una batalla, 80
Historias con hipo, 124
Hitchcock, Alfred, 178–79
Hollywood, 42, 143, 231, 233, 242; studios of in *Noticiero 49*, 8–9; and circulation of films in Cuba, 11; resistance to, 40, 57; genre films of, 43, 83, 110, 230
Hombres sin mujer, 173
Hombres verdes, 139
Homosexuality, 16, 18, 272, 276
Horas del día, Las, 47
Horizontes, 139
Hoz, Pedro de la, 126, 198

Ibarra, Mirta, 42
Identity: revolutionary constructions of national, 6–7, 10, 13; contradictory visions of, 12, 16; impact of global processes on, 13, 29; visions of for future, 13–14; heterogeneity of

proffered in Street Films, 19, 155–58, 237–38; critical formulation of, 19, 210, 275; introduction of emerging values into, 20; highland, 28, 77, 97, 100–102; multiple enactments of, 31; Afro-Cuban, 60–66, 296 (n. 22); iconographies of national identity in *Viva Cuba*, 155–59
Ileasástegui, Dania, 170
Imágenes del Caribe, 64
Imperfect cinema. *See* Cine imperfecto
Independent filmmaking, 20–22, 50, 256–58. *See also* Street Filmmaking
Indocubanos, Los, 110
Infante, Arturo, 18, 24, 70, 184, 193–94
Ingenio, El, 153–54, 173, 184
Insausti, Esteban, 23, 24, 28, 70, 71, 164, 165, 170, 174, 184, 219 (ill.), 225 (ill.), 230 (ill.), 287; premiere of *Existen* at FLC, 72, 206–7, 230; *Luz roja* and *Tres veces dos*, 189–90, 193; admiration of for revolutionary films, 228–29, 262; on working in Hollywood, 230–31; *Larga distancia*, 281–82
Instituto Cubano del Arte e Industria Cinematográficos (ICAIC), 1, 22, 273; early films, 7, 18, 40, 210, 239–40, 261; establishment of, 7–8; crisis and transformation of during Special Period, 11–13, 35–36, 201–2; alliances with, 38–39, 42, 64–65, 71, 76–77; support of for young filmmakers, 50–51, 187–91, 250, 252, 254, 256; role of in Muestra, 55, 240–43, 250–51, 261–64; films depicting rural life, 81–86; and clashes over artistic property rights, 191–93; ongoing challenges of, 192, 226–27, 282–87; Cubanacán production studio, 233;

polemical 1960s and 1970s, 261–64; potential of as distributor for Street Filmmakers, 280–81, 286–87. *See also* Revolutionary film: pioneers of

Instituto Cubano de Radio y Televisión (ICRT), 21–22, 49, 75, 80, 129, 135, 137, 138–40; TVC Casa Productora, 153, 159; reluctance of to program Cuban films, 271–78

Instituto Superior del Arte (ISA), 71–72, 105, 128, 135, 140, 169, 170, 222

Instituto Superior del Diseño, 128, 179

International Festival of New Latin American Cinema. *See* Festival Internacional del Nuevo Cine Latinoamericano

Internet, 11, 151, 182–83, 281

Intruso, El, 70, 184

Japanese animation, 140, 143

Jiménez, José Antonio, 58–59

Jiménez, Luisa María, 154

Jiménez, Rigoberto, 88–89

José Manuel, la mula, y el televisor, 46

Juanchini, Gian Carlos, 46

Jugando al Timeball, 17

Jurassik Cube, 139

Lago, Luis, 232–33

Lamar, Manuel (Lillo), 109

Larga distancia, 231–33

Latin American Cinema, 39–40, 260, 284; EICTV as regional training ground for, 48; resistance of to Hollywood, 57–58; emergence of film auteurs in, 196

Lecuona, 263

León, Luis Leonel, 17, 24, 170

Leyenda americana, Una, 118

Lievesley, Geraldine, 6

Lima Cruz, Adanoe, 139

Literacy, 79–80, 245–46

Loayza, Marcos, 47

López, Ana, 205

López, Ernesto, 276

López, Rigoberto, 60, 144

Lorenzo, Dagmar, 129

Low-budget filmmaking, 15–16, 258, 260, 285; ICAIC competition, 60–61; FLC fostering of, 71; TVS reliance on, 97; Cremata Malberti and, 151, 162–64; Giroud and, 185–87; Insausti and, 218–22

Luis Naranjo, Yurina, 139–40

Luz roja, 70, 189–90, 193, 216–20, 217

Lynn, Verónica, 253

Machado, Carlos, 245

Madagascar, 2–4, 179

Maestro del Cilantro, El, 80

Malberti Cabrera, Iraida, 22, 153, 169

Maná, El, 109

Manos y el ángel, Las, 215–16, 226

Manzanita.com, 182–83

Marcel, Manuel, 38–39

Marcoleta, Llaned, 268

Margins, 224, 272–73; Street Filmmakers' interest in, 16, 268–70; in works of Jorge Luis Sánchez, 51–55; in *Existen*, 206–7; in *Buscándote Havana*, 237–38

María Teresa, 263

Marqueses de Atarés, Los, 62

Martí, José, 101, 118, 156, 254

Martínez, Jorge, 253

Martínez Heredia, Fernando, 13–14, 273

Más se perdió en Cuba, 122

Massip, José, 80, 239, 264

Más vampiros en La Habana, 133, 134, 136

McLaren, Norman, 39, 113, 172

Memorias del subdesarrollo, 53, 179, 223

Memorias de Lucía, 252

Mendieta, Ana, 220

Meñique, 136

Mensajero de los dioses, 60

Mercado de Cine de América Latina (MECLA), 57–58

Mestizaje, 157, 290–91 (n. 20)

Miel para Oshún, 231, 252

Migration, 157–58, 237–38

Miló, Jorge, 154, 161 (ill.)

Minerva traduce el mar, 262

Mobile cinema, 83–86

Montenegro, Carlos, 173

Monte Rouge, 18

Montoya, Homero, 135

Moré, Benny, 55–56, 227

Moreno, Isabel, 253

Morro, El, 224

Mosquitos, el documental, 71

Movimiento Nacional de Video, 27, 36, 38, 58–60, 64, 66

Muerte de un burócrata, La, 43

Muerte y vida en El Morrillo, 263

Muestra de Cine Alternativo de México, 228, 262

Muestra Nacional de Nuevos Realiza-dores, 70–71, 94, 135, 173, 228; sig-nificance of for Street Filmmakers, 29, 46, 189, 191, 239–43, 253, 260–61; founding of, 55, 240; role of in re-flecting on industry missteps, 261–64; Moviendo Ideas, 267–71

Mujer que espera, 252

Mundo Latino, 58, 65

Muñoz Bachs, Eduardo, 85 (ill.), 109, 115 (ill.), 119 (ill.)

My Footsteps in Baraguá, 61

Nace una escuela, 40–41

Nada, 167, 172–73

Nada con nadie, 266

Najmías, Luis, 184, 197

Nation: unbounded in *Madagascar*, 4; constructed through culture, 7, 29; depicted in *Viva Cuba*, 152, 155–59; as empty signifier in *Existen*, 211–12; evolution of concept of, 239

National cinema: transformation of, 5, 19, 27, 152, 174, 204–5, 237–38, 280; and challenges posed by coproduc-tion, 176–77, 281–82; homage paid to, 223; studies of, 307 (n. 2)

National identity. *See* Identity

Negrito cimarrón, El, 114

Negrito cimarrón y la seda del mar-qués, El, 135

Nené traviesa, 135

Neorealism, Italian, 221, 264

New Latin American Cinema, 39–40

New Man, 13, 16, 83

Newsreel, 8–9, 266

Niños, 110

Noa, Pedro, 263

Noguel, Wilber, 142, 268

Nongovernmental organizations (NGOs): alignment of with interna-tional and state organizations, 6, 79, 136, 261; role of in strengthening cul-tural sector, 36, 74, 287; introduction of in Cuba, 67–68, 296 (n. 27)

Nosotros en el Cuyaguateje, 224

Nosotros y el jazz, 62

No te acuestes, 291 (n. 21)

Noticiero 49, 8–9, 283–84
Noticiero ICAIC Latinoamericano, 8–9, 35, 262, 315 (n. 3)
NOW, 226, 228
Núñez, Eslinda, 22
Núñez, Sergio, 290 (n. 15)

Ociel del Toa, 84, 224, 269
Oggún: An Eternal Presence, 61
Omertá, 198, 203
Ortiz, Fernando, 291 (n. 20)
Oscuros rinocerantes enjaulados (muy a la moda), 43–46, 169, 171–72, 228

P.M.—Pasado Meridiano, 262
Padrón, Ernesto, 118, 124, 128, 131, 132, 136
Padrón, Humberto, 17, 24, 170, 291 (n. 22)
Padrón, Ian, 18, 22, 24, 170, 184
Padrón, Juan, 22, 114–36 passim
Páginas del diario de Mauricio, 271, 275
Pájaros tirándole a la escopeta, Los, 179
Palenque de los esclavos cimarrones, El, 114
Pantalla documental, 98
Papeles secundarios, 179
Para curiosos, 131, 136
Parque forestal, 114
Parranda, 70
Partnerships: as strategy for stretching scarce resources, 15, 27, 37, 261, 282; hallmark of NGO success, 47, 59, 72–73, 78–79, 103–4, 136; developed by Street Filmmakers, 152–53, 183–84
Paso de Yabebiri, El, 122
Patata ardiente: Opera de Bushini, La, 132
Patria, 268
Pavón Tamayo, Luis, 272–73, 276–77

Paz, Senel, 7, 174, 189
Pedazo de mí, Un, 53–54
Pedro cero por ciento, 83
Pepe animation films, 112
Pérez, Alejandro, 25 (ill.), 153, 160, 161 (ill), 218–21, 219 (ill.), 229, 232
Pérez, Fernando, 2–4, 5 (ill.), 17, 23, 254, 264, 275; as inspiration for and mentor to Street Filmmakers, 38, 41–42, 54, 179, 190, 223, 308 (nn. 10, 12)
Pérez, Gustavo, 24, 248–52, 251 (ill.)
Pérez, Lou, 290 (n. 6)
Pérez, Manolo, 152, 275
Pérez Ureta, Raúl, 42, 200–202
Personal Belongings, 255–57, 259–60
Perugorría, Jorge, 73 (ill.)
Pimentel, Marcos, 266
Piña Rodríguez, Ernesto, 24, 139–41, 142 (ill.), 170, 184
Pineda Barnet, Enrique, 80, 244, 252–53
Pinilla, Tupac, 19, 291–92 (n. 28)
Por primera vez, 83–84
Posada Carriles, Luis, 132
Prats, Paco, 42, 106, 111, 112, 116, 123–24, 128–29, 134, 137, 143–44, 304 (n. 43)
Premio Flaco, El, 173
Prensa seria, La, 109–10
Preservation of films, challenges to, 283–87
Prieto Armas, Luis Enrique, 296 (n. 29)
Prieto Jiménez, Abel, 74, 276
Primer Congreso de Educación y Cultura, 112
Production companies, fictitious, 183–84
Propietario, El, 141
Protectoras, 269
Puente García, Jeffrey, 24, 184, 269–70
Pujol, Albertico, 154

Quédate conmigo, 94–95, 100–101
Quer Figueredo, Renier, 265
Quinoscopios, 120, 122
Quinquenio Gris, 271–74, 276–77
Quintero, Héctor, 173

Radio Belén, 46, 266
Raggi, Tulio, 109, 114, 118, 122, 124, 125, 128, 135
Raíces de mi corazon, 62
Ramírez, Alejandro, 24
Ramírez, Johanhnn, 128–29
Ramírez, Waldo, 24, 70, 89–93
Ramírez Malberti, Amaury, 153
Ramírez Malberti, Guillermo, 153
Ramos, Alberto, 263
Ray, Benny, 191, 245
Reade, Harry, 112
Redford, Robert, 21, 41
Reloba, Xenia, 114
Remember Girón, 110
Renán, Roberto, 70
Rensoli, Harold, 138–39
Resolver, 90, 284; as strategy employed by Street Filmmakers, 15, 24, 25, 162–64, 245, 251, 287; as represented in *Rey y Reina*, 17; in animation, 123–24
Retrato, El, 262
Retrato de Teresa, El, 264
Revolutionary film: pioneers of, 9, 11, 26, 239, 261, 262–64; as inspiration for Street Filmmakers, 21, 169, 227–29, 252–54, 306 (n. 18); formation of the creators of, 169–71, 306 (n. 19); and Cuban television, 271–78
Rey de la selva, El, 265
Reyes, José, 109
Reyes, Susana Patricia, 17

Rey y Reina, 17, 231
Ring, 180
Rita, 263
Rivas, Daniel, 132
Rivas, Mario, 108, 114, 118, 124, 128, 132, 136
Road movie, 149, 152, 154–57
Rodríguez, Abel, 96
Rodríguez, Alexander, 136
Rodríguez, Carlos, 89, 90 (ill.)
Rodríguez, Ernesto, 70
Rodríguez, Manolito, 153
Rodríguez, Silvio, 116
Rodríguez Abreu, Alina, 24, 191, 237–38, 245, 278
Rodríguez Cabrera, Raúl, 253
Rojas, Orlando, 42, 168 (ill.), 179, 202, 304 (n. 2)
Rolando, Gloria, 58–66, 63 (ill.)
Roldán y Caturla, 263
Romeo, Gonzalo, 253
Rosales, Jaime, 47
Rosenberg, Carole, 73, 168
Ross, Lázaro, 61

Sáez Carvajal, Fernando, 67
Salazar Navarro, Salvador, 56
Salvador, Angélica, 70, 72, 160, 165, 193, 216, 225 (ill.), 229, 230 (ill.), 311 (n. 11)
Salvador, Emiliano, 215–16, 225–26, 229
Sampietro, Mercedes, 195 (ill.), 197, 202
Sánchez, Jorge Luis, 42, 50–56, 51 (ill.), 152, 227, 229, 240
Santos, Isabel, 252, 264
Santos Moray, Mercedes, 263
Saura, Carlos, 199–200
Sed de mirar, 311
Semilla de hombres, 60
Se permuta, 179

Serie homenaje, 139

Serrano, Nelson, 135

Setenta y dos horas, 269

Sexo, historias, y cintas de video, 268

Sociedad General de Autores y Editores (SGAE), 47, 176, 222, 225, 285

Sola: La extensa realidad, 248

Solanas, Fernando "Pino," 41

Solás, Humberto, 7, 9, 10 (ill.), 26, 200–201, 231, 237, 252, 262, 280, 290 (n. 15)

Soto Ricardo, Amado (Asori), 24, 71–72

Sotto, Arturo, 47, 70, 170

Special Period, 124, 104, 106; genesis and conditions of, 1–6; representations of, 1–6, 265; context of for Street Filmmaking, 13–15, 23–24, 28, 90, 274; decline of industry filmmaking during, 35–36, 107, 125–26, 200; visual archive of, 38; Movimiento Nacional as product of, 59; threat posed to island's art scene during, 67–68

State, Cuban: response of to voices for change, 6; interplay between state actors and Street Filmmakers, 242–43, 246–47

Street Filmmaking, 15–24, 153–54, 207, 247–39; factors contributing to emergence of, 14–19, 74–75, 151; dichotomies jettisoned in, 16, 207, 211; film styles of, 16–20; influences on, 145, 150–51, 153–54; marketing and dissemination of, 164–65, 270, 186–87, 240–42, 244–45, 258–60, 281; training of filmmakers, 169–71, 258, 264–67; fictitious production companies, 183–84; newly emerging values as proffered by, 277–78

Sueño, 135

Suite Habana, 17, 23, 221, 271

Sundance Institute, 47, 194, 222

Tabío, Juan Carlos, 8 (ill.), 18, 159, 202, 276

Talavera, Miriam, 42

Taller de Cine y Video, 50, 52

Taller de Línea y 18, 224

Tanner, Harry, 112

Tarrau, Malú, 154, 161 (ill.)

Technology, new, 10–11, 70–72, 108, 128–34, 150–52, 182–83, 207, 280; combined with traditional modes and techniques, 15, 28, 145, 213–14, 221; as strategy for increasing options, 15, 36–37, 284; fostering new modes, 151, 160–64; and migration to digital in animation, 124–25; proffering greater access, 152, 173–74, 251; and complexity of cultural flows, 165; experiment with in *Tres veces dos*, 187–91, 221; and ongoing challenge of archiving, 284–85

Tejera, Susana, 197

Television, Cuban, 53, 86, 178, 214, 248–50, 261, 270–72. *See also* Instituto Cubano de Radio y Televisión

Televisión Latina, 58, 65

Televisión Serrana (TVS), 28, 46, 70, 76, 77–105, 261; alliances with, 39, 72; establishment of, 77–82; in documenting mountain life, 87–93; in engaging local residents, 93–98; as effective model of community media, 98–105

Tenedor plástico, El, 46

Terrorism, 132–33, 165–66, 213, 305–6 (n. 13)

Terroristas no tienen cueva, Los, 132

Tesoro, El, 114
Third Cinema, 294–95 (n. 17)
Tierra conmovida, La, 91–92
Tocar la alegría, 99–100
Todas iban a ser reinas, 249
Todo por Carlitos, 140
Todo por ella, 185–87
Transculturation, 63, 290 (n. 20)
Trapiche, El, 114
Tres veces dos (3 x 2), 187–91, 193–94, 216–22, 246
Tumba francesa, 60
TV Yumurí, 94–95, 100–101

Underground filmmaking, 20
Unemployment, 14–15, 151
UNESCO, 80, 98–99, 104, 153
Unión de Escritores y Artistas de Cuba (UNEAC), 49, 58, 273
Utopia, 13, 14, 16, 211
Utopía, 18, 70, 184
Uz, Laura de la, 3 (ill.)

Valdés, Beatriz, 253
Valdés, Elpidio, 114–18, 122, 125, 136
Valdés, Oscar, 82–83, 144, 262–63
Valdés, Rainer, 135
Valle, Vivian del, 184
Vampiros en La Habana, 120–22, 133, 136
Vaqueros del Cauto, 82–83, 262
Vega, Belkis, 42, 58, 261, 295 (n. 18)
Vega, Hilda Elena, 24, 94, 268
Vega, Larisa, 154
Vega, Pastor, 261, 264
Veinte-cuatro por segundo, 178, 264
Vera, Daniel, 24, 191, 245, 269–70

Viaje más largo, El, 60
Vida es silbar, La, 13, 201
Vidal, Aram, 24, 184, 191, 243–47, 304 (n. 43)
Video, 27, 28, 37, 48–49, 56–59, 77, 87, 95–96, 182, 221, 294 (n. 16); Encuentro Nacional de Video, 59; video art, 70, 180, 207, 308 (n. 6); video clubs, 78, 121, 262, 287; *video cartas,* 96–97; rental of, 137; ICAIC films on, 292–93 (n. 3)
Video clip, 93–94, 181–82, 214
Video de familia, 17, 291 (n. 22)
Vilasís, Mayra, 144
Villafuerte, Santiago, 60
Viva Cuba, 137, 149–59, 280
Viva Papi, 118
Vives, Camilo, 23, 187, 261

Waissbluth, Andrés, 47
Wilder, Billy, 179, 194

Yeyín y la ciudad escondida, 118
Yip, Julia, 42
Yo, ustedes, el viaje, 138
Youth: representations of in Street Films, 18, 244, 247; fascination with culture of in *Oscuros rinocerantes,* 43–46; commitment to strengthened, 126, 133
YouTube, 11, 281
Yúdice, George, 79

Zambrano, Benito, 47
Zona afectada, 71
Zona de silencio, 138

ENVISIONING CUBA

Ann Marie Stock, *On Location in Cuba: Street Filmmaking during Times of Transition* (2009).

Alejandro de la Fuente, *Havana and the Atlantic in the Sixteenth Century* (2008).

Reinaldo Funes Monzote, *From Rainforest to Cane Field in Cuba: An Environmental History since 1492* (2008).

Matt D. Childs, *The 1812 Aponte Rebellion in Cuba and the Struggle against Atlantic Slavery* (2006).

Eduardo González, *Cuba and the Tempest: Literature and Cinema in the Time of Diaspora* (2006).

John Lawrence Tone, *War and Genocide in Cuba, 1895–1898* (2006).

Samuel Farber, *The Origins of the Cuban Revolution Reconsidered* (2006).

Lillian Guerra, *The Myth of José Martí: Conflicting Nationalisms in Early Twentieth-Century Cuba* (2005).

Rodrigo Lazo, *Writing to Cuba: Filibustering and Cuban Exiles in the United States* (2005).

Alejandra Bronfman, *Measures of Equality: Social Science, Citizenship, and Race in Cuba, 1902–1940* (2004).

Edna M. Rodríguez-Mangual, *Lydia Cabrera and the Construction of an Afro-Cuban Cultural Identity* (2004).

Gabino La Rosa Corzo, *Runaway Slave Settlements in Cuba: Resistance and Repression* (2003).

Piero Gleijeses, *Conflicting Missions: Havana, Washington, and Africa, 1959–1976* (2002).

Robert Whitney, *State and Revolution in Cuba: Mass Mobilization and Political Change, 1920–1940* (2001).

Alejandro de la Fuente, *A Nation for All: Race, Inequality, and Politics in Twentieth-Century Cuba* (2001).